Rational behavior and bargaining equilibrium in games and social situations

Rational behavior and bargaining equilibrium in games and social situations

JOHN C. HARSANYI

Professor of Business Administration and of Economics
University of California, Berkeley

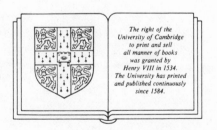

The right of the
University of Cambridge
to print and sell
all manner of books
was granted by
Henry VIII in 1534.
The University has printed
and published continuously
since 1584.

CAMBRIDGE UNIVERSITY PRESS

Cambridge
London   New York   New Rochelle
Melbourne   Sydney

Published by the Press Syndicate of the University of Cambridge
The Pitt Building, Trumpington Street, Cambridge CB2 1RP
32 East 57th Street, New York, NY 10022, USA
10 Stamford Road, Oakleigh, Melbourne 3166, Australia

First published 1977
First paperback edition 1986

Printed in the United States of America

Library of Congress Cataloging in Publication Data

Harsanyi, John C

Rational behavior and bargaining equilibrium in
games and social situations.

Includes bibliographical references.

1. Game theory.
2. Decision-making–Mathematical models.
3. Games of strategy (Mathematics)
4. Social interaction–Mathematical models. I.
Title.
QA269.H37   301.15'54'0184   75-38370

ISBN 0 521 20886 6 hard covers
ISBN 0 521 31183 7 paperback

Contents

Preface

How to define rational behavior (practical rationality) is a philosophical problem of fundamental importance – both in its own right and by virtue of its close connection with the problem of theoretical rationality. The concept of rational behavior is equally fundamental to a number of more specialized disciplines: to *normative* disciplines such as decision theory (utility theory), game theory, and ethics; and to some *positive* social sciences, such as economics and certain, more analytically oriented, versions of political science and of sociology.

This book presents what I believe to be the first systematic attempt to develop a conceptually clear, and quantitatively definite, *general theory of rational behavior*. No doubt, technically more advanced and philosophically more sophisticated versions of such a theory will soon follow. In fact, the first version of this book was completed in 1963, but game theory has been advancing at a very rapid rate since then, and my own thinking has also been changing. Thus, I have revised this manuscript several times to bring it more in line with new developments, but this process must stop if this material is ever to be published. I hope the reader will bear with me if he finds that this book does not cover some recent results, even some of my own. In such a rapidly growing subject as game theory, only journal articles – indeed, only research reports – can be really up to date.

Even if some details of my theory should eventually need modification in the light of later developments, I will feel my book has achieved its purpose if it can convince some readers of one basic point: that it is both possible and eminently desirable to treat decision theory, ethics, and game theory – including the theories of both cooperative and noncooperative games – as special cases of the same general theory of rational behavior.

I wish to express my sincere thanks to the National Science Foundation for its persistent financial support. I also wish to thank Dr. Lloyd S. Shapley of RAND Corporation, Professors Robert J. Aumann and Michael Maschler of Hebrew University, Jerusalem, and Professor Reinhard Selten of the University of Bielefeld, West Germany, for helpful comments. Special thanks are due to Professor Irving H. LaValle of Tulane University, who read the entire manuscript of an earlier version of this book, pointed out errors, and suggested improvements. This list would not be complete without mentioning my wife, Anne, to whom I am indebted not only for her continual moral support but also for many valuable suggestions.

J. C. H.

Berkeley, California
January, 1977

TO ANNE

Part I
Preliminaries

1

Bargaining-equilibrium analysis: a new approach to game theory and to the analysis of social behavior

1.1 Need for a game-theoretical approach yielding determinate solutions

The purpose of this book is to present a new approach to game theory. Based on a *general theory of rational behavior in game situations*, it yields a determinate solution (i.e., a solution corresponding to a unique payoff vector) for each particular game and clearly specifies the strategies by which rational players can most effectively advance their own interests against other rational players.

This new approach, it seems to me, significantly increases the scope and the analytical usefulness of game-theoretical models in the social sciences. It furnishes sharp and specific predictions, both qualitatively and quantitatively, about the outcome of any given game and in particular about the outcome of bargaining among rational players. It shows how this outcome depends on the rewards and penalties that each player can provide for each other player, on the costs that he would incur in providing these rewards or penalties, and on each player's willingness to take risks. Thus it supplies the analytical tools needed for what may be called a *bargaining-equilibrium analysis* of social behavior and of social institutions, i.e., for their explanation in terms of a bargaining equilibrium (corresponding to the "balance of power") among the interested individuals and social groups.

This new approach to game theory also has significant philosophical implications, because it throws new light on the concept of *rational* behavior and on the relationship between rational behavior and *moral* behavior.

When von Neumann and Morgenstern first published *Theory of Games and Economic Behavior* in 1944, many social scientists expressed very high hopes about the revolutionary impact that the theory of games would have on the social sciences. As a matter of fact, many of the conceptual tools developed by von Neumann and Morgenstern (e.g., the concepts of pure and mixed strategies, payoff functions, expected-utility maximization, dominance, side payments, coalitions, and so on) did have a very stimulating influence on the social sciences, as well as on mathematical statistics, operations research, and related disciplines. But the theory of games as such so far has not found extensive applications in the sciences of social behavior.

In my opinion, the main reason for this has been the fact that von Neumann and Morgenstern's approach in general does not yield determinate solutions for two-person nonzero-sum games and for n-person games. To be sure, their approach does

3

provide a very convincing determinate solution for two-person zero-sum games – but it so happens that few, if any, real-life social situations represent games of this particular kind. Even an all-out war is not really a two-person zero-sum game, because the two sides always have a common interest in limiting the intensity of warfare (e.g., by agreeing mutually to refrain from using some particularly destructive weapons).

This means that for purposes of social-science applications the really important parts of game theory are the *theories of two-person nonzero-sum games* and of *n-person games*. Thus, in my opinion, in order to maximize the usefulness of game theory for the analysis of social behavior, we need a game-theoretical approach yielding determinate solutions for both of these two game classes. Only a theory providing determinate solutions can suggest reasonably specific *empirically testable hypotheses* about social behavior and can attempt to *explain* and to *predict* (even in the sense of merely probabilistic prediction) the outcome of social interaction in various real-life social situations. Indeed a theory not yielding a determinate solution cannot even explain how the players can ever agree on *any* specific outcome at all, and how any player, bargaining with another player, can rationally decide to make or not to make any particular concession to him. Likewise only a theory yielding determinate solutions can supply nontrivial *strategy recommendations* to the players in various game situations.

In order to obtain such a theory, I shall adopt a stronger and sharper concept of rational behavior than the one used by von Neumann and Morgenstern and by most other game theorists, and shall define this rational-behavior concept by means of a few additional and more powerful rationality postulates. Analytically the main function of these postulates will be to determine the kinds of *expectations* that a rational player can consistently entertain about other rational players' behavior. I shall try to show that, once we accept this larger and stronger set of rationality postulates, we obtain a theory yielding determinate solutions for *all* classes of "classical" games[1] described in the game-theoretical literature: for two-person and for *n*-person games, for zero-sum and nonzero-sum games, for games with and without transferable utility, for cooperative and noncooperative games, and the like. The solutions that we shall obtain for all these game classes will be simply special cases of the same general theory. In terms of more specific social-science applications, this means that we shall obtain a theory allowing a unified analytical treatment of social situations ranging from, for example, bilateral monopoly (including collective bargaining), duopoly, and oligopoly, to two-sided and many-sided political-power situations, competition for social status, and social conflicts of various kinds.

Of course, in order to obtain determinate predictions for any particular social situation on the basis of our theory, we must always supply specific *factual assumptions* about the players' utility functions, as well as their strategy possibilities, the information available to them, and their ability to communicate and to make binding commitments (binding promises, threats, agreements) to one another. In my opinion game theory – just as individual decision theory (utility theory) of which game theory is a generalization – should be regarded as a purely formal theory lacking empirical content. Both decision theory and game theory state merely what will happen if all participants have consistent preferences, and actually *follow* their own interests as defined by these preferences, in a fully consistent and efficient manner. Empirical content is considered only when we make factual assumptions about the nature of these preferences and about other factual matters (e.g., when we assume that people prefer more money to less money, or make specific assumptions about the economic and political resources – and therefore the strategies – available to the participants in a given social situation).

The advantage of my approach lies in the fact that – once the required factual assumptions have been made – one obtains unique predictions for *all* specific economic, political, and other social situations on the basis of the *same* general theory, without any need for theoretically unjustified arbitrary *ad hoc* assumptions in various particular cases.

More specifically the purpose of my theory is to provide clear, definite, and systematic answers to many important questions arising naturally in the analysis of social behavior but so far left without any satisfactory resolution in social-science literature. For example, what are the conditions that will make it possible for two rational opponents to cooperate in achieving an efficient (Pareto-optimal) outcome? Or what are the conditions that will at least enable them to avoid a direct conflict with all the possible heavy costs that it would entail on both sides? How much cooperation can obtain between two rational opponents who mutually distrust – perhaps with very good reasons – each other's willingness or ability to keep agreements?

Again, if the two players do reach an agreement, what conditions will determine the specific terms on which they will agree? How will agreements based on a rational pursuit of self-interest by both sides differ from agreements based on mutually accepted moral values? Indeed, can two rational players cooperate at all without mutual acceptance of a set of common moral values?

Turning to social situations involving more than two players, when will rational players form two or more *nonoverlapping* coalitions, and when will they form a number of mutually *overlapping* coalitions, so that each player may be a member of several different coalitions and may support different coalitions on different issues? The von Neumann–Morgenstern theory of *n*-person cooperative games, and – on a lower level of abstraction – the Marxian theory of class struggle, as well as the power-blocks theory of international relations, always predict the emergence of two or more nonoverlapping coalitions. In contrast, pluralistic theories of political behavior always predict a complicated network of mutually overlapping coalitions, with the same individual participating in a number of different coalitions or interest groups.

The theory here proposed takes an intermediate position. It predicts the emergence of different coalition structures in different social situations, depending mainly on two classes of variables, viz., on the *communication* possibilities and on the *commitment* possibilities available to the players.[2] If the communication facilities of the game encourage negotiations restricted, at least initially, to some subset of the players, and if the players cannot immediately make irrevokable firm commitments (e.g., if agreements can be unilaterally denounced by the parties), then our theory predicts the emergence of two or more *nonoverlapping* coalitions. But if the players have unbiased communication facilities and unrestricted commitment power, then our theory predicts a pluralistic network of mutually *overlapping* coalitions. Finally, if the communication facilities are biased in favor of negotiations within some sectional group – but, if immediate firm commitments are allowed – then our theory again predicts a pluralistic network of mutually overlapping coalitions. But in this case different coalitions will have *unequal* status in the game: The coalitions formed at earlier stages of the game will have a prior claim to their members' loyalty over all later-formed coalitions; this fact will of course be reflected in the players' final payoffs.

These predictions about the alternative coalition structures that may emerge in n-person cooperative games also point to another aspect of our approach. They illustrate the fact that a satisfactory definition of a given game according to our theory will often require a specification of *additional parameters* to those which by traditional game theory would be included in the definition of the game. For example, for our purposes an n-person cooperative game is not fully defined without exactly specifying the communication and commitment possibilities available to the players.

We must agree with traditional game theory that, if such parameters are left unspecified, any given game can have a wide *variety* of alternative outcomes (even if we assume fully rational behavior on the part of the players). We differ from the traditional approach in that we also want to explain *why* one of these possible outcomes rather than another will emerge in any given case. This is why we need a theory that predicts one specific outcome – that is, a theory that yields a determinate solution – for any given game played by rational players, once we are given enough information about all the basic parameters of the game, including those neglected by classical game theory.

1.2 Restriction of our systematic analysis to classical games

In order to describe the scope of our analysis in more specific terms, we will introduce a distinction between classical and nonclassical games. In this book our interest will be largely restricted to those solution concepts that our theory yields for classical games. Nonclassical games will be considered only incidentally to help our analysis of classical games.

A game will be called a *classical* game if it satisfies the following conditions:

1. It must be a game with *complete information*, where the players have full knowledge of their own and the other players' payoff functions and strategy possibilities.[3]

2. It must be either a fully *cooperative* or a fully *noncooperative* game and cannot be a game of an intermediate status. This means that the players must either be

permitted to make firm and enforceable agreements *before* playing the game, or they must not be permitted to make firm and enforceable agreements in the game at all.

3. It must be a game that can be adequately represented by its *normal form*.[4] That is, the game must be already given in normal form, or it must be possible to convert it into normal form without changing it into an essentially different game.

This last condition requires some explanation. We may distinguish between games with *immediate commitment* and games with *delayed commitment*. In the former the players can freely commit themselves to specific strategies *before* any chance move or personal move has taken place in the game, while in the latter they may be able to do so only *after* one or more chance moves and/or personal moves have been completed.[5] Games with immediate commitment can always be adequately represented by their normal form. But, as I have shown elsewhere [Harsanyi, 1968a, p. 334], a game with delayed commitment is often changed into an essentially different game if it is converted into normal form, so that in this case the normal form is usually not a valid representation of the game as originally defined.

We use the term "classical games" to describe games satisfying our three conditions, because – on the surface at least – all games discussed in classical game-theoretical literature are games of this kind, and all solution concepts of classical game theory are ostensibly solutions for such classical games.

The actual fact, as we shall argue – one of the most important solution concepts of classical game theory, von Neumann and Morgenstern's *stable set* (also known as the von Neumann–Morgenstern solution for n-person cooperative games) – is really a solution concept for a certain class of *nonclassical* bargaining games. These bargaining games are nonclassical games because they are not fully cooperative games. The players cannot make immediately binding commitments at the beginning of the game. Rather, any player whose consent is required for a given agreement is free to upset this agreement (at least during some initial period), if he thinks that he can benefit by doing so. A "stable set" is meant to represent a set of payoff vectors (imputations) that are stable in the sense that (under certain assumptions) no player will have an incentive to upset them in this way, even though the rules of the game would permit him to do so. (It can be shown technically that any stable set corresponds to a certain family of co-polar equilibrium points in an appropriately defined bargaining game. See Harsanyi [1974].)

Although we will restrict our attention largely to the solutions that our theory yields for classical games, in other publications we have also defined solutions, based on the principles of the theory here described, for various classes of nonclassical games, such as games with incomplete information and games with delayed commitment[6] [Harsanyi, 1967, 1968a, 1968b, Harsanyi and Selten, 1972; see also Aumann and Maschler, 1968]. It is my conviction that nonclassical games will have many important applications in the social sciences. But a systematic discussion of nonclassical games is beyond the scope of this book.

1.3   The concept of rational behavior

The fundamental concept of our theory, as of classical game theory, is the concept of rational behavior or of rational choice.

When on the common-sense level we are speaking of rational choice, we are usually thinking of a choice of the most appropriate *means* to a given *end*. For example, we may say that it is "rational" to treat pneumonia with modern antibiotics, because these have been found to be highly effective in achieving the desired medical goal; it is "irrational" to use various traditional folk remedies, because these do not seem to produce the desired result.

Already at a common-sense level, the concept of rational behavior is often a very powerful explanatory principle, because it can account for a large number of possibly quite complicated empirical facts about people's behavior in terms of the goals (or ends) that they are trying to achieve. For instance, a long sequence of complex actions by the patient, his family, and his doctor can often be explained in terms of the simple hypothesis that all these people pursue the patient's recovery as their goal (or as one of their goals).

However, it has been an important achievement of classical economic theory to extend this common-sense concept of rational behavior so that it can cover not only choices among alternative *means* to a given end but also choices among alternative *ends*. Under this more general concept of rationality, our choices among alternative ends are rational if they are based on clear and consistent priorities or preferences. Formally this means that our choice behavior will be rational if it satisfies certain consistency requirements or *rationality postulates*.

Fundamentally the need for choosing among alternative ends arises because in most cases we cannot attain *all* our ends at the same time: If we choose to pursue one particular end, then we have to forego some others. The loss of some other ends is the *opportunity cost* of choosing this particular end. Our choice of any given end will be rational if it is based on clear awareness and careful evaluation of the opportunity costs involved.

Classical economic theory has also shown that, if a given individual's (decision maker's) choice behavior satisfies the appropriate rationality and continuity postulates, then it can be mathematically represented as *maximization* of a well-defined *utility function*. However, the usefulness of simple utility maximization as a definition of rational behavior is largely restricted to the case of *certainty*, in which the outcomes of alternative actions are known to the decision maker in advance, because they cannot be influenced significantly by chance or by the actions of other individuals. But this definition is less useful in the cases of risk and of uncertainty, where the outcomes of some or all available actions depend on unpredictable chance events – with the difference that in the case of *risk* the decision maker knows at least the *objective* probabilities associated with all possible outcomes, whereas in the case of *uncertainty* even these objective probabilities are partly or wholly unknown to him (or perhaps do not exist at all as well-defined numerical probabilities). Even less useful is this definition in *game situations*, where the outcome depends not only on the actions of one rational decision maker but rather on the actions of two or more rational decision makers (players) with possibly divergent interests.

It has remained for modern decision theory to find a more satisfactory definition for rational behavior in the cases of risk and of uncertainty. This has been accomplished by showing that in these cases, if a given decision maker's choice behavior satisfies the appropriate rationality postulates, then it can be represented as *maximization* of his *expected utility*, i.e., as maximization of the mathematical expectation of his cardinal utility function. (In order to establish this result in the case of risk, we need stronger rationality postulates than those used in the case of certainty; and in the case of uncertainty we still need somewhat stronger rationality postulates.)

In the case of *risk* the expected utility to be maximized is defined by using as probability weights the known objective probabilities associated with alternative possible outcomes. In the case of *uncertainty*, in which some or all of these objective probabilities are unknown to the decision maker, these unknown objective probabilities have to be replaced by his own *subjective probabilities* as probability weights. Fundamentally the subjective probabilities that a given decision maker assigns to different events – in the same way as the utilities he assigns to different goals – must be inferred from his actual choice behavior. But intuitively they can be interpreted (at least if the corresponding objective probabilities exist) as the decision maker's personal *estimates* of these objective probabilities, whose true numerical values are unknown to him. On the other hand, these objective probabilities themselves, when they exist, can be interpreted as the long-run *statistical frequencies* of the relevant random events, which, in principle at least, can always be measured by appropriate statistical experiments.

For example, the objective probability of throwing a "head" with a given coin can be interpreted as the long-run frequency of "heads" in a long sequence of trials conducted with this coin. In contrast, a given individual's subjective probability of throwing a "head" can be interpreted as his personal estimate of this unknown long-run frequency. This approach, which defines rational behavior under uncertainty as expected-utility maximization in terms of the decision maker's own subjective probabilities, is often called the *Bayesian approach* [after the Reverend Thomas Bayes (1702-1761), an English writer on probability theory].

Whereas the analysis of rational behavior in the cases of risk and of uncertainty is the task of (individual) decision theory (utility theory), the analysis of rational behavior in *game situations* is of course the task of game theory. (For convenience, we shall subsume the analysis of rational behavior in the case of certainty, also, under individual decision theory.) But according to our preceding discussion, traditional game theory has not provided a sufficiently sharp and specific concept of rational behavior in game situations; to develop such a concept will be one of our main purposes in this book.

We have already pointed out that, as we move from the analysis of the less general cases to the analysis of the more general cases – for example, as we move from *certainty* to *risk* and to *uncertainty* – we need stronger and stronger rationality postulates. As *game situations* represent an even more general case, it is not surprising that for defining rational behavior in game situations we shall need even stronger rationality postulates than we need for defining rational behavior in these three decision-theoretical cases. In effect, in my opinion, the basic weakness of traditional game theory has been that in defining rational behavior in game situations it has tried to restrict itself to using rationality postulates which in their logical content do not go significantly beyond the rationality postulates of individual decision theory.

Technically our theory of rational behavior in game situations will be a direct generalization of the Bayesian theory of rational behavior under uncertainty (see Section 1.4).

In addition to individual decision theory and game theory, we shall add, as a third branch of the general theory of rational behavior, ethics, dealing with rationality in making moral choices and particularly in making moral value judgments.

Individual decision theory deals primarily with rational behavior in situations in which the outcome depends on an individual's (the decision maker's) own behavior. But it can also handle situations where the outcome does depend on other individuals' behavior – as long as it is assumed that their behavior is governed by well-defined deterministic or probabilistic laws rather than by their own rational strategy choices and by their own *rational expectations* about other participants' behaviors. The proposed basic difference between decision-theoretical situations and game situations lies in the fact that the latter involve mutually interdependent reciprocal expectations by the players about each other's behavior; the former do not. (Cf. Sections 1.4 and 6.3 concerning the problem posed by these reciprocal expectations.)

In contrast to individual decision theory, both game theory and ethics deal with rational behavior in a social setting. But *game theory* deals with individuals who rationally pursue their *own* self-interest (as well as all values, both selfish and unselfish, to which their own utility function assigns positive utility) against *other* individuals who just as rationally pursue *their* own self-interest (as well as all their other values included in their own utility functions).

On the other hand, *ethics* deals with a rational pursuit of the interests of *society* as a whole.[7] The basic concept is that of *moral value judgments*. As I have stated in earlier publications [Harsanyi, 1953, 1955, 1958], making a moral value judgment is equivalent to comparing different social situations in terms of the *arithmetic mean of all individuals' cardinal utility levels* in the society. Thus we may say that this arithmetic mean is the quantity that we are trying to maximize when we are making a moral value judgment. (For convenience, I shall briefly restate my arguments in support of this conclusion in Chapter 4.)

To summarize our discussion in this section, we propose to divide the general theory of rational behavior into two main categories (see Table 1.1).

In any given branch of the theory of rational behavior, the analysis in general begins with defining the appropriate rational-behavior concept by means of certain rationality postulates. This definition we shall call the *primary definition* of the

Table 1.1 *General theory of rational behavior*

=====

A. *Individual decision theory* (*utility theory*)
   Deals with rational behavior of an isolated individual under:
   A1. *Certainty*
       The outcome of any possible action is fully predictable.
   A2. *Risk*
       The objective probability of any possible outcome is known.
   A3. *Uncertainty*
       Some or all of these objective probabilities are unknown or even undefined.
B. *Theory of rational behavior in a social setting*
   B1. *Game theory*
       Rational pursuit of self-interest and of personal values against other in-
       dividuals rationally pursuing their own self-interest and their own personal
       values.
   B2. *Ethics*
       Rational pursuit of the interests of society as a whole.

=====

relevant rational-behavior concept. Then it is usually shown that the same rational-behavior concept can also be equivalently characterized by certain mathematical properties, such as maximizing some specified mathematical quantity or satisfying some specified equations. This we will call the *secondary definition* of the relevant rational-behavior concept.[8]

For example, in the three decision-theoretical cases of certainty, risk, and uncertainty, this secondary definition of rational behavior is in terms of utility maximization or expected-utility maximization. In game theory, this secondary definition will be given by the specific solution concepts that we shall propose for different classes of games. In ethics, as we shall argue, this secondary definition is in terms of maximizing the mean utility level of all individuals in the society.

1.4 Analysis of the players' reciprocal expectations and the bargaining problem

As we have already indicated, our theory of rational behavior in game situations will be a direct generalization of the Bayesian theory of rational behavior under uncertainty. Following the Bayesian approach, we shall assume that any player i will express his expectations about the behavior of another player j by assigning *subjective probabilities* to various alternative actions that player j may possibly take.

Yet, as we are dealing with game situations, when the players are assumed to act on the expectation of rational behavior by all other players, we have to go beyond the standard Bayesian approach. Instead of allowing player i to choose his subjective probabilities in any arbitrary way that may occur to him, we must require that the subjective probabilities that he assigns to various possible actions by player j should be consistent with the assumption that player j, like player i himself, will act in a rational manner in playing the game. We will call this requirement the *principle of mutually expected rationality*. One of the main tasks of our theory will be to decide what expectations, and more specifically what subjective probabilities, rational players can reasonably entertain about one another's behavior, in accordance with this principle.

This problem is particularly important in games in which the outcome is decided by explicit or implicit bargaining among the players. It is primarily our analysis of the players' mutual expectations in bargaining situations which enables our theory, unlike earlier approaches to game theory, to define a determinate solution for each particular game.

As we will see, in the case of two-person zero-sum games and in other less important special cases, the outcome of the game does not depend on bargaining between the players, and a determinate solution can be defined on the basis of what we shall call *payoff-dominance* relations (which include dominance relations in von Neumann and Morgenstern's sense, as well as a number of other dominancelike concepts to be defined later). Intuitively speaking, all payoff-dominance relations are based on the principle that, other things being equal, rational players will always prefer strategies (individual strategies as well as joint strategies) that yield higher payoffs.

In most games, however, there is an *indeterminacy problem*, and more particularly a *bargaining problem*, in that payoff-dominance relations in themselves do not furnish a determinate solution: The outcome of the game must be determined by explicit or implicit bargaining among the players. Therefore in order to define determinate solutions for such games we need a clear criterion for rational behavior in bargaining situations.

The criterion at which we will arrive will be a decision rule first proposed by Zeuthen [1930, Chap. IV], which we shall call *Zeuthen's Principle*. It essentially says that at any given stage of bargaining between two rational players the next concession must always come from the party *less willing* to risk a conflict – if each party's willingness to risk a conflict is measured by the highest probability of conflict that he would be prepared to face rather than accept the terms proposed by the other party. We shall see that Zeuthen's Principle is the only decision rule consistent with the expectations (subjective probabilities) that rational players can entertain about each other's bargaining behavior, in accordance with the principle of mutually expected rationality (and with the formal rationality postulates that we shall propose as formalizations of this principle).

Zeuthen's Principle will lead us to the concept of risk-dominance relations, which, as we shall find, will define a determinate solution also for those games for which payoff-dominance relations by themselves would not achieve this.

More particularly, as in the case of *two-person* cooperative games, these risk-dominance relations based on Zeuthen's Principle lead to the Nash solution [Nash, 1950, 1953]. In all other cases they lead to natural generalizations of this solution concept.

In the case of *n-person* cooperative games with *unbiased* communication (and with immediate commitment power) we obtain a solution concept that is a generalization not only of the Nash solution but also of the "modified" Shapley value

[Shapley, 1953; Harsanyi, 1959; Selten, 1960; see also Harsanyi, 1963]. In the case of *n*-person cooperative games with *biased* communication (and with immediate commitment power) we obtain a closely related, but different, solution concept.

Finally, in the case of *noncooperative* games, the risk-dominance relations to be defined will typically select a unique equilibrium point (or a set of equilibrium points that all yield the same payoff vector) as the solution of the game.

It may be noted that the bargaining problem is not the only indeterminacy problem to consider; another type of indeterminacy problem is the *indifference problem*. It is the problem of making – at least probabilistic – predictions about the strategy to be chosen by a given player *i* when he is indifferent between two or more alternative strategies, because any one of them would yield him the same payoff. Our theory requires a solution to this problem, because in general the strategy choice of every other player *j* ($j \neq i$) will depend on the (deterministic or at least probabilistic) prediction that game theory can provide for him on player *i*'s likely strategy choice. We shall argue that in many cases we can solve this problem by making the assumption that player *i* will be *equally likely* to choose any one of the strategies that will yield the same payoff, while in other cases more complicated probabilistic assumptions will be necessary (see Note in Section 6.1).

1.5 Bargaining models versus arbitration models

In the previous section we indicated the proposed distinction between *game theory* and *ethics* and between the game-theoretical and the ethical points of view. Game theory tries to determine what kind of behavior will best serve the *interests of each particular player* in a game played against other players who also are assumed to promote their own interests in the best possible manner. Here the "interests" of each particular player are not meant to be necessarily restricted to selfish considerations; rather, they include all objectives and values, both selfish and unselfish, to which his own utility function assigns positive utility. In contrast, ethics tries to determine what kind of behavior will best serve the *interests of society* as a whole.

Thus the formal definition of any solution concept in game theory must be in terms of game-theoretical rationality postulates, which describe how each player can best advance his own interests in the game; and no use must be made of moral postulates expressing moral value judgments. Of course, game situations in which the players assign positive utility to certain moral values are by no means excluded from game-theoretical analysis. But if we are taking the game-theoretical point of view, then such moral preferences must always be incorporated into each player's utility function (payoff function) instead of used in the formal definition of the solution. Because all values and objectives in which the players are interested have already been incorporated into their payoff functions, our formal analysis of any given game must be based on the assumption that each player has only one interest in the game – to maximize his own payoff.

This approach not only avoids confusion between game-theoretical problems and moral problems but also has the advantage of much greater generality: Because it makes no use of moral value judgments in the formal definition of the solution, it can be used also in cases in which different players have highly dissimilar moral values or possibly pay no attention to moral considerations at all.

In game-theoretical literature that deals with bargaining games a good deal of regrettable confusion has arisen between *arbitration models*, based on moral postulates, and *bargaining models* proper, based on game-theoretical rationality postulates. Arbitration models, such as those of Raiffa [1953] and Braithwaite [1955], try to define solutions to satisfy certain moral criteria (e.g., some notion of "fairness"). In contrast, bargaining models envisage bargaining situations where all parties are interested only in maximizing their own final payoffs. Hence each party will make a concession to another party only because he thinks it would be too *risky*, from his own point of view, not to make this concession – not because he is guided by moral considerations.

Our own solution concepts (for games involving bargaining among the players) will always be based on bargaining models (and not on arbitration models) and will make no use of moral value judgments in defining these solutions.

This confusion that we find in the literature between arbitration models and bargaining models, and more generally between moral considerations and game-theoretical considerations, has no doubt been largely caused by the mistaken assumption that in bargaining situations game-theoretical considerations by themselves, without the use of moral criteria, would fail to yield determinate solutions. However, the purely game-theoretical solution concepts that we will develop will clearly disprove this assumption.

Later we will attempt to show that arbitration models and bargaining models differ not only in their substantive meaning, in the way just described, but also in the formal mathematical postulates that they must use. In particular, we will argue that arbitration models, and indeed ethics and welfare economics quite generally, have to make essential use of *interpersonal comparisons of utility* (see Section 4.10, as well as Sections 4.2 through 4.4). In contrast, bargaining models, and game theory quite generally, have to define solutions invariant with respect to order-preserving linear transformations of any particular player's utility function, which rules out the use of interpersonal utility comparisons (see discussion of Postulate 3 in Section 8.3, as well as the remainder of Chapter 8).

Another, although less important, difference is that arbitration models must use a stronger form of the *joint-efficiency postulate* than bargaining models do. From a moral point of view a given payoff vector u^* is always preferable to another payoff vector u whenever u^* dominates u, even if this is only a *weak* dominance relation. It is our moral duty to help a given individual i, if we can do this without harming anybody else – even if our action does not positively benefit any other individual $j \neq i$ in the society.

In contrast, in a bargaining game, in general only strong dominance relations between payoff vectors are effective. For example, suppose that in a two-person bargaining game a given payoff vector $u^* = (u_1^*, u_2^*)$ assigns to player 1 a higher payoff than another payoff vector $u = (u_1, u_2)$ does but that both payoff vectors assign the same payoff to player 2, so that $u_1^* > u_1$ but $u_2^* = u_2$. Then player 2 will have no incentive to cooperate in achieving u^* rather than u, and so we cannot in general exclude the possibility that the actual outcome of the game will be u rather than u^* or that it will be some probability mixture of the two (cf. Section 8.1).

2

Rational-choice models of social behavior

2.1 The rationality assumption

Like other versions of game theory – and indeed like all theories based on some
notion of perfectly rational behavior – regarding its logical mode, our theory is a
normative (prescriptive) theory rather than a *positive* (descriptive) theory. At least
formally and explicitly it deals with the question of how each player *should* act in
order to promote his own interests most effectively in the game and not with the
question of how he (or persons like him) *will* actually act in a game of this particular type.[1] All the same, the main purpose of our theory is very definitely to help
the *positive* empirical social sciences to predict and to explain real-life human
behavior in various social situations.

To be sure, it has been a matter of continual amazement among philosophers, and
often even among social scientists (at least outside the economics profession), how
any theory of rational behavior can ever be successful in explaining or predicting
real-life human behavior. Yet it is hardly open to doubt that in actual fact such
theories have been remarkably successful in economics and more recently in several
other social sciences, particularly political science, international relations, organiza-
tion theory, and some areas of sociology [see Harsanyi, 1969, and the literature
there quoted].

Needless to say, theories based on some notion of rational behavior (we will call
them rational-behavior or rational-choice theories or, briefly, rationalistic theories),
just as theories based on different principles, sometimes yield unrealistic predictions
about human behavior. Fundamentally, of course, only detailed empirical research
can show us the actual range of social situations for which any specific rationalistic
theory tends to make correct or incorrect predictions.

The point is however, that, in areas in which a given rationalistic theory does
make reasonably realistic predictions, it will often possess *extremely high explanatory power*, in the sense that it may be able to predict a very wide variety of complex empirical facts about people's actual behavior from a very small number of
relatively simple assumptions about their utility functions – that is, about the goals
that they are trying to achieve and about the relative importance that they attach
to each particular goal.

The basic reason for this often quite remarkable explanatory power of rational-
behavior theories lies in a general and fundamental *empirical* characteristic of

human behavior, viz., in its goal-directedness, its goal-seeking orientation. In effect, what we mean by "rational behavior" is essentially behavior showing this goal-directedness to a particularly high degree and in a particularly consistent manner. It is behavior highly adapted, within the possibilities available to the person concerned, to successful achievement of his intended goals. Consequently it is behavior that also admits of *explanation* to a considerable extent in terms of its intended objectives rather than in terms of other "less rational" psychological variables.

Once we know that a given agent – whether a human being, a higher animal, an intelligent organism from another celestial body, or a man-made computer, etc. – is capable of goal-directed behavior of some complexity over a wide range of task situations, we can reasonably expect that his behavior will admit explanation to a large extent in terms of some suitable theory of rational behavior.

To be sure, in spite of this important strain of goal-directedness and rationality in human behavior, human beings often fall quite short of the perfect rationality postulated by normative theories of rational behavior. There are at least two major reasons for this. One lies in the (often unconscious) *emotional* factors pointed out by various psychologists from Freud to Festinger. The other is the *limited information-processing ability* of the human central nervous system, emphasized by Simon's theory of "limited rationality."

For example, as Simon and his associates have pointed out, in chess and in some other parlor games the players are simply *unable* to use their optimal strategies as defined by normative game theory, because finding these optimal strategies would be a computation problem of enormous complexity, far beyond the capabilities of any human being – and indeed even beyond those of the largest and fastest computers now in existence or likely ever to be built in the future [Newell, Shaw, and Simon, 1958]. The same may be true of some real-life economic, political, diplomatic, military, or other game situations of great complexity.

All the same, as the success of rational-behavior theories in economics and other social sciences definitely shows, in actual fact these obvious limitations of human rationality do not generally prevent rational-behavior theories from yielding reasonably good approximate predictions about social behavior over a wide range of social situations. Of course, a good deal of further experimentation with various types of rational-behavior theories will be needed before we can ascertain how far these theories can really take us in explaining and predicting empirical social behavior in each particular field.

In fact, the usefulness of rationalistic theories is not necessarily restricted to situations where people's behavior shows a relatively high measure of overall rationality and consequently admits of actual explanation and prediction by such theories with an acceptable degree of approximation. Even in situations in which rationalistic theories cannot themselves be directly used as explanatory and predictive theories, they may still have considerable *heuristic value* in developing (nonrationalistic) explanatory and predictive theories of social behavior. This is so because even in such situations people's behavior will often conform at least to *some* particularly compelling norms of rationality. Thus it will often be a good heuristic principle to develop behavioral theories consistent with at least certain minimal standards of rationality relevant to that particular social situation, as specified by an appropriate normative theory of rational behavior.

In my opinion the heuristic value of a suitable normative theory of rational behavior is particularly clear if we want to develop fruitful theoretical hypotheses about people's behavior in *game situations*. The history of duopoly and of bilateral-monopoly models, proposed by some of the most eminent economists for over a century and a half, is a good illustration of this point. It shows that even in very simple game situations (involving only two players and having a rather simple logical structure in other respects) it may be virtually impossible to suggest reasonable hypotheses about the players' likely behavior without having a clear systematic idea of what it means to behave *rationally* in the relevant class of game situations. Lacking any clear and consistent definition of rational behavior for these game situations, even such powerful analytical minds as Cournot, Bertrand, Edgeworth, and Hicks have been unable to propose satisfactory models of the two players' behavior and have been unable to avoid the fundamental mistake of ascribing some quite implausible and patently irrational behavior to their two duopolists or bilateral monopolists – without any specific empirical or theoretical justification for assuming such behavior and without even realizing its irrationality.

For example, in Cournot's, Bertrand's, and Edgeworth's duopoly models, the two duopolists make no attempt to reach a jointly efficient cooperative solution. Moreover, they never learn but rather persist in certain mistaken expectations about each other's behavior, in spite of continual disappointments. [For detailed discussion see Fellner, 1960, Chap. II.] On the other hand, in Hicks's [1932] model of collective bargaining (i.e., of bilateral monopoly on the labor market), neither party will put forward the threat of a work stoppage (strike or lockout) of a given duration if such a stoppage would entail positive costs, however small, on him – even if he could extract much better terms from the other party by making such a threat because of the heavy costs that the threatened stoppage would impose on the other party as well. Of course, once a suitable theory of rational behavior in game situations is available, it becomes merely a matter of ordinary routine care to avoid such mistakes in constructing analytical models for economic or noneconomic game situations.

From a slightly different point of view, the heuristic importance of rational-behavior theories is based on the fact that in most cases we cannot really understand and explain a person's behavior (or indeed the behavior of another intelligent organism or even of an intelligent robot) unless we can interpret it *either* as *rational behavior* in this particular situation *or* as an *understandable deviation* from rational behavior. For example, we may be able to interpret it as an understandable mistake, as an understandable emotional reaction, or as an understandable intentionally suboptimal response.[2]

Thus the heuristic value of a clear normative concept of rational behavior will often lie in the fact that it confronts us with the question of explaining why people *deviate* from this concept of rationality in specific ways in various social situations.

By trying to offer an explanation for such deviations, we can often make important advances toward a fruitful explanatory and predictive theory of social behavior in these situations. Indeed, in the long run, normative theories of rational behavior may prove at least as important in the analysis of deviations – or apparent deviations – from rational behavior as in the analysis of human behavior closely conforming to our normative standards of rationality.

In fact, we need a clear concept of rationality, not only if our purpose is to *explain* and *predict* human behavior but also if our aim is merely to *describe* it adequately. In many cases even a mere description of a given player's (e.g., businessman's, trade union leader's, politician's, military commander's, diplomat's) behavior will be seriously incomplete if it contains no *evaluation* of its effectiveness (rationality) in serving this player's own interests in the relevant game situation; and this evaluation can be based only on a suitable normative theory of rational behavior. For example, no satisfactory descriptive historical account of Napoleon's career can fail to mention the brilliance of his military strategies or the incompetence of his foreign policy in many cases.

Finally, besides the "theoretical" purposes of explaining, predicting, and describing human behavior, a normative theory of rational behavior can also be used for the "practical" purpose of providing *strategy recommendations* for the various players. Of course, our theory as it stands provides strategy recommendations for each player only on the assumption that all *other* players in the game will also choose their strategies in a rational manner. In cases where this assumption is felt to be unrealistic, the conclusions of our theory will need appropriate modifications in order to enable each player to take full advantage of – and at the same time also take full precautions against – any irrational behavior that he might anticipate on the part of the other players.

In summary, in the social sciences our theory, and in general all normative theories of rational behavior, can be used for the following analytical purposes:

1. For *conceptual clarification* of how to define rational behavior in various social situations.

2. For *explanation* and *prediction* of people's actual behavior (in cases in which their behavior exhibits high degrees of rationality and therefore admits of explanation in terms of a rationalistic theory).

3. For providing *heuristic criteria* for (nonrationalistic) explanatory and predictive theories of social behavior (even in cases where this behavior deviates from our normative concept of rationality).

4. For providing a descriptive *standard of evaluation* by which to judge the rationality of people's behavior.

5. For providing rational *strategy recommendations* for the various participants.

2.2 Conflicting sectional interests as explanatory variables

Sociology as well as cultural and social anthropology are at present largely dominated by *functionalist* theories, which try to explain social institutions in terms of the functional needs of society, i.e., in terms of certain *common interests* of society as a whole – with little, if any, use of the mutually conflicting *sectional interests* of different social groups as explanatory variables.

We cannot deny that the most general features of a given social institution can often be explained, up to a point, in terms of certain *common* social needs. For example, the very existence and the most basic characteristics of the law-enforcing agencies in any particular society can be accounted for in terms of a common social need for maintaining law and order and for enforcing the decisions of lawful public officials against possible resistance.

It is, however, equally clear that the detailed structure and operation of any given institution, and its structural and operational differences from similar institutions in other societies, can be explained only in terms of the social pressures and counter-pressures by which different social groups have tried to mold this institution in accordance with their own, often conflicting, *sectional* interests. For example, we cannot explain the structure and operation of any law-enforcing agency except by interpreting the latter as a result of a compromise among citizens demanding better police protection, taxpayers demanding greater economies in public expenditures, political reformers fighting against corruption and political bias in the judiciary and in the police, civil liberty organizations fighting against abuses of police power, lawyers protecting their own professional interests and policemen protecting theirs, as well as many other social groups advancing sectional interests of their own.

When we explain institutional *changes*, rather than the institutional conditions of a given moment, the important role that conflicts of interest among various social groups play as explanatory variables becomes even more obvious. [For further discussion of conflicts of interest as explanatory variables and for further criticism of functionalist theories, see Harsanyi, 1968c, 1969.]

In effect, in economics, political science, international relations, as well as in economic, political, and social history, conflicts of interest have always been recognized as major explanatory variables of social behavior. This insight has given rise to many valuable explanatory theories in these disciplines. Even in sociology and in anthropology the prevalence of functionalist doctrines has not completely suppressed explanatory theories of this type.

In the past, however, all explanatory theories of this kind have always suffered from a *fundamental logical defect* because of the absence of any clear theoretical model to yield determinate predictions about the behavior that intelligent individuals, or social groups led by intelligent individuals, are likely to display in conflict-of-interest situations. Moreover, there has been a tendency to regard the common interests of society and the divergent sectional interests of various social groups as alternative and mutually incompatible explanatory variables, and little attempt has been made to bring both classes of explanatory variables together within the same theoretical model.

Thus Marxist writers and other social scientists who have stressed the importance of conflicting class or group interests have found little room in their theories for the common interests of different social classes or social groups. Conversely, functionalists and others stressing the importance of the common interests of society have found little room for conflicting sectional interests. Indeed, a well-known German sociologist, Ralf Dahrendorf, has gone as far as explicitly asserting the strange doctrine that the general interests of society and the conflicting sectional interests of various social groups simply *cannot* be used as explanatory variables within the same model [Dahrendorf, 1958, p. 127].

Our theory of rational behavior in game situations enables us to overcome these difficulties. It yields determinate predictions about the behavior of intelligent individuals in all specific conflict-of-interest situations. Moreover, it shows how we can take account, within the same theoretical model, of any conflicts of interest that may exist among different players and also of any common interest they may have in reaching a peaceful agreement and in cooperating to achieve their shared common objectives.

2.3 The problem of dominant loyalties and the balance-of-power problem

Any interaction among individuals or social groups with partly or wholly divergent interests always gives rise to two different (although interrelated) problems, which ought to be clearly distinguished from each other for analytical purposes. One is a problem of social psychology: Given a free choice, to what extent will people in various social situations give priority first to their own *individual interests* in the narrowest sense; second to the *sectional interests* of their own family, business corporation, occupational group, social class, ethnic group, national community, or any other social group to which they belong, and third to the *general interests* of human society as a whole? This may be called the problem of *dominant loyalties*. From a formal point of view it is essentially a question about the nature of each individual's (or social group's) utility function – about how much weight this utility function assigns to individual, to various sectional, and to general interests and objectives.

The second problem belongs to a different level of analysis. It is assumed that all participants' utility functions are *given*, including their tastes for different commodities, their willingness to take risks, their value attitudes, and in particular the priorities that they want to assign to individual, sectional, and general interests. The question now to be asked is this: Given all parties' utility functions, what factors will determine the relative influence that each party's utility function (or each party's interests) will have on the final outcome? This may be called the *balance-of-power* problem.

As we have seen, the problem of dominant loyalties is a problem of social psychology.[3] In any case, it is *not* a game-theoretical problem and cannot be solved by game-theoretical methods, because game theory regards the players' utility functions as *given*. In contrast, the balance-of-power problem *is* clearly a game-theoretical problem and indeed is the central problem of game theory as a whole. It is, of course, also the central problem for our theory of rational behavior in game situations.

3

Rational behavior under certainty, risk, and uncertainty

3.1 Sure prospects and risky prospects

In Section 1.3 we briefly summarized the main results of individual decision theory (utility theory). In this chapter we will discuss these results in more detail. Recall that we speak of *certainty* when any action that the decision maker can take can have only *one* possible outcome, known in advance. We speak of *risk* or *uncertainty* when at least some of the actions available to the decision maker can have two or more alternative outcomes, without his being able to discern which particular outcome will actually arise in any given case.

More particularly we speak of *risk* when the objective probabilities (long-run frequencies) associated with all possible outcomes are known to the decision maker. We speak of *uncertainty* if at least some of these objective probabilities are unknown to him (or are not even well defined).

For example, I make a *risky* decision when I buy a lottery ticket offering known prizes with known probabilities. In contrast, I make an *uncertain* decision when I bet on horses or when I make a business investment, because in the case of horse races and business investments the objective probabilities of alternative outcomes are not known.

To describe the expected results of any given human action under certainty, risk, and uncertainty, we are introducing the concepts of "sure prospects," "risky prospects," and "uncertain prospects." We are also introducing the term "alternatives" as a common name for sure prospects, risky prospects, and uncertain prospects.

Since in the case of *certainty* the decision maker knows the actual outcome of any action that he may take, a *sure prospect* is simply any specific *outcome*. Therefore we shall use the terms "sure prospect" and "outcome" interchangeably.

Thus a sure prospect may involve possession of given amounts of money and/or physical commodities. It may also involve specification of certain noneconomic conditions, such as occupying a certain social position or being in a certain state of health. We shall assume that a sure prospect can always be characterized by specifying the values of a finite number of variables, i.e., by specifying a vector with a finite number of components. Therefore the set X of all sure prospects will be regarded as (a subset of) a finite-dimensional Euclidean space.

In contrast, in the case of *risk*, if the decision maker takes some particular action, then in general all that he can predict are the probabilities of alternative possible outcomes (sure prospects) that may result from his action. Therefore we have to define a *risky prospect*, or more exactly a *simple* risky prospect, as a probability distribution over the set X of all sure prospects. If the number of different sure prospects involved is finite, we shall write

$$B = (A_1, p_1; A_2, p_2; \ldots; A_k, p_k) \tag{3.1}$$

This notation is meant to indicate that the risky prospect B consists in having probability p_1 of obtaining A_1, having probability p_2 of obtaining A_2, and so on. A_1, $A_2, \ldots, A_k$ are called the *components* of B, while B itself is called a *probability mixture* of $A_1, A_2, \ldots, A_k$. The probabilities $p_1, \ldots, p_k$ of course must always satisfy the conditions

$$p_i \geqq 0 \qquad i = 1, \ldots, k \tag{3.2}$$

and

$$\sum_{i=1}^{k} p_i = 1 \tag{3.3}$$

Besides *simple* risky prospects, whose components are sure prospects, we shall also consider *composite* risky prospects, whose components (or at least some of them) may be themselves risky prospects or uncertain prospects. (See below; the intuitive meaning of such composite prospects will be discussed in connection with our notational conventions for risky and for uncertain prospects.) The set of all risky prospects, both simple and composite, will be called Y.

In the special case where $k = 2$, we will often use the notation

$$C = (A, p; B, 1 - p) \tag{3.4}$$

For risky prospects we will use the following notational conventions.

Notational conventions for risky prospects

Convention 1. Unity probability. Let $p = 1$. Then

$$(A, p; B, 1 - p) = (A, 1; B, 0) = A \tag{3.5}$$

That is, a risky prospect (say, a lottery ticket) yielding outcome A with probability 1, and yielding any alternative outcome B with probability 0, is the same thing as the full certainty of obtaining A.

In view of Convention 1 any sure prospect A can be formally written as a risky prospect $(A, 1; B, 0) = A$; thus sure prospects are formally special cases of risky prospects. Consequently, $X \subseteq Y$.

Convention 2. Commutativity.

$$(A, p; B, 1 - p) = (B, 1 - p; A, p) \tag{3.6}$$

That is, it does not matter in what order we list the prizes of a lottery so long as each prize remains associated with the same probability (say, A with probability p, and B with probability $1 - p$).

Convention 3. Addition of probabilities. Let $A_1 = A_2$. Then

$$(A_1, p_1; A_2, p_2; A_3, p_3; \ldots; A_n, p_n) \tag{3.7}$$

$$= (A_1, p_1 + p_2; A_3, p_3; \ldots; A_n, p_n)$$

That is, if $A_1 = A_2$, then, by the Addition Law for probabilities, the total probability of winning A_1 is $(p_1 + p_2)$.

Convention 4. Multiplication of probabilities. This is also called the "principle of two-stage lotteries." Let

$$C = (A, p; B, 1 - p) \tag{3.8}$$

and

$$E = (C, q; D, 1 - q) \tag{3.9}$$

Then

$$E = (A, pq; B, (1 - p)q; D, 1 - q) \tag{3.10}$$

Intuitively E can be interpreted as a two-stage lottery. At stage 1, the holder of this lottery ticket E will have probability q of winning lottery ticket C and will have probability $(1 - q)$ of winning prize D. If he wins C, then he will also participate in stage 2 of the lottery, where he will have probability p of winning prize A and will have probability $(1 - p)$ of winning prize B. Thus, by the Multiplication Law for probabilities (assuming that the outcomes of the stage-one and stage-two lotteries are statistically independent), he will have a total probability pq of winning A, a total probability $(1 - p)q$ of winning B, and a total probability $(1 - q)$ of winning D.

Convention 4 really involves two assumptions:

1. It involves the assumption that risky prospects obey the Multiplication Law of the probability calculus, which we have used in computing the probabilities pq, $(1 - p)q$, and $(1 - q)$ associated with the prizes A, B, and D, respectively.

2. At the same time, Convention 4 also assumes that the decision maker will be indifferent between a one-stage lottery and a two-stage lottery, as long as both of them yield him the same *prizes* with the same *probabilities*. This assumption follows from the general principle that the utility of any risky prospect to the decision maker will depend only on the prizes and the probabilities associated with them but will not depend on the physical processes used to generate these probabilities. For example, it does not matter whether a given probability $r = pq$ is generated by drawing lots, or by turning a roulette wheel, or by casting a die. In the same way it does not matter whether this probability is generated by *one* random event (e.g., by one lottery drawing) or by *two* random events (e.g., by two lottery drawings, corresponding to the two stages of a composite lottery).

3.2 Uncertain prospects

In the case of uncertainty, if the decision maker takes some particular action, then in general all he can predict is that his action will result in one of two or more alternative outcomes $A_1, A_2, \ldots, A_k$, where the objective probabilities associated with these alternative outcomes $A_1, A_2, \ldots, A_k$ are not known. We shall use the notation

$$B = (A_1|e_1; A_2|e_2; \ldots; A_k|e_k) \tag{3.11}$$

to indicate that, under the uncertain prospect B, outcome A_1 will obtain if event e_1 occurs, but outcome A_2 will obtain if event e_2 occurs, and so on.

For example, B may be a bet in a horse race, yielding prize A_1 if horse 1 wins, yielding prize A_2 if horse 2 wins, and so on. We shall require that the events e_1, $e_2, \ldots, e_k$ should always represent a set of mutually *exclusive* and *exhaustive* possibilities. That is, these k events must be chosen in such a way that always one and only one of them will occur in any given case. Thus in our example it must be true that always one and only one of the horses listed will win. (If this is not true, e.g., because the horse race might be cancelled, then this possibility will have to be included among the events $e_1, \ldots, e_k$.)

The possible outcomes $A_1, \ldots, A_k$ will be called the *components* of the uncertain prospect B, while B will be called the *contingency mixture* of $A_1, \ldots, A_k$ (because it will give rise to one of these outcomes $A_1, \ldots, A_k$, contingent on which of the events $e_1, \ldots, e_k$ will occur). The events $e_1, \ldots, e_k$ will be called the *conditioning events*.

We will consider *composite* uncertain prospects B, whose components $A_1, \ldots, A_k$ (or at least some of them) are themselves uncertain prospects and/or risky prospects. The set of all uncertain prospects, both simple and composite, will be called Z.

We will also use the term *mixed* composite prospects, as a common name for "risky" prospects having "uncertain" prospects as components, and "uncertain" prospects having "risky" prospects as components. In contrast, composite "risky" prospects having only "risky" prospects as components, and composite "uncertain" prospects having only "uncertain" prospects as components, will be called *pure* composite prospects.

In the special case where $k = 2$ we will often use the notation

$$C = (A|e; B|\bar{e}) \tag{3.12}$$

in which $\bar{e}$ denotes the event consisting in the nonoccurrence of event e; $\bar{e}$ is called the *complementary* event to e because the two together exhaust all possibilities. Of course, $\bar{\bar{e}} = e$. That is, if $\bar{e}$ does not occur, e does occur.

Notational conventions for uncertain prospects

Convention 1*. Full certainty.

$$(A|e; A|\bar{e}) = A \tag{3.13}$$

That is, if the same alternative A obtains both if event e *does* occur and if it does *not* occur, then A obtains with full certainty.

In view of Convention 1*, any *sure* prospect A can be written formally as an *uncertain* prospect, so that sure prospects can be regarded as special cases of uncertain prospects. Therefore $X \subseteq Z$. Indeed, as A can also be a risky prospect, we also have $Y \subseteq Z$. On the other hand, Convention 1 of Section 3.2 implies that $Z \subseteq Y$, because alternative A in Equation (3.5) can be an uncertain prospect. Consequently $Y = Z$. Nevertheless, for convenience of exposition we shall go on calling this set $Y = Z$ sometimes the set of all *risky* prospects and sometimes the set of all *uncertain* prospects, depending on the context.

Convention 2*. Commutativity.

$$(A|e; B|\bar{e}) = (B|\bar{e}; A|e) \tag{3.14}$$

That is, we can list the components of an uncertain prospect in any order that we wish, as long as each component remains associated with the same conditioning event (e.g., A with event e, and B with event $\bar{e}$).

Consider the following situation. Suppose that the outcome depends on the occurrence or nonoccurrence of *two* different statistically independent events e and f.[1] Thus there are four possible cases, viz., $ef, \bar{e}f, e\bar{f}$, and $\bar{e}\bar{f}$. Let us assume that these will give rise, respectively, to the outcomes A, B, A^*, and B^*. We can represent this situation by a double-entry table (see Table 3.1).

Table 3.1

	e	$\bar{e}$
f	A	B
$\bar{f}$	A^*	B^*

Table 3.2

	e	$\bar{e}$
p	A	B
$1-p$	A^*	B^*

Convention 3* below asserts that, using our notation for uncertain prospects, the situation represented by Table 3.1 can be described in three different but equivalent ways.

Convention 3*. Three equivalent descriptions for pure *composite uncertain prospects.*

$$(A|ef; B|\bar{e}f; A^*|e\bar{f}; B^*|\bar{e}\bar{f}) \tag{3.15}$$

$$= \{(A|e; B|\bar{e})|f; (A^*|e; B^*|\bar{e})|\bar{f}\}$$

$$= \{(A/f; A^*|\bar{f})|e; (B|f; B^*|\bar{f})|\bar{e}\}$$

Here the first expression lists each element of the matrix separately, together with the two relevant conditioning events. In contrast, the second expression displays the two uncertain prospects $(A|e; B|\bar{e})$ and $(A^*|e; B^*|\bar{e})$, corresponding to the two *row vectors* (A, B) and $(A*, B*)$ in the matrix, indicating that the first uncertain prospect will arise if event f *does* occur while the second will arise if event f does *not* occur. Finally, the third expression displays the two uncertain prospects $(A|f; A*|\bar{f})$ and $(B|f; B*|\bar{f})$, corresponding to the two *column vectors*

$$\begin{pmatrix} A \\ A* \end{pmatrix} \quad \text{and} \quad \begin{pmatrix} B \\ B* \end{pmatrix}$$

in the matrix, indicating that the first uncertain prospect will arise if event e *does* occur, while the second will arise if event e does *not* occur. Convention 3* asserts that all three expressions are equivalent, because all of them describe the situation represented by Table 3.1.

Convention 3* enables us to restrict our attention largely to two-component uncertain prospects, because it shows how we can build up many-component uncertain prospects from two-component ones.

Now let us change our assumptions. Suppose that the situation is like that represented by Table 3.1, except that the objective probabilities associated with events f and $\bar{f}$ are *known* and are in fact p and $(1 - p)$. But the probabilities associated with events e and $\bar{e}$ are again assumed to be *unknown* (see Table 3.2). Convention 4* below asserts that this situation again admits of two different but equivalent descriptions.

Convention 4. Two equivalent descriptions for* mixed *composite prospects.*

$$\{(A|e; B|\bar{e}), p; (A*|e; B*|\bar{e}), 1 - p\} \tag{3.16}$$

$$= \{(A, p; A*, 1 - p)|e; (B, p; B*, 1 - p)|\bar{e}\}$$

Both sides of the equation are *mixed* composite prospects. More particularly the expression on the left side is a *risky* prospect whose two components are the *uncertain* prospects $(A|e; B|\bar{e})$ and $(A*|e; B*|\bar{e})$ corresponding to the two *rows* of the matrix. In contrast, the expression on the right side is an *uncertain* prospect whose two components are the *risky* prospects $(A, p; A*, 1 - p)$ and $(B, p; B*, 1 - p)$ corresponding to the two *columns* of the matrix. Convention 4* asserts that these two expressions are equivalent, because both of them describe the situation represented by Table 3.2.

3.3 Utility maximization in the case of certainty

To describe a given decision maker's choice behavior, we shall use the concepts of "preference" and of "indifference." We shall say that A is *preferred* (or is *strictly preferred*) to B by the decision maker if he always (i.e., with probability 1) chooses A rather than B whenever he has to choose between them. We shall say that he is *indifferent* between A and B (or that A and B are *equivalent* for him) if he is equally likely to choose either (i.e., if he chooses either with probability $\frac{1}{2}$).

Under the idealized model of perfectly rational choice that we will use, clear preference and clear indifference will be the only two possibilities. That is, we will assume that, if A and B are the only two alternatives, then the decision maker can choose A (or B) only with probability 1, 0, or $\frac{1}{2}$. But, e.g., he cannot choose A (say) with a probability $\frac{2}{3}$, which would represent an attitude intermediate between clear preference for A and clear indifference between A and B, indicating that the decision maker could not consistently make up his mind about the relative value of A and of B to him, contrary to our concept of perfect rationality.

The following notations will be used: "$A > B$" will mean* "A is preferred (or strictly preferred) to B." "$A \sim B$ will mean "A is indifferent (or equivalent) to B."

Besides "strict preference" and "indifference," we shall also use the concept of "nonstrict preference," denoted by $\gtrsim$. "$A \gtrsim B$" will mean "A is at least as desirable as B," or "A is preferred to B or is at least equivalent to B." More formally we define

$$\text{"} A \gtrsim B \text{"} \quad \text{means} \quad \text{"either} \quad A > B \quad \text{or} \quad A \sim B \text{"} \tag{3.17}$$

So far we have used "strict preference" and "indifference" as our basic concepts and have defined "nonstrict preference" in terms of them. Although this is probably the intuitively more natural approach, for reasons of mathematical convenience in our formal analysis we shall reverse this procedure. We shall make "nonstrict preference" our basic concept and shall define both "strict preference" and "indifference" in terms of "nonstrict preference." Thus we shall define

$$\text{"} A > B \text{"} \quad \text{means} \quad \text{"} A \gtrsim B \quad \text{but } not \quad B \gtrsim A \text{"} \tag{3.18}$$

and

$$\text{"} A \sim B \text{"} \quad \text{means} \quad \text{"} A \gtrsim B \quad \text{and } also \quad B \gtrsim A \text{"} \tag{3.19}$$

If "strict preference" and "indifference" were used as basic concepts, then these two relations could be characterized by the following three axioms:

Axiom (a). Transitivity of strict preference. Suppose that $A > B$ and $B > C$. Then also $A > C$.

Axiom (b). Transitivity of indifference. Suppose that $A \sim B$ and $B \sim C$. Then also $A \sim C$.

Axiom (c). Principle of trichotomy. For any pair of sure prospects A and B, there are three mutually exclusive possibilities: *either $A > B$ or $A \sim B$ or $B > A$.*

Axioms (a) and (b) are consistency requirements; Axiom (c) expresses the requirement that the decision maker should be able to *compare* any two sure pros-

---

*In my manuscript, "A is preferred to B" was denoted as $A \succ B$, and the notation "$A > B$" was reserved for denoting "A is larger than B." In the printed text, both statements will be expressed by "$A > B$." The context will make it clear which meaning is intended.

pects A and B concerning their relative desirability. If he did not find A preferable to B, or B preferable to A, but did not feel indifferent between them, this would mean he would be simply unable to compare these two alternatives: This is the case that Axiom (c) is meant to exclude.

To be sure, both everyday observation and laboratory experiments show that people's actual choice behavior does not always conform to these three axioms. For example, people sometimes make intransitive choices, choosing A in preference to B, choosing B in preference to C, but then choosing C in preference to A. Again at times they seem unable to determine whether they prefer, for example, A to B or B to A or are indifferent between the two. Such deviations from our axioms, of course, do not affect their usefulness as axioms of a *normative* theory of rational behavior. We can always take the point of view that deviations from these axioms simply represent "irrational" behavior attributable, e.g., to various limitations in people's information-processing ability.

On the other hand, if we want to use these axioms in *positive* (explanatory or predictive) theories, then we must recognize that the axioms cannot be taken literally and are no more than convenient simplifying assumptions. But, as we argued in Section 2.1, theories based on such simplifying assumptions often do furnish fairly realistic predictions; and even in situations where this is not the case they may have considerable heuristic value.

Axioms (a), (b), and (c), which are stated in terms of "strict preference" and "indifference," are equivalent to the following two axioms, stated in terms of "nonstrict preference" (cf. Lemma 1 below).

Axiom (a*). Transitivity of nonstrict preference. Suppose that $A \gtrsim B$ and $B \gtrsim C$. Then also $A \gtrsim C$.

Axiom (b*). Completeness or connectedness of nonstrict preference. For any pair of sure prospects A and B, *either* $A \gtrsim B$ *or* $B \gtrsim A$ (or both). That is, A and B must be connected by a nonstrict preference relation at least in one direction but may be so connected in both directions.

Again Axiom (a*) is a consistency requirement, while Axiom (b*) expresses the requirement that any two sure prospects A and B must be comparable as to their relative desirability.

If a given relation, such as the relation $\gtrsim$, is both transitive and connected, then it is called a *complete preordering* [Debreu, 1959, pp. 7–8]. Thus we can replace Axioms (a*) and (b*) by the single statement that "nonstrict preference" is a complete preordering over the set X of all sure prospects.

The logical relationship between our two sets of axioms can be described as follows:

Lemma 1. Axioms (a), (b), and (c), together with Definition (3.17), imply Axioms (a*) and (b*). Conversely Axioms (a*) and (b*), together with Definitions (3.18) and (3.19), imply Axioms (a), (b), and (c).

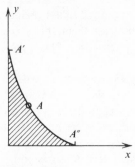

Figure 3.1

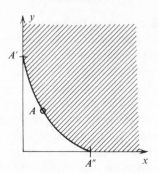

Figure 3.2

Proof of the lemma is trivial once we replace the relevant relations by their definitions (in the way indicated in the text of the lemma).

We will now introduce a few more definitions.

Let A be a given sure prospect. Let $I(A)$ be the set of all sure prospects B such that $A \gtrsim B$. [Thus $I(A)$ is the set of all sure prospects B inferior or equivalent to A.] Then $I(A)$ is called the *inferior set* for A. For example, suppose that there are only two commodities; let the x-coordinate represent the decision maker's stocks of commodity 1, and let the y-coordinate represent his stocks of commodity 2 (see Figure 3.1). The indifference curve $A'A''$ is the locus of all points (x, y) equivalent to point A for the decision maker. Then $I(A)$ is the set consisting of all points lying below and to the left of $A'A''$ and of all points lying on $A'A''$ itself.

Similarly let $S(A)$ be the set of all sure prospects C such that $C \gtrsim A$. [Thus $S(A)$ is the set of all sure prospects C superior or equivalent to A.] Then $S(A)$ is called the *superior set* for A. $S(A)$ is the set consisting of all points lying above and to the right of $A'A''$ and of all points lying on $A'A''$ itself (see Figure 3.2).

Let U be a real-valued function defined over the set X of all sure prospects, with the property that

$$U(A) \geqq U(B) \quad \text{iff} \quad A \gtrsim B \quad \text{in terms of the preferences of} \tag{3.20}$$
$$\text{individual } i$$

Here "iff" denotes "if and only if." Then U is called a *utility function* for individual i. We shall also say that U is a utility function *representing* i's preferences. It is easy to see that, if U satisfies condition (3.20), then individual i's choice behavior will be such *as if* he tried to *maximize* this utility function U by his choices.

Condition (3.20) is of course completely equivalent to the condition that

$$U(A) > U(B) \quad \text{iff} \quad A > B \tag{3.21}$$

$$U(A) = U(B) \quad \text{iff} \quad A \sim B$$

$$U(A) < U(B) \quad \text{iff} \quad B > A$$

We now state the following two axioms.

Axioms for rational behavior under certainty[2]

Axiom 1. Complete preordering. The relation of "nonstrict preference" is a complete preordering over the set X of all sure prospects. [That is, it satisfies Axioms (a*) and (b*).]

Axiom 2. Continuity. For any sure prospect A, both its inferior set $I(A)$ and its superior set $S(A)$ are closed sets.

Axiom 2 can also be stated as follows. Suppose that the sequence of sure prospects $B_1, B_2, \ldots$ converges to a given sure prospect B_0, and suppose that $A \gtrsim B_i$ for $i = 1, 2, \ldots$. Then also $A \gtrsim B_0$.

Likewise, suppose that the sequence of sure prospects $C_1, C_2, \ldots$ converges to a given sure prospect C_0, and suppose that $C_i \gtrsim A$ for $i = 1, 2, \ldots$. Then also $C_0 \gtrsim A$.

Intuitively Axiom 2 essentially asserts that there is a continuous relationship between the physical characteristics of a given sure prospect (e.g., the physical composition of a given commodity basket) and its relative desirability: A small change in the former will produce only a small change in the latter.

We can now state:

Theorem 3.1. Existence of a utility function. Suppose that the preferences of a given decision maker among sure prospects satisfy Axioms 1 and 2. Then there exists a continuous utility function U representing his preferences among sure prospects, and his choice behavior will be such *as if* he tried to maximize this utility function U.

For proof see Debreu [1959, pp. 55–59].

Note that the utility function U whose existence has been established by this theorem is an *ordinal utility function*, i.e., it is a utility function *unique only up to order-preserving monotone transformations*. That is, let V be another function defined over the set X of all sure prospects. Then V will also be a utility function representing the same decision maker's preferences if and only if it satisfies an equation of the form

$$V(A) = F\{U(A)\} \quad \text{for all} \quad A \in X \tag{3.22}$$

where F is a strictly increasing function (also called an order-preserving monotone transformation). This is so because, if U satisfies condition (3.20), then so will any function V defined by an equation of the form (3.22). Thus, if U is a utility function representing the preferences of a particular individual, then so will be also $V = U^3$ or $V = e^U$, and so on.

This means that for the purpose of expressing the decision maker's preferences only those properties of the utility function U that are invariant under order-preserving monotone transformations are relevant. These are called the *ordinal properties* of the utility function U. The term "ordinal utility function" is used to remind us of the fact that only the ordinal properties of the utility function U are relevant.

3.4   Expected-utility maximization in the case of risk

In the case of risk, our purpose will be to establish the existence of a utility function having the *expected-utility property*. We will say that a given utility function U has this property if it equates the utility of any risky prospect $C = (A, p; B, 1 - p)$ to its expected utility, i.e., to the expected value (mathematical expectation) of the utility function U for this risky prospect C. In other words, U will have the expected-utility property if and only if

$$U(C) = U(A, p; B, 1 - p) = p \cdot U(A) + (1 - p) \cdot U(B) \tag{3.23}$$

Obviously, if a given individual i has a utility function U possessing this property, then his choice behavior will be such *as if* he tried to maximize the *expected value* of this utility function U. A utility function U having the expected-utility property is called a *von Neumann–Morgenstern* utility function.

If we merely wanted to establish the existence of *some* utility function for the decision maker over risky prospects, all we would have to do is extend Axioms 1 and 2 (which we used in the case of certainty) to risky prospects. Among the axioms that we will use in the case of risk, Axioms 1* and 2* below are in fact essentially extensions of Axioms 1 and 2 risky prospects. But to ensure the existence of a utility function possessing the *expected-utility property* we will need a third axiom, Axiom 3*, which has no counterpart among the axioms we have used in the case of certainty.

We will now state two definitions. First we define the set $I^* = I^*(B; A, C)$, the *inferior probability set* for alternative B with respect to alternatives A and C, as follows. I^* is the set of all probability numbers p satisfying the condition:

$$B \gtrsim (A, p; C, 1 - p) \tag{3.24}$$

That is, I^* includes all probability numbers p such that the corresponding probability mixture $(A, p; C, 1 - p)$ would be inferior, or at best equivalent, to alternative B from the decision maker's point of view.

Next we define the set $S^* = S^*(B; A, C)$, the superior *probability set* for alternative B with respect to alternatives A and C, as follows. S^* is the set of all probability numbers q satisfying the condition

$$(A, q; C, 1 - q) \gtrsim B \tag{3.25}$$

That is, S^* includes all probability numbers q such that the corresponding probability mixture $(A, q; C, 1 - q)$ would be superior, or at worst equivalent, to alternative B from the decision maker's point of view.

Axioms for rational behavior under risk[3]

Axiom 1*. Complete preordering. The relation of "nonstrict preference" is a complete preordering over the set Y of all risky prospects.

Axiom 2*. Continuity. For any alternative B, with respect to any pair of alternatives A and C, both the superior probability set $S^*(B; A, C)$ and the inferior probability set $I^*(B; A, C)$ are closed sets.

Axiom 2* can also be stated as follows. Suppose that the sequence of probability numbers $p_1, p_2, \ldots$ converges to a given probability number p_0, and suppose that $B \gtrsim (A, p_i; C, 1 - p_i)$ for $i = 1, 2, \ldots$. Then also $B \gtrsim (A, p_0; C, 1 - p_0)$.

Likewise suppose that the sequence of probability numbers $q_1, q_2, \ldots$ converges to a given probability number q_0, and suppose that $(A, q_i; C, 1 - q_i) \gtrsim B$ for $i = 1, 2, \ldots$. Then also $(A, q_0; C, 1 - q_0) \gtrsim B$.

Intuitively Axiom 2* essentially asserts that the utility value of a risky prospect $D(p) = (A, p; C, 1 - p)$ depends *continuously* on the probability number p. That is, a small change in p will have only a small effect on the utility value of $D(p)$.

Axiom 3*. Monotonicity in prizes. Suppose that $A^* > A$ and $p > 0$. Then

$$(A^*, p; B, 1 - p) > (A, p; B, 1 - p) \qquad (3.26)$$

Conversely, if relationship (3.26) holds, then $A^* > A$.

That is, the utility value of a lottery ticket will increase if a given prize A is replaced by a preferred prize A^*, provided that the probability p of winning A (and A^*) is not 0 (in which case of course it makes no difference whether we replace A by A^* or not). Conversely, if replacing A by A^* makes the lottery ticket more valuable, then A^* must be a prize preferable to A for the decision maker.

Note that, instead of this *monotonicity principle*, as our third axiom we could also use the *substitution principle* (which appears as Lemma 1 below). While the monotonicity principle states that replacing a given prize by a *more* desirable prize will *increase* the value of a lottery ticket (as long as $p \neq 0$), the substitution principle asserts that replacing a given prize by an *equally* desirable prize will leave the value of the lottery ticket *unchanged*. We are using the monotonicity principle, rather than the substitution principle, because of the close connection that the former has to the *dominance principle* used in game theory.

Note also that our monotonicity principle is closely related to Savage's *sure-thing principle* [Savage, 1954, pp. 21–26]. But the sure-thing principle is a little weaker because it asserts only that the value of a lottery ticket cannot *decrease* if a given prize A is replaced by a more valuable prize A^*. In contrast, our monotonicity principle makes the stronger claim that in such a case the value of a lottery ticket will definitely *increase* (as long as the probability p of winning A or A^* is larger than 0).

Theorem 3.2. Existence of a utility function with the expected-utility property for risky prospects.[4] Suppose that a given decision maker's preferences among risky prospects satisfy Axioms 1*, 2*, and 3* and are also consistent with the identity relationships stated by Conventions 1, 2, and 3 of Section 3.1. Then there exists a utility function $U = U(A)$ representing his preferences and having the expected-utility property. Consequently his choice behavior will be such as if he wanted to maximize the expected value of this utility function U.

Before proving this theorem, we will first prove 10 lemmas.

Lemma 1.[5] Suppose that $A^* \sim A$. Then

$$(A^*, p; B, 1 - p) \sim (A, p; B, 1 - p) \tag{3.27}$$

Conversely, if relationship (3.27) holds, and if $p > 0$, then $A^* \sim A$.

Lemma 1 follows directly from Axiom 3*.

Lemma 2.

$$(A, p; A, 1 - p) = A \tag{3.28}$$

That is, if a given risky prospect yields A with probability 1, then it is equivalent to the full certainty of obtaining A. (Intuitively Lemma 2 expresses the same basic principle as Convention 1 does. But formally it is a different statement from Convention 1, so we must show that it is implied by our notational conventions.)

Proof. By Conventions 1 and 2,

$$(B, 0; A, 1) = A \tag{3.29}$$

Consequently

$$(A, p; A, 1 - p) = \{(B, 0; A, 1), p; A, 1 - p\} \tag{3.30}$$

But by Conventions 3 and 4,

$$\{(B, 0; A, 1), p; A, 1 - p\} = (B, 0; A, 1) = A \tag{3.31}$$

where the last equality follows from (3.29). By (3.30) and (3.31),

$$(A, p; A, 1 - p) = A \tag{3.32}$$

as desired.

Lemma 3. Suppose that $A > B$ and $0 < p < 1$. Then

$$A > (A, p; B, 1 - p) > B \tag{3.33}$$

That is, the utility value of any probability mixture of A and B lies between that of A and that of B.

Proof. By Axiom 3*, we can write

$$(A, p; A, 1 - p) > (A, p; B, 1 - p) > (B, p; B, 1 - p) \tag{3.34}$$

In view of Lemma 2, however, (3.34) implies (3.33) as desired.

Lemma 4. Suppose that

$$A > B \tag{3.35}$$

and

$$0 < p < q < 1 \tag{3.36}$$

Then

$$(A, q; B, 1 - q) > (A, p; B, 1 - p) \tag{3.37}$$

That is, the utility value of any probability mixture of two outcomes will increase, if we increase the probability associated with the *more* desirable outcome, and decrease the probability associated with the *less* desirable outcome.

Proof. Let

$$r = \frac{p}{q} \quad \text{so that} \quad p = qr \tag{3.38}$$

By (3.36) we can write

$$0 < r < 1 \tag{3.39}$$

Let

$$C = (A, q; B, 1 - q) \tag{3.40}$$

By Lemma 3, in view of (3.35),

$$C > B \tag{3.41}$$

Let

$$D = (C, r; B, 1 - r) \tag{3.42}$$

By Lemma 3, in view of (3.41),

$$C > D \tag{3.43}$$

But, by Conventions 3 and 4, in view of (3.40) and (3.42),

$$D = \{(A, q; B, 1 - q), r; B, 1 - r\} = (A, qr; B, 1 - qr) \tag{3.44}$$

By (3.38), this can also be written as

$$D = (A, p; B, 1 - p) \tag{3.45}$$

By (3.40), (3.43), and (3.45), we can write

$$C = (A, q; B, 1 - q) > D = (A, p; B, 1 - p) \tag{3.46}$$

as desired.

Lemma 5. Suppose that $A > B > C$. Then there exists a probability number p, with $0 < p < 1$, such that

$$(A, p; C, 1 - p) \sim B \tag{3.47}$$

Moreover, this number p is unique.

Proof. Consider the inferior and the superior probability sets $I^* = I^*(B; A, C)$ and $S^* = S^*(B; A, C)$. Neither of these two sets is empty because $0 \in I^*$ and $1 \in S^*$. By Axiom 2*, both I^* and S^* are closed sets. Moreover, their union is the whole closed interval $[0, 1]$. Consequently I^* and S^* must have at least one point p in common, because otherwise I^* and S^* would represent a decomposition of the closed interval $[0, 1]$ into two disjoint closed subsets, which is impossible. But, by definitions (3.18), (3.24), and (3.25), this common point p must have property (3.47), and so a number p having this property does exist. Also $0 < p < 1$, because $p = 0$ would imply $B \sim C$, while $p = 1$ would imply $B \sim A$, contrary to our assumption that $A > B > C$.

Indeed p is the only number having property (3.47). Suppose that there were two numbers, say, $p = p^*$ and $p = p^{**}$, having this property, with

$$p^* > p^{**} \tag{3.48}$$

Then we could write

$$(A, p^*; C, 1 - p^*) \sim B \sim (A, p^{**}; C, 1 - p^{**}) \tag{3.49}$$

Yet, by Lemma 4, in view of (3.48), we could also write

$$(A, p^*; C, 1 - p^*) > (A, p^{**}; C, 1 - p^{**}) \tag{3.50}$$

which contradicts (3.49). Thus there can be only one number p with property (3.47). This completes the proof.

It may happen that in the set Y of all risky prospects under consideration there is a *most preferred* (maximal) prospect Q and there is a *least preferred* (minimal) prospect R, with

$$Q > R \tag{3.51}$$

and with

$$Q \gtrsim A \gtrsim R \quad \text{for all} \quad A \in Y \tag{3.52}$$

However, if this is not the case, then we will arbitrarily select some highly desirable prospect and call it Q, and will arbitrarily select some highly undesirable prospect and call it R, such that $Q > R$. Let $Y^* = Y^*(Q, R)$ be the set of all risky prospects A such that $Q \gtrsim A \gtrsim R$. Thus Y^* is the set of all risky prospects lying between Q and R in utility. If the set Y of risky prospects does contain a maximal and a minimal element, then $Y^* = Y$. Otherwise Y^* will be a proper subset of Y.

By restricting our analysis temporarily to set Y^* we can simplify our proofs and can give a direct intuitive interpretation to the expected-utility maximization theorem (in terms of "characteristic probabilities" - see below).

Let A be any risky prospect in set Y^*. Because $Q \gtrsim A \gtrsim R$ and $Q > R$, by Lemma 5, we can always find a unique probability $p = p_A$ such that

$$(Q, p_A; R, 1 - p_A) \sim A \tag{3.53}$$

We shall call p_A the *characteristic probability* of this prospect A. We can now state:

Lemma 6. The function

$$U(A) = p_A \quad \text{for all} \quad A \in Y^* \tag{3.54}$$

is a utility function that represents the decision maker's preferences among risky prospects in set Y^*. Moreover,

$$U(Q) = p_Q = 1 \quad \text{and} \quad U(R) = p_R = 0 \tag{3.55}$$

Proof. We have to show that $U(A) = p_A$ satisfies Condition (3.20) [or, equivalently, Condition (3.21)] for all alternatives A in set Y^*. That is, we have to show that

(i) $p_A = p_B$ implies $A \sim B$, and
(ii) $p_A > p_B$ implies $A > B$, whereas, conversely,
(iii) $A \sim B$ implies $p_A = p_B$, and
(iv) $A > B$ implies $p_A > p_B$.

Now, in view of Definition (3.53), we can write

$$A \sim (Q, p_A; R, 1 - p_A) \quad \text{and} \quad B \sim (Q, p_B; R, 1 - p_B) \tag{3.56}$$

Hence $p_A = p_B = p$ implies $A \sim (Q, p; R, 1 - p) \sim B$, which establishes conclusion (i).

Next suppose that $p_A > p_B$. Then, by Lemma 4, in view of (3.56), we must have $A > B$, which establishes conclusion (ii).

Now suppose that $A \sim B$. Then we cannot have $p_A > p_B$, because, by conclusion (ii), this would imply $A > B$. Nor can we have $p_A < p_B$, because, by conclusion (ii), this would imply $B > A$. Therefore we must have $p_A = p_B$, which establishes conclusion (iii).

Finally suppose that $A > B$. Then we cannot have $p_A = p_B$, because, by conclusion (i), this would imply $A \sim B$. Nor can we have $p_A < p_B$, because, by conclusion (ii), this would imply $B > A$. Therefore we must have $p_A > p_B$ which establishes conclusion (iv).

To establish statement (3.55), we note that, by Conventions 1 and 2, $Q = (Q, 1; R, 0)$, while $R = (Q, 0; R, 1)$. This completes the proof.

Lemma 7. The utility function $U(A) = p_A$ has the expected-utility property.

Proof. Let

$$C = (A, q; B, 1 - q) \tag{3.57}$$

We have to show that

$$p_C = q p_A + (1 - q) p_B \tag{3.58}$$

where p_A, p_B, and p_C are the characteristic probabilities satisfying

$$A \sim (Q, p_A; R, 1 - p_A) \tag{3.59}$$

$$B \sim (Q, p_B; R, 1 - p_B) \tag{3.60}$$

and

$$C \sim (Q, p_C; R, 1 - p_C) \tag{3.61}$$

By Convention 3, in view of (3.57), (3.59), and (3.60), we can write

$$C \sim \{(Q, p_A; R, 1 - p_A), q; (Q, p_B; R, 1 - p_B), 1 - q\} \tag{3.62}$$

$$= \{Q, qp_A + (1 - q)p_B; R, (1 - q)p_A - (1 - q)p_B\}$$

By conclusion (iii) in the proof of Lemma 6, (3.61) and (3.62) together imply (3.58), as desired.

Lemmas 6 and 7 together establish Theorem 3.2 for the risky prospects belonging to set $Y^* = Y^*(Q, R)$. The proof of Lemma 7 also shows that the expected-utility maximization theorem as restricted to set Y^* can be written in the form of Equation (3.58); written in this form it has a very natural intuitive interpretation: *It is a direct consequence of the Multiplication and Addition Laws of the probability calculus.*

We now extend the utility function U to the whole set Y (in case $Y^* \neq Y$) as follows:

Let $A > Q$. Then, by Lemma 5, we can always find a unique probability r_A such that

$$(A, r_A; R, 1 - r_A) \sim Q \tag{3.63}$$

We now define

$$U(A) = \frac{1}{r_A} \tag{3.64}$$

Obviously under this definition, if $A > Q$, then $U(A) > U(Q) = 1$, since $0 < r_A < 1$.

Alternatively let $R > A$. Then, again by Lemma 5, we can always find a unique probability t_A such that

$$(A, t_A; Q, 1 - t_A) \sim R \tag{3.65}$$

We now define

$$U(A) = 1 - \frac{1}{t_A} \tag{3.66}$$

Clearly under this definition, if $R > A$, then $U(A) < U(R) = 0$, since $0 < t_A < 1$.

It remains to be shown that this extended function U is still a utility function with the expected-utility property, i.e., that U still exhibits properties (3.21) and (3.23).

Let Q^o and R^o be two risky prospects such that $Q^o > Q$ and $R > R^o$, and let $Y^o = Y^o(Q^o, R^o)$ be the set of all risky prospects A with $Q^o \gtrsim A \gtrsim R^o$. For each A in Y^o, let p_A^o be the unique probability satisfying

$$(Q^o, p_A^o; R^o, 1 - p_A^o) \sim A \tag{3.67}$$

Then we can state:

Lemma 8. The function

$$U^o(A) = p_A^o \tag{3.68}$$

is a utility function and has the expected-utility property.

Proof. Lemma 8 directly follows from Lemmas 6 and 7 if we choose Q^o as our prospect Q and choose R^o as our prospect R.

Lemma 9. For all $A \in Y^o(Q^o, R^o)$ we can write

$$U^o(A) = \alpha U(A) + \beta \tag{3.69}$$

where

$$\alpha = U^o(Q) - U^o(R) > 0 \tag{3.70}$$

whereas

$$\beta = U^o(R) \tag{3.71}$$

Proof. We will distinguish three cases.

Case 1: $Q^o \gtrsim A > Q$. In this case $U(A)$ is defined by (3.63) and (3.64). But, by Lemma 8, (3.63) implies that

$$r_A U^o(A) + (1 - r_A) U^o(R) = U^o(Q) \tag{3.72}$$

which in turn implies (3.69), in view of (3.70) and (3.71).

Case 2: $Q \gtrsim A \gtrsim R$. In this case $U(A)$ is defined by (3.53) and (3.54). But, by Lemma 8, (3.53) implies that

$$p_A U^o(Q) + (1 - p_A) U^o(R) = U^o(A) \tag{3.73}$$

which in turn again implies (3.69).

Case 3: $R > A \gtrsim R^o$. In this case $U(A)$ is defined by (3.65) and (3.66). But, by Lemma 8, (3.65) implies that

$$t_A U^o(A) + (1 - t_A) U^o(Q) = U^o(R) \tag{3.74}$$

which in turn once more implies (3.69).

Finally the inequality stated in (3.70) follows from the facts that $Q > R$ and that, by Lemma 8, U^o has property (3.21).

Lemma 10. The extended function U is a utility function with the expected-utility property for all prospects A in the set $Y^o(Q^o, R^o)$.

Proof. In view of Lemma 9, for all $A \in Y^o(Q^o, R^o)$ we can write

$$U(A) = \alpha * U^o(A) + \beta *$$ (3.75)

where

$$\alpha * = 1/\alpha > 0$$ (3.76)

whereas

$$\beta * = -\beta/\alpha$$ (3.77)

By (3.75) and (3.76), U is a strictly increasing function of U^o. But, by Lemma 8, U^o has property (3.21). Therefore U must have the same property. Again, by (3.75), U is a linear transform of U^o. But, by Lemma 8, U^o has property (3.23). It is easy to verify that this implies that any linear transform of U^o will also have this property. Therefore U will have both properties (3.21) and (3.23) over the whole set $Y^o(Q^o, R^o)$. This completes the proof.

Clearly the prospects Q^o and R^o mentioned in Lemmas 8 through 10 can be chosen arbitrarily, so that the set $Y^o(Q^o, R^o)$ can be made to cover as wide a range of possible utility levels as desired. Consequently Lemma 10 implies that Theorem 3.2 is true for the *whole set* Y of risky prospects.

Note: We have seen that in the case of certainty the decision maker's choice behavior can be analyzed in terms of an *ordinal* utility function, *unique only up to monotone transformations.* [See Equation (3.22) and the subsequent discussion.] This implies that only those properties of his utility function that are invariant under all monotone transformations can have a behavioral meaning: These we have called the *ordinal properties* of his utility function.

In contrast, in the case of risk, the decision maker's behavior can best be analyzed in terms of a utility function possessing the expected-utility property (often called a von Neumann–Morgenstern utility function). Theorem 3.2 establishes the existence of such a utility function, if the decision maker's choice behavior satisfies the appropriate consistency requirements. Such a utility function is *unique up to order-preserving linear transformations* and is therefore called a *cardinal* utility function. That is, let U and V be two utility functions representing the same decision maker's preferences between risky prospects, and suppose that U has the expected-utility property. Then, in order that V should likewise possess the expected-utility property, it is both sufficient and necessary that V should uniformly satisfy an equation of the form

$$V(A) = aU(A) + b \quad \text{for all} \quad A \in Y \tag{3.78}$$

where a and b are both real-valued constants with $a > 0$.

To put it differently, suppose that a given decision maker's choice behavior satisfies our axioms, and we want to define a utility function U with the expected-utility property for him. Then we are free to choose a *zero point* and a *utility unit* for U in any way that we wish. But once these two parameters have been chosen, the utility function U will be uniquely determined. [Choosing a zero point and a utility unit for U is, of course, equivalent to choosing two alternatives Q and R, with $Q > R$, and assigning the utility value $U(Q) = 1$ to the former, while assigning the utility value $U(R) = 0$ to the latter. We have already seen that once Q and R are chosen, the utility function U is uniquely determined by Equations (3.54), (3.64), and (3.66).]

3.5 Expected-utility maximization in the case of uncertainty

In the case of uncertainty, in accordance with the Bayesian approach, our purpose will be to establish the existence of a utility function that has the *expected-utility property*, not only in terms of objective probabilities known to the decision maker but also in terms of his own *subjective probabilities*, which he assigns to events whose objective probabilities are unknown to him. That is, we want to establish the existence of a utility function U defining the utility $U(C)$ of any uncertain prospect $C = (A \mid e; B \mid \bar{e})$ as

$$U(C) = U(A \mid e; B \mid \bar{e}) = p^e U(A) + (1 - p^e) U(B) \quad \text{with} \quad 0 \leqq p^e \leqq 1 \tag{3.79}$$

where the quantity p^e, called the decision maker's subjective probability for event e, depends only on event e itself and not on alternatives A and B. That is, for any other uncertain prospect $C^* = (A^* \mid e; B^* \mid \bar{e})$ with the same conditioning event e we should be able to write in a similar fashion

$$U(C^*) = U(A^* \mid e; B^* \mid \bar{e}) = p^e U(A^*) + (1 - p^e) U(B^*) \tag{3.80}$$

where p^e is the *same* quantity as in (3.79), regardless of the choice of A^* and B^*. The quantity $p^{\bar{e}} = 1 - p^e$ is called the decision maker's subjective probability for the complementary event $\bar{e}$.

Various alternative sets of axioms can be used to establish the existence of a utility function U and of subjective probabilities p^e, which together satisfy Equation (3.79). The axioms most commonly used for this purpose were proposed by Savage [1954]. Under his approach no formal distinction is made between *objective* and *subjective* probabilities. (He actually uses the term "personal probabilities" to describe what we call "subjective probabilities.") Rather, *all* probabilities used by the decision maker are considered to be *subjective* probabilities, even those that are based on long-run frequencies known to him. Accordingly Savage's theory does not require the assumption that there are any objective probabilities known to the decision maker at all.

However, there is a price for avoiding this assumption. One of Savage's seven postulates, Postulate 4, is equivalent to assuming that the decision maker entertains at least consistent *qualitative* subjective probabilities for alternative events – in the sense that in the appropriate choice situations he will act on the basis of his judgement concerning whether a given event e or the complementary event $\bar{e}$ is *more likely* (or whether he feels that they are equally likely). In our notations Savage's Postulate 4 asserts:

Postulate S4. Existence of consistent qualitative subjective probabilities.[6] Suppose that $A \gtrsim B$ and $A^* \gtrsim B^*$. Suppose also that

$$C = (A \mid e; B \mid \bar{e}) \gtrsim D = (B \mid e; A \mid \bar{e}) \tag{3.81}$$

Then also

$$C^* = (A^* \mid e; B^* \mid \bar{e}) \gtrsim D^* = (B^* \mid e; A^* \mid \bar{e}) \tag{3.82}$$

In other words, if the decision maker (nonstrictly) prefers C to D, then he must feel that e is *at least as* likely to occur as $\bar{e}$ is (otherwise he would prefer to associate the more valuable prize A with $\bar{e}$ and the less valuable prize B with e, rather than the other way around). But then he must likewise (nonstrictly) prefer C^* to D^* for the same reason. Thus Postulate S4 assumes that, when the decision maker chooses between C and D or between C^* and D^*, he will form a *qualitative* probability judgment, at least implicitly, about whether event e or event $\bar{e}$ is more likely to occur. This judgment will be independent of the prizes A, B, A^*, and B^*.

To be sure, Postulate S4 assumes only a *qualitative* probability judgment on the part of the decision maker and does not explicitly assume any *quantitative* probability judgment (about numerical subjective probabilities) on his part – but it comes dangerously close to doing precisely this. The statement that $\text{Prob}(e) \geq \text{Prob}(\bar{e})$ is exactly equivalent to the statement that $\text{Prob}(e) \geq \frac{1}{2}$, while $\text{Prob}(\bar{e}) \leq \frac{1}{2}$, because $\text{Prob}(e) + \text{Prob}(\bar{e}) = 1$. By means of our axioms we are trying to prove the proposition that the decision maker's choice behavior will be such as if it were based on judgments concerning numerical subjective probabilities; in my view Postulate S4 comes undesirably close to assuming from the outset the actual proposition that we are trying to prove.

Anscombe and Aumann [1963], and also Pratt, Raiffa, and Schlaifer [1964], have shown that Postulate S4 and any similar assumption can be dispensed with if we are willing to assume that the decision maker knows at least *some* objective probabilities. Indeed it is sufficient if he knows the objective probabilities associated with the behavior of *one* random mechanism capable of producing all probabilities between zero and unity. This may be, for example, a random mechanism whose output is a random variable with a uniform continuous probability distribution (or with any other absolutely continuous probability distribution known to the decision maker). In fact, from a practical point of view, it may be even a random device that produces a known discrete probability distribution (such as repeated throws of a given fair coin), if the latter can at least suitably *approximate*, even if it cannot always exactly *reach*, any probability between 0 and 1).

The random mechanism whose statistical behavior is assumed to be known to the decision maker will be called the *canonical random mechanism*, and events defined in terms of possible alternative outcomes of this mechanism will be called *canonical events*. (Thus the canonical events are the events whose objective probabilities are assumed to be known to the decision maker.) Finally a risky prospect $(A, p; B, 1 - p)$ will now have to be interpreted as a situation in which *either A or B* will obtain depending on the occurrence or nonoccurrence of some canonical event e whose objective probability is p. In terms of our notation this means that $(A, p; B, 1 - p) = (A \mid e; B \mid \bar{e})$, where p is the objective probability of e, known to the decision maker.

The statement that the decision maker *knows* the objective probability of every canonical event e can be interpreted as saying that he knows the long-run *frequency* of this event. This is the interpretation most convenient to use in many cases. But we can also use the following interpretation. We may interpret this statement as saying that *in the case of canonical events* the decision maker will assess the (qualitative) probability of each event in a consistent manner, in accordance with Postulate S4. Thus we may say that the main result established by Anscombe and Aumann, and again by Pratt, Raiffa, and Schlaifer, is the fact that we need not assume that the decision maker has consistent qualitative subjective probabilities for *all* events; rather, it is sufficient to assume that he has such probabilities for *canonical* events, possibly representing merely the behavior of *one* suitably chosen random mechanism. From this assumption (in conjunction with our axioms and notational conventions) we can derive as a *theorem* that our decision maker's behavior will have consistent subjective probabilities and will satisfy Postulate S4 with respect to *all* events.

We will now state our axioms for uncertainty, which are based on those of Anscombe and Aumann [1963].

Axioms for rational behavior under uncertainty

Axiom 1**. *Complete preordering.* The relation of "nonstrict preference" is a complete preordering over the set Z of all uncertain prospects.

Axiom 2**. *Expected-utility property for risky prospects.* The decision maker has a utility function U which to any risky prospect $C = (A, p; B, 1 - p)$ assigns the utility

$$U(C) = U(A, p; B, 1 - p) = pU(A) + (1 - p)U(B) \qquad (3.83)$$

Axiom 2** can also be stated by saying that the decision maker's preferences among risky prospects satisfy Axioms 1*, 2*, and 3*, as well as Conventions 1, 2, and 3. By Theorem 3.2 these axioms and conventions together imply Equation (3.83).

Axiom 3**. *Monotonicity in prizes for uncertain prospects (Sure-thing principle for uncertain prospects).* Suppose that $A^* \gtrsim A$. Then

$$(A^* | e; B | \bar{e}) \gtrsim (A | e; B | \bar{e}) \tag{3.84}$$

That is, if a given prize A is replaced by a more valuable prize A^*, this *cannot decrease* the value of a lottery ticket – even if the probability of winning prize A or A^* is not known. Axiom 3** is obviously a natural analogue to Axiom 3*.

Thus our three axioms for uncertainty do nothing more than *reaffirm* and *extend* our axioms for risk. Axiom 2** merely reaffirms Axioms 1* to 3* for *risky* prospects, whereas Axioms 1** and 3** extend Axioms 1* and 3*, respectively, from *risky* prospects to *uncertain* prospects. But none of these axioms involves any fundamentally new assumption going essentially beyond our axioms for risk.

Lemma 1. Suppose that $A^* \sim A$. Then

$$(A^* | e; B | \bar{e}) \sim (A | e; B | \bar{e}) \tag{3.85}$$

That is, if a given prize A is replaced by an equivalent prize A^*, this will not change the value of a lottery ticket. This lemma is obviously a direct analogue of Lemma 1 of Section 3.4 and may be called a substitution principle for uncertain prospects.

Proof. In view of Definition (3.19), the lemma directly follows from Axiom 3**.

Lemma 2. Let U be the utility function defined by the relationship

$$U(A) = p_A \tag{3.86}$$

where p_A is the *characteristic probability* of prospect A as defined by Condition (3.53). Let $C = (A | e; R | \bar{e})$. Then

$$U(C) = U(A | e; R | \bar{e}) = p_A \cdot U(Q | e; R | \bar{e}) \tag{3.87}$$

Proof. In view of Lemma 1 and Statement (3.53), we have

$$(A | e; R | \bar{e}) \sim \{(Q, p_A; R, 1 - p_A) | e; R | \bar{e}\}$$
$$= \{(Q, p_A; R, 1 - p_A) | e; (R, p_A; R, 1 - p_A) | \bar{e}\} \tag{3.88}$$

since $R = (R, p_A; R, 1 - p_A)$. But, in view of Convention 4*,

$$\{(Q, p_A; R, 1 - p_A) | e; (R, p_A; R, 1 - p_A) | \bar{e}\}$$
$$= \{(Q | e; R | \bar{e}), p_A; (R | e; R | \bar{e}), 1 - p_A\}$$
$$= \{(Q | e; R | \bar{e}), p_A; R, 1 - p_A\} \tag{3.89}$$

where the last equality follows from the fact that, by Convention 1*, $(R \mid e; R \mid \bar{e}) = R$. In view of (3.88) and (3.89), we can write

$$(A \mid e; R \mid \bar{e}) \sim \{(Q \mid e; R \mid \bar{e}), p_A; R, 1 - p_A\} \tag{3.90}$$

Taking utilities on both sides and using Axiom 2**, we obtain

$$U(A \mid e; R \mid \bar{e}) = p_A U(Q \mid e; R \mid \bar{e}) + (1 - p_A) U(R) \tag{3.91}$$

Because $U(R) = 0$, this gives us Equation (3.87), as desired.

Theorem 3.3. Existence of a utility function with the expected-utility property in terms of the decision maker's subjective probabilities. Let us define

$$p^e = U(Q \mid e; R \mid \bar{e}) \tag{3.92}$$

and

$$p^{\bar{e}} = U(Q \mid \bar{e}; R \mid e) \tag{3.93}$$

We call the quantities p^e and $p^{\bar{e}}$ the decision maker's *subjective probabilities* for event e and for event $\bar{e}$, respectively. Then

$$p^e + p^{\bar{e}} = 1 \tag{3.94}$$

and

$$U(A \mid e; B \mid \bar{e}) = p^e \cdot U(A) + p^{\bar{e}} \cdot U(B) \tag{3.95}$$

In other words, the utility function U defined by Equation (3.86) has the desired expected-utility property in accordance with Equation (3.79).

Proof. Equation (3.94) is a special case of Equation (3.95) and can be obtained from the latter by setting $A = B = Q$. Therefore it is sufficient to prove Equation (3.95).

Let us define

$$C = \{(A \mid e; R \mid \bar{e}), \tfrac{1}{2}; (R \mid e; B \mid \bar{e}), \tfrac{1}{2}\} \tag{3.96}$$

$$D = \{(A, \tfrac{1}{2}; R, \tfrac{1}{2}) \mid e; (R, \tfrac{1}{2}; B, \tfrac{1}{2}) \mid \bar{e}\} \tag{3.97}$$

$$D^* = \{(A, \tfrac{1}{2}; R, \tfrac{1}{2}) \mid e; (B, \tfrac{1}{2}; R, \tfrac{1}{2}) \mid \bar{e}\} \tag{3.98}$$

$$C^* = \{(A \mid e; B \mid \bar{e}), \tfrac{1}{2}; (R \mid e; R \mid \bar{e}), \tfrac{1}{2}\} \tag{3.99}$$

$$= \{(A \mid e; B \mid \bar{e}), \tfrac{1}{2}; R, \tfrac{1}{2}\}$$

Now, by Convention 3*, $C = D$. By Convention 2, $D = D^*$. By Convention 3*, $D^* = C^*$. Consequently $C = C^*$, and so we can write

$$\{(A \mid e; R \mid \bar{e}), \tfrac{1}{2}; (R \mid e; B \mid \bar{e}), \tfrac{1}{2}\} = \{(A \mid e; B \mid \bar{e}), \tfrac{1}{2}; R, \tfrac{1}{2}\} \tag{3.100}$$

Taking utilities on both sides and using Axiom 2* we obtain

$$\tfrac{1}{2} U(A\,|\,e; R\,|\,\bar{e}) + \tfrac{1}{2} U(R\,|\,e; B\,|\,\bar{e}) = \tfrac{1}{2} U(A\,|\,e; B\,|\,\bar{e}) + \tfrac{1}{2} U(R) \tag{3.101}$$

But $U(R) = 0$. Moreover, by Lemma 2 and by Equations (3.92) and (3.93), we have

$$U(A\,|\,e; R\,|\,\bar{e}) = p_A \cdot U(Q\,|\,e; R\,|\,\bar{e}) = U(A) \cdot p^e \tag{3.102}$$

and

$$U(B\,|\,\bar{e}; R\,|\,e) = p_B \cdot U(Q\,|\,\bar{e}; R\,|\,e) = U(B) \cdot p^{\bar{e}} \tag{3.103}$$

Consequently Equation (3.101) can also be written as

$$p^e \cdot U(A) + p^{\bar{e}} \cdot U(B) = U(A\,|\,e; B\,|\,\bar{e}) \tag{3.104}$$

which is the same as Equation (3.95). This completes the proof.

Note 1: The utility function $U(A) = p_A$ used in Theorem 3.3 is the same utility function as that used in Theorem 3.2. Consequently it is a *cardinal* utility function and is *unique up to order-preserving linear transformations.*

Note 2: Equations (3.92) and (3.93) define the subjective probabilities of events e and $\bar{e}$ in terms of the utilities that the decision maker assigns to the uncertain prospects $F = (Q\,|\,e; R\,|\,\bar{e})$ and $G = (Q\,|\,\bar{e}; R\,|\,e)$, respectively. But, in view of Equation (3.86), these utilities themselves are defined in terms of the corresponding characteristic probabilities, by setting $U(F) = p_F$ and $U(G) = p_G$. This means that the *subjective* probability p^e of any event e is defined as being equal to the objective probability $p = \mathrm{Prob}(e^*)$ of some canonical event e^*, which satisfies the equivalence relationship

$$(Q\,|\,e; R\,|\,\bar{e}) \sim (Q\,|\,e^*; R\,|\,\bar{e}^*) = (Q, p; R, 1 - p) \tag{3.105}$$

In other words, we can say that the canonical event e^* is, in the decision maker's judgment, *equally likely* to event e, because, if we replace e by e^* as conditioning event in the uncertain prospect $(Q\,|\,e; R\,|\,\bar{e})$, then this will not change the utility of the latter to him. Thus the *known* probability p of a canonical event e^* is used to measure the decision maker's estimate of the *unknown* probability of event e.

Note 3: Theorem 3.3 defines the subjective probabilities p^e and $p^{\bar{e}}$ of events e and $\bar{e}$ in terms of the utilities of the prospects F and G, whose components are the prospect Q (with utility 1) and the prospect R (with utility 0). But these definitions do not involve the prospects A and B mentioned in the theorem. Thus the subjective probability p^e of any event e is *independent* of the choice of A and B, in agreement with Postulate S4. Consequently Theorem 3.3 *implies* Postulate S4. However, our proof of the theorem *has made no use* of the postulate, or of any similar assumption, with reference to events outside the special class of canonical events. (We have seen that the assumption that the decision maker knows the probabilities of canonical events essentially amounts to assuming that his behavior follows Postulate S4, at least with respect to canonical events e^*.)

3.6 Our postulates of rational expectations and the principle of best information

As we stated in Section 1.4, our theory of rational behavior in game situations will represent a generalization of Bayesian decision theory. In accordance with the Bayesian approach, we will assume that each player i will express his expectations about the behavior of any other player j by assigning *subjective probabilities* to alternative actions (or alternative strategies) that player j may choose. But, contrary to the Bayesian approach *as it is often interpreted*, we shall considerably *restrict* player i's freedom in selecting his subjective probabilities. For we require that the probabilities selected by player i should be consistent with the assumption that player j, like player i himself, is a rational individual and will act rationally in the game, pursuing his own interests in an effective manner. This requirement will be called the *principle of mutually expected rationality*. In our formal theory this principle will be stated by way of introducing certain rationality postulates, to be called *postulates of rational expectations*, specifying the expectations that an intelligent player can rationally entertain about another intelligent player's behavior.

In my opinion, in actual fact this use of the principle of mutually expected rationality and of the corresponding rationality postulates is in full agreement with the true meaning of the Bayesian approach. To be sure, if we look only at the formal axioms and notational conventions of Bayesian decision theory (as stated in Sections 3.2 and 3.5), then the decision maker is free to choose his subjective probabilities in any way that he desires, as long as his choices are consistent with the basic laws of the probability calculus (in particular, with the Addition and the Multiplication Laws). But in any practical application of the Bayesian approach there is always an implicit recognition of the principle that the decision maker must choose his subjective probabilities in a rational manner, i.e., in the light of the best information available to him. We will call this the *principle of best information*.

Our own principle of mutually expected rationality is essentially a *specialization* of this principle of best information. It represents an application of the latter principle to game situations in which each player has good reasons to believe, on the basis of the best information available to him, that the other players are also intelligent individuals, likely to display rational behavior in the game.

The main reason that the principle of best information is usually not included among the formal axioms of Bayesian decision theory is that it is not needed to establish the main results of the theory. In particular it is not needed to establish the expected-utility maximization theorem (our Theorem 3.3). Moreover, stating the principle in a precise and logically satisfactory manner poses some difficult and, thus far, partly unsolved analytical problems.[7]

In contrast, as we will see, the more restricted principle of mutually expected rationality poses no similar problems and can be translated without difficulty into specific formal rationality postulates. These rationality postulates will play an essential role in establishing the main results of our theory.

4

Morality and social welfare

A CONSTRUCTIVE APPROACH

4.1 Disregard of one's personal identity – a model for moral value judgments

In Section 1.3 we divided the general theory of rational behavior into individual decision theory, ethics, and game theory. In Chapter 3 we summarized the main results of *individual decision theory*, following Debreu [1959], Herstein and Milnor [1953], and Anscombe and Aumann [1963]. In this chapter we will review the main results of our own work in *ethics* and will discuss a related result by Fleming [cf. Harsanyi, 1953, 1955, and 1958; Fleming, 1952]. Most of these results were originally developed for the purposes of welfare economics but will be discussed here from a more general ethical point of view. The remaining chapters of this book will deal with *game theory*.

People often take a friendly (positive) or an unfriendly (negative) interest in other people's well-being. Technically this means that the utility function of a given individual *i* may assign positive or negative utility to the *utility level* as such of some other individuals *j*, or to the objective economic, social, biological, and other conditions determining the latter's utility levels. The question naturally arises: What factors will decide the relative importance that any given individual's utility function will assign to the well-being of various other individuals or social groups? We have called this question the problem of *dominant loyalties* (Section 2.3). This question obviously requires a rather complicated answer. But that much is clear that, according to common experience, people in most cases tend to give lesser weight to other people's interests than to their own, and tend to give lesser weight to the interests of complete strangers than to the interests of people close to them.

However, there are occasions when people make, or are at least expected to make, a special effort to assess social situations from an impartial and impersonal point of view, giving *equal weight* to the legitimate interests of each participant. For example, we expect judges and public officials to be guided by such impartial criteria when they act in their official capacities as the guardians of unbiased justice and of general social interests (i.e., of the "public interest"). Indeed *every person* is expected to follow such impartial criteria when he makes *moral value judgments*.

Since Adam Smith, moral philosophers have often pointed out that the moral point of view is essentially the point of view of a *sympathetic* but *impartial* observer. It is the point of view of a person taking a positive sympathetic interest in the welfare of *each* participant but having no partial bias in favor of *any* participant.

Originally the moral point of view is that of an *outsider*, not that of an interested party. Given a conflict of interest between two or more individuals, the natural inclination of each party will be to judge the situation from his own one-sided point of view. An impartial moral point of view will be taken only by an outside observer whose personal interests are not involved – or by such interested parties who make a *special effort* to look at the situation with the eyes of an impartial observer. Obviously one does not have to *be* an outsider in order to take the moral point of view; but one has to make a serious attempt to judge the situation *as if* one *were* a detached outsider: Otherwise one is simply not engaged in the activity called "making a moral value judgment."

These considerations suggest the following model. Society consists of n individuals, referred to as individuals $1, \ldots, i, \ldots, n$. Suppose that individual i wants to make a *moral value judgment*. This will always involve comparing two or more social situations concerning their relative merits from a moral point of view. These social situations may be alternative patterns of social behavior (alternative moral rules), alternative institutional frameworks, alternative government policies, alternative patterns of income distributions, and so forth. Mathematically any social situation can be regarded as a *vector* listing the economic, social, biological, and other variables that will affect the well-being of the individuals making up the society. Different social situations will be called $A, B, \ldots$. Let U_i be the von Neumann–Morgenstern cardinal utility function of individual i ($i = 1, \ldots, n$). Thus $U_i(A)$ will denote the (cardinal) utility level that individual i enjoys (or would enjoy) in social situation A.

Now if individual i wants to make a moral value judgment about the merits of alternative social situations $A, B, \ldots$, he must make a serious attempt not to assess these social situations simply in terms of his own personal preferences and personal interests but rather in terms of some impartial and impersonal criteria. For example, if individual i expresses certain views about how rich men and poor men, or motorists and pedestrians, or teachers and students, and so on, should behave toward each other, these views will qualify as true moral value judgments only if they are not significantly influenced by the fact that he himself happens to be a rich man or a poor man, a motorist or a pedestrian, a teacher or a student. Likewise, for example, if he expresses some views about the merits of alternative government policies, these views will qualify as true moral value judgments, only if they are not significantly influenced by the fact that he himself is a member of the social group directly favored (or disfavored) by these government policies.

Individual i's choice among alternative social situations would certainly satisfy this requirement of impartiality and impersonality, if he simply *did not know in advance* what his own social position would be in each social situation – so that he would not know whether he himself would be a rich man or a poor man, a motorist or a pedestrian, a teacher or a student, a member of one social group or a member of another social group, and so forth. More specifically this requirement would be satisfied if he thought that he would have an *equal probability* of being *put in the place* of any one among the *n* individual members of society, from the first individual (say, the one in the *best* social position) to the *n*th individual (say, the one in the *worst* social position). But then, technically, his choice among alternative social situations would be a choice among alternative *risky prospects*. Hence, by Theorem 3.2, his choice would be rational only if it maximized his *expected utility*. Now under our model any given social situation *A* would yield him the expected utility

$$W_i(A) = \frac{1}{n} \sum_{j=1}^{n} U_j(A) \tag{4.1}$$

because he would have the same $1/n$ chance of being put in the place of each individual j $(j = 1, \ldots, i, \ldots, n)$ and therefore of obtaining the utility amount $U_j(A)$, representing individual j's utility level in situation A. In other words, in making moral value judgments individual i would evaluate each social situation A in terms of the *average utility level* that the *n* individual members of society would enjoy in this situation.

To be sure, in real life, when an individual is making a moral value judgment about the merits of alternative social situations, he will often have a very clear idea of what his own social position is or would be in any given social situation. But his value judgment will still qualify as a true moral value judgment as long as he judges these social situations essentially in the same way as he would do *if he did not have this information* – that is, as long as he judges each situation A in terms of the quantity $W_i(A)$ defined by Equation (4.1).

This function W_i that individual i will use in evaluating various social situations from a moral point of view will be called his *social welfare function*, because it can be interpreted as indicating the social welfare level associated, in i's opinion, with each particular social situation. We may also say that W_i indicates the value that i ascribes to each social situation from a *social* or *moral* point of view. In contrast, i's own utility function U_i indicates the value that he ascribes to each social situation from his *personal* point of view.

Thus under our model each individual i in effect has two different preference scales. The preferences expressed by his social welfare function W_i may be called his *moral* or *social preferences*, while those expressed by his utility function U_i may be called his *personal preferences*.[1] By definition his actual choice behavior will be governed by his personal preferences, whereas his moral value judgments will be governed by his moral preferences. Accordingly only his personal preferences can be called his "preferences" in the strict sense of the word. His moral preferences are only "conditional preferences," because they indicate merely what he *would* prefer *if* he gave equal weight to each individual's interests in choosing between alternative social situations. We may also say that they represent his preferences only in those – possibly very rare – moments when he is forcing a very special impartial moral attitude on himself.

The personal and the moral preferences of a given individual may be quite dissimilar. An egoist's personal preferences may give little, if any, weight to other people's interests; his moral preferences, by definition, will give the same weight to any other individual's interests as to his own. Hence it can easily happen that his personal and his moral preferences will rank two social situations A and B in the opposite way. It is quite possible that $U_i(A) > U_i(B)$ but that $W_i(A) < W_i(B)$. For example, A may be a social situation in which i would have a very high income while most individuals would have very low incomes, whereas B may be a social situation in which all individuals, including i himself, would have moderately high incomes. Because i would be personally better off in A than in B, he may prefer A to B from his own personal point of view but may very well admit that B would represent the more desirable situation from a social or moral point of view.

We can now state:

Theorem 4.1. The social-welfare function as the arithmetic mean of individual utilities. In making moral value judgments, i.e., in judging alternative social situations from a moral (or social) point of view, a rational individual will rank these situations according to the *arithmetic mean* of the utility levels that the individual members of society would enjoy in this situation.

Note. By Equation (4.1), the social welfare function W_i of all individuals i will be identical, so that the subscript i can be omitted, and we can write $W_i = \cdots = W_n = W$. But this conclusion follows only if:

1. All individuals i have full information about the von Neumann–Morgenstern *utility functions* of all individuals j making up the society.

2. All individuals i agree on how to make *interpersonal utility comparisons* among different members j of society.

3. All individuals i agree on which particular individuals j are *"members of society"* in the sense that their utility functions U_j should enter the definition of the social welfare function W.

If these conditions are not satisfied (see Sections 4.4 through 4.6), then, of course, the social welfare function W_i of different individuals i need not be the same.

4.2 Interpersonal comparisons of utility: consistency requirements

Our model is based on the assumption that, in order to construct his social welfare function W_i, each individual i will try to assess the utilities $U_j(A)$ that any *other* individual j would derive from alternative social situations A and will try to compare these with the utilities $U_i(A)$ that he *himself* would derive from these (or from other) social situations. That is, he will try to make *interpersonal utility comparisons*. Moreover, we have assumed that i will attempt to assess these utilities $U_j(A)$ by some process of *imaginative empathy*, i.e., by imagining himself to be *put in the place* of individual j in social situation A.

This must obviously involve his imagining himself to be placed in individual j's *objective position*, i.e., to be placed in the objective conditions (e.g., income, wealth, consumption level, state of health, social position) that j would face in social situation A. But it must also involve assessing these objective conditions in terms of j's own *subjective attitudes* and *personal preferences* (as expressed by j's own utility function U_j) - rather than assessing them in terms of i's own subjective attitudes and personal preferences (as expressed by his own utility function U_i).

For example, suppose that j likes meat and dislikes fish, while i himself has opposite food preferences. Then it would be clearly absurd for i to assess j's food consumption in terms of i's own taste and claim that j would be better off if j had to eat fish (which j dislikes) than if he could eat meat (which j likes) - simply because i himself happens to like fish and to dislike meat.

This is, of course, merely the familiar *principle of consumers' sovereignty*, often discussed in the literature of welfare economics: The interests of each individual must be defined fundamentally in terms of his *own* personal preferences and not in terms of what somebody else thinks is "good for him." In the context of interpersonal comparisons of utility, this principle can be best described as the *principle of acceptance*, because it requires us to accept each individual's own personal preferences as the basic criterion for assessing the utility (personal welfare) that he will derive from any given situation. We will argue that this principle needs certain qualifications. But with appropriate qualifications we regard it as one of the most important principles of welfare economics, ethics, and political philosophy.

Now suppose that individual i is trying to make an interpersonal utility comparison between the utility $U_i(A)$ that he himself would derive from some social situation A, and the utility $U_j(B)$ that another individual j would derive from some social situation B. (Our discussion is meant to cover both the case in which $A = B$ and the case in which $A \neq B$.) Let A_i denote i's *personal position* in social situation A (i.e., the objective conditions that would face individual i in social situation A). Likewise let B_j denote j's personal position in social situation B. In view of these definitions we can write

$$U_i(A_i) = U_i(A) \quad \text{and} \quad U_j(B_j) = U_j(B) \tag{4.2}$$

Finally, let P_i and P_j denote i's and j's *subjective attitudes* (including their personal preferences), respectively.

Then by the principle of acceptance (consumers' sovereignty), when i is trying to make an interpersonal utility comparison between the utility levels $U_i(A) = U_i(A_i)$ and $U_j(B) = U_j(B_j)$, this will really amount to trying to decide whether he himself would *prefer* to be in the objective position A_i with his *own* subjective attitudes P_i, or rather to be in the objective position B_j with j's subjective attitudes P_j (or whether he would be indifferent between these two hypothetical alternatives). In symbols, it would amount to deciding which one he would prefer of the two hypothetical alternatives $[A_i, P_i]$ and $[B_j, P_j]$.

Thus let A be a social situation where all individuals' diets consist mainly of fish, and let B be a social situation where all individuals' diets consist mainly of meat. Suppose that individual i has a *mild* preference for fish, while individual j has a very *strong* preference for meat (with a violent distaste for fish). Then individual i, his taste P_i being what it is, will obviously prefer fish to meat, which means that he will prefer $[A_i, P_i]$ to $[B_i, P_i]$. But he will presumably also recognize that it is better (less inconvenient) to eat meat with a *mild* distaste for meat than it is to eat fish with a *strong* distaste for fish. Therefore he will prefer $[B_i, P_i]$ to $[A_j, P_j]$. In terms of the language of interpersonal utility comparison, he will recognize that j would derive more disutility (i.e., would derive less utility) from eating fish than (i) himself would derive from eating meat.

Hypothetical alternatives of the form $[A_i, P_i]$ or $[B_j, P_j]$, and so on, will be called *extended alternatives*. A given individual's (say, i's) preferences among such extended alternatives will be called his *extended preferences*. (For a similar approach, see Sen [1970, p. 152].)

No doubt there is an important difference in logical status between an individual's *personal preferences* (i.e., his preferences as usually defined in economics) and his *extended preferences*. The former are preferences between *real* alternatives, for example, between eating meat and eating fish. The latter are preferences between partly *imaginary* alternatives, for example, between eating meat with one's actual taste and eating fish with a taste quite different from one's actual taste. Accordingly an individual's personal preferences will manifest themselves *both* in his actual choice behavior *and* in his verbal statements of preference, whereas in general his extended preferences can manifest themselves *only* in his verbal statements.[2]

More formally the extended alternatives underlying interpersonal utility comparisons will be defined as follows. Let X_j be the set of all individual positions A_j that a given individual j ($j = 1, \ldots, i, \ldots, n$) can obtain under any possible social situation A. We will assume that this set X_j is the *same* for all individuals j. (That is, in principle any individual j could be given, e.g., any possible income level and any possible social position.) Therefore we write $X_i = \cdots = X_n = X$. (But for convenience we will continue to denote the elements of set X by the symbols $A_j, B_j, \ldots$, with subscript j, when they refer to an individual position occupied by individual j – even though, e.g., position A_j of individual j may be the same objective position as position B_k of individual k is.)

We will also consider risky prospects (probability mixtures) whose components are different individual positions $A_j, B_j, \ldots$ of the same individual j. The set of all such risky prospects will be called Y. Mathematically Y can be defined as the set of all probability distributions over set X.

We now define a *pure extended alternative* as a pair $[A_j, P_j]$, where A_j is an element of set X or of set Y, while P_j represents the subjective attitudes of some individual j ($j = 1, \ldots, i, \ldots, n$). The set of pure extended alternatives for all n individuals will be called Φ.

We will also consider risky prospects (probability mixtures) whose components are pure extended alternatives, possibly belonging to two or more different individuals, for example, probability mixtures of $[A_j, P_j]$ and $[B_k, P_k]$. These will be called *mixed extended alternatives,* and the set of these latter, Ψ. Mathematically Ψ can be defined as the set of all probability distributions over set Φ.

These notations make it natural to adopt the following notational convention.

Notational convention for extended alternatives

Convention 1°. Relationship between risky prospects and mixed extended alternatives.

$$[(A_j, p; B_j, 1 - p), P_j] = ([A_j, P_j], p; [B_j, P_j], 1 - p) \tag{4.3}$$

Both sides of the equation refer to a situation in which individual j has the subjective attitudes P_j and is facing the risky prospect $(A_j, p; B_j, 1 - p)$. Therefore they refer to the same situation.

Our model of moral value judgments (stated in Section 4.1) presupposes that individual i's extended preferences satisfy the following consistency axioms.

For convenience we will use the phrase "the axioms for rational behavior under risk" as a short reference to Axioms 1*, 2*, and 3* of Section 3.3, as well as to Conventions 1, 2, and 3 of Section 3.1.

Consistency axioms for extended preferences

Axiom 1°. Rationality of individual i's extended preferences. Individual i's extended preferences among mixed extended alternatives in set Ψ satisfy the axioms for rational behavior under risk.

This axiom is needed to establish that, in making moral value judgments, individual i will try to maximize the expected utility $W_i(A)$ defined by Equation (4.1).

Axiom 2°. Agreement between individual i's extended preferences and each individual's personal preferences. Let A_j and B_j be two risky prospects in set Y, and let j be one of the n individuals $1, \ldots, i \ldots, n$. Suppose that $A_j \gtrsim B_j$ in terms of individual j's *personal preferences.* Then also $[A_j, P_j] \gtrsim [B_j, P_j]$ in terms of individual i's *extended preferences.*

In interpreting Axiom 2° we have to distinguish two cases. In the special case where $j = i$, the axiom directly follows from the definition of extended preferences. To say that individual i prefers $[A_i, P_i]$ to $[B_i, P_i]$ is the same thing as saying that, his subjective attitudes P_i being what they are, he prefers position A_i to position B_i.

In contrast, in the case where $j \neq i$, the axiom is not a tautology but rather is a restatement of the *principle of acceptance* (consumers' sovereignty). It expresses the fact that individual i will evaluate the personal position of another individual j in terms of j's own personal preferences.

In view of Axiom 1° we can define an *extended-utility function* $V_i = V_i[A_j, P_j]$ for individual i over all extended alternatives $[A_j, P_j]$ with $j = 1, \ldots, i, \ldots, n$ and over all probability mixtures of such alternatives, so that V_i will have the expected-utility property.

In view of Axiom 2°, for each individual j we can define a utility function U_j such that

$$U_j(A_j) = V_i[A_j, P_j] \quad \text{for all} \quad A_j \in Y \tag{4.4}$$

From the fact that V_i has the expected-utility property, and from Equations (4.3) and (4.4), it follows that U_j will also have the expected-utility property and therefore will be a von Neumann–Morgenstern utility function for individual j. This in turn implies that the *personal preferences* of each individual j among risky prospects in set Y satisfy the axioms for rational behavior under risk. Thus this fact need not be assumed as a separate axiom but rather already follows from Axioms 1° and 2° in conjunction with Convention 1°.

Under our model, in making moral value judgments individual i will treat any social situation A as if it were an equiprobability mixture of the n extended alternatives $[A_1, P_1], \ldots, [A_n, P_n]$. Since V_i has the expected-utility property, to this probability mixture he will assign the utility value

$$W_i(A) = \frac{1}{n} \sum_{j=1}^{n} V_i[A_j, P_j] \tag{4.5}$$

By Equations (4.4) and (4.2) this can be written as

$$W_i(A) = \frac{1}{n} \sum_{j=1}^{n} U_j(A_j) = \frac{1}{n} \sum_{j=1}^{n} U_j(A) \tag{4.6}$$

which is the same as Equation (4.1).

4.3 Interpersonal comparisons of utility: conversion ratios

The extensive-utility function V_i of a given individual i is indeterminate up to the choice of a zero point and a utility unit, so that we really have a two-parameter family of equally acceptable utility functions V_i, any one of which can be used to represent individual i's extended preferences. By the same token, each individual j has a two-parameter family of equally acceptable von Neumann–Morgenstern utility functions U_j, any one of which can be used to represent his personal preferences. But, of course, if we choose one of these utility functions V_i and one of these utility functions U_j at random, then the two together in general will not satisfy Equation (4.4).

However, if a given extended utility function V_i of individual i and a given von Neumann–Morgenstern utility function U_j of some individual j do jointly satisfy Equation (4.4), then we will call them *congruent*. Congruence between two utility functions V_i and U_j has an obvious intuitive interpretation: It means that they have the *same zero point* and the *same utility unit*. [If this were not the case, they could not have identically the same numerical value for all positions A_j of individual j in accordance with Equation (4.4).]

Now suppose that the utility functions U_j and U_k of two different individuals j and k are both congruent with the *same* extended utility function V_i of individual *i*. Then U_j and U_k are themselves also called *congruent*. This again can be interpreted as an indication that (according to individual *i*'s interpersonal utility comparisons) these two utility functions have the *same zero point* and the *same utility unit*.

If U_j and U_k are congruent, then they have the following property. Let A_j and B_k be individual positions for individuals *j* and *k*, respectively, such that

$$U_j(A_j) = U_k(B_k) \tag{4.7}$$

Then this will be an indication of the fact that individual *i* feels *indifferent* between the corresponding two extended alternatives $[A_j, P_j]$ and $[B_k, P_k]$. This is so because, in view of (4.4), Equation (4.7) can also be written as

$$V_i[A_j, P_j] = V_i[B_k, P_k] \tag{4.8}$$

which implies that individual *i* is indifferent between these two extended alternatives. This result can also be stated as follows. If U_j and U_k are congruent-utility functions, then a numerical equality between two utility levels $U_j(A_j)$ and $U_k(B_k)$ can be regarded as indicating that (according to individual *i*'s interpersonal utility comparisons) these two utility levels represent the "same amount of utility." (This property, of course, is a direct implication of the fact that the two utility functions have the same zero point and the same utility unit.)

Let U_j and U_k again be two congruent utility functions, and let $U_k{}^* = U_k + c$ where *c* is a positive or negative constant. Then U_j and $U_k{}^*$ will not be congruent to each other, but they will still have the *same utility unit* (while having different zero points) as judged by individual *i*.

According to Equation (4.5), individual *i* should define his social welfare function W_i in terms of utility functions $U_1, \ldots, U_n$, which are all *congruent* to the same extended-utility function V_i and are therefore also congruent to one another. But this is not really strictly necessary, because, if individual *i* replaces some utility function U_j by another utility function $U_j{}^* = U_j + c$, having a different zero point, this will merely introduce an irrelevant additive constant c/n into his social-welfare function W_i and therefore will not affect the ranking of alternative social situations by W_i.

Accordingly all we have to require is that individual *i* should define W_i in terms of utility functions $U_1, \ldots, U_n$ expressed in terms of the *same utility unit* (as judged by individual *i* himself). On the other hand, this requirement is essential: If in Equation (4.1) he used utility functions U_j expressed in unequal utility units, then he would change the *relative weights* that his social-welfare function W_i would give to the different individuals' interests and in particular would violate the requirement of assigning equal weight to each individual. For example, suppose that he would choose to express individual *j*'s utility in terms of a *larger* utility unit than he would use for the other individuals' utilities. This would decrease the numerical value $U_j(A)$ of *j*'s utility function U_j for any given social situation *A* and would therefore make his social-welfare function W_i relatively *insensitive* to *j*'s personal interests.

Thus, when individual i is constructing his social-welfare function W_i, the only way that he is really required to make interpersonal utility comparisons is by trying to compare the *utility units* of the different individuals' utility functions $U_1, \ldots,$ $U_i, \ldots, U_n$. Suppose that he begins with individual utility functions $U_1, \ldots,$ $U_i, \ldots, U_n$ expressed in arbitrary (and therefore in general presumably unequal) utility units. Then his basic task will be to choose *conversion ratios* $q_1, \ldots,$ $q_i, \ldots, q_n$, which in his best judgment will convert all these utility functions into the same common utility unit, by setting $U_1^* = q_1 U_1, \ldots, U_n^* = q_n U_n$. (Of course, he can always choose $q_i = 1$. That is, he need not change the utility unit in which he is expressing his own utility.)

4.4 Interpersonal comparisons of utility: the question of interobserver validity

Our model of moral value judgments requires that individual i be able to make *internally consistent* interpersonal comparisons of utility in accordance with Axioms 1° and 2°. But it does not require that he be able to make interpersonal comparisons of utility possessing *interobserver* validity, in the sense of being in agreement with interpersonal comparisons of utility made by other observers. In the terminology that we used in Section 4.3, it is not required that the extended preferences of different observers should *agree* between all pairs of extended alternatives $[A_j, P_j]$ and $[B_k, P_k]$. For example, individual i may prefer the former to the latter, while a different observer, individual h, may prefer the latter to the former. (Agreement is necessary only in the special case in which the two extended alternatives in question refer to the same individual so that $j = k$: In this case, by Axiom 2°, the extended preferences of all observers must go in the same direction, because they must all agree with individual j's *own* personal preferences.)

Let $U_1, \ldots, U_h, \ldots, U_i, \ldots, U_n$ be again von Neumann–Morgenstern utility functions representing the personal preferences of individuals $1, \ldots, h, \ldots,$ $i, \ldots, n$ and expressed in arbitrary utility units. Let W_h and W_i be the social-welfare functions of individuals h and i, respectively. As both h and i must accept the utility functions $U_1, \ldots, U_n$ as representing the personal preferences of the relevant individuals, both social-welfare functions (apart from possible irrelevant additive constants) must be of the mathematical form

$$W(A) = \frac{1}{n} \sum_{j=1}^{n} q_j U_j(A) \qquad (4.9)$$

However, our model does *not* necessarily imply that individuals h and i will choose the *same* conversion ratios $q_1, \ldots, q_n$; and, of course, if they do choose different ratios, then their social-welfare functions W_h and W_i will give different relative weights to the various individuals' interests.

At the same time, even if our model does not directly require that interpersonal comparisons of utility should have interobserver validity, most people actually making such comparisons would hardly engage in this activity if they did not expect that their judgments concerning the relative magnitude of two different individuals' utility levels would have some degree of objective validity. They may very well admit that such judgments are often subject to considerable margins of error, and indeed they may tend to feel quite uncertain about their judgments in some cases. But in many other cases they will feel reasonably confident in their judgment that, e.g., individual *j* in situation *A* would reach a *higher* utility level than individual *k* would reach in situation *B*; or equivalently they would feel quite sure that "any reasonable person" would prefer to be in situation *A* with *j*'s subjective attitudes rather than to be in situation *B* with *k*'s subjective attitudes. In this section we would like to investigate whether there is any rational basis for this feeling that such interpersonal utility comparisons tend to have some degree of "objective" interobserver validity.

If all individuals' personal preferences were identical, then we could ascribe the same utility function *U* to all individuals and could always make interpersonal utility comparisons in terms of this common utility function *U*. Moreover, all *inter*personal utility comparison could be reduced to *intra*personal utility comparisons. If we wanted to know whether a given apple would give more utility to Peter (who just had a heavy meal) than to Paul (who had only a very light meal), we could simply ask whether Peter himself would derive more utility from an apple after a heavy meal or after a light meal.[3]

Of course, in actuality different individuals often have very different personal preferences and very different utility functions. But the possibility of meaningful interpersonal utility comparisons will remain, as long as the different individuals' choice behavior and preferences are at least governed by the *same basic psychological laws*. For in this case each individual's preferences will be determined by the same general causal variables. Thus the differences we can observe between different people's preferences can be predicted, at least in principle, from differences in these causal variables, such as differences in their biological inheritance, in their past life histories, and in their current environmental conditions. This means that if Peter had Paul's biological makeup, had Paul's life history behind him, and were currently subject to Paul's environmental influences, then he would presumably have the *same* personal preferences as Paul has now and would ascribe the *same* utility as Paul does now to each particular situation.

Let P_j again denote individual *j*'s *subjective attitudes* (including his preferences), and let R_j denote a vector consisting of all *objective causal variables* needed to explain these subjective attitudes denoted by P_j. Our discussion suggests that the extended utility function V_i of each individual *i* should really be written as $V_i = V_i[A_j, R_j]$ rather than as $V_i = V_i[A_j, P_j]$. Written in this form, the utility function $V_i = V_i[A_j, R_j]$ indicates the utility that individual *i* would assign to the objective position A_j if the causal variables determining his preferences were R_j. Because the mathematical form of this function is defined by the basic psychological laws governing people's choice behavior, this function V_i must be the same for all individuals *i*, so that, for example,

$$V_h[A_j, R_j] = V_i[A_j, R_j] \tag{4.10}$$

for each pair of individuals h and i. In the special case in which $h = j$, we can write

$$V_i[A_j, R_j] = V_j[A_j, R_j] = U_j(R_j) \tag{4.11}$$

That is, individual i (or individual h) would have the *same* preferences and would assign the *same* utility to any objective situation A_j as individual j now does, if the causal variables determining his preferences took the same value R_j as do the causal variables determining j's preferences.

In other words, even though the "ordinary" utility functions U_i and U_j of two individuals i and j may be quite different, their *extended* utility functions V_i and V_j will be identical. This is so because, by the definition of the causal-variables vectors R_i and R_j, all differences between the two utility functions $U_i(A_i) = V_i[A_i, R_i]$ and $U_j(A_j) = V_j[A_j, R_j]$ must be attributed to differences between the vectors R_i and R_j and not to differences between the mathematical form of the two functions V_i and V_j.

Yet, if the two individuals have the same extended utility function $V_i = V_j = V$, then we are back in a world of identical utility functions. Hence individual i will be able in principle to reduce any *inter*personal utility comparison that he may wish to make between himself and individual j to an *intra*personal utility comparison between the utilities that he is *in fact* assigning to various situations and the utilities that he *would* assign to them *if* the vector of causal variables determining his preferences took the value R_j (which is the value that the vector of these causal variables takes in the case of individual j).

For example, if I want to compare the utility that I would derive from a new car with the utility that a friend would derive from a new sailboat, then I must ask myself what utility I would derive from a sailboat if I had taken up sailing for a regular hobby as my friend has done, and if I could suddenly acquire my friend's expert sailing skill, and so forth. In practice, of course, we may not know the actual values of some important causal variables for the relevant individuals. For instance, the utility that my friend would derive from a sailboat may depend on certain of his psychological character traits of which I am unaware. But in principle I could always determine the values of such causal variables by psychological measurement, historical research, and so forth. In other cases we may know the relevant causal variables but may be unable to predict their actual effect on a given person's preferences and on his utility function because of our imperfect knowledge of the relevant psychological laws. For example, I may know that my friend has an introvert personality but may not know how this fact will affect the utility that he will derive from a sailboat. But again in principle such questions could be answered by appropriate experimental tests or by inferences drawn from the general psychological laws of human behavior, assuming that these laws were known to us.

Therefore, given enough information about the relevant individuals' psychological, biological, social, and cultural characteristics, as well as about the general psychological laws governing human behavior, *inter*personal utility comparisons in principle should be no more problematic than *intra*personal utility comparisons are between the utilities that the *same* person would derive from various alternatives under different conditions.[4]

In actuality interpersonal utility comparisons between people of similar cultural background, social status, and personality are probably quite reliable and are likely to show a high degree of interobserver validity – at least if the observers making these comparisons are familiar with the personal conditions of the people concerned. But, of course, we must reckon with much larger margins of error when we compare utilities for people of very different backgrounds and personalities. Yet advances in our theoretical understanding of the general psychological laws that govern human behavior and in our information about the relevant person's cultural and personal characteristics will tend to decrease this margin of error for any given utility comparison. If we knew more about human nature in general and about Peter and Paul in particular, then we could better judge the influence that differences in their personalities and their environment will have on their utility functions.

To conclude, our model of moral value judgments shows an interesting analogy with the results obtained in individual decision theory. In decision theory we found that a rational individual will try to base his actions on the *objective probabilities* of the relevant events. But if these are not known to him, then he will use his own *subjective probabilities* for these events – representing his best *estimates* of these objective probabilities – formally in the same way as he would use their true objective probabilities, if these were known to him.

Likewise, under our model of moral value judgments, a rational individual will try to base his social-welfare function on the "true" conversion ratios between the various individuals' utility units (i.e., on the conversion ratios that would presumably be used by observers who had full information about these individuals' personal characteristics and about the general psychological laws governing human behavior). But if he does not have enough information to ascertain these "true" conversion ratios, then he will use his best *estimates* of the latter, formally in the same way as he would use the "true" conversion ratios, if these were known to him.

4.5 The boundary problem for our "society"

Our model as it stands obviously gives us no criterion to decide *who* those individuals are whose utility functions ought to be included in our social-welfare function. It gives no criterion to define the *boundaries* of the society or moral community whose members ought to feel direct moral concern for one another's well-being and ought to feel moral solidarity with one another. This problem we will call the *boundary problem* for the society.

Of course, in practice it is often sufficient to say that our society must certainly include at least all normal human beings now living. But for theoretical reasons, and in many cases also for practical reasons, we would like to have an operationally meaningful *analytical* criterion that could help us to decide whether to include, e.g., higher animals, human idiots, unborn babies in their mothers' wombs, more distant future generations – or even to decide under what conditions the inhabitants of other celestial bodies, or man-made robots, would qualify or would fail to qualify.

We surely should like to include any agent who is able to enter into some creative cooperative relationship with us. But even if this criterion could perhaps serve as a sufficient condition for inclusion, it probably would be too restrictive as a necessary condition (e.g., most human idiots would fail this test). In any case, at this stage we are still very far from being able to translate any criterion of this kind into operationally meaningful behavioral terms.

4.6 The principle of individual self-determination: some qualifications

When a given individual i tries to construct his social-welfare function W_i, he will often have rather insufficient information about the personal preferences (and, more fundamentally, about the choice behavior) of some other individuals j. As a result, even if i does his best to follow the principle of acceptance and to define the interests of each individual j in terms of the latter's own utility function U_j, his actual estimate U_j' of this utility function U_j may differ in important ways from j's true utility function U_j. It is, of course, another question whether individual i can ever have any justification for *deliberately* replacing j's true utility function by another utility function U_j', when he is constructing his social function W_i in accordance with Equation (4.1).

Consider two cases: In the first case individual i may feel that individual j's actual preferences should be disregarded in certain matters, because j's preferences are based on *factual errors*. For example, i may argue that j wants a certain medicine only because j has a mistaken belief about the efficacy of this medicine in curing a particular disease. Or he may argue that j wants to move to New York only because j does not know how serious the traffic problem is there, and so forth. (Thus j's alleged factual errors may be both about *causal* - or technical - relationships and about *noncausal* facts.) Instead of using j's *actual* utility function U_j, which represents j's actual manifest preferences, i may wish to use a *corrected utility function* U_j', representing i's own estimate of what j's preferences *would* be *if* j had better information about the relevant facts.

It seems that in many cases the use of corrected utility functions U_j' by individual i will not be at all inconsistent with the principle of acceptance. Individual i can sometimes rightly claim that the corrected utility function U_j' will better represent individual j's "true" preferences than would the utility function U_j, based on j's manifest choice behavior. For example, in many cases it will be reasonable to assume that what a sick person really wants is not a specific medicine but rather the best treatment available, even if the latter involves using another medicine than he actually has in mind.

However, in many other cases this assumption will not be correct. People often want to be free to make their own mistakes - at least as long as these are not very *costly* mistakes. They may prefer to be treated in accordance with their manifest preferences, even if they are fully aware of the possibility that these preferences may possibly be based on erroneous factual information. Thus i will be justified in using a corrected utility function U_j' only if he thinks that j himself would *approve* of this – at least if j were made aware of the possibility that his actual preferences were based on factual mistakes and of the likely costs of these mistakes to him.

In the second case individual i may feel that individual j's preferences should be disregarded in certain matters, because j's preferences conflict with i's own *fundamental value judgments*. Instead of using j's actual utility function U_j, i may wish to use a *censored utility function* U_j'' that disregards j's actual preferences in those matters in which i could not satisfy j's preferences "with good conscience."

Whereas using a *corrected* utility function U_j', as we have argued, is not necessarily inconsistent with the principle of acceptance, using a *censored* utility function U_j'' certainly is. But we feel that in this respect the principle has no unqualified validity. In our opinion individual i will be perfectly justified in disregarding j's actual preferences in cases where the latter are based on clearly *antisocial* attitudes, e.g., on sheer hostility, malice, envy, and sadism. After all, the entire basis for i's interest in satisfying j's preferences is human sympathy. But human sympathy can hardly impose on i the obligation to respect j's preferences in cases where the latter are in clear conflict with human sympathy. For example, human sympathy can hardly require that i should help sadists to cause unnecessary human suffering – even if a very large number of sadists could obtain a very high utility from this activity. [For a contrary view, see Smart, 1961, p. 16.]

This problem is somewhat analogous to the problem of defining boundaries for the society or moral community to which individual i should extend his moral sympathy (see Section 4.5). If i uses a censored utility function U_j'' for a given individual j, this is equivalent to excluding certain aspects of j's personality from the moral solidarity that i otherwise entertains toward j and toward all other members of society. With regard to his antisocial preferences j will be treated as if he were not a member of the society at all – though j's preferences in other matters will be given the same weight as that given to the preferences of all other members of society.

4.7 Rule utilitarianism versus act utilitarianism: the concept of critical rule utilitarianism

So far we have dealt only with the question of how a rational man will judge alternative *social situations* from a moral point of view. But, of course, any theory of moral value judgments must also answer the question of how a rational man will judge the moral value of individual *human actions* as morally right or wrong.

The simplest answer to this question would be to say that a given action α by individual i will be morally right if α maximizes i's social-welfare function W_i. This view is called *act utilitarianism* in the philosophical literature, because as a criterion of moral value it uses the social usefulness of individual acts. However, this view has curious implications. Most of us feel that, with the exception of very special cases, it is morally right to repay our debts and morally wrong not to do so. Yet suppose that i has borrowed money from a man much richer than himself. Then, by repaying his debt, i would presumably *reduce* the value of his social-welfare function W_i, because by doing so he would take away money from himself (who has a high marginal utility for it) and would give it to his rich creditor (who probably has a low marginal utility for it).

The point is, of course, that we must not look at individual acts of debt repayment in isolation. Repaying debts is a common (at least in a high percentage of cases) and socially useful practice, because it encourages lending, including lending by rich people to poor people. A common practice of repaying debts - and more generally a common practice of complying with contractual obligations - is useful because of its effects on people's *expectations* and *incentives*. Thus the proper question is not whether society will be better off if individual *i* repays his debts on one particular occasion. Rather it is whether society will be better off if it accepts as a *general moral rule* that (except for cases of extreme hardship and the like) people should *always* repay their debts.

In other words, the question we have to ask is: If we were given the task of choosing a moral rule to regulate people's behavior in a certain type of situation, which would be the *moral rule whose adoption would best serve the social interest* (i.e., whose adoption would maximize our social-welfare function)? If *R* is this socially most beneficial moral rule, and if *R* requires action α in a given situation, then in this situation doing α will be morally right, and not doing α will be morally wrong. Thus basically the criterion of social usefulness applies to alternative *rules* of behavior and not to alternative individual *actions* in isolation. In contrast to act utilitarianism, this view is called *rule utilitarianism*.

We can state the rule utilitarian position also as follows: When individual *i* is considering what to do in a particular situation, he often will not be morally free to do just anything that he may wish to do because he may have *special obligations* toward various other people (arising out of his status as, e.g., a parent, relative, friend, or citizen, or arising out of voluntary contracts or other commitments that he had made in earlier periods). Therefore he cannot simply choose the action that would maximize his social-welfare function W_i; rather he must maximize W_i *subject to the constraint of not violating any of his existing special obligations*. For example, he may not be morally free to give his money to the person who needs it most - because in many situations he will have to give priority to repaying his debts, or to maintaining his family, or to paying his taxes, and so on, over mere philanthropy. But, of course, these special obligations themselves have priority only because it is assumed that in the long run society as a whole will be better off, and our social-welfare function will assume a higher value, if people give priority to fulfilling their special obligations over good deeds of other sorts.

In other words, the rule utilitarianism requires us to apply the yardstick of social usefulness primarily to *social institutions,* such as private property, the right to enter into legally and morally binding contracts, the nuclear family, the state, and so forth. As far as these institutions pass the test of social usefulness we are morally bound to comply with the special obligations arising from these institutions: We have to respect private property, fulfill our contractual obligations, care for our family, and pay our taxes - regardless of whether these acts maximize our social-welfare function in any given case in the short run.

To sum up, our model of moral value judgments leads to an ethical position that clearly belongs to the *utilitarian* tradition, because it finds the basic criterion for morality in social welfare or social utility - itself defined in terms of the utilities of the individual members of society. But our position represents a doubly qualified form of utilitarianism:

1. It represents *rule* utilitarianism, not *act* utilitarianism. Social utility is used primarily as a criterion to judge alternative moral rules and indeed alternative institutional arrangements for society, rather than to judge individual human actions as such (though we do apply the criterion of social utility directly to individual actions within the limits set by the actor's special obligations, given the existing institutional arrangements of society).

2. We do not always feel obliged to accept other people's utility functions uncritically but rather feel free to "correct" them for factual errors and even to "censor" them for antisocial attitudes. Thus our position may be called *critical rule utilitarianism*, as distinguished from ordinary rule utilitarianism, which would simply accept people's utility functions as they are, i.e., which would follow the principle of acceptance without any qualification.

TWO AXIOMATIC APPROACHES AND CONCLUDING REMARKS

4.8 The first axiomatic approach to an additive social-welfare function

In the first part of this chapter we presented our model for moral value judgments, which implies that the social-welfare function of a rational individual must take the form of the arithmetic mean of individual utilities. In this part we present two sets of axioms which in our view must be satisfied by any reasonable social-welfare function and which also lead to the conclusion that a social-welfare function must be a linear combination of individual utilities. A social-welfare function of this form will be called *additive*. The arithmetic mean of individual utilities is, of course, one special type of additive social-welfare functions. The case for an additive social-welfare function is obviously greatly strengthened by the existence of at least three essentially independent arguments in its favor.[5]

To state our axioms we will use the following definitions. Let X^* be the set of all possible social situations. Let Y^* be the set of all risky prospects (probability mixtures) whose components are social situations in set X^*. Thus Y^* is the set of all probability distributions over set X^*. We will again use the phrase "the axioms for rational behavior under risk" as a short reference to Axioms 1^*, 2^*, and 3^* of Section 3.4, as well as to Conventions 1, 2, and 3 of Section 3.1.

We will again distinguish between a given individual's *personal preferences*, ranking different alternatives from his personal point of view, and his *moral preferences* (or social preferences), ranking these alternatives from a moral (or social) point of view.

First set of axioms for an additive social-welfare function

Axiom 1^{oo}. Rationality of individual i's moral preferences. In choosing among risky prospects in set Y^* from a moral (or social) point of view, individual i's preferences satisfy the axioms for rational behavior under risk. (That is, if individual *i* had to choose among different risky prospects as a guardian of the general social interest, then he would follow the rules of rational behavior.)

Axiom 2°°. Rationality of each individual's personal preferences. In choosing among risky prospects in set Y^* from his personal point of view, each individual $j(j = 1, \ldots, i, \ldots, n)$ will display preferences consistent with the axioms for rational behavior under risk.

Axiom 3°°. Positive relationship between the moral preferences of individual i *and the personal preferences of all individual members of the society.* Let *A* and *B* be two risky prospects in set Y^*. Suppose that *A* is (at least nonstrictly) preferred over *B* by all individuals *j* in the society from their own personal points of view. Then *A* will also be (at least nonstrictly) preferred over *B* by individual *i* from a moral (or social) point of view.

Among these three axioms only Axiom 3°° represents a moral value judgment – and even this is a rather weak and noncontroversial value judgment. Axiom 1°°, even though it is a rationality requirement rather than a moral value judgment, has been more controversial in the literature. It has been argued that rationality postulates defining rational behavior under risk, and in particular the monotonicity principle (our Axiom 3*), apply only to individual choice and do not apply to social choice. They apply only to the *personal* preferences of a rational individual but do not apply to his *social* (moral) preferences.

In our opinion this argument is quite unconvincing. Axiom 1°° deals with individual *i*'s social preferences, while Axiom 2°° deals with his (and all other individuals') personal preferences. Thus Axiom 1°° tells us how he will act if he is guided by impartial social interests, whereas Axiom 2°° tells us how he will act when he is guided by his personal interests. Why should he be less bound by the formal criteria of rationality when he is pursuing general social objectives than when he is pursuing purely personal objectives? If there is any difference, then, it seems to me, he is under a stronger obligation to act rationally in the former case.

Perhaps the objections to Axiom 1°° arise from the feeling that "social preferences" are somehow the preferences of some collective entity called "society," which is not subject to the same rationality requirements as individual human beings are. But, of course, we have always been careful to emphasize that under our definition the "social preferences" or "moral preferences" of individual *i* are the preferences of an *individual human being*, when he is taking a "moral point of view" and is trying to judge alternative social situations with the eyes of an impartial but sympathetic observer. They have nothing to do with the hypothetical preferences of any personified collective entity called "society."

These axioms imply the following theorem:

Theorem 4.2. The social-welfare function as a weighted sum of individual utilities. The social-welfare function W_i of individual *i*, representing his moral (or social) preferences will have the mathematical form

$$W_i(A) = \sum_{j=1}^{n} a_j U_j(A) \qquad (4.12)$$

where $a_1, \ldots, a_i, \ldots, a_n$ are positive constants.

Before proving the theorem we shall prove four lemmas.

Lemma 1. The personal preferences of each individual j can be represented by a utility function U_j, possessing the expected-utility property.

In view of Theorem 3.2, this lemma directly follows from Axiom 2^{oo}.

Lemma 2. The moral preferences of individual i can be represented by a utility function W_i, possessing the expected-utility property (and called his social-welfare function).

In view of Theorem 3.2, this lemma directly follows from Axiom 1^{oo}.

Lemma 3. W_i is a single-valued function of $U_1, \ldots, U_n$.

Proof. We must show that, if two risky prospects A and B yield the same utility $U_j(A) = U_j(B)$ to every individual j, then they also yield the same social-welfare value $W_i(A) = W_i(B)$. But this statement directly follows from Axiom 3^{oo}.

Lemma 4. W_i is a linear homogeneous function of $U_1, \ldots, U_n$. That is, if we have

$$U_j(A) = kU_j(B) \quad \text{for} \quad j = 1, \ldots, n \qquad (4.13)$$

with the same number k for each U_j, then

$$W_i(A) = kW_i(B) \qquad (4.14)$$

Proof. Let Q be a social situation yielding zero utility for each individual, so that

$$U_j(Q) = 0 \quad \text{for} \quad j = 1, \ldots, n \qquad (4.15)$$

Since we are free to choose the zero point of the social-welfare function W_i in any way we wish, we will set

$$W_i(Q) = 0 \qquad (4.16)$$

Consider three cases.

Case I. Suppose that $0 \leq k \leq 1$. Let us define

$$B^* = (B, k; Q, 1 - k) \qquad (4.17)$$

By Lemma 1, we can write

$$U_j(B^*) = kU_j(B) + (1 - k) \cdot 0 = kU_j(B) \quad \text{for} \quad j = 1, \ldots, n \qquad (4.18)$$

By Lemma 2, we can write

$$W_i(B^*) = kW_i(B) + (1 - k) \cdot 0 = kW_i(B) \tag{4.19}$$

By (4.18), $U_j(B^*) = U_j(B)$ for all j. Therefore, by Lemma 3 and Equation (4.19),

$$W_i(A) = W_i(B^*) = kW_i(B) \tag{4.20}$$

as desired.

Case II. Suppose that $k > 1$. Let $m = 1/k$. Then $0 < m < 1$. Then, by our result in Case I, if we have

$$U_j(A) = kU_j(B) = \frac{1}{m} U_j(B) \quad \text{for} \quad j = 1, \ldots, n \tag{4.21}$$

that is, if we have

$$U_j(B) = mU_j(A) \quad \text{for} \quad j = 1, \ldots, n \tag{4.22}$$

then also

$$W_i(B) = mW_i(A) = \frac{1}{k} W_i(A) \tag{4.23}$$

Hence

$$W_i(A) = kW_i(B) \tag{4.24}$$

as desired.

Case III. Suppose that $k < 0$. We could actually omit consideration of Case III without any real loss of generality, because we could restrict all utility functions U_j to nonnegative values by choosing the zero prospect Q so as to represent a low enough utility level for each individual. But for completeness, let us now suppose that $k < 0$. Let us define

$$p = \frac{1}{1 - k}. \quad \text{Clearly} \quad 0 < p < 1 \tag{4.25}$$

Let C be a social situation such that

$$(C, p; B, 1 - p) \sim Q \quad \text{for all individuals } j \tag{4.26}$$

so that, by Lemma 1,

$$U_j(Q) = 0 = pU_j(C) + (1 - p) U_j(B) \quad \text{for} \quad j = 1, \ldots, n \tag{4.27}$$

By (4.13), (4.25), and (4.27),

$$U_j(A) = kU_j(B) = \frac{p - 1}{p} U_j(B) = U_j(C) \tag{4.28}$$

On the other hand, by (4.26) and by Lemma 2,

$$W_i(Q) = 0 = pW_i(C) + (1 - p) W_i(B) \tag{4.29}$$

and therefore

$$W_i(C) = \frac{p-1}{p} W_i(B) = kW_i(B) \tag{4.30}$$

But since $U_j(A) = U_j(C)$ for each individual j, in view of Lemma 3,

$$W_i(A) = W_i(C) = kW_i(B) \tag{4.31}$$

as desired, where the last equality follows from (4.30). This completes the proof for all possible values of k.

Proof of Theorem 4.2. Consider a set of social situations $B^1, \ldots, B^n$, such that each social situation $B^j (j = 1, \ldots, n)$ yields the utility $U_j(B^j) = 1$ to individual j but yields zero utility to all other individuals. Let us write

$$W_i(B^j) = a_j \quad \text{for} \quad j = 1, \ldots, n \tag{4.32}$$

Because individual j will prefer B^j to Q, while all other individuals will be indifferent between the two, by Axiom 3^{oo}, we must have

$$W_i(B^j) = a_j > W_i(Q) = 0 \tag{4.33}$$

Also consider another set of social situations $C^1, \ldots, C^n$, such that $C^j (j = 1, \ldots, n)$ yields the utility

$$U_j(C^j) = U_j(A) \tag{4.34}$$

to individual j but yields zero utility to all other individuals. Clearly situation C^j yields $U_j(A)$ times as much utility to each individual j as situation B^j does. Hence, by Lemma 4 and by (4.32),

$$W_i(C^j) = a_j U_j(A) \quad \text{for} \quad j = 1, \ldots, n \tag{4.35}$$

Finally let D be the equiprobability mixture of the n social situations $C^1, \ldots, C^n$. Then, by Lemma 1 and by (4.34), we can write

$$U_j(D) = \frac{1}{n} U_j(C^j) = \frac{1}{n} U_j(A) \quad \text{for} \quad j = 1, \ldots, n \tag{4.36}$$

On the other hand, by Lemma 2 and by (4.35), we can write

$$W_i(D) = \frac{1}{n} \sum_{j=1}^{n} W_i(C^j) = \frac{1}{n} \sum_{j=1}^{n} a_j U_j(A) \tag{4.37}$$

By (4.36), A yields n times as much utility as D does to each individual j. By Lemma 4, this implies that

$$W_i(A) = nW_i(D) \tag{4.38}$$

Yet (4.37) and (4.38) imply (4.12). This completes the proof of the theorem.

Theorem 4.2 is obviously a weaker statement than Theorem 4.1, because it does not allow the inference that all individuals' utility functions, if they are expressed in the *same* utility unit, must be given the *same* weight in the social-welfare function. To obtain this conclusion we would have to add a further axiom, such as:

Axiom 4°°. Symmetry. If the n individuals' utility functions $U_1, \ldots, U_n$ are expressed in the same utility unit, then the social-welfare function W_i must be a symmetric function of these individual utility functions.

If we add Axiom 4°° to our other three axioms, we can then infer that in Equation (4.12) $a_1 = \cdots = a_n = a$. Of course, we are free to choose $a = 1/n$, in which case Equation (4.12) will become identical with Equation (4.1).

4.9 A second axiomatic approach to an additive social-welfare function

We will now derive essentially the same conclusion from a different set of axioms, those of Fleming [1952]. Fleming's approach makes no use of the expected-utility property of the individual utility functions U_j and of the social-welfare function W_i and therefore does not need as strong rationality axioms as Axioms 1°° and 2°°. On the other hand, it needs Axiom 4°°°, below, which is a stronger ethical axiom than Axiom 3°°.

For convenience we use the phrase "the axioms for rational behavior under certainty" as a short reference to Axioms 1 and 2 of Section 3.3. These axioms are, of course, significantly weaker than the axioms defining rational behavior under risk. In particular they do not contain the monotonicity principle (or the substitution principle). Therefore Axioms 1°°° and 2°°°, below, are weaker than Axioms 1°° and 2°° of the preceding section.

Second set of axioms for an additive social-welfare function

Axiom 1°°°. Weak rationality of individual i's moral preferences. In choosing among alternative social situations A in set X^* from a moral (or social) point of view, individual i's preferences satisfy the axioms for rational behavior under certainty.

Corollary. Individual i's moral preferences can be represented by a continuous utility function W_i^*, called his social-welfare function. W_i^* is an *ordinal* social-welfare function, unique only up to order-preserving monotone transformations.[6]

Axiom 2°°°. Weak rationality of each individual's personal preferences. In choosing among alternative social situations A in set X^* from a personal point of view, the preferences of each individual $j(j = 1, \ldots, i, \ldots, n)$ satisfy the axioms for rational behavior under certainty.

Corollary. The personal preferences of each individual j can be represented by a continuous utility function U_j^*. For each individual j, U_j^* is an *ordinal* utility function, unique only up to order-preserving monotone transformations.[7]

Axiom 3°°°. This is identical to Axiom 3°° of Section 4.8.

Definition 1. Let A and B be two social situations in set X^*. Any individual j indifferent between A and B will be called *unconcerned* about the choice between A and B. In contrast, any individual k who (strictly) prefers A to B, or who (strictly) prefers B to A, will be called a *concerned* individual.

Definition 2. By the *direction* of a given individual's preferences between two situations A and B we shall mean the question of whether he (strictly) prefers A to B, or (strictly) prefers B to A, or whether he is indifferent between A and B.

Axiom 4°°°. Independence of individual i's moral preferences of the utility levels of unconcerned individuals. Suppose that individuals j and k are the only two individuals concerned with a choice between the two social situations A and B and that they have opposite preferences in this matter so that

$$U_j^*(A) = \alpha_j > U_j^*(B) = \beta_j \tag{4.39}$$

whereas

$$U_k^*(A) = \alpha_k < U_k^*(B) = \beta_k \tag{4.40}$$

and

$$U_m^*(A) = \alpha_m = U_m^*(B) = \beta_m \quad \text{for all} \quad m \neq j, k \tag{4.41}$$

Then the direction of individual i's moral preferences between A and B will depend only on the utility vectors $\alpha_{jk} = (\alpha_j, \alpha_k)$ and $\beta_{jk} = (\beta_j, \beta_k)$, describing the utility levels of the two *concerned* individuals j and k in these two stiuations, but will not depend on the utility levels α_m and β_m that the *unconcerned* individuals m would enjoy in these two situations.

More particularly suppose that $\overline{A}$ and $\overline{B}$ are two other social situations, such that

$$U_j^*(\overline{A}) = U_j^*(A) = \alpha_j \qquad U_j^*(\overline{B}) = U_j^*(B) = \beta_j \tag{4.42}$$

and

$$U_k^*(\overline{A}) = U_k^*(A) = \alpha_k \qquad U_k^*(\overline{B}) = U_k^*(B) = \beta_k \tag{4.43}$$

Moreover, suppose that

$$U_m^*(\overline{A}) = \overline{\alpha}_m = U_m^*(\overline{B}) = \overline{\beta}_m \quad \text{for all} \quad m \neq j, k \tag{4.44}$$

so that j and k are also the only two individuals concerned with a choice between $\overline{A}$ and $\overline{B}$. Then the direction of i's moral preferences between $\overline{A}$ and $\overline{B}$ will be the *same* as the direction of his moral preferences between A and B. This will be true even if

$$\overline{\alpha}_m = \overline{\beta}_m \neq \alpha_m = \beta_m \quad \text{for some or all} \quad m \neq j, k \tag{4.45}$$

That is, the direction of i's moral preferences between $\bar{A}$ and $\bar{B}$ will not depend on the utility levels $\bar{\alpha}_m = \bar{\beta}_m$ that the unconcerned individuals m would derive from $\bar{A}$ and $\bar{B}$, and, in particular, it will not depend on whether these utility levels $\bar{\alpha}_m = \bar{\beta}_m$ are equal or unequal to the utility levels $\alpha_m = \beta_m$ that these unconcerned individuals would derive from the first two situations A and B.

In other words, it is assumed that j and k are the *only* two individuals concerned with a choice between A and B (and also with a choice between $\bar{A}$ and $\bar{B}$). Therefore, when individual i is trying to decide whether A or B is morally preferable (or whether $\bar{A}$ or $\bar{B}$ is morally preferable), he should consider only the relative importance of j's and k's interest in this matter and should not be influenced by the utility levels that the other individuals m would assign to A and B (or to $\bar{A}$ and $\bar{B}$). This is so because by assumption each of these other individuals m would assign the *same* utility level $\alpha_m = \beta_m$ to A as to B (and would also assign the same utility level to $\bar{A}$ and $\bar{B}$), so that in choosing between A and B (or between $\bar{A}$ and $\bar{B}$) the interests of these individuals m need not be considered.

In assessing the plausibility of Axiom 4^{ooo}, it must be understood that the axiom is by no means inconsistent with the common practice of judging the "fairness" of income distribution in one part of society in the light of the income distribution existing in other parts of the society. For example, it is often argued that it would be "unfair" to refuse wage increases to workers in industry A after large wage increases were received by workers of comparable skill in other industries.

This argument is not necessarily inconsistent with Axiom 4^{ooo}, because the latter requires only that our moral value judgment about the *utility distribution*[8] in industry A be independent of the economic conditions in other industries. But in practice what is directly given to us is the income distribution rather than the utility distribution in a given industry. Axiom 4^{ooo} does not necessarily imply that in judging the *income distribution* in industry A we should disregard the income levels prevailing in other industries, because the utility that each individual in the industry derives from his income will presumably itself depend on the incomes that other individuals of comparable skill and social position receive both inside and outside the industry. In fact, it is this very relationship that may make it "unfair" not to give workers in industry A similar wage increases to those granted in other industries: They might suffer significant losses in utility (in psychological satisfaction), if their relative economic position fell significantly below that of workers of comparable skill in other industries.

Theorem 4.3. Suppose that there are at least three individuals in the society and that Axioms 1^{ooo} to 4^{ooo} hold. Then there exists a social-welfare function W_i representing individual i's *moral* preferences, and there exist utility functions $U_1, \ldots, U_i, \ldots, U_n$ representing the *personal* preferences of the individuals $1, \ldots, i, \ldots, n$ belonging to the society such that

$$W_i(A) = \sum_{j=1}^{n} U_j(A) \tag{4.46}$$

for all social situations A in set X^*. These functions $U_1, \ldots, U_n$ and W_i are *cardinal* utility and *cardinal* social-welfare functions, unique up to order-preserving linear transformations.

The proof of the theorem will be based on actually constructing functions U_1, $\ldots, U_n$ and W_i satisfying Equation (4.46).

Construction procedure. In accordance with the corollaries to Axioms 1^{ooo} and 2^{ooo}, we will assume that some utility function U_j^* has already been defined for each individual $j(j = 1, \ldots, i, \ldots, n)$, and that some social-welfare function W_i^* has already been defined for individual i (whose moral preferences we are considering). But, of course, in general these functions U_j^* and W_i^* will not satisfy Equation (4.46), except by accident, and our task will be to construct new utility functions U_j and a new social-welfare function W_i that do satisfy the equation.

As part of our construction procedure we will define a set of social situations B_j^m for $j = 1, \ldots, n$, with m ranging over all integers (of either sign), such that for all values of m

$$U_j(B_j^m) = W_i(B_j^m) = m \qquad (4.47)$$

while

$$U_k(B_j^m) = 0 \quad \text{for all} \quad k \neq j \qquad (4.48)$$

We shall also define another set of social situations C^m, with m again ranging over all integers, such that for all values of m

$$U_1(C^m) = U_1(B_1^m) = m \qquad (4.49)$$

$$U_2(C^m) = 1 \qquad (4.50)$$

$$U_j(C^m) = U_j(B_1^m) = 0 \quad \text{for} \quad j = 3, \ldots, n \qquad (4.51)$$

and

$$W_i(C^m) = W_i(B_1^{m+1}) = m + 1 \qquad (4.52)$$

We now choose two social situations B^* and C^* such that

$$U_2^*(B^*) < U_2^*(C^*) \qquad (4.53)$$

whereas

$$U_j^*(B^*) = U_j^*(C^*) \quad \text{for} \quad j = 1 \quad \text{and} \quad j = 3, \ldots, n \qquad (4.54)$$

By Axiom 3^{oo} this implies that

$$W_i^*(B^*) < W_i^*(C^*) \qquad (4.55)$$

Obviously the new utility and social-welfare functions U_j and W_i to be constructed will have to preserve the ordinal properties of the old functions U_j^* and W_i^* and therefore will have to satisfy relationships similar to (4.53), (4.54), and (4.55).

Consequently we can set

$$U_1(B^*) = W_i(B^*) = 0 \tag{4.56}$$
$$U_2(C^*) = W_i(C^*) = 1 \tag{4.57}$$

and

$$U_j(B^*) = U_j(C^*) = 0 \quad \text{for} \quad j = 1 \quad \text{and} \quad j = 3, \dots, n \tag{4.58}$$

We now define

$$B_j^0 = B^* \quad \text{for} \quad j = 1, \dots, n \tag{4.59}$$

and

$$C^0 = C^* \tag{4.60}$$

These definitions obviously ensure that the functions $U_1, \dots, U_n$ and W_i to be constructed will satisfy Conditions (4.47) to (4.52) for $m = 0$.

We will now actually define the situations B_j^m $(j = 1, \dots, n)$ and C^m for *positive* values of m. Suppose that $B_j^{m-1} (j = 1, \dots, n)$ and C^{m-1} have already been defined in such a way that they satisfy Conditions (4.47) through (4.52). We now define B_j^m for each individual $j (j = 1, \dots, n)$ as a social situation such that

$$U_k{}^*(B_j^m) = U_k{}^*(B^*) \quad \text{for all} \quad k \neq j \tag{4.61}$$

whereas

$$W_i{}^*(B_j^m) = W_i{}^*(C^{m-1}) \tag{4.62}$$

Because U_k and W_i must have the same ordinal properties as $U_k{}^*$ and $W_i{}^*$ do, we can write

$$U_k(B_j^m) = U_k(B^*) = 0 \quad \text{for all} \quad k \neq j \tag{4.63}$$

and

$$W_i(B_j^m) = W_i(C^{m-1}) = (m - 1) + 1 = m \tag{4.64}$$

where the last equality follows from the fact that C^{m-1} satisfies Condition (4.52). Consequently

$$W_i(B_j^m) = m > W_i(B_j^{m-1}) = m - 1 \tag{4.65}$$

whereas, in view of (4.48) and (4.63),

$$U_k(B_j^m) = U_k(B_j^{m-1}) = 0 \quad \text{for all} \quad k \neq j \tag{4.66}$$

But (4.65) and (4.66) imply, in view of Axiom $3^{\circ\circ\circ}$, that

$$U_j(B_j^m) > U_j(B_j^{m-1}) = m - 1 \tag{4.67}$$

Therefore we can set

$$U_j(B_j^m) = m \tag{4.68}$$

Next we define C^m as a social situation such that

$$U_1{}^*(C^m) = U_1{}^*(B_1{}^m) \tag{4.69}$$

whereas

$$U_j{}^*(C^m) = U_j{}^*(C^*) \quad \text{for} \quad j = 2, \dots, n \tag{4.70}$$

Consequently

$$U_1(C^m) = U_1(B_1{}^m) = m \tag{4.71}$$

where the second equality follows from (4.68). Moreover,

$$U_2(C^m) = U_2(C^*) = 1 \tag{4.72}$$

and

$$U_j(C^m) = U_j(C^*) = 0 \quad \text{for} \quad j = 3, \dots, n \tag{4.73}$$

In view of (4.63), (4.68), (4.71), (4.72), and (4.73),

$$U_j(C^m) > U_j(B_1{}^m) \quad \text{for} \quad j = 2 \tag{4.74}$$

but

$$U_j(C^m) = U_j(B_1{}^m) \quad \text{for} \quad j = 1 \quad \text{and} \quad j = 3, \dots, n \tag{4.75}$$

Consequently, in view of Axiom $3^{\circ\circ\circ}$, we must have

$$W_i(C^m) > W_i(B_1{}^m) = m \tag{4.76}$$

Therefore we can set

$$W_i(C^m) = m + 1 \tag{4.77}$$

In view of (4.63), (4.64), (4.68), (4.71), (4.72), (4.73), and (4.77), our definitions of $B_j{}^m$ and of C^m satisfy Conditions (4.47) through (4.52).

Once the situations $B_j{}^m (j = 1, \dots, n)$ and $C^{\cdots}$ have been defined, we can define $B_j{}^{m+1}$ (for $j = 1, \dots, n$) and C^{m+1} by the same procedure, and so forth.

To define the social situations $B_j{}^m$ and C^m for *negative* values of m, we proceed as follows. Suppose that the situations $B_j{}^{m+1}$ (for $j = 1, \dots, n$) and C^{m+1} have already been defined in such a way that they satisfy Conditions (4.47) through (4.52). We now define C^m as a social situation such that

$$U_j{}^*(C^m) = U_j{}^*(C^*) \quad \text{for} \quad j = 2, \dots, n \tag{4.78}$$

and

$$W_i{}^*(C^m) = W_i{}^*(B_1{}^{m+1}) \tag{4.79}$$

Consequently

$$U_2(C^m) = U_2(C^*) = 1 \tag{4.80}$$

and

$$U_j(C^m) = U_j(C^*) = 0 \quad \text{for} \quad j = 3, \ldots, n \tag{4.81}$$

whereas

$$W_i(C^m) = W_i(B_1{}^{m+1}) = m + 1 \tag{4.82}$$

where the last equality follows from the fact that $B_1{}^{m+1}$ satisfies Condition (4.52). As C^{m+1} satisfies Equations (4.50) through (4.52), while C^m satisfies Equations (4.80) through (4.82), we can write

$$U_j(C^m) = U_j(C^{m+1}) \quad \text{for} \quad j = 2, \ldots, n \tag{4.83}$$

but

$$W_i(C^m) = m + 1 < W_i(C^{m+1}) = m + 2 \tag{4.84}$$

In view of Axiom $3^{\circ\circ\circ}$, this means that we must have

$$U_1(C^m) < U_1(C^{m+1}) = m + 1 \tag{4.85}$$

Therefore we can set

$$U_1(C^m) = m \tag{4.86}$$

Next we define the social situations $B_j{}^m$, first for $j = 1$ and then separately for all other values of $j (j = 2, \ldots, n)$. We define $B_1{}^m$ as a social situation such that

$$U_1{}^*(B_1{}^m) = U_1{}^*(C^m) \tag{4.87}$$

whereas

$$U_j{}^*(B_1{}^m) = U_j{}^*(B^*) \quad \text{for} \quad j = 2, \ldots, n \tag{4.88}$$

Consequently

$$U_1(B_1{}^m) = U_1(C^m) = m \tag{4.89}$$

and

$$U_j(B_1{}^m) = U_j(B^*) = 0 \quad \text{for} \quad j = 2, \ldots, n \tag{4.90}$$

As $B_1{}^{m+1}$ satisfies Conditions (4.47) and (4.48), we can write

$$U_1(B_1{}^m) = m < U_1(B_1{}^{m+1}) = m + 1 \tag{4.91}$$

and

$$U_j(B_1{}^m) = U_j(B_1{}^{m+1}) \quad \text{for} \quad j = 2, \ldots, n \tag{4.92}$$

By Axiom $3^{\circ\circ\circ}$, this means that we must have

$$W_i(B_1{}^m) < W_i(B_1{}^{m+1}) = m + 1 \tag{4.93}$$

where the last equality follows from the fact that B^{m+1} satisfies Condition (4.47).

Therefore we can set

$$W_i(B_1{}^m) = m \tag{4.94}$$

Finally we define $B_j{}^m$ for the other individuals $j = 2, \ldots, n$ as a social situation such that

$$U_k{}^*(B_j{}^m) = U_k{}^*(B^*) \quad \text{for all} \quad k \neq j \tag{4.95}$$

whereas

$$W_i{}^*(B_j{}^m) = W_i{}^*(B_1{}^m) \tag{4.96}$$

Consequently

$$U_k(B_j{}^m) = U_k(B^*) = 0 \quad \text{for all} \quad k \neq j \tag{4.97}$$

and

$$W_i(B_j{}^m) = W_i(B_1{}^m) = m \tag{4.98}$$

As $B_j{}^{m+1}(j = 2, \ldots, n)$ satisfies Condition (4.48), we can write

$$U_k(B_j{}^m) = U_k(B_j{}^{m+1}) \quad \text{for all} \quad k \neq j \tag{4.99}$$

but

$$W_i(B_j{}^m) = m < W_i(B_j{}^{m+1}) = m + 1 \tag{4.100}$$

By Axiom $3^{\circ\circ\circ}$, this means that we must have

$$U_j(B_j{}^m) < U_j(B_j{}^{m+1}) = m + 1 \tag{4.101}$$

where the last equality follows from the fact that $B_j{}^{m+1}$ satisfies Condition (4.47). Therefore we can set

$$U_j(B_j{}^m) = m \tag{4.102}$$

In view of (4.80), (4.81), (4.82), (4.86), (4.89), (4.90), (4.94), (4.97), (4.98), and (4.102), our last definitions of C^m and of $B_j{}^m$ (for $j = 1, \ldots, n$) satisfy Conditions (4.47) through (4.52). Once situations C^m and $B_j{}^m$ have been defined, we can define situations C^{m-1} and $B_j{}^{m-1}$ ($j = 1, \ldots, n$) by the same procedure, and so forth.

Finally, for every social situation A satisfying

$$U_j{}^*(A) = U_j{}^*(B_1{}^m) \tag{4.103}$$

for given values of j and m, we define

$$U_j(A) = U_j(B_1{}^m) = m \tag{4.104}$$

Likewise, for any social situation A^* satisfying

$$W_i{}^*(A^*) = W_i{}^*(B_1{}^m) \tag{4.105}$$

for some given value of m, we define

$$W_i(A^*) = W_i(B_1{}^m) = m \tag{4.106}$$

These definitions uniquely determine the values of the $(n + 1)$ functions $U_1, \ldots,$ U_n and W_i at all points where these functions take (positive, negative, or zero) integer values. Our next task is to show that at all points where these functions have been defined they satisfy Equation (4.46).[9]

Consider the vector

$$u = (u_1, \ldots, u_n) \tag{4.107}$$

where

$$u_j = U_j(A) \quad \text{for} \quad j = 1, \ldots, n \tag{4.108}$$

We will call u the utility vector for the social situation A and will write

$$u = U(A) \tag{4.109}$$

In what follows, unless stated otherwise, we will assume that, for all utility vectors u, all components $u_1, \ldots, u_n$ are integers.

Lemma 1. Let A and A^* be two social situations with the utility vectors $u = (u_1, \ldots, u_n) = U(A)$ and $u^* = (u_1{}^*, \ldots, u_n{}^*) = U(A^*)$. Suppose that $u_j = 0$, and suppose that u^* differs from u only in the fact that its jth and kth components are interchanged, so that

$$u_k{}^* = u_j = 0 \tag{4.110}$$

whereas

$$u_j{}^* = u_k \tag{4.111}$$

and

$$u_h{}^* = u_h \quad \text{for all} \quad h \neq j, k \tag{4.112}$$

Then

$$W_i(A^*) = W_i(A) \tag{4.113}$$

Proof. We know that the lemma is true at least in the special case where

$$u_h{}^* = u_h = 0 \quad \text{for all} \quad h \neq j, k \tag{4.114}$$

This is so because, as $u_j{}^* = u_k$ is an integer, we can write

$$u_j{}^* = u_k = m \tag{4.115}$$

But, in view of (4.110), (4.114), and (4.115), we can write

$$U(A) = U(B_k{}^m) \quad \text{and} \quad U(A^*) = U(B_j{}^m) \tag{4.116}$$

Therefore, in view of Equation (4.47) and Axiom $3^{\circ\circ\circ}$, we have

$$W_i(A) = W_i(B_k{}^m) = m \quad \text{and} \quad W_i(A^*) = W_i(B_j{}^m) = m \tag{4.117}$$

which verifies that the lemma is true in this special case.

However, in view of Equation (4.112), in comparing the two social situations A and A^*, all individuals $h \neq j$, k must be classified as *unconcerned* individuals indifferent between these two social situations. Consequently, in view of Axiom $4^{\circ\circ\circ}$, if the lemma is true in the special case in which Condition (4.114) holds, it must be true also in the more general case where for some or all individuals $h \neq j$, k this condition fails to hold [as long as Condition (4.112) does hold].

Lemma 2. Let A and A^* be again two social situations with the utility vectors $u = U(A)$ and $u^* = U(A^*)$. Suppose that u and u^* differ only in their jth and kth components so that

$$u_j{}^* = u_j + 1 \tag{4.118}$$

$$u_k = 1 \tag{4.119}$$

$$u_k{}^* = 0 \tag{4.120}$$

whereas

$$u_h{}^* = u_h \quad \text{for all} \quad h \neq j, k \tag{4.121}$$

Then

$$W_i(A^*) = W_i(A) \tag{4.122}$$

Proof. We know that the lemma is true in the special case where

$$u_h{}^* = u_h = 0 \quad \text{for all} \quad h \neq 1, 2 \tag{4.123}$$

and where in particular

$$j = 1 \quad \text{and} \quad k = 2 \tag{4.124}$$

To show this, let us write

$$u_1 = m \quad \text{and therefore} \quad u_1{}^* = m + 1 \tag{4.125}$$

Then obviously

$$U(A) = U(C^m) \tag{4.126}$$

whereas

$$U(A^*) = U(B_1{}^{m+1}) \tag{4.127}$$

Hence, in view of Equation (4.52) and Axiom $3^{\circ\circ\circ}$, we can write

$$W_i(A) = W_i(C^m) = m + 1 \quad \text{and} \quad W_i(A^*) = W_i(B_1{}^{m+1}) = m + 1 \tag{4.128}$$

which verifies that the lemma holds in this special case.

Now we propose to show that the lemma holds, even if Condition (4.124) is not satisfied, as long as Condition (4.123) is satisfied. To show this, let $\bar{A}$ and $\bar{A}^*$ be two other social situations, with the utility vectors $\bar{u} = U(\bar{A})$ and $\bar{u}^* = U(\bar{A}^*)$. Suppose that the utility vector $\bar{u} = U(\bar{A})$ can be obtained from the utility vector

$u = U(A)$ by interchanging the first and the jth components and by interchanging the second and the kth components. Likewise suppose that $\bar{u}^* = U(\bar{A}^*)$ can be obtained from $u^* = U(A^*)$ by means of the same procedure. Then the social situations $\bar{A}$ and $\bar{A}^*$ will come under the special case already discussed, and we can write

$$W_i(\bar{A}^*) = W_i(\bar{A}) \tag{4.129}$$

On the other hand, by Lemma 1, we have

$$W_i(\bar{A}) = W_i(A) \quad \text{and} \quad W_i(\bar{A}^*) = W_i(A^*) \tag{4.130}$$

Consequently

$$W_i(A) = W_i(A^*) \tag{4.131}$$

which shows that the lemma holds, even if Condition (4.124) is not satisfied.

Finally we will now show that the lemma holds, even if Condition (4.123) also fails to be satisfied. This is so because in comparing the two situations A and A^* all individuals $h \neq j, k$ must be classified as *unconcerned* individuals. Hence, by Axiom $4^{\circ\circ\circ}$, Condition (4.123) is irrelevant.

Lemma 3. Let A and A^* be two social situations with $u = U(A)$ and $u^* = U(A^*)$. Suppose that u and u^* differ only in their jth and kth components so that

$$u_j^* = u_j + 1 \tag{4.132}$$

whereas

$$u_k^* = u_k - 1 \tag{4.133}$$

and

$$u_h^* = u_h \quad \text{for all} \quad h \neq j, k \tag{4.134}$$

Then

$$W_i(A^*) = W_i(A) \tag{4.135}$$

Proof. First consider the special case where for some particular individual $g \neq j$, k we have

$$u_g^* = u_g = 0 \tag{4.136}$$

Let A^{**} be a third social situation with $u^{**} = U(A^{**})$. Suppose that

$$u_j^{**} = u_j = u_j^* - 1 \tag{4.137}$$

$$u_k^{**} = u_k - 1 = u_k^* \tag{4.138}$$

$$u_g^{**} = 1 \tag{4.139}$$

and

$$u_h^{**} = u_h^* = u_h \quad \text{for all} \quad h \neq j, k, g \tag{4.140}$$

By Lemma 2, we can write

$$W_i(A^*) = W_i(A^{**}) = W_i(A) \tag{4.141}$$

which shows that the lemma holds in the special case where Condition (4.136) is satisfied.

However, in comparing A and A^*, individual g is an *unconcerned* individual. Hence, by Axiom 4^{ooo}, the lemma holds, even if Condition (4.136) is not satisfied.

Lemma 4. Let A and A^* be two social situations with $u = U(A)$ and $u^* = U(A^*)$. Suppose that

$$\sum_{j=1}^{n} u_j^* = \sum_{j=1}^{n} u_j \tag{4.142}$$

Then

$$W_i(A^*) = W_i(A) \tag{4.143}$$

Proof. The lemma follows from the fact that, in view of (4.142), u^* can be obtained from u by repeated one-unit utility transfers satisfying Lemma 3.

Lemma 5. Let A be a social situation for which all u utility values $U_1(A), \ldots,$ $U_n(A)$ are integers. Then

$$W_i(A) = \sum_{j=1}^{n} U_j(A) \tag{4.144}$$

in accordance with Equations (4.46).

Proof. Let

$$\sum_{j=1}^{n} U_j(A) = m \tag{4.145}$$

Consider the social situation $B_1{}^m$. In view of Equations (4.47) and (4.48), we have

$$\sum_{j=1}^{n} U_j(B_1{}^m) = m = W_i(B_1{}^m) \tag{4.146}$$

Consequently, by Lemma 4,

$$W_i(A) = W_i(B_1{}^m) = m \tag{4.147}$$

as desired.

Proof of Theorem 4.3. By using the same procedure we can define the functions $U_1, \ldots, U_n$ and W_i at all points where their values are positive, negative, or zero multiples of some freely chosen small positive number ϵ and can show that at all these points Equation (4.46) will be satisfied. By an appropriate limiting process we can extend the definitions of these functions to all social situations A in set X^*. By continuity, Equation (4.46) will be satisfied at all such points A.

Clearly the functions $U_1, \ldots, U_n$ and W_i satisfying Equation (4.46) are *cardinal* utility and *cardinal* social welfare functions, unique up to order-preserving linear transformations. This is so because nonlinear transformations would destroy the property expressed by Equation (4.46). This completes the proof of the theorem.

Note: Theorem 4.3 looks somewhat stronger than Theorem 4.2, because it seems to set the coefficients $a_1, \ldots, a_n$ of Equation (4.12) equal to unity. But this fact is merely a consequence of the procedure by which we have defined the functions $U_1, \ldots, U_n$ and W_i used in Theorem 4.3. Had we used a slightly different procedure we would have obtained arbitrary positive values for the coefficients $a_1, \ldots, a_n$ in the same way as we did in Theorem 4.2. Axioms 1^{ooo} to 4^{ooo} as such do not assign any specific values to these coefficients. (However, by Axiom 3^{ooo}, they all must be positive.) Just as in the case of Theorem 4.2, we would need an additional axiom (e.g., Axiom 4^{oo} of Section 4.8) if we wanted to impose the formal requirement on these coefficients that they must take the same numerical value with $a_1 = \cdots = a_n = a$.[10]

4.10 The unavoidable need for interpersonal comparisons of utility in ethics

We have seen that, if individual i defines his social-welfare function W_i in terms of Theorem 4.1, then he must make use of *interpersonal utility comparisons* in order to ensure that the utility functions $U_1, \ldots, U_i, \ldots, U_n$ are all expressed in the same utility unit. The same is true if he defines his social-welfare function W_i in terms of Theorem 4.2 or 4.3 in conjunction with Axiom 4^{oo}, because this axiom also requires that these utility functions be expressed in the same utility unit. However, it may appear that he can avoid interpersonal utility comparisons if he defines his social-welfare function W_i in terms of Theorem 4.2 or 4.3 *without* any use of Axiom 4^{oo} [that is, if he defines W_i by Equation (4.12) with arbitrary positive coefficients $a_1, \ldots, a_n$].

In actuality I propose to show that he *cannot* avoid interpersonal utility comparisons even if he follows this latter approach, as long as he wants to choose the coefficients $a_1, \ldots, a_n$ of his social-welfare function W_i in a rational manner. This is so because the only way that individual i can judge how much relative weight a given set of coefficients $a_1, \ldots, a_n$ actually assigns to each individual's interests is by converting all n individuals' utility functions $U_1, \ldots, U_n$ into the same utility unit – which, of course, involves making interpersonal utility comparisons. For example, suppose that he originally tentatively defined his social-welfare function W_i as

$$W_i(A) = \sum_{j=1}^{n} a_j U_j(A) \tag{4.148}$$

Converting the utility functions $U_1, \ldots, U_n$ into the same utility unit, he will obtain the new utility functions

$$U_j^*(A) = q_j U_j(A) \qquad j = 1, \ldots, n \tag{4.149}$$

Thus his social-welfare function will take the form

$$W_i(A) = \sum_{j=1}^{n} a_j q_j U_j(A) = \sum_{j=1}^{n} a_j^* U_j(A) \tag{4.150}$$

with

$$a_j^* = a_j q_j \qquad j = 1, \ldots, n \tag{4.151}$$

Only by computing these normalized coefficients $a_1^*, \ldots, a_n^*$ can individual i judge the actual weight that this social-welfare function W_i assigns to each individual. The original coefficients $a_1, \ldots, a_n$ in themselves cannot give him this information.

For instance, suppose that individual i's moral code requires that he give a much greater weight to individual i's interests than he would give to any other individual's interests (which, of course, implies that his moral code is inconsistent with our Axiom 4^{oo}). This means that, after converting all individuals' utility functions into the same utility unit, the normalized coefficient a_1^* ought to be much larger than the normalized coefficients $a_2^*, \ldots, a_n^*$ are in his social-welfare function W_i. But individual i cannot predict the relative sizes of the normalized coefficients a_1^*, $\ldots, a_n^*$ by looking merely at the coefficients $a_1, \ldots, a_n$, without trying to estimate the conversion ratios $q_1, \ldots, q_n$ by means of interpersonal utility comparisons.

To conclude, whether individual i's moral code includes our egalitarian Axiom 4^{oo} or not, he cannot define his social-welfare function W_i in a rational manner, and cannot make moral value judgments in a rational fashion, without attempting interpersonal utility comparisons. This is, of course, not surprising. Sooner or later individual i will have to decide whether he should use his scarce resources to satisfy the needs of one particular individual or another. But he cannot decide this rationally without paying at least *some* attention to the question of which individual's needs have a greater psychological urgency – or equivalently which individual would derive a higher utility from a satisfaction of his needs. Yet this will mean making interpersonal utility comparisons.[11]

4.11 The role of moral attitudes in social conflicts

Although the main subject matter of this book is game theory, our discussion of some basic problems of ethics serves two main purposes.

On the level of conceptual analysis, because both ethics and game theory are branches of the general theory of rational behavior, any clarification of the nature of *moral* rationality is likely to help us in understanding the nature of *game-theoretical* rationality. Both the similarities and the differences between the two concepts of rationality will be instructive (cf. Section 1.5). One important difference that we have already discussed is the unavoidable use of interpersonal utility comparisons in ethics (Section 4.10), in contrast to their inadmissibility (as we will argue) in game theory.

On the level of empirical applications, models of social behavior guided by impersonal and impartial moral criteria can usefully supplement purely game-theoretical models. It seems that the principal mechanism for resolving conflicts of interest in society is bargaining among the directly interested parties; and the appropriate theoretical tools for the analysis of this mechanism are game-theoretical bargaining models and game-theoretical models of other types. But we must not overlook the fact that in such conflict situations the outcome is often decided by the intervention of more or less "disinterested" third parties (such as "public opinion"), whose behavior may be guided to a large extent by impartial "moral" criteria. Moreover, the interested parties themselves may be influenced to some degree by such "moral" considerations. For this reason an analytical theory of moral value judgments can throw considerable light on the various parties' policy goals and on the actual outcome in conflict-of-interest situations.

Part II
General principles

5

Some basic concepts of game theory

5.1 Introduction

The main concern of this book is with *game situations* (situations of strategic inter-dependence), in which the outcome depends on mutual interaction between two or more rational individuals, each of them pursuing his own interests (and his own values) against the other individuals, who are likewise pursuing their own interests (and their own values). In earlier chapters we discussed situations of *individual independence* (certainty, risk, and uncertainty), in which the outcome depends on the actions of only one individual (and possibly on chance). We also discussed *moral situations*, in which the outcome does depend on interaction between two or more individuals but in which this outcome and these individuals' actions are evaluated, not in terms of their own individual interests but rather in terms of the interests of society as a whole – as seen by an impartial but sympathetic observer. However, all of this was merely a preliminary to our analysis of game situations.

Following von Neumann and Morgenstern [1944] it is customary to analyze what we call game situations by using parlor games – already existing ones or ones specially constructed for this very purpose – as analytical models. (More specifically, what are used as models are *games of strategy*, where the outcome depends at least in part on a rational choice of strategy by the participants rather than on mere physical skill or on mere chance.) Hence the term "game situations" and the name "*game theory*," for the theory analyzing such situations, arise.

The actively participating individuals in a game situation (or the actively participating social groups or organizations if they are regarded as the basic units of the analysis) are called the *players*. Depending on the number of players, a game situation is called a *two-person* game, a *three-person* game, and so forth. (Sometimes what we have called situations of individual independence are also called *one-person* games. But unless we indicate otherwise, we will not include these under the concept of "games.") Games with more than two players, called *n-person* games, give rise to special problems, absent from two-person games, because of the possibility that the players may form *coalitions*, which will be discussed later.

It is often partially a matter of analytical convenience which particular participants are regarded as *active* players and which are regarded as mere *passive* participants, who are simply parts of the active players' physical environment, more or less on a par with the material equipment used by the latter in the game. In general a given individual can be treated as a mere passive participant not in-

cluded in the game proper only if his strategy (i.e., his pattern of behavior) is regarded as *given* and if no attempt is to be made to *explain* his strategy in terms of
game-theoretical rationality considerations. In practice this means that a duopoly
situation or a war, for example, can often be treated as a *two-person* game, with
the two duopolist entrepreneurs or the two opposing army commanders (or alternatively the two duopolist business firms or the two opposing armies as units)
regarded as the sole active players. But this can be done only if the customers
(and employees) of the two duopolists or the soldiers of the two armies follow
some relatively simple and standardized strategies. For instance, the customers
may simply follow the rule of always buying at the cheapest market, without
ever trying to influence the market conditions themselves (e.g., by bargaining
or by forming cooperative purchasing organizations); or the soldiers may simply
obey the orders of their respective army commanders (or disobey these orders
only according to some *given* statistical laws) without making any attempt to
obtain some independent influence on army policies. But if the customers or the
soldiers follow more independent strategies, then they must be assigned the status
of active players, because, in this case, excluding their strategies from our game-
theoretical analysis would mean assuming away a major part of our analytical
problem.

In any game situation the *rules of the game* must specify what *actions* each
player can take at any particular stage of the game, how much *information* he will
have available to guide his actions, and what the *consequences* of his actions will
be both for himself and for the other players. A game situation with fully specified
rules is called a *game*. Thus chess or bridge is a game, but so is a specific war or a
specific duopoly situation.

In real parlor games the rules are essentially matters of arbitrary *convention*.
But in social situations analyzed as game situations, what the game theorist may
subsume under the "rules of the game" includes:

1. The *social conventions* observed by the players (e.g., legal or moral rules).

2. The *laws of nature* (e.g., the physical, chemical, and biological laws governing
the performance of the human body and of the material equipment used).

3. The initial *distribution of resources* (e.g., bodily strength, economic resources,
military equipment) among the players − including the initial distribution of *information, technological knowledge, and practical skills*.

Besides the rules of the game, the description of a game situation must also include the (cardinal) *utility functions* of the players. Again, if we want to assume
that the players will act in a certain manner (e.g., that they will abide by agreements made with other players), then it may be a matter of analytical convenience
whether this assumption is included in the *rules* of the game or is incorporated
into the players' utility functions (by postulating that contrary behavior would
be very costly to them, e.g., because of heavy penalties imposed on violators).

5.2 The extensive form of a game

Deviating somewhat from everyday language, in game theory all of the alternative
"moves" or "actions" among which a given player can choose at a particular

moment are called his *choices*. The term *move* itself is reserved for the *set* of *all* alternative choices among which he can make his selection at that particular stage of the game. For convenience of exposition (to keep closer to everyday language), we will also use *choice point* to refer to the same concept. Thus we will say, "Player 3 at his second 'move' – or at his second 'choice point' – will have five alternative 'choices' available."

Both in parlor games and in real-life situations the course of the game at some points may depend on *chance events*, i.e., on events whose outcome the players are unable to predict, while they may or may not know at least the objective probability distribution of the possible outcomes. For example, in parlor games the course of the game may depend on a throw of dice or on a deal of cards; in real-life situations it may depend on the vagaries of the weather, on the chance events deciding the outcome of a given battle, or on the more-or-less unpredictable results of technological research.

A chance event influencing the course of the game can be formally treated as a "move" by an imaginary player personifying chance, who by convention is always allotted the serial number 0. The rules of the game must specify, when this player 0 has a "move," his alternative "choices" for a given move (i.e., what the possible outcomes are of the chance event in question) and the *probabilities* associated with each alternative "choice" (i.e., with each alternative outcome).

Chance events (regarded as the "moves" of this imaginary player 0) are called *chance moves*, whereas the moves of the other (real) players are called *personal moves*.

A particular sequence of choices by the players, from the beginning of the game to its end, is called a *play*. Thus a play can be regarded as a full description of how the game was (or could have been) played on some particular occasion. (In ordinary language we often use the word "game" itself in this sense, e.g., when we speak of a particular chess "game" that two masters played against each other on some particular occasion.)

The logical structure of a game can be represented by means of a *game tree* (see Figure 5.1).[1]

The lines of the tree are called *branches*. Each branch is said to originate from its lowest point. A point from which two or more branches originate is called a *node*. The points at the top, where a branch ends but where no new branch originates, are called *end points*.

Each node represents a *move* or *choice point* for some player, while the branches originating from this node represent the alternative *choices* that he has at that point. The serial number of the *player* whose move a given node represents is indicated by a large number to the right of that node. On the other hand, the branches (choices) belonging to the same node are numbered by small numbers to the left of each branch. In the case of branches originating from a node that belongs to player 0 (i.e., in the case of a node representing a chance move), we have to indicate the *probabilities* associated with each branch (each possible outcome of the chance move). This we have done by writing these probabilities in brackets after the number 0, to the right of the relevant node. (For instance, at

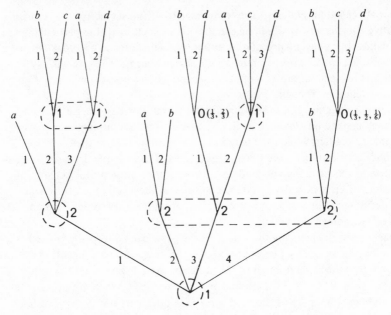

Figure 5.1

the farthest right node the branches 1, 2, and 3 are associated with probabilities $\frac{1}{3}, \frac{1}{2}, \frac{1}{6}$, in that order.)

The game (rather, a given particular "play") starts at the lowest node, called the *starting node*, and then gradually moves upward – along a route depending on the actual choices of the players at each choice point – until an *end point* is reached. (Of course, the game tree of almost any real game would be much more extensive than the one we have drawn for illustrative purposes.) For every end point of the game tree, the rules of the game must specify the corresponding *outcome*, i.e., the specific result that would arise for all players if the game came to an end at that end point.[2] In Figure 5.1 one of the letters a, b, c, or d is written next to each end point to indicate the corresponding outcome.

The *utility function* of each player will determine the utility – called the *payoff* – that he will derive from any particular physical outcome. (If a given player takes sympathetic or antipathetic interest in other players' well-being, then the utility that he derives from any given outcome will depend not only on his own personal position under this outcome but also on other players' personal positions under it.) The set of all payoffs (listed in the order of the players' serial numbers[3]) that the various players would derive from a given outcome is called a *payoff vector*.

It is often convenient when drawing a game tree to indicate directly the *payoff vectors* associated with each end point instead of indicating the physical *outcomes* that underlie these payoff vectors, as we have done.

A game tree can also be used to indicate the amount of *information* that each player will have at every particular stage of the game. Depending on the amount of information available to the players, we distinguish between games with *complete* and *incomplete* information and again between games with *perfect* and *imperfect* information. We speak of a game with *complete* information if the players have full information about the *rules* of the game, which is the same as saying that they have full information about the extensive form of the game.[4] In particular they must know their own and the other players' strategical possibilities, and the amount of information available to each player, as well as their own and the other players' utility functions. If this is not true, then we speak of a game with *incomplete* information. We may also say that in a game with incomplete information the players are not quite sure of the precise nature of the game that they are playing. In this book we will deal only with games with complete information (cf. Section 1.2). [On games with incomplete information, see Harsanyi, 1967, 1968a, and 1968b; Harsanyi and Selten, 1972.]

On the other hand, even if the players have complete information about the rules of the game and their utility functions, they may or may not have full information about the other players' (or possibly even about their own) previous personal moves and/or about the outcomes of previous chance moves. For example, in many card games the players often discard their cards face down, so that the other players will not know which particular cards have been discarded by a given player, which represents ignorance about these players' personal moves. Likewise the players will usually have no information about which particular cards have been dealt out to the other players, which means ignorance about the outcomes of chance moves. Similarly, in real life the government of a given country may have little or no information about the war preparations of another country; or a given firm may have little or no information about the investment and research plans and even about the results of past research by other firms (which are determined partly by chance).

We speak of a game with *perfect* information if each player, at any choice point when he has to decide on his next move, always has full information about *all personal and chance moves* that have already taken place in the game. Otherwise we speak of a game with *imperfect* information. Our discussion will cover both games with perfect and with imperfect information (within the class of games with complete information).

To sum up, the distinction between games with complete and with incomplete information refers to the amount of information that the players have about the basic parameters of the game situation, i.e., about the *independent variables* (the rules of the game and the players' utility functions). In contrast, the distinction between games with perfect and imperfect information refers to the amount of information that the players have about the past history of this particular play, i.e., about the past behavior of the *dependent variables* (personal and chance moves).

A special case of imperfect information is *imperfect recall*, which means that some player(s) may fail to remember even *his* (or their) *own* previous moves in the game. Thus, we speak of a game with *perfect recall* or of *imperfect recall*, depending on whether the players always have full recollection about all their own earlier moves or not. Games with imperfect recall are meant to model game situations in which some of the "players" are in fact *teams* or *organizations* consisting of two or more individuals. In such cases, it is often convenient to assume that this "player" may lack information also about some of his *own* earlier moves, in the sense that one individual acting for this "player" may not know the moves made by other individuals acting for the same "player." For example, in the game of bridge North and South (and again East and West) act as a team with identical interests and can be regarded as one "player" who alternates between "remembering" only North's past moves (when he is acting as North) and "remembering" only South's past moves (when he is acting as South) – although both North's and South's moves are to be considered as the moves of this one composite "player."

Lack of information about previous moves will have the effect that a given player, when he has to decide on his next move, will not know what his exact position is on the game tree, i.e., which of two or more nodes (choice points) represents his present position. We can indicate this by drawing a dotted line around those nodes among which the player cannot distinguish. Such nodes form an *information set*. For example, on Figure 5.1 we have assumed that if player 1 at the starting choice point (i.e., at the lowest node of the tree) chooses one of branches 2, 3, or 4, then player 2 will not know which branch player 1 has chosen and therefore will not know which node, of the three nodes at the top of these branches, represents his own actual position after player 1's move. Thus these three nodes belong to the *same* information set, which is indicated by the dotted line around them. On the other hand, we have assumed that player 2 will always know whether player 1 has chosen branch 1 or has chosen *one* (but not which one) of the three other branches. Therefore the node at the top of branch 1 belongs to another information set than the nodes at the tops of branches 2, 3, and 4.

For each information set I of a given player i, the rules of the game must specify the number, K, of the alternative choices (physical actions) he can take if he is in this information set. Suppose we number these alternative choices as $1, \ldots,$ $k, \ldots, K$. Then, the game tree must have exactly K branches originating in *each* of the nodes belonging to this information set I. Moreover, the branches originating in each of these nodes must be numbered as $1, \ldots, k, \ldots, K$ to indicate *which* branch represents any particular choice k. Branches having the same serial number k and, therefore, representing the same physical action by player i are called *corresponding branches*.

In case a player at a given choice point knows all previous moves of the play, he will know exactly which node of the game tree represents his *present* position, i.e., he will be able to distinguish this node from all others. Such a node is said to form a one-node information set, and this is indicated by drawing a separate dotted circle around it. (Of course, no information sets have to be defined for the fictitious player 0 who merely personifies chance.)

To conclude, a *game tree* is a configuration of *nodes* and *branches* running without any closed loops from its *starting node* to its *end points* and indicating:

1. Which node belongs to which *player* (the players being numbered as 1, 2, ..., *n* and the number 0 being assigned to a fictitious player personifying chance).

2. The *probabilities* associated with the branches originating from nodes belonging to player 0.

3. The *information sets* into which each (real) player's nodes are divided, and the *corresponding branches* at different nodes of the same information set.

4. The physical *outcomes* associated with each end point of the game tree.

4'. Or alternatively the *payoff vectors* associated with each end point of the game tree.

If the game tree indicates only physical outcomes (as stated in 4), then a full characterization of the game must also include the *utility functions* of the players. But if the game tree indicates directly the corresponding *payoff vectors* (as stated in 4'), then it will itself fully characterize the game.

Characterization of a game by means of a game tree (such that it indicates payoff vectors rather than physical outcomes) is called the *extensive form* of that game.

The game-tree (or extensive-form) representation formally requires that the players should make their moves in a definite *time order*, i.e., that two or more players should never make moves at the same time. (As we will see, this convention is the exact opposite of the convention adopted in the normal-form representation of a game, where all players are *always* assumed to make their choices at the same time.) But this requirement does not result in any real loss of generality, if appropriate assumptions are made about the *information* available to the players. For example, suppose that, at a given stage of the game, players *i* and *j* are required to make their moves at the same time. Then, from the standpoint of game theory, the only important point about this fact is the inability of either player to *know* the other player's move when he decided his own. Thus it does not make any difference if, for the purposes of a game-tree representation, we formally assume that, e.g., player *i* moves first and player *j* moves second – as long as we also assume that, in spite of the assumed "time order," player *j* will not know what player *i*'s move has been when he chooses his own. (Or equivalently we can assume that player *j* moves first, as long as we also assume that player *i*, now supposedly moving after player *j*, will not know what player *j*'s move has been when he chooses his own move.)

Since the game tree of a given game (if the payoff vectors associated with each end point are indicated) gives full information about the rules of the game and also about the players' utility functions (as far as these are relevant for analyzing the game), we can also define a game with complete information as a game in which the players know all the information displayed by the game tree.

In particular, in a game with complete information the players will know the objective probabilities associated with various possible outcomes of any chance move (chance event) in the game. This means that in such games any chance event will involve *risk* rather than uncertainty.

Games involving chance events with probabilities unknown to some or to all players are always games with incomplete information. In view of Theorem 3.3

of Section 3.5, rational players will always assign subjective probabilities to the various possible outcomes of such chance events, which means that games involving *uncertain* chance events can be analyzed somewhat similarly to games involving only *risky* chance events. But there are two important differences:

1. The *objective* probabilities actually governing the course of the game will be in general different from the *subjective* probabilities entertained by the various players.

2. The subjective probabilities that *different* players assign to the same event will also be different in general from one another.

5.3   The normal form of a game

Instead of assuming that every player decides on each move only just before he has to carry it out, we can also assume that each player decides *in advance*, before the game actually starts, what move he will make *in any possible situation* that may arise. A full description of what move a given player would make in every possible situation is called a *strategy*. Thus a strategy must specify *which particular branch* of the game tree a given player would choose *at any particular node* representing a choice point of this player – or, more exactly, since he cannot distinguish between nodes belonging to the same information set, a strategy must specify which branch (rather, which set of equivalent branches) he would choose *in any particular information set* that he has in the game.

More formally let us number the information sets of a given player i as the 1st, 2nd, . . . , rth. Let $x_1, x_2, . . . , x_r$ each be the serial number of some particular branch that player i may choose while being located in his 1st, 2nd, . . . , rth information set. Then this sequence of numbers, $x_1, x_2, . . . , x_r$, will be called a possible *strategy* (*pure* strategy) of player i.

We can imagine that the game is played in the following way. The players *simultaneously* (and therefore without knowing the choices of the other players) choose their strategies. Then the game is played in accordance with the strategies chosen by the players. Finally all players receive their payoffs as specified by the rules of the game.

Once the players have chosen their strategies, their payoffs can be computed even without going through the physical motions of actually playing the game in accordance with these strategies. For example, it would be quite sufficient for the players to inform the umpire of their strategy choices, and then the umpire could compute their final payoffs. Indeed he could simply program a computer to perform the necessary computations.

More exactly, if the game contains chance moves, then in general the strategies chosen by the players will not determine the actual *values* u_i of the players' payoffs but rather will determine only *probability distributions* over these payoffs. For instance, we may have to conclude that, given this particular choice of strategies by the players, player 1 may obtain the payoff $u_1 = 2$ (with probability $\frac{1}{3}$) or may obtain the payoff $u_1 = 8$ (with probability $\frac{2}{3}$), depending on the outcome of certain chance move(s) in the game. However, in view of Theorem 3.2 of Section 3.4, each player will be interested only in the *expected value* of his payoff. Thus in our example the expected value of player 1's payoff - called his *expected payoff* - would be $\bar{u}_1 = \frac{1}{3} \cdot 2 + \frac{2}{3} \cdot 8 = 6$; and a strategy combination yielding him this expected payoff $\bar{u}_1 = 6$ would be completely equivalent for him to a strategy combination yielding him the actual payoff $u_1 = 6$ with full certainty. For this reason we can regard each player's expected payoff $\bar{u}_i$ as if it were his actual payoff u_i and can simply denote it by the symbol u_i rather than by the symbol $\bar{u}_i$.

More formally, suppose the strategy combination $\sigma_1, \ldots, \sigma_i, \ldots, \sigma_n$ chosen by the n players can yield player i various alternative payoffs $u_i^1, \ldots, u_i^k$ with the probabilities $p^1, \ldots, p^k$, respectively; then in the normal form of the game we define player i's payoff as the expected value

$$u_i = \sum_{i=1}^{k} p^j u_i^j \tag{5.1}$$

Thus we obtain the following model. There are n players. Any given player i has a choice among m_i different strategies.[5] At the same time, each player chooses one of the m_i strategies available to him. Let $\sigma_1, \ldots, \sigma_n$ be the strategies chosen by players $1, \ldots, n$. Then the rules of the game will determine the payoff u_i of a given player i as a *function* of the strategies chosen by himself and by all the other players; that is

$$u_i = U_i(\sigma_1, \ldots, \sigma_n) \tag{5.2}$$

We can also write the entire payoff vector $u = (u_1, \ldots, u_n)$ as a vector-valued function of the strategies chosen by the players:

$$u = U(\sigma_1, \ldots, \sigma_n) \tag{5.3}$$

The function $U = (U_1, \ldots, U_n)$ is called the *payoff function* of the game while its ith component, the function U_i, is called the payoff function of player i.

This characterization of the game, specifying the number of *players*, the number of alternative *strategies* available to each player, and the *payoff function* of the game, is called the *normal form* of the game. While the use of the *extensive form* of a game corresponds to the assumption that the players decide on each move separately, the use of the *normal form* corresponds to the model where each player chooses a full strategy as a whole in advance.

Thus the normal form of the game amounts essentially to reducing a given game - in which every player may have a large number of consecutive moves - to a simpler game in which every player has only *one* move, viz., the choice of a full strategy. But this simplification is, of course, achieved at a cost. Even for quite simple games, each particular strategy may be a very *complicated* logical structure (it will involve the choice of one particular branch of the game tree for each one of a possibly very large number of information sets), and the *number* of alternative strategies available to a given player may be astronomical.

This complexity of strategies, as well as their enormous number, in most games is the essential reason that in practice the players of a game hardly ever choose full strategies in advance as envisaged by the normal-form model. But, in view of the theoretical equivalence of the two representations, for the purposes of a general theory of game situations the use of the normal-form representation has great advantages in terms of analytical simplicity.[6]

In the case of *two-person* games the payoff function for the normal form of the game can be conveniently represented by means of a double-entry table or *matrix* (see Example 1).

	B_1	B_2	B_3
A_1	$(4,-5)$	$(0,0)$	$(-8,1)$
A_2	$(0, 6)$	$(7,0)$	$(1,2)$

Example 1

Player 1's pure strategies are denoted by $A_1, A_2, \ldots, A_k$ and correspond to the *rows* of the matrix, while player 2's pure strategies are denoted by $B_1, B_2, \ldots, B_n$ and correspond to the *columns*.[7] The two numbers enclosed in parentheses in each cell indicate the payoffs that the two players would receive if they used the strategies corresponding to the relevant row and column. (For example, according to our table, if player 1 used strategy A_2 and player 2 used strategy B_1, then player 1 would receive the payoff $u_1 = 0$, while player 2 would receive the payoff $u_2 = 6$.)

5.4   Coalitions and strategies

We now introduce a few more game-theoretical concepts that we will need later.

The set of all n players will be denoted by N. Any set S of s different players, with $S \subseteq N$, will be called a *coalition*.[8] The set $\bar{S} = N - S$, consisting of all players not in S, is called the *complementary coalition* to S. A "coalition" consisting of one player i alone, denoted as $S = (i)$, is called a *solo coalition*. Any coalition smaller than N is called a *sectional coalition*, while N itself is called the *all-player coalition*.

Apart from his pure strategies σ_i as defined in Section 5.3, any player i will be assumed to be allowed the use of *mixed* strategies also. A mixed strategy $\tilde{\sigma}_i$ is a *probability mixture* of pure strategies, i.e., a decision by player i to assign the probabilities $p_i^1, \ldots, p_i^k$ to the pure strategies $\sigma_i^1, \ldots, \sigma_i^k$ and then to let a chance mechanism (e.g., a throw of dice) yielding the required probabilities decide which particular pure strategy $\sigma^j (j = 1, \ldots, k)$ he will use on any particular occasion. The vector $p = (p^1, \ldots, p^k)$ is called the *probability vector* of the mixed strategy $\tilde{\sigma}_i$. Any pure strategy σ_i will be identified with that particular mixed strategy which concentrates *all* probability on the pure strategy σ_i.

A set σ^S of s (pure or mixed) strategies that contains exactly one strategy σ_i for each player i in S, is called a *strategy s-tuple*, or a *joint strategy*, of coalition S. If all component strategies σ_i are pure strategies, then we call σ^S a *pure* joint strategy; if any σ_i is a mixed strategy, then we call σ^S a *mixed* joint strategy.

Among mixed joint strategies σ^S we distinguish *individually randomized* and *jointly randomized* strategies. By *individual* randomization we mean an arrangement under which each player i decides by a *separate* and independent chance mechanism which particular individual pure strategy σ_i he should use on each given occasion. That is, an individually randomized joint mixed strategy $\tilde{\sigma}^S$ is simply a combination of s independent individual joint strategies $\tilde{\sigma}_i^S$, used by the s members of coalition S. On the other hand, by *joint* randomization we mean an arrangement under which all s players in a coalition S use *one* and the same chance mechanism to decide which particular joint pure strategy σ^S they should use on each given occasion. That is, a jointly randomized joint mixed strategy $\tilde{\sigma}^S$ is a probability mixture of various *joint* pure strategies $(\sigma^S)_1, \ldots, (\sigma^S)_k$ of coalition S as a whole. Thus under individual randomization the individual pure strategies σ_i used by the different members i of coalition S are statistically *independent*, whereas under joint randomization the players can establish any degree of statistical *correlation* among their individual strategies. Consequently *individually* randomized strategies can be regarded as that special case of *jointly* randomized strategies where the players i in a coalition S decide to have zero correlation between each other's individual strategies. We will assume that the players are free to use *individually* randomized joint strategies *both* in cooperative and in noncooperative games but can use *jointly* randomized joint strategies only in cooperative games (more precisely, the use of such strategies is restricted to cooperative games with free communication among the players, which we call *vocal* cooperative games).

In the special case in which we deal with a strategy s-tuple of the all-player coalition $S = N$, and so $s = n$, we speak of a *strategy n-tuple* σ^N. If $s = 2$, we speak of a *strategy pair*.

5.5 Dominance

Let $u^* = (u_1^*, \ldots, u_n^*)$ and $u = (u_1, \ldots, u_n)$ be two payoff vectors (utility vectors) for the n players. We will say that the payoff vector u^* *strongly dominates* the payoff vector u, if u^* assigns higher payoffs to all n players, that is, if $u_i^* > u_i$ for all i.

On the other hand, we will say that u^* *weakly dominates* u, if u^* assigns higher payoffs to *some* player(s) and at the same time assigns at least equally high payoffs to all *other* players, that is, if $u_i^* > u_i$ for *some* i, but $u_i^* \geq u_i$ for *all* i.

If in a given set P of payoff vectors there is some payoff vector u^* that is not strongly dominated by any other payoff vector u in P, then u^* is called a *weakly efficient* payoff vector in P. On the other hand, if u^* is not dominated, even weakly, by any other payoff vector u in P, then u^* is called an *efficient* (or a

strongly efficient) payoff vector in *P*. Obviously any (strongly) efficient payoff
vector is also weakly efficient, but the converse is not true.

Thus for any payoff vector to be weakly (or strongly) efficient in some set *P* is
the same thing as to be a *maximal element* in *P* under the relation of strong dominance (or of weak dominance).

5.6   Payoff space. Payoff conservation laws

The *n*-dimensional Euclidean space consisting of all possible utility vectors $u =$
$(u_1, \ldots, u_n)$ for the *n* players is called the utility space U^n.

The set *P* of all payoff vectors *u* that the *n* players of the game can actually
achieve by any joint strategy σ^N that the rules of the game make available to
them we call the *payoff space* of the game.[9]

In a *cooperative* game (see Section 5.15) where the players are free to use
jointly randomized strategies, the payoff space *P* of the game is always a *convex*
set. That is, if u^* and u^{**} are two points of *P*, then any probability mixture of u^*
and u^{**}, i.e., any point $u = pu^* + (1 - p)u^{**}$, with $0 \leq p \leq 1$, is also in *P*. Geometrically this means that all points *u* on the straight-line segment connecting u^*
and u^{**} will lie in *P*.

The set of all *strongly efficient* (not even *weakly* dominated) points *u* in *P* is
called the *upper boundary H* of *P*. The set H^* of all points *u* that are at least
weakly efficient, i.e., are not *strongly* dominated (though possibly being weakly
dominated) in *P*, is called the *extended* upper boundary of *P*. Of course, $H^* \supset H$.
If *P* is a convex set of *n* dimensions, then H^* (as well as *H*) will be in general a
hypersurface of $(n - 1)$ dimensions. In the special case $n = 2$, *H* (as well as H^*)
will be a curve in the utility plane U^2 and will be called for obvious geometrical
reasons the *upper right boundary* (or the extended upper right boundary) of *P*.

If the sum of all players' payoffs, $\bar{u} = \Sigma u_i$, is equal to *zero* for all points *u* in the
payoff space *P*, then we say that the game is *zero-sum*. Intuitively this means that,
whatever one player wins, the other players must lose, and vice versa – in other
words, the players' utilities in the game follow a certain *conservation law*, in that
net utility is neither created nor destroyed but is merely transferred from one
player to another. A game in which this is not true is called *nonzero-sum*.

A game in which the sum of all players' payoffs, $\bar{u} = \Sigma u_i$, is equal to a constant
(which may or may not be zero) is called a *constant-sum* game. The contrary is a
variable-sum game. Any constant-sum game is trivially equivalent to a zero-sum
game, because it can be converted into a zero-sum game by changing the zero
point of any player's utility function. (Alternatively we may say that a constant-
sum game is equivalent to a situation where the players play a zero-sum game and,
in addition, also receive – or have to pay out – certain fixed amounts; this latter
fact has no influence on their strategical possibilities in the zero-sum game
itself.)

Finally consider a game which is not constant-sum but in which all points of the
payoff space satisfy an equation of the form $\Sigma a_i u_i = $ const., with constant coeffi-

cients $a_i > 0$. Such a game may be called a *constant-weighted sum* game. It still will be trivially equivalent to a zero-sum game, because it can be converted into a zero-sum game by order-preserving linear transformations of the players' utility functions.[10] Zero-sum, constant-sum, and constant-weighted sum games together will be called *generalized* zero-sum games.

Geometrically, since all points u in the payoff space P of a generalized zero-sum game satisfy an equation of the form $\Sigma a_i u_i$ = const., they always lie on an $(n - 1)$-dimensional hyperplane H. Since $a_i > 0$ for all $i = 1, \ldots, n$, H will cut all positive axes at obtuse angles. Such a hyperplane is called a hyperplane with *positive slopes* in all directions. (Any straight line L orthogonal to such a hyperplane will be called a straight line with *negative slopes* in all directions.) In the case of a zero-sum game proper, or of a constant-sum game, we can take $a_1 = \cdots = a_n = 1$.

Empirically the simplest way in which a generalized zero-sum game can arise is a situation where the total amount of money or other values possessed by all the players together is *constant,* and the game can only redistribute this amount among them – and where all players' utility functions are *linear* in money or in these other values.

But there are also other possibilities. For example, any two-person game can be treated as a two-person zero-sum game if there are only *two* possible outcomes for each player, say, "victory" and "defeat" – with no possibility for "larger" or "smaller" victories and defeats. In such a case no special linearity assumption is needed concerning the players' utility functions in order to assure the zero-sum property, because we can always assign the utility $v = +1$ to "victory" and the utility $d = -1$ to defeat, making their joint payoff $\bar{u}$ identically zero, as $\bar{u} = v + d = (+1) + (-1) = 0$.

On the other hand, if the game also has a third possible outcome, representing neither a "victory" nor a "defeat" for either player but rather a "draw" between the two players, the game will not be zero-sum unless we make special assumptions about the utilities that the two players will assign to this "draw" situation. In particular we may assume that for each player a "draw" is exactly half way in utility between a "victory" and a "defeat" – that is, each player would be indifferent between a "draw" and a fifty–fifty chance of "victory" and of "defeat." In this case the utility of a "draw" to each player would be $d^* = (v + d)/2 = 0$, so that in a "draw" situation the two players' joint payoff $\bar{u}$ would again be zero since $\bar{u} = 2d^* = 0$. It is easy to verify that, if the game has more than three possible outcomes, then even stronger linearity assumptions regarding the players' utility functions are needed to ensure the zero-sum property.

Some games lacking the zero-sum (and even the generalized zero-sum) property may satisfy a considerably weaker utility conservation law, the transferable-utility property. Let G be a game (given in extensive form). Suppose that in G each player i has moves by which he can transfer any amount of utility that he wishes to transfer to any other player j (e.g., by giving him money or commodities) in such a way that their joint payoff $\bar{u}_{ij} = u_i + u_j$ remains constant, j's utility gain being exactly equal to i's own utility loss, without this move having any effect on the payoffs u_k of the other players $k \neq i, j$. In this case we say that G is a game with *transferable utility*, and the moves described will be called *conservative transfer moves*.

To put it differently, in a zero-sum game all possible moves by the players are conservative, because no moves can change the players' joint payoff away from zero. In contrast, the transferable-utility property does not mean an absence of nonconservative moves; it means merely a presence of conservative moves, permitting the players to transfer unlimited amounts of utility from one another without changing their joint payoff.

If G is given in normal form rather than in extensive form, then the transferable-utility property can be defined as follows: Let $u = (u_1, \ldots, u_n)$ and $u^* = (u_1^*, \ldots, u_n^*)$ be any two utility vectors corresponding to the same joint payoff $\bar{u} = \Sigma u_i = \Sigma u_i^*$ for the n players. Let S be the set of all players i for whom $u_i^* < u_i$. Thus S contains those players who would lose utility by moving from u to u^*. Suppose that the n players have some joint strategy $\sigma = (\sigma_1, \ldots, \sigma_n)$ yielding the payoff vector $u = U(\sigma)$. Then, if G is to have the transferable-utility property, it must be possible for the players in S to achieve the other payoff vector u^* by switching to some alternative strategies σ_i^*. In other words, the n players must have another joint strategy $\sigma^* = (\sigma_1^*, \ldots, \sigma_n^*)$ yielding the other payoff vector $u^* = U(\sigma^*)$, such that $\sigma_j^* = \sigma_j$ for all players j not in set S. (That is, in order to achieve u^* only the players S have to change their strategies.)[11]

Again it is convenient to say that a game has transferable utility *in a generalized sense* if it can be converted into a game with transferable utility by applying order-preserving linear transformations to the players' utility functions (more particularly, by changing the *units of measurement* for the players' utilities).

Like a zero-sum game, a game with transferable utility most naturally arises in situations where the players are free to transfer money to one another without transfer costs (or gains) and where all players' utility functions are *linear* in money. However, unlike in zero-sum or constant-sum games, in games with transferable utility the players in general *can* make joint utility gains or losses of variable amounts, depending on the efficiency of their strategies and in particular on the degree of cooperation between them. (For example, a bargaining game in which the players can divide \$100 among them, if they can agree on how to divide it, but lose the \$100 if they cannot agree, is obviously not a constant-sum game. But it is a game with transferable utility if the players' utilities are linear in money.)

The payoff space P of a game with transferable utility in a generalized sense is bounded by two parallel hyperplanes with positive slopes in all directions, called the *upper boundary H* and the *lower boundary I*, and consists of all points of the utility space U^n lying on or between H and I. Both these hyperplanes extend to infinity in all directions. H will have the equation $\Sigma a_i x_i = c_1, a_i > 0$, while I will have the equation $\Sigma a_i x_i = c_2$ with $c_1 > c_2$. If the game has transferable utility in the strict sense, then we can write $a_1 = \cdots = a_n = 1$.

In theoretical physics we find that the mathematical theory of a physical system is greatly simplified if the system is known to follow certain special conservation laws (e.g., the theory of what are called "conservative forces" is much simpler than the theory of nonconservative forces). Likewise in game theory, games satisfying utility-conservation laws, such as zero-sum games and games with transferable utility, admit analysis in terms of simpler principles than do games of more general types. It is therefore not surprising that the theory of these games (in particular, the von Neumann and Morgenstern solution for the two-person zero-sum game and the Shapley value for the n-person cooperative game with transferable utility) has earlier reached maturity than has the theory of more general games. But the bargaining models to be discussed in this book will enable us to develop a general theory not confined to games satisfying these restrictive assumptions.

5.7 Payoff-dominance relations: reply-dominance

Suppose that a given strategy σ_i^* can be expected under certain conditions to yield player i a payoff higher (or at least no lower) than some alternative strategy σ_i^{**} would yield him. Then we will say that σ_i^* has *payoff-dominance* over σ_i^{**}. Likewise suppose that a given joint strategy σ_*^S can be expected under certain conditions to yield each member of coalition S (where $S \subset N$ or $S = N$) a payoff higher (or at least no lower) than some alternative joint strategy σ_{**}^S would yield him. Again we will say that σ_*^S has *payoff-dominance* over σ_{**}^S. We will consider several types of payoff-dominance relations.[12] In this section we define two such relations, to be called strong and weak *reply-dominance*.

Consider an n-tuple of strategies $\sigma = (\sigma_1, \ldots, \sigma_{i-1}, \sigma_i, \sigma_{i+1}, \ldots, \sigma_n)$. Let σ^i denote the $(n-1)$-tuple that remains if we omit from σ its ith component, the strategy σ_i. Thus $\sigma^i = (\sigma_1, \ldots, \sigma_{i-1}, \sigma_{i+1}, \ldots, \sigma_n)$. Hence σ^i denotes a combination of strategies (i.e., a joint strategy) that the other $(n-1)$ players use or may use against player i. We often write the strategy n-tuple $\sigma = (\sigma_1, \ldots, \sigma_i, \ldots, \sigma_n)$ itself in the form

$$\sigma = (\sigma_i, \sigma^i) \tag{5.4}$$

Likewise (σ_i^*, σ^i) will denote the strategy n-tuple that we obtain from σ if we replace the strategy σ_i by the strategy σ_i^*, and so forth.

Let σ_i^* and σ_i^{**} be two strategies of player i, and let σ^i be a strategy combination of the other players. We will say that σ_i^* is a *better reply* to σ^i than σ_i^{**} is, if σ_i^* yields player i a higher payoff than σ_i^{**} does, if the other players use the strategy combination σ^i against him, that is, if

$$U_i(\sigma_i^*, \sigma^i) > U_i(\sigma_i^{**}, \sigma^i) \tag{5.5}$$

To be a better reply is obviously a payoff-dominance relation. Therefore in the case just described we also say that σ_i^* has *strong reply-dominance* over σ_i^{**} against σ^i, or simply that σ_i^* *strongly reply-dominates* σ_i^{**} against σ^i.

On the other hand, if at least the *weak* inequality corresponding to (5.5) is satisfied, then we say that σ_i^* is *at least as good a reply* to σ^i as σ_i^{**} is, or that σ_i^* has *weak reply-dominance* over σ_i^{**}, or that σ_i^* *weakly reply-dominates* σ_i^{**}, against σ^i.

5.8 Best-reply strategies

Suppose that a given strategy $\sigma_i{}^*$ yields player i the highest payoff among all strategies available to him when the other players use the strategy combination σ^i, so that

$$U_i(\sigma_i{}^*, \sigma^i) = \max_{\sigma_i \in \Sigma_i} \ U_i(\sigma_i, \sigma^i) \tag{5.6}$$

where Σ_i is player i's strategy space, i.e., the set of all mixed strategies available to him. (Note that we regard pure strategies as special cases of mixed strategies. Therefore player i's pure strategies are also elements of Σ_i.) Then we shall say that $\sigma_i{}^*$ is player i's *best reply* to σ^i.

If $\sigma_i{}^*$ is a best reply to σ^i, this obviously means that player i has no better reply to σ^i. In other words, if $\sigma_i{}^*$ is a best reply to σ^i, then $\sigma_i{}^*$ is a *maximal element* [cf. Debreu, 1959, p. 8] in the strategy space Σ_i, under the relation of *strong* reply-dominance as against σ^i.

If $\sigma_i{}^*$ is the only strategy of player i that satisfies Equation (5.6), then it will be called player i's *only best reply* to σ^i. If $\sigma_i{}^*$ has this property, then player i will not have even a strategy *weakly* reply-dominating $\sigma_i{}^*$. In other words, if $\sigma_i{}^*$ is his *only* best reply to σ^i, then $\sigma_i{}^*$ is a *maximal element* also under the relation of *weak* reply-dominance as against σ^i.

Lemma 1. Let $\Sigma_i{}^* = \Sigma_i{}^*(\sigma^i)$ be the set of all best-reply strategies that player i has against a given strategy combination σ^i of all other players. This set $\Sigma_i{}^*$ will be always a convex subset of player i's strategy space Σ_i.

Proof. We must show that, if $\sigma_i{}^*$ and $\sigma_i{}^{**}$ are two best replies to σ^i, then any probability mixture $\bar{\sigma}_i = p\sigma_i{}^* + (1 - p)\sigma_i{}^{**}$ of two such strategies will also be a best reply to σ^i. Now

$$U_i(\sigma_i{}^*, \sigma^i) = U_i(\sigma_i{}^{**}, \sigma^i) = \max_{\sigma_i \in \Sigma_i} \ U_i(\sigma_i, \sigma^i) = u_i \tag{5.7}$$

But

$$U_i(\bar{\sigma}_i, \sigma^i) = pU_i(\sigma_i{}^*, \sigma^i) + (1 - p) U_i(\sigma_i{}^{**}, \sigma^i) = pu_i + (1 - p)u_i = u_i \tag{5.8}$$

This shows that $\bar{\sigma}_i$ yields the same payoff u_i as $\sigma_i{}^*$ and $\sigma_i{}^{**}$ themselves do against σ^i. Hence $\bar{\sigma}_i$ is also a best reply to σ^i, which is what we wanted to show.

Lemma 2. Let $\sigma_i{}^* = p^1 \sigma_i{}^{(1)} + \cdots + p^k \sigma_i{}^{(k)}$ be a mixed strategy of player i, with $p^j > 0$ for $j = 1, \ldots, k$, and, of course, with $\Sigma p^j = 1$. Suppose that $\sigma_i{}^*$ is a best reply to some strategy combination σ^i of the other players. Then each pure strategy $\sigma_i{}^{(j)}$ used in $\sigma_i{}^*$ with a positive probability p^j is likewise a best reply to σ^i, and so is any arbitrary probability mixture $\sigma_i{}^{**} = q^1 \sigma_i{}^{(1)} + \cdots + q^k \sigma_i{}^{(k)}$ of these pure strategies $\sigma^{(1)}, \ldots, \sigma^{(k)}$.

Proof. We have

$$U_i(\sigma_i^*, \sigma^i) = \sum_{j=1}^{k} p^j U_i(\sigma_i^{(j)}, \sigma^i) = \max_{\sigma_i \in \Sigma_i} U_i(\sigma_i, \sigma^i) = u_i \qquad (5.9)$$

We want to show that

$$U_i(\sigma_i^{(j)}, \sigma^i) = u_i \quad \text{for} \quad j = 1, \ldots, k \qquad (5.10)$$

and also that

$$U_i(\sigma_i^{**}, \sigma^i) = \sum_{j=1}^{k} q^j U_i(\sigma_i^{(j)}, \sigma^i) = u_i \qquad (5.11)$$

Now suppose that Equation (5.10) would not hold for all strategies $\sigma_i^{(j)}$ that have positive probability weights p^j in σ_i^*. Then, in view of Equation (5.9), we could find at least one strategy $\sigma_i^{(j)}$ such that

$$U_i(\sigma_i^{(j)}, \sigma^i) > u_i \qquad (5.12)$$

But this would mean that σ_i^* would not be a best reply to σ^i, contrary to our assumptions. Therefore Equation (5.10) must hold for all strategies $\sigma_i^{(j)}$. Finally, Equation (5.11) follows immediately from Equation (5.10). (Cf. Lemma 1.)

We will now introduce a certain generalization of the concept of best reply, the *subjective best reply*. Suppose that player i has no definite expectations about the strategy combination σ^i that the other $(n-1)$ players will use but has only some subjective probability distribution $P_i(\sigma^i)$ over all possible strategy combinations σ^i that the other $(n-1)$ players may follow. Let $\tilde{\sigma}^i$ represent that probability mixture of all possible strategy combinations σ^i which correspond to this subjective probability distribution $P_i(\sigma^i)$. Mathematically $\tilde{\sigma}^i$ will be a jointly randomized joint strategy of the $(n-1)$ players other than player i. We will call $\tilde{\sigma}^i$ the *mean strategy combination* that player i expects the other players to use. Finally let σ_i^* be that strategy of player i which would maximize his payoff against $\tilde{\sigma}^i$ so that

$$U_i(\sigma_i^*, \tilde{\sigma}^i) = \max_{\sigma_i \in \Sigma_i} U_i(\sigma_i, \tilde{\sigma}^i) \qquad (5.13)$$

We will call σ_i^* player i's *subjective best reply* to the other players' expected mean strategy combination $\tilde{\sigma}^i$. It differs from an ordinary best-reply strategy in being a best reply, not to some specific combination σ^i of the pure or mixed strategies used by the other players, but rather to some *mean* strategy combination $\tilde{\sigma}^i$, expressing the *subjective probability distribution* $P_i(\sigma^i)$ that player i entertains over alternative possible strategy combinations σ^i of the other players.

In the same way we can also define the concept of *subjective better reply* and say that one strategy σ_i^* is subjectively a better reply than another strategy σ_i^{**} is to the other players' expected mean strategy combination $\tilde{\sigma}^i$.

5.9 Equilibrium points

Let $\sigma = (\sigma_1, \ldots, \sigma_n)$ be a strategy n-tuple such that the strategy σ_i of *every* player i
is a best reply to the strategy combination $\sigma^i = (\sigma_1, \ldots, \sigma_{i-1}, \sigma_{i+1}, \ldots, \sigma_n)$ used
by the other $(n - 1)$ players. Then σ is called an *equilibrium point*. Any strategy
σ_i occurring as a component in some equilibrium point $\sigma = (\sigma_1, \ldots, \sigma_i, \ldots, \sigma_n)$ is
called an *equilibrium strategy*. The payoff vector $u = U(\sigma)$ that results if all players
use strategies corresponding to a given equilibrium point σ is called an *equilibrium
payoff vector*, and each component $u_i = U_i(\sigma)$ of such a vector $u = (u_1, \ldots,
u_i, \ldots, u_n)$ is called an *equilibrium payoff*. For example, consider a two-person
game (see Example 2). This game has two equilibrium points in pure strategies, viz.,
the strategy pairs (A_1, B_1) and (A_2, B_2). The corresponding equilibrium payoff
vectors are $U(A_1, B_1) = (8, 4)$ and $U(A_2, B_2) = (14, 10)$. The game also has an
equilibrium point in mixed strategies $(\frac{1}{5}A_1 + \frac{4}{5}A_2, \frac{1}{3}B_1 + \frac{2}{3}B_2)$. This yields the
equilibrium payoffs $(8, 10)$.

	B_1	B_2
A_1	(8, 4)	(11, 0)
A_2	(2, 9)	(14, 10)

Example 2

Nash [1950a, 1951] proved the following important theorem:

Theorem 5.1. Every finite game has at least one equilibrium point.

An equilibrium point $\sigma = (\sigma_1, \ldots, \sigma_n)$ is called *strong* if each player's equilibrium strategy σ_i is not merely *a* best reply to the other players' strategy combination σ^i but is in fact the *only* best reply to σ^i.[13] An equilibrium point that is not
strong is called *weak*.

In our last example both pure-strategy equilibrium points are *strong*. For instance, A_1 is player 1's only best reply to B_1, and B_1 is player 2's only best reply
to A_1. In contrast, the mixed-strategy equilibrium point is *weak*, because $\sigma_1 =
\frac{1}{5}A_1 + \frac{4}{5}A_2$ is *not* the only best reply by player 1 to $\sigma_2 = \frac{1}{3}B_1 + \frac{2}{3}B_2$, and σ_2 is
not the only best reply by player 2 to σ_1. Indeed in this game *any* strategy of
player 1, whether pure or mixed, is a best reply to σ_2, and *any* strategy of player 2,
whether pure or mixed, is a best reply to σ_1. More generally:

Lemma 1. Any equilibrium point $\sigma = (\sigma_1, \ldots, \sigma_i, \ldots, \sigma_n)$ having one or more
mixed-strategy components σ_i is a *weak* equilibrium point.

Proof. Let $\sigma_i = p^1 \sigma_i^{(1)} + \cdots + p^k \sigma_i^{(k)}$ with $p^j > 0$ for $j = 1, \ldots, k$. Then, by
Lemma 2 of Section 5.8, all the component strategies $\sigma_i^{(1)}, \ldots, \sigma_i^{(k)}$ as well as all

their probability mixtures will be best replies to σ^i. Hence σ_i is not the only best reply to σ^i, and therefore σ is a weak equilibrium point.

An equilibrium point of which all components are *pure* strategies can be either strong or weak. We have already seen examples for strong pure-strategy equilibrium points. In contrast, the equilibrium point (A_1, B_1) is weak in Example 3, because A_1 is *not* the only best reply to B_1 (even though B_1 itself *is* the only best reply to A_1). In fact, besides A_1, A_2 and all probability mixtures of A_1 and A_2 are best replies to B_1.

	B_1	B_2
A_1	(2, 2)	(5, 1)
A_2	(2, 3)	(3, 4)

Example 3

5.10 Maximin strategies and maximin payoffs

Let Σ^i be the set of all strategy combinations $\sigma^i = (\sigma_1, \ldots, \sigma_{i-1}, \sigma_{i+1}, \ldots, \sigma_n)$ that the other players can use against player i. Clearly Σ^i can also be defined as the Cartesian product $\Sigma^i = \Sigma_1 \times \cdots \times \Sigma_{i-1} \times \Sigma_{i+1} \times \cdots \times \Sigma_n$, where $\Sigma_1, \ldots, \Sigma_n$ are the strategy spaces of players $1, \ldots, n$, respectively.

If player i uses a given strategy σ_i, then the very lowest payoff $\overline{U}_i(\sigma_i)$ that he can obtain is given by

$$\overline{U}_i(\sigma_i) = \min_{\sigma^i \in \Sigma^i} U_i(\sigma_i, \sigma^i) \tag{5.14}$$

This payoff $\overline{U}_i(\sigma_i)$ is called player i's *security level* for this strategy σ_i. The highest security level that player i can obtain by any strategy σ_i is given by

$$\check{u}_i = \max_{\sigma_i \in \Sigma_i} \overline{U}_i(\sigma_i) = \max_{\sigma_i \in \Sigma_i} \min_{\sigma^i \in \Sigma^i} U_i(\sigma_i, \sigma^i) \tag{5.15}$$

This highest security level $\check{u}_i$ is called player i's *maximin payoff* from the game. It represents the highest payoff that he can count on even under the most pessimistic expectations about the strategy choices of the other players. Any strategy $\check{\sigma}_i$ having this payoff $\check{u}_i$ as its security level - i.e., any strategy $\check{\sigma}_i$ satisfying $\overline{U}_i(\check{\sigma}_i) = \check{u}_i$ - is called a *maximin strategy*.

In a finite game (and more generally in any game with a compact payoff space) a maximin payoff $\check{u}_i$, and one or more maximin strategies $\check{\sigma}_i$, will always exist for every player i.

If all components $\check{\sigma}_1, \ldots, \check{\sigma}_n$ of a given strategy n-tuple $\check{\sigma} = (\check{\sigma}_1, \ldots, \check{\sigma}_n)$ are maximin strategies, then $\check{\sigma}$ will be called a *maximin point*.[14]

Lemma 1. The payoff $\bar{u}_i = U_i(\bar{\sigma})$ of any player i at an equilibrium point $\bar{\sigma} = (\bar{\sigma}_1, \ldots, \bar{\sigma}_i, \ldots, \bar{\sigma}_n) = (\bar{\sigma}_i, \bar{\sigma}^i)$ will be always at least as large as his maximin payoff $\check{u}_i$.

Proof. As $\bar{\sigma}$ is an equilibrium point, $\bar{\sigma}_i$ must be a best reply to $\bar{\sigma}^i$. Therefore

$$\bar{u}_i = U_i(\bar{\sigma}_i, \bar{\sigma}^i) = \max_{\sigma_i \in \Sigma_i} U_i(\sigma_i, \bar{\sigma}^i) \tag{5.16}$$

Let $\check{\sigma}_i$ be a maximin strategy of player i. Then

$$\check{u}_i = \bar{U}_i(\check{\sigma}_i) = \min_{\sigma^i \in \Sigma^i} U_i(\check{\sigma}_i, \sigma^i) \tag{5.17}$$

In view of Equations (5.16) and (5.17),

$$\bar{u}_i = U_i(\bar{\sigma}_i, \bar{\sigma}^i) \geq U_i(\check{\sigma}_i, \bar{\sigma}^i) \geq \bar{U}_i(\check{\sigma}_i) = \check{u}_i \tag{5.18}$$

This completes the proof.

An equilibrium point σ will be called *profitable* to player i if it yields him a payoff higher than his maximin payoff, i.e., if $U_i(\sigma) > \check{u}_i$, and will be called *unprofitable* to him if it yields him exactly his maximin payoff, i.e., if $U_i(\sigma) = \check{u}_i$. By Lemma 1, the case $U_i(\sigma) < \check{u}_i$ cannot occur. An equilibrium point is called *uniformly profitable* if it is profitable to *all* players. It is called *partially profitable* if it is profitable to some players but is unprofitable to some other players.

Lemma 2. The set $\check{\Sigma}_i$ of all maximin strategies of any given player i is always a convex set.

Proof. Let $\check{\sigma}_i$ and $\hat{\sigma}_i$ be two maximin strategies of player i. We have to show that any probability mixture

$$\bar{\sigma}_i = p\check{\sigma}_i + (1 - p)\hat{\sigma}_i \tag{5.19}$$

of two such strategies is itself also a maximin strategy. Now

$$\bar{U}_i(\bar{\sigma}_i) = \min_{\sigma^i \in \Sigma^i} U_i(\bar{\sigma}_i, \sigma^i) = \min_{\sigma^i \in \Sigma^i} [pU_i(\check{\sigma}_i, \sigma^i) + (1 - p)U_i(\hat{\sigma}_i, \sigma^i)]$$

$$\geq p \min_{\sigma^i \in \Sigma^i} U_i(\check{\sigma}_i, \sigma^i) + (1 - p) \min_{\sigma^i \in \Sigma^i} U_i(\hat{\sigma}_i, \sigma^i) = p\check{u}_i + (1 - p)\check{u}_i = \check{u}_i$$

$$\tag{5.20}$$

Hence

$$\bar{U}_i(\bar{\sigma}_i) \geq \check{u}_i \tag{5.21}$$

But we cannot have $\bar{U}_i(\bar{\sigma}_i) > \check{u}_i$, because by definition

$$\check{u}_i = \max_{\sigma_i \in \Sigma_i} \bar{U}_i(\sigma_i) \tag{5.22}$$

Consequently $\overline{U}_i(\overline{\sigma}_i) = \check{u}_i$, and therefore $\overline{\sigma}_i$ is a maximin strategy of player i, as desired.

5.11 Simple dominance

It may happen that a given strategy σ_i^* of player i is a better reply than another strategy σ_i^{**} is, not only against a given strategy combination σ^i of the other players but rather against *all* possible strategy combinations σ^i available to them. That is, it may happen that

$$U_i(\sigma_i^*, \sigma^i) > U_i(\sigma_i^{**}, \sigma^i) \quad \text{for all} \quad \sigma^i \in \Sigma^i \tag{5.23}$$

In this case we shall say that strategy σ_i^* *strongly dominates* strategy σ_i^{**}.

If no other strategy of player i has strong dominance over a given strategy σ_i, i.e., if σ_i is a *maximal element* in player i's strategy space Σ_i under the relation of strong dominance, then σ_i is called a *weakly admissible* strategy.[15]

On the other hand, we will say that strategy σ_i^* *weakly dominates* strategy σ_i^{**} if σ_i^* is a *better* reply to *some* strategy combinations σ^i of the other players and is *at least as good* a reply to all *other* strategy combinations σ^i. That is, we require that σ_i^* should satisfy Condition (5.23) for *some* σ^i and should satisfy the corresponding weak inequality for *all* σ^i.

Clearly dominance, whether strong or weak, is a payoff-dominance relation. We will sometimes call it "simple" dominance in order to distinguish it from "joint" dominance, to be defined below.

If no other strategy of player i has even weak dominance over a given strategy σ_i, i.e., if σ_i is a *maximal element* under the relation of weak dominance, then σ_i is called an *admissible* (or a *strongly admissible*) strategy. Obviously any (strongly) admissible strategy is also weakly admissible, but the converse is not true.

5.12 Joint dominance

Let σ^* and σ^{**} be two joint strategies (pure, individually randomized, or jointly randomized) for the n players. We say that σ^* has *strong joint dominance* over σ^{**} if the payoff vector $U(\sigma^*)$ strongly dominates[16] the payoff vector $U(\sigma^{**})$, that is, if σ^* yields every player i a higher payoff

$$U_i(\sigma^*) > U_i(\sigma^{**}) \tag{5.24}$$

than σ^{**} does.

We say that σ^* has *weak joint dominance* over σ^{**} if the payoff vector $U(\sigma^*)$ weakly dominates the payoff vector $U(\sigma^{**})$, that is, if σ^* yields *all* players at least as high payoffs as σ^{**} does, and at the same time yields some players definitely higher payoffs. Clearly, both strong and weak joint dominance are payoff-dominance relations.

Let Σ denote the n players' joint-strategy space, i.e., the set of all joint strategies available to them. In a cooperative game Σ will include *jointly* randomized joint strategies, whereas in a noncooperative game, apart from pure joint strategies, Σ will include only *individually* randomized joint strategies. Let Σ^* be any subset in Σ.

Suppose that the joint strategy σ is in Σ^* and that there is no other joint strategy σ' in Σ^* such that σ' would have *strong* joint dominance over σ. That is, we are assuming that σ is *maximal* in Σ^* under the relation of strong joint dominance. Then we say that σ is an *efficient* (or a weakly efficient) joint strategy in Σ^*.

If there is not even a strategy σ' having *weak* joint dominance over σ – i.e., if σ is maximal even under weak dominance – then we say that σ is *strongly efficient* in Σ^*.

Reply-dominance (Section 5.8), simple dominance (Section 5.11), and joint dominance are the main types of payoff-dominance relations that we will use in our analysis.

5.13   Centroid strategies

Let Σ_i^* be some subset of the space Σ_i of all (pure and mixed) strategies available to player i. Let σ_i^* be the equiprobability mixture of all strategies σ_i in this set Σ_i^*. Thus geometrically σ_i^* will be the centroid (center of gravity) of this set Σ_i^*. We will call σ_i^* the *centroid strategy* of Σ_i^*.

Let $\Sigma_i^*(\sigma^i)$ be the set of all best-reply strategies σ_i that player i has against the strategy combination σ^i of the other $(n-1)$ players. Let σ_i^* be the centroid strategy of this set $\Sigma_i^*(\sigma^i)$. Then σ_i^* itself will also be a best reply to σ^i because, by Lemma 1 of Section 5.11, the set $\Sigma_i^*(\sigma^i)$ is always convex, and therefore its centroid σ_i^* will be an element of this set. We will call this strategy σ_i^* the *centroid best reply* to σ^i.

Let $\sigma = (\sigma_1, \ldots, \sigma_n)$ be an equilibrium point with the property that every player's equilibrium strategy σ_i is a centroid best reply to the other players' strategy combination σ^i. Then σ will be called a *centroid equilibrium point*.

Lemma 1. Every *strong* equilibrium point σ is a *centroid* equilibrium point.

Proof. If σ is a strong equilibrium point, then each set $\Sigma_i^*(\sigma^i)$ for $i = 1, \ldots, n$ will contain only the one strategy σ_i. Consequently this strategy σ_i will be the centroid strategy of $\Sigma_i^*(\sigma^i)$.

However, *weak* equilibrium points in general are *not* centroid equilibrium points. Let $\sigma = (\sigma_1, \ldots, \sigma_n)$ be any equilibrium point. Let $\sigma_1^*, \ldots, \sigma_n^*$ be the centroid best replies to the strategy combinations $\sigma^1, \ldots, \sigma^n$ corresponding to σ. Then in general the strategy n-tuple $\sigma^* = (\sigma_1^*, \ldots, \sigma_n^*)$ will *not* be an equilibrium point. Consequently, if a given equilibrium point $\sigma = (\sigma_1, \ldots, \sigma_n)$ is not already a centroid equilibrium point, then in general we cannot transform it into one simply by replacing each equilibrium strategy σ_i with an appropriate centroid–best-reply strategy σ_i^*.

Let $\breve{o}_i{}^*$ be the centroid of the set $\breve{\Sigma}_i$ of player i's maximin strategies. Then $\breve{o}_i{}^*$ itself will also be a maximin strategy, because, by Lemma 2 of Section 5.13, $\breve{\Sigma}_i$ is a convex set, and so its centroid will be an element of this set. We will call $\breve{o}_i{}^*$ player i's *centroid maximin strategy*.

5.14 Games with strictly identical interests, with strictly opposite interests, and with mixed interests

We can distinguish the following main classes of games:

1. Games where the players have strictly *identical interests*.
2. Games where the players have strictly *opposite interests*.
3. Games where the players have *mixed interests*, i.e., where their interests are partly similar and partly dissimilar.[17]

In games with strictly *identical* interests each player's payoff is a strictly *increasing* function of any other payoff over the entire payoff space P of the game. Hence, if u and u^* are two different payoff vectors in P, then either u must strongly dominate u^*, or u^* must strongly dominate u. If the players are free to use mixed strategies, then this condition can be satisfied only if the payoff space P is a segment of a straight line with a *positive slope* in all directions (see Figure 5.2).

If the payoff space P of such a game is a compact set (i.e., if it is bounded and closed), then it will include its own upper boundary point $\bar{u}$, and the latter will strongly dominate all other points u of P and so will represent the only efficient point of P. Hence, as long as the players are free to coordinate their strategies (see Section 5.15, below), this point $\bar{u}$ will obviously represent the only rational outcome of the game.

While a game with strictly identical interests can have any number of players, a game with strictly *opposite* interests can have only two players. This is so because two players, of course, can have opposite preferences between any two points u and u^* of the payoff space of the game. But a third player would have to be *either* indifferent between u and u^* *or* agree in his preference with one of the two other players: He obviously could not have an opposite preference to *both* of the two other players at the same time.

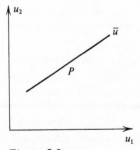

Figure 5.2

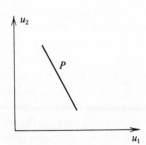

Figure 5.3

Thus a game with strictly opposite interests must be a two-person game. More-over, each player's payoff must be a strictly *decreasing* function of the other player's payoff over the entire payoff space P of the game. If the players are free to use mixed strategies, then this condition can be satisfied only if P is a segment of a straight line with a *negative slope* in the (u_1, u_2) plane (see Figure 5.3), i.e., if the game is a generalized *two-person zero-sum* game (see Section 5.6).

5.15 Cooperative and noncooperative games

In a game with *mixed* interests the payoff space will not be a line segment but rather will contain at least three points not lying on the same straight line. Indeed, if mixed strategies are permitted, then the payoff space will always cover a more-than-one-dimensional (typically an n-dimensional) connected region of the n players' n-dimensional joint utility space.

In games with strictly identical or with mixed interests, the players always have some common interests that they could in principle promote by agreeing on a mu-tually advantageous joint strategy. But in practice such agreements make sense only if the players can be reasonably sure that such agreements would be *stable*, i.e., would be kept if they were agreed upon. An agreement can be stable for two reasons.

One reason is that it may be *self-enforcing*: The payoff function of each player may be such that it gives him a clear incentive to follow the joint strategy agreed upon, at least as long as he expects the other players to do the same. Technically this means that an agreement can be self-enforcing only if the joint strategy agreed upon is an *equilibrium point*. Actually we will argue that even equilibrium points are not always stable (i.e., self-enforcing). While *strong* equilibrium points (as de-fined in Section 5.9) always possess full stability, *weak* equilibrium points do so only under special conditions.

An agreement may be stable also because it is *enforceable*: The rules of the game may be such that they require the players to keep agreements that they have entered into (even if they could increase their payoffs by breaking them).

In a game with strictly *identical* interests all *efficient* agreements are self-enforcing (because they will be agreements to use strategies corresponding to some strong equilibrium point). But in the case of games with *mixed* interests we must distinguish between games where the rules of the game make agreements always fully binding and enforceable and games where agreements have no binding force. The former are *cooperative games*; the latter are *noncooperative* games.

More generally we assume that in cooperative games not only *agreements* be-tween two or more players, but also *unilateral commitments* (threats and promises) made by the players, will be fully binding and strictly enforced. The opposite is true in noncooperative games.

In empirical situations what may make agreements and other commitments en-forceable may be special law-enforcing agencies (e.g., courts of law, administrative officials, police), the pressure of public opinion, prestige and credibility considerations, or moral attitudes (which can be regarded as internalized penalties for breaking agreements).

Finally, in games with strictly *opposite* interests (i.e., two-person zero-sum games), no useful purpose could be served by agreeing on some joint strategy, because the players have no common interests at all which they could promote by such agreements.

Thus it is convenient to include games with strictly identical interests among cooperative games and to include games with strictly opposite interests among non-cooperative games. This gives the following classification:

A. *Cooperative* games, including
   (a) Games with strictly *identical* interests.
   (b_1) Games with *mixed* interests, where agreements and other commitments are *enforceable*.
B. *Noncooperative* games, including
   (b_2) Games with *mixed* interests, where agreements and other commitments are *not enforceable*.
   (c) Games with strictly *opposite* interests (two-person zero-sum games).

Of course, there are various intermediate cases between fully cooperative and fully noncooperative games. For example, in some games certain classes of agreements may be enforceable; others may be unenforceable. Or the same agreements may or may not be enforceable, depending on various specified conditions (e.g., only agreements concluded in the last stage of the game may be fully enforceable). Most of these intermediate cases will not be discussed in this book. (They represent "nonclassical" games – cf. Section 1.2.) We will discuss, however, the intermediate case of *almost-noncooperative* games. These are defined as games in which the players can be trusted to keep agreements or other commitments as long as they have no positive incentive to break the latter (even though they may have no positive incentive *not* to break these agreements or commitments either). This means that in such games, unlike in fully noncooperative games, not only will strong equilibrium points be stable but weak equilibrium points will be also. The concept of almost-noncooperative games can be justified by assuming that in such games there is a commitment-enforcing agency but that it can impose only very small fines (not exceeding some very small positive number ϵ) on the players for violating any agreement or other commitment. This assumption may be described by saying that in these games agreements and other commitments are *ϵ-enforceable*.

Our definitions both for cooperative and for noncooperative games are more general than the customary definitions, which would require *free* preplay *communication* among the players in the case of cooperative games and the *absence* of *any* preplay communication in the case of noncooperative games. We have chosen these broader definitions, because this will enable us to observe the effects of *independently* varying the two variables of commitment enforceability and of free communication.

Our analysis will be based on the following principle, which we will call the principle of *tacit bargaining*.[18] Assuming that the players are sufficiently intelligent, any payoff-distribution agreement that they could reach by explicit bargaining they can also reach by tacit understanding alone if every player realizes that this payoff distribution represents the only rational solution of the game.

Thus our definitions of both cooperative and noncooperative games cover both *vocal games*, where the players are free to communicate, and *tacit games*, where they are not (as well as various intermediate cases).

6

Rationality postulates for game situations

6.1 Introduction

The rationality postulates (axioms) that we will use in our analysis of game situations fall into two main classes:

A. Postulates of *rational behavior* in a narrower sense, stating rationality criteria for *strategies* to be used by the players.

B. Postulates of *rational expectations*, stating rationality criteria for the *expectations* that rational players can entertain about each other's strategies.

Postulates of Class A in themselves would not be sufficient. We have defined game situations as situations in which each player's payoff depends not only on his own strategy but also on the other players' strategies. If a player could regard the other players' strategies as *given*, then the problem of rational behavior for him would be reduced to a straightforward maximization problem, viz., to the problem of choosing a strategy maximizing his own expected payoff. But the point is precisely that he *cannot* regard the other players' strategies as given independently of his own. If the other players act rationally, then their strategies will depend on the strategy that they expect *him* to follow, in the same way that his own strategy will depend on the strategies that he expects *them* to follow. Thus there is, or at least appears to be, a vicious circle here. The only way that game theory can break this vicious circle, it seems to me, is by establishing criteria for deciding what *rational expectations* intelligent players can consistently hold about each other's strategies.

Our postulates of Class A can be divided into Subclasses A* and A**. Subclass A* consists of four postulates, all of them asserting in different ways that, other things being equal, rational players will *prefer* strategies yielding *higher* payoffs. Subclass A** consists of a single postulate stating that, other things being equal, rational players will be *indifferent* between strategies yielding *equal* payoffs, and will choose between such strategies in a random manner.

Technically all the postulates in Subclass A* are based on payoff-dominance relations: Postulates A2 and A3 are based on two variants of reply-dominance, while Postulates A1 and A4 are based on two variants of simple dominance[1] (although Part II of Postulate A4 can also be interpreted as based on joint dominance). Specifically what Postulates A1, A2, and A3 assert is that a rational player will choose a strategy that is a *maximal element* (i.e., one that is undominated) with respect to the relevant payoff-dominance relation.[2] The intuitive meaning of this is that a rational player will not be satisfied until he has found a strategy that cannot be improved upon further, i.e., a strategy *maximal* in the relevant sense.

Our four postulates of Subclass A* are closely related to certain axioms and theorems of individual decision theory (utility theory). Postulates A1 and A4 are essentially specialized forms of the Monotonicity Principle (Sure-Thing Principle) that appeared as Axiom 3* and as Axiom 3** in Chapter 3. On the other hand, Postulates A2 and A3 are specialized forms of the utility maximization and of the expected-utility maximization theorems appearing as Theorems 3.1, 3.2, and 3.3.[3]

Class A** consists of a single postulate, Postulate A5. It envisages a situation in which a given player i has to choose a strategy σ_i from some set Σ_i* of "equally good" strategies, all expected to yield him the same payoff. The postulate asserts that in such a situation he will be *equally likely* to choose any one of these "equally good" strategies σ_i. This means that his behavior will be such *as if* he chose the centroid strategy σ_i* of this set Σ_i*.

This postulate (or some similar postulate) follows from the customary operational definition of *equality* between two utilities. For example, let $\sigma_i{}'$ and $\sigma_i{}''$ be two strategies in set Σ_i*. If player i were found to choose (say) strategy $\sigma_i{}'$ more often, i.e., with a *higher probability*, than he chooses strategy $\sigma_i{}''$, then this would be taken as an indication that he attaches a *higher utility* to $\sigma_i{}'$ than he attaches to $\sigma_i{}''$. He would not be regarded as attaching the same utility to both strategies unless he were found to choose them with the same probability.

Note that Postulate A5 does not assert that player i will *intentionally* choose the centroid strategy σ_i*. Rather it asserts that he will be equally likely to choose *any* strategy σ_i in set Σ_i*, which is, of course, *behaviorally equivalent* to choosing the centroid strategy σ_i* of this set. If player i intentionally chooses strategy σ_i*, then he would presumably generate the probabilities that σ_i* assigns to various pure strategies by using some mechanical chance device, e.g., by flipping a coin. However, under our assumptions these probabilities will be generated not by a mechanical device of this kind but rather by what amounts to an unconscious chance mechanism inside player i's central nervous system.[4]

Note. It is easy to visualize situations where one may wish to replace our Postulate A5 by a more general assumption. For example, suppose that set Σ_i* contains five different strategies, which we shall call $X_1, \ldots, X_5$. Let us assume that these five strategies fall naturally into two different classes, viz., class X^o, consisting of strategies X_1 and X_2; and class X^{oo}, consisting of strategies, X_3, X_4, and X_5. In this case all will depend on the specific method by which player i chooses his strategy. One possibility is that he will disregard the fact that the five strategies can be divided into two classes and will simply choose one of the five strategies at random (with any one of them having the same chance of being selected). In this case each strategy will have probability $\frac{1}{5}$ of being chosen, in accordance with Postulate A5.

However, another possibility is that player i will first choose between classes X^o

and X^{oo} at random (both classes having an even chance). Only then will he choose a strategy from this class at random (again giving equal chance to all strategies within the class). In this case the probability of being chosen will be $\frac{1}{4}$ for strategies X_1 and X_2, and will be $\frac{1}{6}$ for strategies X_3, X_4, and X_5.

As this example shows, in general the probability distribution of a given player's strategy choices over any set Σ_i^* of "equally good" strategies will depend crucially on the specific nature of the decision-making processes that this player will use in choosing his strategy – even assuming that these processes do operate in accordance with some kind of equiprobability principle. Clearly, from a game-theoretical point of view, the nature of each player's decision-making processes – and the specific probability distributions generated by them – must be regarded as part of the *data* in the same way as each player's utility function must be regarded as part of the data (independent variables) determining the nature of the game situation.

Thus under our theory every player is characterized by two pieces of information. One is his *utility function*, governing his choices between alternatives of *unequal* utility. The other is a certain family of probability distributions $\Pi_i(\sigma_i; \Sigma_i^*)$ governing his strategy choices in situations where he has to choose a strategy σ_i from some set Σ_i^* of strategies, all of which are expected to yield him the *same* payoff (the same utility).

It is reasonable to assume that in many cases player i's decision-making processes will be sufficiently uniform to permit derivation of all these probability distributions $\Pi_i(\sigma_i; \Sigma_i^*)$ as conditional distributions from one fundamental probability distribution $\Pi_i(\sigma_i) = \Pi_i(\sigma_i; \Sigma_i)$, defined over his entire strategy space Σ_i. That is to say, in the very special case where all of player i's strategies happen to be "equally good," i.e., where $\Sigma_i^* = \Sigma_i$, player i's strategy choice will be directly governed by this fundamental probability distribution $\Pi_i(\sigma_i)$. But in the more usual case where the set Σ_i^* of "equally good" strategies is a (possibly quite small) proper subset of player i's strategy space Σ_i, his strategy choice will be governed by the corresponding *conditional* probability distributions $\Pi_i(\sigma_i; \Sigma_i^*) = \Pi_i(\sigma_i | \sigma_i \in \Sigma_i^*)$.

Our Postulate A5 as it stands is equivalent to the assumption that the fundamental probability distribution $\Pi_i(\sigma)$ – and therefore also all the conditional probability distributions $\Pi_i(\sigma_i; \Sigma_i^*)$ – are *uniform* distributions. But it is easy to verify that all our results in what follows could be easily restated in such a way that they would correspond to more general assumptions about the mathematical form of the probability distributions $\Pi_i(\sigma_i; \Sigma_i^*)$, governing any given player's choices among "equally good" strategies.

We assume that every game G will be preceded by a bargaining game $B(G)$, in which the players will try to agree on their payoffs and on specific strategies for obtaining these payoffs.[5] Only after this bargaining game has been completed will the players play the main game G itself, implementing the agreed-upon strategies and obtaining the corresponding payoffs. We can analyze this bargaining game $B(G)$ by assuming that each player i has a *bargaining strategy* β_i that has the nature of a *decision rule* telling him whether to make a *concession* (i.e., whether to accept a lower payoff than he has asked for thus far) at any particular stage of the bargaining game or not. When we speak of "strategies" rather than "bargaining strategies," we will always mean strategies σ_i in the main game G.

Suppose that at a given stage of the bargaining game $B(G)$ one of the players proposes some joint strategy σ for use in the main game G. Then the bargaining strategy β_i of every other player i must specify whether he is to agree at this stage to this proposed joint strategy σ or not. By $A_i(\beta_i)$ we will denote the set of all joint strategies σ agreeable to player i at a given stage of the bargaining game $B(G)$, as determined by his bargaining strategy β_i.

As we will see, there are games in which a given player i cannot rationally expect more than his maximin payoff $\breve{u}_i$. Such games will be called *unprofitable* to this player i. All other games will be called *profitable* to player i.

6.2 The rationality postulates

We will now state our *postulates of rational behavior for game situations*.

Class A. Postulates of rational behavior in a narrower sense

> *Subclass A*. Postulates of preference for strategies yielding higher payoffs (payoff-dominance postulates)*

A1. *Maximin postulate.* In any game G *unprofitable* to you, always use a maximin strategy $\breve{\sigma}_i$. (In other words, if you cannot hope to obtain *more* than your maximin payoff $\breve{u}_i$ anyhow, then use a strategy fully assuring you at least *that much*.)

A2. *Best-reply postulate.* In a game G *profitable* to you, as far as your binding agreements with other players allow, always use a strategy σ_i representing a *best reply* to the strategy combination σ^i used by the other ($n - 1$) players. (This postulate implies that in a *profitable* noncooperative game the strategies used by the players will always represent an *equilibrium point*. For reasons that we will discuss, the postulate does not apply to *unprofitable* noncooperative games. Finally, in the case of *cooperative* games the postulate does not limit the players' choice to equilibrium points, because, as soon as the players *agree* on any joint strategy σ which is not an equilibrium point, the postulate ceases to be operative.)

A3. *Subjective-best-reply postulate (Bayesian expected-utility maximization postulate).* In a bargaining game $B(G)$ associated with a game G profitable to you, as far as your binding agreements with other players allow, always use a bargaining strategy β_i representing your *subjective* best reply to the mean bargaining-strategy combination $\tilde{\beta}^i$ that you expect the other players to use. [In a bargaining game $B(G)$ in general the players will not know each other's bargaining strategies in advance and will have thus to rely on the subjective probabilities that they assign to various possible combinations of the other players' bargaining strategies. Hence we cannot require more than that each player's bargaining strategy β_i should be a *subjective* best reply to the other players' expected mean bargaining-strategy combination. In contrast, in the main game G itself we can require that the strategy σ_i of each player i should be an *actual* best reply to the strategy combination used, in fact, by the other players, because our theory yields sufficiently definite predictions to enable each player to satisfy this stronger requirement in choosing his own strategy.]

A4. *Acceptance-of-higher-payoffs postulate.*

Part I. Let σ and σ^* be two joint strategies available to the n players, both of them consistent with our other rationality postulates. Suppose that σ^* would yield you (player i) a higher payoff $U_i(\sigma^*) > U_i(\sigma)$. Let us assume that, at a given stage of the bargaining game $B(G)$, the set $A_i(\beta_i)$ of all joint strategies acceptable to you (as determined by your bargaining strategy β_i) would include the joint strategy σ. Then this set $A_i(\beta_i)$ must also include the joint strategy σ^* more favorable to you. (In other words, if you are willing to agree to some joint strategy σ, then you must be even more willing to agree to another joint strategy σ^* yielding you a higher payoff than σ would.)

Part II. Let $\beta = (\beta_1, \ldots, \beta_i, \ldots, \beta_n)$ and $\beta^* = (\beta_1{}^*, \ldots, \beta_i{}^*, \ldots, \beta_n{}^*)$ be two possible n-tuples of bargaining strategies for the n players, both of them consistent with our other rationality postulates, but β^* yielding you (player i) a higher payoff than β would. Suppose that, in the absence of any special agreement to the contrary, you and all the other players would use bargaining strategies corresponding to the n-tuple β. Then you must be willing to enter into an agreement under which you and all the other players will shift to bargaining strategies corresponding to the n-tuple β^*.

> *Subclass A**. Postulate of indifference between strategies yielding equal payoffs*

A5. *Equiprobability or centroid postulate.* Let $\Sigma_i{}^*$ be a subset of player i's strategy space Σ_i. Suppose that all strategies σ_i in this set $\Sigma_i{}^*$ would be equally consistent with our other rationality postulates and that player i expects all of them to yield him the same payoff u_i. Then player i will be *equally likely* to use any particular strategy σ_i in this set $\Sigma_i{}^*$. Hence his behavior will be such *as if* he used the *centroid strategy* $\sigma_i{}^*$ of this set $\Sigma_i{}^*$.

Class B. Postulates of rational expectations

B1. *Mutually expected-rationality postulate.* In the same way that you will follow the present postulates (i.e., Postulates A1 through A5 and B1 through B3), if you are a rational player, you must expect, and act on the expectation, that *other* rational players will likewise follow these rationality postulates.

B2. *Symmetric-expectations postulate.* You cannot choose your bargaining strategy β_i on the expectation that a rational opponent will choose a *different* bargaining strategy from your own and, in particular, that he will choose a bargaining strategy *more concessive* than you would choose in the same situation. (That is, if you, in *his* place, would refuse a given concession and would regard this refusal as a rational decision on your own part, then you cannot expect that another player, no less rational than you are, will take a more accommodating attitude in this situation.)[6]

B3. *Expected-independence-of-irrelevant-variables postulate.* You cannot expect a rational opponent to make his bargaining strategy β_j dependent on variables whose *relevance* for bargaining behavior *cannot be established* on the basis of the present rationality postulates. (The purpose of this postulate is to exclude some completely arbitrary decision rules, e.g., making the players' payoffs proportional to their telephone numbers. We need the present postulate, because many of these arbitrary decision rules would be quite consistent with all our other rationality postulates. The present postulate, however, rules them out on the ground that there is no reason to regard, e.g., telephone numbers as *relevant* variables in deciding the players' payoffs.)

In Chapter 8 we will restate Postulate B3 in a more specific and therefore analytically more useful form by explicitly naming those variables which under our theory can and those which under our theory cannot rationally influence an intelligent player's bargaining behavior. But at this point an unduly long digression would be required to decide which particular variables belong to either category.

6.3   The postulates of rational expectations: their weaker and their stronger form

We do not always need all three postulates of rational expectations (Class B). In the analysis of the two extreme cases of games with strictly identical interests and of games with strictly opposite interests (and in some other rather special cases), we need only *one* of these, the postulate of mutually expected rationality (Postulate B1). This is so because, as we will see, the solution of these games is fully determined by certain payoff-dominance relations: Thus all we have to assume is that each player himself will act in accordance with these relations and will expect the other player(s) to do the same. These games will be called *games determined by payoff-dominance relations.* Moreover, we will call Postulate B1 our *weak postulate of rational expectations*, whereas our postulates of Class A together with Postulate B1 will be called our *weak rationality postulates.*

In contrast, in games with mixed interests in general, the payoff-dominance relations existing in the game by themselves will fail to determine a unique solution, and the outcome of the game will depend on bargaining among the players. Such games will be said to involve an *indeterminacy problem* and more particularly a *bargaining problem.* Here we will need all three of the postulates of Class B in order to obtain a unique solution. These three postulates together will be called our *strong postulates of rational expectations*, whereas the latter together with the postulates of Class A will be called our *strong rationality postulates*.

We will see that our *strong* rationality postulates imply a certain rationality criterion for bargaining behavior, to be called Zeuthen's Principle. This principle says essentially that in bargaining situations the next concession must always come from that particular player who can least afford risking a conflict by not making the next concession. On the basis of Zeuthen's Principle we will define a new class of dominancelike relations, to be called *risk-dominance* relations. The term refers to the fact that they are based on comparing the *risks* (i.e., the subjective probabilities) of a conflict that different players are willing to face in preference to making a concession. This fact sets them apart from *payoff-dominance* relations, based on comparing the *payoffs* associated with alternative strategies.

We will find that these risk-dominance relations do select a unique solution even in games in which the payoff-dominance relations by themselves would not do so. Such games will be called *games determined by bargaining* or *games determined by risk-dominance relations*.

6.4 Analysis of games with strictly identical interests

To illustrate how our rationality postulates can be used in the analysis of games with strictly identical interests, consider the simple two-person game in Example 1.

	B_1	B_2
A_1	(100, 100)	(200, 200)
A_2	(0, 0)	(201, 201)

Example 1

Even without using any formal rationality postulates, by sheer common sense, rational players will obviously use the strategy pair (A_2, B_2), which jointly dominates any other possible strategy pair and which yields both players the highest possible payoffs $u_1 = u_2 = 201$. Formally this conclusion can be established as follows: Let (β_1, β_2) be a pair of bargaining strategies that would make the players agree to use the strategy pair (A_2, B_2) in the main game. By Part II of Postulate A4, whatever bargaining strategies the players start with, they will end up with the bargaining strategies (β_1, β_2) or with some equivalent bargaining strategies. Therefore they will always agree to use the strategy pair (A_2, B_2) in the main game.

Explicitly this reasoning has made no use of the postulates of Class B. But implicitly it does presuppose Postulate B1. If player 1 did not expect player 2 to act rationally (i.e., in accordance with our preceding analysis), then player 1 could not rationally use strategy A_2. In particular, if he expected player 2 to be misguided enough to use strategy B_1 (instead of using strategy B_2, as we would recommend), then player 1 would be obviously well advised to shift to strategy A_1. Thus his use of strategy A_2 does depend on Postulate B1.

6.5   Analysis of two-person zero-sum games

Consider the two-person zero-sum game in Example 2. (Contrary to the usual practice, we are indicating both players' payoffs explicitly.)

	B_1	B_2	B_3
A_1	(5, -5)	(2, -2)	(7, -7)
A_2	(6, -6)	(0, 0)	(-3, 3)
A_3	(-8, 8)	(1, -1)	(10, -10)

　　　Example 2

　　　The von Neumann–Morgenstern solution for two-person zero-sum games requires that both players use *maximin* strategies. (Of course, if we analyzed the game wholly in terms of player 1's payoffs, as is usually done, then a maximin strategy of player 2 would have to be described as a minimax strategy.) In our example this means that the players should use the strategy pair (A_1, B_2). Under our theory the justification of the von Neumann–Morgenstern solution lies in the following facts:

1. A two-person zero-sum game is *unprofitable* to both players. That is, if the other player plays rationally, then neither player $i(i = 1, 2)$ can hope to obtain more than his maximin payoff $\check{u}_i$.

2. Therefore, by Postulate A1, both players should use maximin strategies.

To illustrate the first point, in Example 2 player 1 cannot hope to obtain more than $\check{u}_1 = 2$, because by using strategy B_2 player 2 *can* keep him down to this payoff level[7] and *will* actually do so if he acts rationally, since it is in his interest to do so. By the same token, player 2 cannot hope to obtain more than $\check{u}_2 = -2$, because by using strategy A_1 player 1 *can* keep him down to this payoff level[8] and *will* actually do so if he acts rationally, since it is in his interest to do so.

More formally, by making use of Postulate A2, we can show that a two-person zero-sum game is unprofitable to both players. In view of this postulate, the highest payoff that any player can obtain in a noncooperative game, if the other player or players act rationally, is his highest equilibrium payoff. But in a two-person zero-sum game the equilibrium payoff that either player i would obtain at any equilibrium point equals his maximin payoff $\check{u}_i$. Therefore in a two-person zero-sum game neither player can obtain more than this if his opponent acts rationally, which means that the game is unprofitable to both players. (By the same reasoning, *any* noncooperative game is unprofitable to a given player if all equilibrium points of the game are unprofitable to him.)

Note that in order to show that a two-person zero-sum game is unprofitable to either player, we must make essential use, at least implicitly, of Postulate B1. That is to say, if either player did not expect the other player to act rationally (i.e., to act in accordance with our rationality postulates), then his maximin payoff would no longer be the highest payoff that he could rationally hope to achieve. Therefore it might be no longer true that the best thing for him to do would be to use a maximin strategy. For instance, if player 1 in Example 2 expected player 2 to be foolish enough to use strategy B_3, then he could rationally expect to obtain the payoff $u_1 = 10$ (much larger than his maximin payoff $\check{u}_1 = 2$); but in order to accomplish this he would have to use strategy A_3. (His maximin strategy A_1 would yield him only $u_1 = 7$.)

Going over to the second point, in order to bring out the intuitive meaning of Postulate A1, we introduce the concept of the *truncated game* $T(G)$, which is defined as follows: We take the payoff matrix on the original game G, eliminate all payoffs of player 1 exceeding his maximin payoff $\check{u}_1$, and replace them by the quantity $\check{u}_1$. Likewise we eliminate all payoffs of player 2 exceeding his maximin payoff $\check{u}_2$, and replace them by the quantity $\check{u}_2$. In our example this procedure will give us the truncated game in Example 3. (Notice that in general the truncated

	B_1	B_2	B_3
A_1	(2, -5)	(2, -2)	(2, -7)
A_2	(2, -6)	(0, -2)	(-3, -2)
A_3	(-8, -2)	(1, -2)	(2, -10)

Example 3

game is no longer a zero-sum game, but this does not matter for our analysis.) The purpose of constructing the truncated game is to eliminate those payoffs that the players cannot rationally expect to achieve against a rational opponent and, by this method, to enable the players to evaluate their various strategies in a more realistic manner. For example, in the original payoff matrix, for player 1 strategy A_1 does not dominate strategies A_2 and A_3 (because in the case of strategy A_2, $6 > 5$; and in the case of strategy A_3, $10 > 7$). But in the truncated game, A_1 does dominate the other two strategies, because those entries (viz., 6 and 10), where the other two strategies had an advantage over A_1, have been eliminated since these entries cannot be achieved against a rational opponent. We can now state:

Lemma 1. Let $\check{\sigma}_i$ be a maximin strategy, and let σ_i be a nonmaximin strategy, in the original game G. Then in the truncated game $T(G)$, $\check{\sigma}_i$ will have (at least) weak simple dominance over σ_i.

Proof. To fix our ideas, suppose that $\check{\sigma}_i = \check{\sigma}_1$ and $\sigma_i = \sigma_1$ are strategies of player 1. (The case in which they are strategies of player 2 can be treated similarly.) By definition, in the original game G, $\check{\sigma}_1$ will have the security level $\check{u}_1$, where $\check{u}_1$ is player 1's maximin payoff. In contrast, σ_1 will have some security level $\bar{u}_1 < \check{u}_1$. Therefore in the truncated game $T(G)$, in the row corresponding to $\check{\sigma}_1$, all entries representing player 1's payoff will be equal to $\check{u}_1$. On the other hand, in the row corresponding to σ_1 at least one entry will be $\bar{u}_1 < \check{u}_1$. But all entries u_1 in this row will satisfy $u_1 \leqq \check{u}_1$. Therefore $\check{\sigma}_1$ will have (at least) weak simple dominance over σ_1.

Lemma 2. A given strategy $\check{\sigma}_i$ will be *maximal* (undominated) in the truncated game $T(G)$ with respect to weak simple dominance if and only if $\check{\sigma}_i$ is a maximin strategy in the original game G.

Proof. By Lemma 1, if $\check{\sigma}_i$ is a maximin strategy, it will be undominated by any nonmaximal strategy σ_i. (In fact, dominance will go the other way around.) On the other hand, $\check{\sigma}_i$ will also be undominated by any other maximin strategy $\check{\sigma}_i{}'$, because, in the rows (or columns) corresponding to both $\check{\sigma}_i$ and $\check{\sigma}_i{}'$, all entries for player i's payoff will be $\check{u}_i$, so that neither of these two strategies will dominate the other. Finally $\check{\sigma}_i$ will be undominated *only if* it is a maximin strategy, because, by Lemma 1, every nonmaximin strategy σ_i is dominated by the maximin strategies of player i.

Therefore we can state Postulate A1 also as follows:

Postulate A1*. In a game G unprofitable to you, always use a strategy $\check{\sigma}_i$ that is maximal (undominated) under weak simple dominance in the corresponding truncated game $T(G)$.

6.6   Note on simple dominance

It is often asserted in the game-theoretical literature that a rational player i will always use some strategy σ_i undominated by any other strategy $\sigma_i{}'$ of the same player (in terms of strong or even of weak simple dominance). This statement will be called the Dominance Principle. Our own theory does not use this principle in its unqualified form. It uses only two – quite restricted – forms of the principle, Postulates A1 and A4. The former asserts the Dominance Principle about strategies in the truncated game $T(G)$ derived from a game G unprofitable to the relevant player, whereas the latter asserts an essentially similar principle about strategies in the bargaining game $B(G)$. But in general we do not assert the Dominance Principle about strategies in the original game G.

The reason is that we do not regard the principle as a rationality postulate of general validity. Consider, for instance, the two-person nonzero-sum game in Example 4. (As we will see, this kind of game is called a Prisoner's Dilemma game.) By Postulates A1 and A2, if this game is played as a *noncooperative* game, then its solution must be the strategy pair (A_2, B_2). But if it is played as a *co-*

	B_1	B_2
A_1	(10, 10)	(-10, 11)
A_2	(11, -10)	(1, 1)

Example 4

operative game, then, by Part II of Postulate A4, its solution will be the strategy pair (A_1, B_1), which is the only efficient joint strategy in the game. This will be true even though the strategies A_1 and B_1 are both *strongly dominated* by strategies A_2 and B_2. This example shows that the Dominance Principle, even if restricted to *strong* simple dominance, has no general validity, at least in the case of cooperative games: It may be perfectly rational for the players to use strongly dominated strategies.

In the case of (profitable) noncooperative games it is true, of course, that under our theory no *strongly* dominated strategy can be a rational strategy. But this is true only because, by Postulate A2, a rational strategy must be an equilibrium strategy, and an equilibrium strategy cannot be strongly dominated by another strategy. However, in certain cases it will be rational for some players to use *weakly* dominated strategies. For example, consider the game in Example 5. In

	B_1	B_2
A_1	(1, 1)	(10, 10)
A_2	(0, 0)	(10, 10)

Example 5

this game there are two classes of equilibrium points. Class I consists of the one strategy pair $s^* = (A_1, B_1)$, while Class II consists of all strategy pairs of the form $s(p) = (pA_1 + (1-p)A_2, B_2)$ with $0 \leq p \leq 10/11$. The one equilibrium point s^* in Class I is strong and is therefore stable. But in Class II, according to the criteria that we will state later, only the centroid equilibrium point $s^{**} = s(\frac{1}{2}) = (\frac{1}{2}A_1 + \frac{1}{2}A_2, B_2)$ is stable. This is true even though the strategy $\frac{1}{2}A_1 + \frac{1}{2}A_2$ that player 1 would use at s^{**} is weakly dominated by strategy A_1 and all strategies of the form $pA_1 + (1-p)A_2$ he would use at those equilibrium points of Class II itself for which $\frac{1}{2} < p \leq 10/11$. Under our theory, if player 1 expects player 2 to use strategy B_2, then player 1 will use strategies A_1 and A_2 with equal probabilities. (In other words, the fact that A_1 would do better than A_2 would do against B_1 - which makes A_1 weakly dominate A_2 - does not matter, since player 1 would expect player 2 to use B_2.)

Of course, if the players' choice is restricted to s^* and s^{**}, he will choose s^{**}, since $U(s^*) = (1, 1)$, while $U(s^{**}) = (10, 50)$, and therefore s^{**} jointly dominates s^*. Consequently the solution of the game is s^{**}, even though s^{**} uses the weakly dominated strategy $(\frac{1}{2}A_1 + \frac{1}{2}A_2)$.

7

The four basic problems facing the players of a game

7.1 The four basic problems

Playing a game effectively means solving the problem of choosing a rational strategy. It is convenient to divide this problem into several subproblems, which are in general not independent of one another but are at least logically distinguishable:

1. *The enforcement or stability problem*. This consists in identifying the *stable* joint strategies, i.e., those which can be adopted by means of enforceable or self-enforcing agreements and therefore, once agreed upon, will in fact be implemented by the players.

2. *The joint-efficiency problem*. Let E be the set of all payoff vectors u that can be achieved by means of stable joint strategies. Then the joint-efficiency problem consists in finding the set E^* of all efficient (undominated) payoff vectors u^* in E.

3. *The payoff-distribution or bargaining problem*. This consists in agreeing on one particular efficient payoff vector u^{**} of set E^*. This problem can be further subdivided into:

   (a) *The bargaining problem* in a narrower sense.
   (b) *The threat problem*, i.e., the problem of choosing *optimal threat strategies* for the purpose of strengthening one's own bargaining position against the other players.
   (c) *The coalition problem*, i.e., the problem of deciding what coalitions one should try to join in order to strengthen one's bargaining position.

4. *The strategy-coordination problem*. This consists in agreeing on one particular joint strategy for achieving the payoff vector u^{**} selected by the players.

In this chapter we offer a brief general overview of how our theory deals with each of these problems. In the following chapters we will discuss the specific solution concepts that our theory provides for various classes of games.

7.2 The enforcement or stability problem

Our theory deals with this problem by means of Postulates A1, A2, and A5. We have already seen that in a *cooperative* game *every* possible joint strategy will be stable as soon as the players have agreed to adopt it. In a *noncooperative* game, however, only *strong* equilibrium points have full stability. If $\sigma = (\sigma_1, \ldots, \sigma_n)$ is a weak equilibrium point, then at least one player i will be able to switch from his equilibrium strategy σ_i to some other strategy τ_i *without positive penalty*, even if all other players stick to their own equilibrium strategies $\sigma_1, \ldots, \sigma_{i-1}, \sigma_{i+1}, \ldots, \sigma_n$. (Of course, player i cannot achieve any *positive gain* either by shifting to τ_i, since σ is an equilibrium point. But this fact in itself is insufficient to assure full stability.)

To illustrate the reasons that we restrict Postulate A2 to *profitable* games, consider the two-person noncooperative game in Example 1. The only equilibrium

	B_1	B_2	$B^* = \frac{1}{2}B_1 + \frac{1}{2}B_2$	$\bar{B} = \frac{2}{5}B_1 + \frac{3}{5}B_2$
A_1	(60, 24)	(0, 44)	(30, 34)	(24, 36)
A_2	(20, 84)	(40, 4)	(30, 44)	(32, 36)
$A^* = \frac{4}{5}A_1 + \frac{1}{5}A_2$	(52, 36)	(8, 36)	(30, 36)	
$\bar{A} = \frac{1}{4}A_1 + \frac{3}{4}A_2$	(30, 64)	(30, 14)		(30, 36)

Example 1

point in this game is the strategy pair $\sigma^* = (A^*, B^*)$, where $A^* = \frac{4}{5}A_1 + \frac{1}{5}A_2$ and $B^* = \frac{1}{2}B_1 + \frac{1}{2}B_2$. But this is a *weak* equilibrium, and, what is more important for our present analysis, it is *unprofitable* to both players, because the payoffs $U_1(\sigma^*) = 30$ and $U_2(\sigma^*) = 36$ are only the maximin payoffs of the two players. Each of them could achieve the same payoff by using his *maximin* strategy, which is $\bar{A} = \frac{1}{4}A_1 + \frac{3}{4}A_2$ in the case of player 1 and is $\bar{B} = \frac{2}{5}B_1 + \frac{3}{5}B_2$ in the case of player 2. Indeed in our opinion each player will be *better off* actually by using his *maximin* strategy $\bar{A}$ or $\bar{B}$ than he would be by using his *equilibrium* strategy A^* or B^*. For instance, if player 1 uses strategy $\bar{A}$, then he can be *absolutely sure* of obtaining the payoff $\check{u}_1 = 30$. In contrast, if he uses strategy A^*, then he will obtain the same payoff 30 only if the other player also uses his equilibrium strategy B^*. But if player 2 uses some other strategy (viz., B_2), then his payoff may fall as low as 8. Yet player 1 has no reason to expect that player 2 will in fact stick to the equilibrium strategy B^*, because player 2 will not suffer any kind of penalty if he shifts to another strategy while player 1 himself uses strategy A^*. Accordingly Postulate A1 suggests that in games of this type the players should use maximin strategies instead of trying to reach an equilibrium point.

Our example also illustrates the fact that *weak* equilibrium points are in general unstable.

To illustrate the use of Postulate A5, consider the two-person noncooperative game in Example 2. In this game all possible pairs of mixed strategies[1] are equilib-

	B_1	B_2
A_1	(3, 3)	(1, 3)
A_2	(3, 1)	(1, 1)

Example 2

rium points, and all of them are *weak* equilibrium points. If the game were played as a cooperative game – or even as an almost-noncooperative game[2] – then the players presumably would agree to use the strategy pair (A_1, B_1), which would yield them the payoffs $u_1 = u_2 = 3$. But we are assuming that this is a strictly non-cooperative game in which such an agreement would have no binding force. There-fore, by Postulate A5, each player will be *equally likely* to use *any* of his mixed strategies. Thus his behavior will be such *as if* he always used his centroid equilib-rium strategy $A^* = \frac{1}{2}A_1 + \frac{1}{2}A_2$ (in the case of player 1) or $B^* = \frac{1}{2}B_1 + \frac{1}{2}B_2$ (in the case of player 2). Hence we define the *solution* of the game as the *centroid equilibrium point* $\sigma^* = (A^*, B^*)$, which will yield the two players the expected payoffs $u_1{}^* = u_2{}^* = 2$.

More generally we call a uniformly profitable equilibrium point σ *stable* in a noncooperative game if it is a *centroid equilibrium point*. (By this definition *strong* equilibrium points are always stable because they are always centroid equilibrium points.)

If an equilibrium point σ is partially profitable, i.e., if it is profitable to some player(s) i but is unprofitable to some other player(s) j, then we call it *stable* if:

1. For each player i, the strategy σ_i is his *centroid best reply* to the strategy com-bination σ^i used by the other $(n-1)$ players.

2. For each player j, the strategy σ_j is his *centroid maximin strategy*.

Here the first requirement is based on Postulates A2 and A5, whereas the second requirement is based on Postulates A1 and A5.

On the other hand, in almost-noncooperative games, *all* uniformly profitable equilibrium points are stable, even if they are *not* centroid equilibrium points, whereas partially profitable equilibrium points are stable if they satisfy the second requirement, even if they fail to satisfy the first. This is why we have argued that, in our example, the players can agree to use the equilibrium point (A_1, B_1) if the game is played as an almost-noncooperative game: In such a game an agreement of this kind will have binding force.

Many discussions in the literature assume that all equilibrium points are stable and therefore seem to have in mind almost-noncooperative rather than strictly noncooperative games. (However, under our theory even in the former class of games equilibrium points must satisfy *some* – rather weak – special stability re-quirements if they are to be stable.)

Note. As we have already stated, under our theory a *strong* equilibrium point is always *stable*. It remains to be shown that this statement is consistent with stabil-ity conditions (1) and (2), based on Postulates A1, A2, and A5 – even in the case of *strong* equilibrium points *unprofitable* to one or more players. This will be shown by proving the following two lemmas.

Lemma 1. Let $\sigma = (\sigma_1, \ldots, \sigma_j, \ldots, \sigma_n)$ be a *strong* equilibrium point *unprofitable* to player j. Then player j's equilibrium strategy σ_j will be a maximin strategy and will be, in fact, his *only* maximin strategy in the game.

Proof. Suppose that σ_j is *not* a maximin strategy or that σ_j is at least not the *only* maximin strategy that player j has. Then in either case player j must have at least one maximin strategy $\check{\sigma}_j$ different from σ_j. Let $\check{u}_j$ be player j's maximin payoff. Because $\sigma = (\sigma_j, \sigma^j)$ is *unprofitable* to player j, we have

$$U_j(\sigma_j, \sigma^j) = \check{u}_j \tag{7.1}$$

As σ_j is a best reply to σ^j, we have

$$U_j(\sigma_j, \sigma^j) \geqq U_j(\check{\sigma}_j, \sigma^j) \tag{7.2}$$

As $\check{\sigma}_j$ is a maximin strategy, we have

$$U_j(\check{\sigma}_j, \sigma^j) \geqq \check{u}_j \tag{7.3}$$

But (7.1), (7.2), and (7.3) together imply that

$$U_j(\sigma_j, \sigma^j) = U_j(\check{\sigma}_j, \sigma^j) = \check{u}_j \tag{7.4}$$

Consequently *both* σ_j and $\check{\sigma}_j$ are best replies to σ^j, and therefore σ is *not* a *strong* equilibrium, point contrary to our assumptions. Hence both the assumption that σ_j is *not* a maximin strategy and the assumption that σ_j is not the *only* maximin strategy of player j lead to contradiction. This proves the lemma.

Lemma 2. Let σ be a *strong* equilibrium point unprofitable to some player(s) j and (possibly) profitable to some other player(s) i. Then each equilibrium strategy σ_i of such a player i will satisfy stability condition (1), and each equilibrium strategy σ_j of such a player j will satisfy stability condition (2). Therefore σ will be a stable equilibrium point.

Proof. Since σ is a strong equilibrium point, each strategy σ_i will be player i's *only* best reply to the strategy combination σ^i of the other players and therefore will be his *centroid* best reply to σ^i. On the other hand, by Lemma 1, each strategy σ_j will be player j's *only* maximin strategy and therefore will be his *centroid* maximin strategy. But this means that each σ_i will satisfy condition (1) and that each σ_j will satisfy condition (2), as desired.

7.3 The joint-efficiency problem

Let P be the payoff space of the game, i.e., the set of all payoff vectors that can be achieved by *any* joint strategy available to the players. Let E be the *enforceable set*, i.e., the set of all payoff vectors that can be achieved by any *stable* joint strategy (as defined in Section 7.2). In cooperative games $E = P$, but in noncooperative games E will be a subset (usually a very small subset) of P.

By Part II of Postulate A4, rational players will try to achieve an efficient payoff vector u *within* this enforceable set E. (That is, they will try to achieve some payoff vector u in E such that it is not dominated, or at least is not strongly dominated, by any other payoff vector u' in E.) Thus, under our theory, such efficiency considerations can operate only *within* the enforceable set E. This gives rise to the Prisoner's Dilemma Paradox:[3] The players cannot do any better than obtain some payoff vector $u^* \in E$, even though another mutually preferred payoff vector $u \in P$ but $\notin E$, with $u_i > u_i^*$ for all players i, would be physically available to them.

For instance, consider the game in Example 3 (discussed in Section 6.6). If this is played as a *cooperative* game, then the players can enter into a binding agreement to use the strategy pair (A_1, B_1) and can in this way obtain the highest payoffs physically available to them, viz., $u_1 = u_2 = 10$. We will call (A_1, B_1) the *cooperative solution* of the game.

	B_1	B_2
A_1	(10, 10)	(-10, 11)
A_2	(11, -10)	(1, 1)

Example 3

However, (A_1, B_1) is not an equilibrium point; in fact, the strategy pair (A_2, B_2) is the only equilibrium point of the game. Therefore, if the game is played as a *noncooperative* (or even as an almost-noncooperative) game, then any agreement to use (A_1, B_1) would be unstable and surely would be violated by the players; both of them know this. Hence the players cannot do any better than to use the equilibrium strategy pair (A_2, B_2), even though this will give them only the much lower payoffs $u_1^* = u_2^* = 1$. [(A_2, B_2) is a *strong* equilibrium point and is therefore fully stable.] We will call (A_2, B_2) the *noncooperative solution.*

A different type of Prisoner's Dilemma Paradox arises in Example 2 of Section 7.2: There the strategy pair (A_1, B_1), representing the cooperative solution, is actually an equilibrium point. But the players cannot use it in a *strictly* non-cooperative game, because it is an *unstable* equilibrium point. (The coordination problem in Example 6, to be discussed in Section 7.5, gives rise to a Prisoner's Dilemma situation of another type. The same is true of the bargaining deadlock in Example 5, to be discussed in Section 7.4.)

7.4 The payoff-distribution or bargaining problem

The bargaining problem in a narrower sense

A bargaining problem arises whenever two players' preferences between any pair of efficient payoff vectors u^* and u^{**} in the enforceable set E are *not identical*. This means that a bargaining problem will arise if:

1. One player prefers u^* to u^{**}, while the other player prefers u^{**} to u^*.
2. One player has a clear preference between u^* and u^{**} (either way), while the other player is indifferent between them.

But this means:

Lemma 1. A bargaining problem will arise whenever E contains *more than one* efficient payoff vector.

Proof. Let u^* and u^{**} be two efficient payoff vectors in E. In order to avoid both conditions 1 and 2 it would be necessary that either (a) *all* players should prefer u^* to u^{**}, which would mean that $u_i^* > u_i^{**}$ for all players i; or (b) *all* players should prefer u^{**}, i.e., that $u_i^{**} > u_i^*$ for all players i.

But (a) would mean that u^* would strongly dominate u^{**}, so that u^{**} would not be efficient, whereas (b) would mean that u^{**} would strongly dominate u^*, so that u^* would not be efficient. Thus both cases would be inconsistent with our assumption that both u^* and u^{**} are efficient payoff vectors in E. This means that, if there is more than one efficient payoff vector in E, then condition 1 or condition 2 (or both) will be satisfied; therefore there will be a bargaining problem in the game.

As an example, consider the two-person noncooperative game in Example 4. The

	B_1	B_2
A_1	(2, 1)	(-1, -100)
A_2	(0, 0)	(1, 2)

Example 4

game has three equilibrium points. Two of them, $\sigma^* = (A_1, B_1)$ and $\sigma^{**} = (A_2, B_2)$, are in pure strategies and are strong, and therefore stable, equilibrium points. The third, $\tau = (\frac{2}{103} A_1 + \frac{101}{103} A_2, \frac{1}{2} B_1 + \frac{1}{2} B_2)$, is in mixed strategies and is unstable. Hence the enforceable set E consists of the two payoff vectors $u^* = U(\sigma^*) = (2, 1)$ and $u^{**} = U(\sigma^{**}) = (1, 2)$. Both of them are efficient because they do not dominate each other. Player 1 would obviously prefer u^*, while player 2 would prefer u^{**}. Hence the choice between u^* and u^{**}, and between the corresponding equilibrium points $\sigma^* = (A_1, B_1)$ and $\sigma^{**} = (A_2, B_2)$, is a bargaining problem.

Luce and Raiffa [1957, p. 110] have argued that, in a game such as this, equilibrium point σ^* will have "psychological dominance" over equilibrium point σ^{**}. Their reasoning is that, in case of a conflict, i.e., if the two players could not agree on which equilibrium point should be chosen, each player would presumably use the equilibrium strategy corresponding to the equilibrium point that *he* would prefer. Thus player 1 would choose strategy A_1, while player 2 would choose strategy B_2. Hence in a conflict the two players' payoffs would be $\bar{u}_1 = U_1(A_1, B_2) = -1$ and $\bar{u}_2 = U_2(A_1, B_2) = -100$. Accordingly player 2 would be *much more afraid* of a conflict than player 1 would be, and both players would know this. Therefore player 2 would be under strong psychological pressure to yield and to accept the equilibrium point σ^* preferred by player 1. This is what Luce and Raiffa mean by the statement that σ^* would have "psychological dominance" over σ^{**}.

As previously stated, our theory deals with the bargaining problem in terms of Zeuthen's Principle, to be discussed in later chapters. But it may be worth mentioning that Zeuthen's Principle leads to the same conclusion as Luce and Raiffa's analysis does and defines the equilibrium point $\sigma^* = (A_1, B_1)$ as the solution of the game. (Indeed Zeuthen's Principle, as applied to small two-person noncooperative games, can be regarded as a mere quantitative reformulation of Luce and Raiffa's purely qualitative notion of psychological dominance.)

To illustrate certain difficulties that arise in analyzing bargaining problems, let us consider the two-person noncooperative game in Example 5. This game, like Example 4, has two stable equilibrium points, viz., $\sigma^* = (A_1, B_1)$ and $\sigma^{**} = (A_2, B_2)$. By similar reasoning as before, the conflict situation would presumably lead to the strategy pair (A_1, B_2). But now $U_1(A_1, B_2) = U_2(A_1, B_2) = -10$. Thus the two players will be "equally afraid" of a conflict and will be under the same psychological pressure to yield (or not to yield). Hence neither σ^* nor σ^{**} will have "psychological dominance" over the other.

	B_1	B_2
A_1	(2, 1)	(-10, -10)
A_2	(0, 0)	(1, 2)

Example 5

Because the game is completely *symmetrical* between the two players and also between the two stable equilibrium points, it is clear that no mathematical principle of *any kind* (including, of course, Zeuthen's Principle) can help us to choose one equilibrium point over the other. In cases such as this we say that there is a *bargaining deadlock* between the two players (as well as between the two equilibrium points). Our theory suggests that in such situations the two players cannot hope to agree on which stable equilibrium point to choose. Since the third equilibrium point is in mixed strategies and would be unstable, the game must be classified as *unprofitable* to both players, and therefore by Postulate A1 they should use their maximin strategies $\check{A} = \frac{1}{13} A_1 + \frac{12}{13} A_2$ and $\check{B} = \frac{12}{13} B_1 + \frac{1}{13} B_2$, even though these will yield them only their maximin payoffs $\check{u}_1 = \check{u}_2 = \frac{2}{13}$.

Of course, if the game were played as a cooperative game, then the players could agree on a jointly randomized joint strategy, e.g., on the use of each stable equilibrium point with a probability $\frac{1}{2}$, yielding them the expected payoffs $u_1 = u_2 = 1\frac{1}{2}$. But in a noncooperative game the use of jointly randomized joint strategies is not permitted.

The threat problem

By a threat we mean a *binding commitment* undertaken by a given player i to implement some retaliatory strategy or *threat strategy* $\theta_i \in \Sigma_i$ in case he cannot reach an agreement with some other player(s) on the final payoffs of the game. Thus we are restricting our definition to "serious" threats meant to be implemented if the relevant situation were to arise, as distinguished from mere "bluffs" involving no serious intention of implementation. Because binding commitments can be made only in *cooperative* games, the problem of choosing the most effective threat strategies arises only in the latter.

The purpose of a threat is always to increase the costs of a possible conflict to the opponent(s), in order to make him (or them) more reluctant to risk a conflict. But any threat will tend to increase the costs of a conflict also to the player making a threat, because it involves a (conditional) commitment on his part to implement some threat strategy θ_i, which may be quite a costly operation. Indeed typically the more *damaging* a given threat strategy is against the opponent(s), the more *costly* it will be to implement.

Yet as far as a given threat commitment increases the conflict costs of the player so committed, his reluctance to risk a conflict will increase; therefore his bargaining position against his opponent(s) may worsen rather than improve. Thus the problem of finding an optimal threat strategy in a given game amounts to finding the best *compromise* between trying to *increase* the opponent's conflict costs and trying to *decrease* those of one's own.

The problem of defining optimal threat strategies in a *two-person* cooperative game has been solved by Nash [1953]. (We will discuss Nash's theory in Chapter 9. Chapters 11 and 12 will discuss optimal threat strategies in n-person cooperative games.)

The coalition problem

This problem arises only in n-person cooperative games, because these are the only ones in which coalitions can form.

Both the threat problem and the coalition problem refer to behavior in conflict situations. But when the players choose threat strategies, they decide how to deal with their prospective *opponents* in case of a conflict. In contrast, when they choose a coalition structure for the game, they decide who will be their *allies* in case of a conflict. But both in choosing threat strategies and in choosing coalition partners, each player's only aim is to strengthen his bargaining position against those of the other players.

Our treatment of the coalition problem will be based on what we call the *Principle of Full-Coalition Formation:* Under our theory, if there is free and unbiased communication among the n players, then *all* the $(2^n - 1)$ possible coalitions will be established by the players. Every possible subset R of the players will have *some* common interests against the rest of the players and will form a coalition to protect these common interests in bargaining with the other players. Thus our model will closely resemble what political scientists call the pluralistic model of society.

In contrast, starting with von Neumann and Morgenstern [1944], most game-theoretical approaches so far have been based on the assumption that in any particular n-person cooperative game the players will split into two or more mutually disjoint coalitions, so that only a small fraction of all possible coalitions will actually come into existence. Under our own theory such a coalition structure, suppressing some possible coalitions for the sake of others, can arise only if there is a strong *bias* in the communication network of the game, which will favor the emergence of some particular coalitions and hinder the emergence of others.

Our bargaining model for the n-person cooperative game (Chapter 10) will show that it is perfectly *feasible* for all the $(2^n - 1)$ possible coalitions to operate at the same time, and in particular that no logical difficulty arises from the assumption that each player will be simultaneously a member of a large number of different and mutually overlapping coalitions and will support different coalitions on different issues, as determined by his own personal interests. Under our model each coalition R will serve the interests of its members i primarily by guaranteeing them certain payoffs w_i^R, called "dividends," the final payoff u_i of each player i to be the *sum* of all dividends w_i^R that he receives from the various coalitions R of which he is a member. Each member i of a given coalition R will have an interest in cooperating with the other members in trying to *increase* the dividends w_i^R from this coalition R and in trying to *decrease* the dividends $w_j^{\bar{R}}$ from the complementary coalition $\bar{R}$ (consisting of all players j not belonging to R). Our model specifies each player's optimal strategy under these assumptions.

For instance, in a three-person cooperative game, for some purposes players 1 and 2 will be in coalition against player 3; for other purposes players 1 and 3 will be in coalition against player 2; for still other purposes players 2 and 3 will be in coalition against player 1. Finally, on issues affecting the common interests of all three players, all three will act as one grand coalition.

A different and more selective coalition structure can emerge only if there is some *communication bias.* For instance, it may happen that coalition (12) will be the *only* two-person coalition coming into existence, so that players 1 and 2 will side on *all* issues against player 3; but this can happen only if players 1 and 2 can reach a final cooperative agreement against player 3, *before* player 3 could intervene and disrupt such an agreement by offering one of the other two players a higher payoff. If the communication network is unbiased, then every player will be in a position to intervene *before* the other two players have formed an all-purpose alliance against him, and therefore all such possibly attempted alliances will be unstable. The only stable arrangement will be a situation where *all* three possible pairs of players [viz., (12), (13), and (23)] form coalitions for limited purposes, instead of *one* pair of players forming an all-purpose alliance against the third player.

Stated differently, if the communication network of a three-person cooperative game is *symmetric* with respect to the three players, then the game will give rise to a *symmetric* coalition structure in which none of the three possible two-person coalitions will have a privileged position. Only if the communication network itself is asymmetric can the coalition structure be dominated by one of the three possible two-person coalitions.

7.5 The strategy-coordination problem

Two strategy n-tuples σ and $\overline{\sigma}$ are called *equivalent* if they yield the same payoffs to all players, i.e., in vector notation, if

$$U(\sigma) = U(\overline{\sigma}) = u = (u_1, \ldots, u_n) \tag{7.5}$$

Let σ and $\overline{\sigma}$ be two such equivalent strategy n-tuples. Suppose that the players will obtain the payoff vector $u = U(\sigma) = U(\overline{\sigma})$ not only if all players i use the strategies σ_i corresponding to σ, or if all of them use the strategies $\overline{\sigma}_i$ corresponding to $\overline{\sigma}$, but also if *some* players use the strategies σ_i, while the *other* players use the strategies $\overline{\sigma}_i$. That is, suppose that

$$U(\sigma^S, \overline{\sigma}^{\overline{S}}) = u \quad \text{for all} \quad S \subset N, \quad \text{where} \quad \overline{S} = N - S \tag{7.6}$$

More generally let Σ^* be a set of any number of equivalent strategy n-tuples $\sigma^1, \ldots, \sigma^k, \ldots$, all yielding the same payoff vector

$$u = U(\sigma^1) = \cdots = U(\sigma^k) = \cdots \tag{7.7}$$

Let $\sigma_i{}^k$ denote the ith component of σ^k.

Let $\zeta_1 = (\zeta_1, \ldots, \zeta_n)$ be a strategy n-tuple such that $\zeta_1 = \sigma_1{}^k, \zeta_2 = \sigma_2{}^m, \ldots$ where $\sigma^k, \sigma^m, \ldots \in \Sigma^*$ but where $k = $ or $\neq m$. That is, different components ζ_1, $\zeta_2, \ldots$ of ζ may (but need not) be chosen from different strategy n-tuples σ^k, $\sigma^m, \ldots$ in Σ^*. Then we can say that ζ is a *recombination* of the strategy n-tuples $\sigma^1, \ldots, \sigma^k, \ldots$ in set Σ^*.

The strategy n-tuples $\sigma^1, \ldots, \sigma^k, \ldots$ in set Σ^* are *strictly coeffective* if *all* their possible recombinations ζ yield the same payoff vector

$$u = U(\zeta) = U(\sigma^1) = \cdots = U(\sigma^k) = \cdots \tag{7.8}$$

as the original strategy n-tuples $\sigma^1, \ldots, \sigma^k, \ldots$ themselves would yield.

We will say that a given game G involves a nontrivial *strategy-coordination problem*, if G contains at least one set Σ^* of mutually *equivalent*, but *not* strictly coeffective, strategy n-tuples $\sigma^1, \ldots, \sigma^k, \ldots$. The strategy-coordination problem arises from the fact that, even if all players *agreed* to try to achieve the payoff vector $u = U(\sigma^1) = \cdots = U(\sigma^k) = \cdots$ corresponding to these strategy n-tuples, in general they *could* actually achieve this payoff vector u only if they managed somehow to coordinate their strategies, i.e., if either *all* of them chose strategies corresponding to σ^1, or *all* of them chose strategies corresponding to σ^2, and so forth. In contrast, if *some* players i chose strategies $\sigma_i{}^1$ corresponding to σ^1 while *other* players j chose strategies $\sigma_j{}^2$ corresponding to σ^2, and so forth, then they would in general obtain a payoff vector $U(\zeta)$ different from u.[4]

A coordination problem can always be easily overcome if the players are free to communicate, i.e., if the game is played as a *vocal* game. In this case any one of the players can propose one particular strategy n-tuple σ^k from set Σ^* as the joint strategy to be used by the players; and his proposal will be immediately accepted by the other players, because they will be indifferent between all the strategy n-tuples σ^k in set Σ^*, yet will realize the need for the same strategy n-tuple to be used by all players.

However, in a *tacit* game the players may be unable to overcome a coordination problem – except to the extent to which they can coordinate their strategies by reliance on sheer chance, in accordance with Postulate A5 (see below).

Consider the two-person game in Example 6. (Since the two players have strictly identical interests in this game, under our theory it will always be played as a co-operative game.) If the players can communicate, they will choose either the strategy pair (A_1, B_1) *or* the strategy pair (A_2, B_2) – it does not matter which – and will obtain the payoffs $u_1 = u_2 = 2$.

	B_1	B_2
A_1	(2, 2)	(0, 0)
A_2	(0, 0)	(2, 2)

Example 6

However, if they cannot communicate, then, according to Postulate A5, each player i ($i = 1, 2$) will be *equally likely* to choose either one of his two pure strategies; moreover, the two players' choices will be statistically independent. Hence their behavior will be such *as if* they had chosen the centroid-strategy pair $s = (\frac{1}{2} A_1 + \frac{1}{2} A_2, \frac{1}{2} B_1 + \frac{1}{2} B_2)$. In other words, if they try to achieve the payoff vector $U(A_1, B_1) = U(A_2, B_2) = (2, 2)$, then on the average they will actually achieve only the payoff vector $U(s) = (1, 1)$. Thus the players will be *unable* to achieve the payoff vector $(2, 2)$, even though it appears twice in the payoff matrix of the game.

This suggests the following definition: In a given tacit game G, let $\Sigma^*(u)$ be the set of all stable strategy n-tuples σ yielding a given payoff vector $u = U(\sigma)$. Let σ^* be the centroid-strategy n-tuple for $\Sigma^*(u)$, as defined in Section 5.13. Because $\Sigma^*(u)$ in general will not be a convex set, this centroid-strategy n-tuple σ^* itself need not be an element of $\Sigma^*(u)$. Thus it is quite possible that σ^* will yield a payoff vector u' different from u so that $U(\sigma^*) = u' \neq u$.

However, suppose that this centroid-strategy n-tuple σ^* does yield the same payoff vector $u = U(\sigma) = U(\sigma^*)$ as the strategy n-tuples σ in set $\Sigma^*(u)$ do. In this case we say that the strategy n-tuples σ in $\Sigma^*(u)$ are *simply coeffective*.

Clearly, if these strategy n-tuples are *strictly* coeffective (as defined earlier in this section), then they are also *simply* coeffective. But the converse is not true.

Finally suppose that (1) The strategy n-tuples σ in $\Sigma^*(u)$ are at least *simply coeffective*, and that (2) The centroid-strategy n-tuple σ^* is an *eligible* (i.e., a stable) strategy n-tuple in game G.

Then we can say that this centroid-strategy n-tuple σ^* as well as the corresponding payoff vector u are *accessible* to the players. If either or both conditions are not met, then σ^* and u are called *inaccessible*.

Equivalently we may say that the centroid-strategy σ^* as well as the corresponding payoff vector $u = U(\sigma^*)$ are *accessible* if and only if σ^* itself is also an element
of the set $\Sigma^*(u)$ of stable equivalent strategy n-tuples.

In the preceding definition, Condition (1) is necessary because, by Postulate A5,
if the players are trying to achieve the payoff vector u, then they will actually
achieve the payoff vector $U(\sigma^*)$. Therefore their attempt to achieve u will be un-
successful unless $U(\sigma^*) = u$ as Condition (1) requires.

On the other hand, Condition (2) is necessary because the players' actual behavior
will correspond to the centroid-strategy n-tuple σ^* and not to the various other
strategy n-tuples σ in set $\Sigma^*(u)$. Therefore Postulate A2 will not be satisfied unless
σ^* itself is stable. The stability of the strategy n-tuples σ in set $\Sigma^*(u)$ will not be
sufficient.

Accordingly in tacit games we must replace the *enforceable set E* by the (usually
smaller) *accessible set F* defined as the set of all accessible payoff vectors u. Efficiency considerations and (tacit) bargaining between the players must be restricted
to this smaller set F rather than to the set E.

To facilitate the analysis of tacit bargaining in games without free communication, we use the concept of *semivocal* games. These are defined as games in which
the players can communicate sufficiently to be able to tell each other when they
are willing to make a *concession*, i.e., to accept a lower payoff; but they cannot
communicate sufficiently to be able to *coordinate* their strategy choices when this
would be desirable. This means that the players can choose only accessible payoff
vectors satisfying the definition just given but are not restricted in their bargaining
behavior in any other way.

Our formal theory is limited to fully *vocal* and to *semivocal* games and does not
explicitly cover fully *tacit* games (where verbal communication even for bargaining
purposes is disallowed). But we postulate that the solution that our theory assigns
to a given *semivocal* game is also the solution for the corresponding fully *tacit*
game. This assumption is based on what may be called the Tacit-Bargaining Principle: Sufficiently intelligent players can reach any agreement that they would
reach by explicit bargaining, also by mere tacit bargaining.[5] (To my knowledge,
this principle was first stated by Fellner [1949]. He calls tacit bargaining "quasi-
bargaining" and tacit agreements "quasi-agreements.")

7.6 Formal definition of the solution

In any given game G, any joint strategy $\bar{\sigma}$ of the n players consistent with our
rationality postualtes is called a *rational joint strategy* or a *particular strategy solution*. The set $\bar{\Sigma}$ of all particular strategy solutions $\bar{\sigma}$ is called *the (complete) strategy solution*.

Let G be a game profitable to player i. In this case, under our theory all rational
joint strategies $\bar{\sigma}$ will yield the *same* payoff $u_i = U_i(\bar{\sigma})$ to player i, with $u_i > \check{u}_i$,
where $\check{u}_i$ is player i's maximin payoff. Now let

$$\bar{u} = (\bar{u}_1, \ldots, \bar{u}_n) \tag{7.9}$$

be a payoff vector defined as follows:

$$\bar{u}_i = u_i = U_i(\bar{\sigma}) \quad \text{if } G \text{ is profitable to player } i \tag{7.10a}$$

$$\bar{u}_i = \check{u}_i \qquad \text{if } G \text{ is unprofitable to player } i \tag{7.10b}$$

We will call $\bar{u}$ the *solution payoff vector* or the *bargaining equilibrium point* of the game. The payoffs $\bar{u}_i$ themselves will be called the *solution payoffs* of the various players.

Finally we define the *solution* of game G as the ordered pair $\delta = \{\bar{u}, \overline{\Sigma}\}$, where $\bar{u}$ is the solution payoff vector and $\overline{\Sigma} = \{\bar{\sigma}\}$ is the complete strategy solution.

The solution defined in this way has the following properties.

Lemma 1. For any player i, his solution payoff $\bar{u}_i$ satisfies

$$\bar{u}_i \geq \check{u}_i \tag{7.11}$$

Proof. The game is called "profitable to player i" only if all particular strategy solutions $\bar{\sigma}$ have the property that $U_i(\bar{\sigma}) = \bar{u}_i > \check{u}_i$. Otherwise the game is called "unprofitable to player i." But then, by Equation (7.10b), $\bar{u}_i = \check{u}_i$. Thus in either case $\bar{u}_i \geq \check{u}_i$.

Lemma 2. Let $\bar{\sigma}$ be any particular strategy solution. If the game is *profitable* to player i, then, by (7.10a), we can write

$$\bar{u}_i = U_i(\bar{\sigma}) \tag{7.12}$$

But if the game is *unprofitable* to player i, then (7.12) may not hold. Instead we may have

$$\bar{u}_i > U_i(\bar{\sigma}) \tag{7.13}$$

Proof. To show that (7.13) rather than (7.12) may obtain, consider the two-person noncooperative game in Example 7. This game has only one equilibrium point, $\sigma^* = (\frac{3}{5}A_1 + \frac{2}{5}A_2, \frac{1}{2}B_1 + \frac{1}{2}B_2)$. It would yield the equilibrium payoffs $u_1{}^* = 25$ and $u_2{}^* = 12$. However, this is a *weak* equilibrium point and therefore is *unstable*.

	B_1	B_2
A_1	(30, 20)	(20, 0)
A_2	(40, 0)	(10, 30)

Example 7

Player 1's only maximin strategy is the pure strategy $\bar{A} = A_1$, and his maximin payoff is $\check{u}_1 = 20$. Player 2's only maximin strategy is the mixed strategy $\bar{B} =$

$\frac{3}{5}B_1 + \frac{2}{5}B_2$, and his maximin payoff is $\check{u}_2 = 12 = u_2{}^*$. (Thus σ^* is not only *weak* but is also unprofitable to player 2, which is a further reason for its instability.)

Because the game has no stable equilibrium point, it is unprofitable to both players. Therefore, by Postulate A1, the two players should use their maximin strategies $\bar{A}$ and $\bar{B}$. Thus the only particular strategy solution is the strategy pair $\bar{\sigma} = (\bar{A}, \bar{B})$. The solution payoff vector is $\bar{u} = (\check{u}_1, \check{u}_2) = (20, 12)$. However, $U_1(\bar{\sigma}) = 26 > \check{u}_1 = 20$. This shows that $U_i(\bar{\sigma})$ may satisfy (7.13) instead of satisfying (7.12). This completes the proof.

7.7 Discussion: definition of the solution payoffs in unprofitable games

We suggested in Example 7 that the solution payoff of player 1 should be defined as $\bar{u}_1 = \check{u}_1 = 20$, even though the only particular strategy solution of the game, the strategy pair $\bar{\sigma} = (\bar{A}, \bar{B})$, would yield him the payoff $U_1(\bar{\sigma}) = 26$. Perhaps it would be more appropriate to designate this latter payoff $U_1(\bar{\sigma}) = 26$ as player 1's solution payoff, since this is the payoff corresponding to the strategy solution $\bar{\sigma} = (\bar{A}, \bar{B})$.

The reason that under our theory this payoff $U(\bar{\sigma}) = 26$ cannot be regarded as the solution payoff lies in the fact that the strategy pair $\bar{\sigma} = (\bar{A}, \bar{B})$ is highly *unstable*. Indeed it is even more unstable than the weak equilibrium point σ^*, because it is not an equilibrium point at all, not even a weak one. Therefore the strategy pair $\bar{\sigma} = (\bar{A}, \bar{B})$ cannot serve as a focus of stable expectations by the players. In other words, player 1 cannot act on the firm expectation that player 2 will use strategy $\bar{B}$; and player 2 cannot act on the firm expectation that player 1 will use strategy $\bar{A}$. This can be shown as follows: If player 1 did confidently expect player 2 to use $\bar{B}$, then he himself would not use $\bar{A} = A_1$ but rather would use his own best reply to $\bar{B}$, which is the strategy A_2. Likewise, if player 2 did confidently expect player 1 to use $\bar{A}$, then he himself would not use $\bar{B} = \frac{3}{5}B_1 + \frac{2}{5}B_2$ but rather would use his own best reply to $\bar{A}$, which is the strategy B_1. Thus the assumption that the two players will *use* the strategy pair $\bar{\sigma} = (\bar{A}, \bar{B})$ is *inconsistent* with the assumption that they will firmly *expect* each other to do so.

The point is that in Example 7 *all* possible strategy pairs are *unstable*. The strategy solution $\bar{\sigma} = (\bar{A}, \bar{B})$ is certainly no exception. This is precisely why our theory suggests that in such games the players should use maximin strategies. Because *all* strategy pairs are unstable, the players simply *cannot* formulate stable and consistent expectations about each other's strategies. However, the effectiveness of a player's maximin strategy in securing his maximin payoff is *independent* of the strategy (or strategies) that the other player(s) will choose. Thus in order to use a maximin strategy he *does not have to be able to formulate definite expectations* about the other players' strategies. If he uses a maximin strategy, he may obtain his maximin payoff, or he may obtain a higher payoff than this. But if he cannot formulate definite expectations (not even definite probabilistic expectations) about the other players' strategies, then he cannot rationally *count* on obtaining more than his maximin payoff. It is for this reason that our theory defines the solution payoffs as the players' maximin payoffs in such games.

7.8   The solutions for unprofitable games as "quasi-solutions"

The preceding discussion shows that there is an important conceptual difference
between the solutions that our theory defines for games profitable to all players
and the solutions that it defines for games unprofitable to all players.[6]   In the
former the solution essentially depends on the *expectations* that the players entertain about each other's strategies, in accordance with our postulates of Class B
(postulates of rational expectations), while in the latter the solution is independent
of the players' expectations, even more so since in most cases the players will
be unable to formulate stable and consistent expectations about each other's
strategies.

There is also another difference, closely related to the former. In *profitable*
games any particular strategy solution $\bar{\sigma}$ represents one possible way in which
the players can rationally *cooperate* in the game in order to advance their common interests. Of course, in *noncooperative* games the scope for rational cooperation among the players is smaller than in cooperative games, because it is restricted
to stable joint strategies.[7]   Likewise in *tacit* games the scope for cooperation is
smaller than in *vocal* games, because it is restricted to strategy n-tuples posing no
unsurmountable strategy-coordination problems. But as long as the game is profitable to some or all players, there is always *some* possibility of rational cooperation
among these latter players; and the strategy solutions $\bar{\sigma}$ that our theory defines for
such games will always involve some degree of mutual cooperation.

In contrast, in a game *unprofitable* to all players, there is simply no possibility
of rational cooperation among the players. Therefore each player must set an objective for himself that can be attained *without* any cooperation (and indeed against
any possible resistance) from the other players. Securing at least his own maximin
payoff is such an objective. This is why Postulate A1 suggests that in such games
each player should concentrate on securing at least his maximin payoff by using a
maximin strategy.

One may very well take the point of view that only those solutions which are
based on consistent reciprocal expectations – i.e., solutions defined for games *profitable* to all players or at least to some of the players – are alone true "solutions" in
the full sense of the word. For games *unprofitable* to all players our theory does
not provide such solutions; rather it shows that for these games no such solutions
can be defined. What our theory suggests is that in such games, as a practical
matter, the players should at least protect their maximin payoffs by using maximin
strategies. But it may be argued that this suggestion does not deserve to be called a
"solution," because it lacks many of the desirable properties of true solutions. It
may be called a "quasi-solution." One may even argue that it is just another way
of saying that such games have *no* true solutions.

In what follows we will make no terminological distinction between "solutions"
proper and "quasi-solutions." Both will be simply called "solutions," in accordance
with the definition stated in Section 7.8. But the difference in conceptual status
between the two should be kept in mind.

Part III
Solutions for specific classes of games

8

Two-person simple bargaining games: the Nash solution

8.1 Definitions and assumptions

We will first consider only *vocal* cooperative games. We make the following assumptions. The two players can achieve *any* payoff vector $u = (u_1, u_2)$ within the payoff space P of the game, if they can agree *which* particular payoff vector u to adopt, i.e., if they can agree how to divide the payoffs between them. The players are free to use jointly randomized mixed strategies, which make the payoff space P a convex set. Moreover, P is assumed to be bounded and closed, i.e., compact. We also exclude the degenerate case in which the payoff space is a segment of a straight line with u_i = const. for either player i: Any such case will always have to be treated as a strictly noncooperative game, since player i would have no incentive whatever to cooperate with the other player.

Among cooperative games we will distinguish two cases, depending on the nature of the conflict situation that would emerge if the two players could not agree on their final payoffs $u_1 = \bar{u}_1$ and $u_2 = \bar{u}_2$. In a *simple bargaining game* the rules of the game themselves fully specify the *conflict-payoff* vector or *conflict point* $c = (c_1, c_2)$ to which the players would be confined in such a conflict situation. This means that the players have essentially only one conflict strategy, viz., simple noncooperation.

In contrast, in a *general cooperative game*, if a conflict situation arises, then the players will have a choice between alternative conflict strategies (retaliatory strategies) of different "intensity," with different *damaging effects* on the opponent but also with different *costs* to the user.

Accordingly in a simple bargaining game the disagreement payoffs c_1 and c_2 are independent variables regarded as *given*, whereas in a general cooperative game they are dependent variables to be *predicted* by our theory, together with the final payoffs $\bar{u}_1$ and $\bar{u}_2$.

8.2 The classical approach to the bargaining problem

Classical economic theory cannot make a determinate prediction about the outcome of a bargaining situation, even in the case of a simple bargaining game. But it does reach the important conclusion that any agreement concluded between two rational bargainers must satisfy the following two rationality requirements:

1. *Individual rationality.* The agreement must represent, for *both* players, a

situation at least as favorable as the conflict situation that would emerge in the absence of any agreement. That is, if $\bar{u}_1$ and $\bar{u}_2$ are the payoffs to be received by the players under the agreement, then $\bar{u}_i \geq c_i$ ($i = 1, 2$). Geometrically the vector $\bar{u} = (\bar{u}_1, \bar{u}_2)$ must lie at least as *high* and at least as far to the *right* as the conflict point $c = (c_1, c_2)$. That is, in Figure 8.1, if the payoff space is represented by the enclosed area, then $\bar{u}$ must lie in the triangular area *cde*.

2. *Joint rationality (joint efficiency)*. The agreement will represent a situation that could not be improved upon any further to *both* players' advantage (because rational players would not accept a given agreement if some alternative arrangement could make both of them better off). Hence the agreement payoff vector $\bar{u}$ must be *efficient*, i.e., it must not be dominated (at least in a strong sense) by any other payoff vector u in the payoff space. Geometrically this means that $\bar{u}$ must lie on the upper right boundary *adeb* of the payoff space in Figure 8.1. (This upper right boundary corresponds to Edgeworth's [1881] "contract curve.")

These two requirements together imply that $\bar{u}$ must lie on the arc *de*. Thus this arc *de* represents the set of possible agreement points $\bar{u}$ between rational players, which Luce and Raiffa [1957] call the *negotiation set* of the game. (It also corresponds to what Pigou [1960] has called the "range of possible bargains.") The end points *d* and *e* of the negotiation set may be called the *concession limits* of player 1 and player 2, respectively, because they represent the *least favorable* efficient agreement points that these players might possibly accept. If *d* were adopted as the agreement point, then the entire gain achieved by cooperation would go to player 2, while player 1 would be no better off than he would be at the conflict point *c*. The converse would be true if *e* were adopted as the agreement point. Finally agreement points $\bar{u}$ lying between *d* and *e* would mean *dividing* the net gain of their cooperation in some proportion between the two players.

Thus classical economic theory predicts that the agreement point $\bar{u}$ will lie *within* the negotiation set *de*. But it does not predict the actual position of $\bar{u}$ *between* the two parties' concession limits *d* and *e*. That is, it fails to tell how the net gain of cooperation will be divided between the two parties. Hence classical eco-

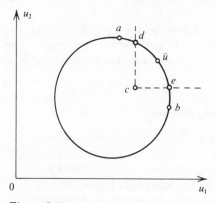

Figure 8.1

nomic theory does not overcome the *indeterminacy problem* associated with bargaining situations and does not furnish a determinate solution for the bargaining problem.

We are now in a position to state the reasons for this. The fundamental reason is that the two rationality requirements used by classical economic theory do not go beyond what we have called the *weak* rationality postulates for game situations, which do not suffice to overcome the indeterminacy problem.

Moreover, classical economic theory makes no essential use of *cardinal* utility functions but rather is based on purely *ordinal* utility. (Although earlier authors did sometimes assume cardinal utility, none of their conclusions in positive economics essentially depended on the use of cardinal utility.[1]) But it is easy to see that no theory based on mere ordinal utility functions can yield a determinate solution for the bargaining problem.[2]

This last difficulty is connected with a deeper one. Bargaining by its very nature represents decision making under *uncertainty*. The two players can reach agreement only if they make concessions to each other. The fundamental reason that a rational player will make a concession to his opponent will always be that he feels that the *risk*[3] (i.e., the subjective probability of a conflict) associated with a refusal of this concession would outweigh the advantages of holding out for better terms. Thus logically a determinate theory of rational behavior in bargaining situations presupposes a sufficiently specific theory of rational behavior under risk and/or uncertainty. Yet classical economics did not possess such a theory.

Even von Neumann and Morgenstern's *Theory of Games and Economic Behavior* [1944] did not furnish a determinate solution for the bargaining problem, because their analysis, also, was based on "weak" rationality postulates. But their approach did lay the foundations for further advance in this field by giving game theory the concepts of cardinal utility functions and of expected-utility maximization under risk and uncertainty.

8.3 The Nash solution

John Nash [1950b] was the first to realize that von Neumann and Morgenstern's concept of cardinal utility functions leads to a determinate theory, if we make use of some very natural additional rationality postulates.

Formally Nash represents the bargaining process between the players by means of the following bargaining model. Each player i ($i = 1, 2$) chooses a real number u_i, called his *payoff demand*. The two players have to choose their payoff demands u_1 and u_2 simultaneously and independently of each other. If the payoff vector $u = (u_1, u_2)$ lies in the payoff space P of the game, then we say that the two players' payoff demands are mutually *compatible*. And in this case each player i will receive the payoff u_i that he has been asking for. In contrast, if $u = (u_1, u_2) \notin P$, then we say that the players' payoff demands are *incompatible*, which will give rise to a conflict between them. In this case each player i will receive only his conflict payoff c_i.

Nash's bargaining model is obviously a game (a bargaining game) in *normal form*, because each player has only one move (consisting in the choice of his payoff demand), and the two players have to make their moves at the same time and independently of each other; there are no chance moves.

Nash's basic assumption is that a bargaining situation has a determinate solution at least in one special case, viz., in case the situation is completely *symmetrical* with respect to the two players. In this case it is a natural prediction that the two players will agree on *equal* payoffs to both of them, because neither player will have any reason to grant to his opponent better terms than the latter is prepared to grant to him. (For instance, everybody would expect that two duopolists with exactly the same cost functions, market connections, capital resources, and so forth, and with exactly similar personalities, would reach an agreement yielding equal profits to both of them.) In brief, a symmetric game must have a unique symmetric solution. By adopting this symmetry postulate, Nash goes beyond both classical economics and the von Neumann–Morgenstern theory.[4] Fundamentally the justification of this postulate is based on the analysis of the two players' mutual *expectations* about each other's behavior: In a symmetric game neither player can *rationally expect* that a rational opponent will grant him better terms than he himself is willing to concede.

At the same time this solution must also satisfy the classical joint-efficiency requirement. Hence the solution (or agreement point) of a fully symmetric bargaining game must lie at the point $\bar{u}$ where the 45° line drawn through the origin intersects the upper right boundary of the payoff space (see Figure 8.2).

Nash then extends this solution concept also to asymmetric bargaining games by assuming that the solution must be invariant with respect to certain mathematical transformations. More particularly Nash's main postulates are as follows:

1. *Joint efficiency.* The solution $\bar{u} = (\bar{u}_1, \bar{u}_2)$ lies on the upper right boundary H of the payoff space P.

A simple bargaining game is called *symmetric* if its conflict point $c = (c_1, c_2)$ lies on the $u_1 = u_2$ line and its payoff space P is symmetric with respect to the same line.

2. *Symmetry.* The solution $\bar{u}$ of a symmetric game lies on the line $u_1 = u_2$.

3. *Linear invariance.* Let G be a simple bargaining game with solution $\bar{u}$. Let G^* be the game that results from G if we subject one player's utility function U_i to an order-preserving linear transformation T, leaving the other player's utility function U_j unchanged. Then the solution $\bar{u}^*$ of this new game G^* will be the image of $\bar{u}$ under this transformation T, i.e., $\bar{u}^* = T\bar{u}$.

4. *Independence of irrelevant alternatives (invariance with respect to irrelevant restrictions of the payoff space).* Let G again be a simple bargaining game with payoff space P, conflict point c, and solution $\bar{u}$. Let G^* be a game obtained from G by restricting the payoff space to the smaller set $P^* \subset P$, in such a way that c and $\bar{u}$ remain in the new payoff space P^*, c being the conflict point also for G^*. Then $\bar{u}$ will be the solution also of the new game G^*. (For example, in Figure 8.3, if we exclude the shaded area from the payoff space, the position of the solution $\bar{u}$ will not be altered.)

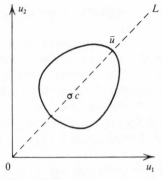

Figure 8.2

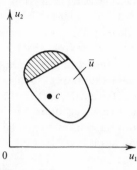

Figure 8.3

Since we have already discussed the first two postulates, we will now comment only on Postulates 3 and 4.

Postulate 3 says essentially that, if we express the players' payoffs in terms of money or commodities, and so forth (rather than in utility units), then their payoffs will be independent of the *unit* of measurement and the *zero point* that we choose for each player's utility function. Two issues are here involved:

1. Even a cardinal utility function is unique only up to order-preserving linear transformations. That is, the utility unit and the zero point of utility are always matters of arbitrary choice. Therefore these two parameters can have no influence on the outcome in "real" terms (i.e., in terms of the physical or the monetary payoffs or more generally in terms of the joint strategy to be agreed upon by the players).

2. The postulate allows us to choose each player's utility unit (and zero point) *independently* of the other player's. This means that the solution is assumed to be independent of *interpersonal comparisons* of utility between the players. (If interpersonal comparisons of utility were not regarded as irrelevant, then we could permit only such utility transformations that would not destroy *equality* between the two players' utility units: If we wanted to change one player's utility unit, we would always have to change the other player's utility unit in a similar way.)

Assumption 2 is motivated by the fact that (at least under our own interpretation – Nash's own statements are not quite clear on this point) Nash's model is meant to be a *bargaining model*, not an *arbitration model*. Interpersonal comparisons of utility, as we saw in Chapter 4, do have an important role in ethical contexts. But we are now envisaging a bargaining situation in which ethical considerations play no essential part.

In this bargaining situation each player is assumed to maximize his own expected utility on the basis of his expectations (i.e., his subjective probability distribution) concerning his opponent's possible bargaining strategies.[5] But if a person's behavior is guided by expected-utility maximization, then, *given* his expectations (i.e., given his subjective probabilities), his behavior will be *invariant* with respect to order-preserving linear transformations of his utility function: That is, we will obtain the same predictions about his behavior regardless of how we choose the unit and the zero point of his utility.

Each player will not only know that his *own* behavior has this invariance property but will also expect that his *opponent's* behavior will have the same property. This means that each player's *expectations* concerning his opponent's behavior will be invariant with respect to linear transformations of both his own and his opponent's utility functions. Yet, if both players' behavior (given their expectations) and also their expectations possess this invariance property, then the same must be true about the final outcome that *results* from their behavior, guided by their mutual expectations.

Thus the outcome will be independent of interpersonal comparisons of utility, simply because such comparisons do not enter, at any point, into either player's strategy choice based on expected-utility maximization.

A possible interpretation of Postulate 4 would regard it directly as a rationality postulate. If we excluded from the payoff space some potential agreement points that *would not be chosen anyhow* by the players, this should make no difference to the final outcome (irrelevance of unchosen alternatives).[6]

But we prefer Nash's [1953, p. 138] own interpretation of Postulate 4, which makes it essentially an *"institutional" assumption* about the bargaining process. Mathematically the role of the postulate is to make the solution $\bar{u}$ depend only on the *local* properties of the payoff space P (or more exactly on the local shape of the upper right boundary of P) around the solution point $\bar{u}$, so that distant parts of the payoff space will have no influence on the position of $\bar{u}$. This corresponds to the institutional fact that bargaining by its very nature consists in gradually *narrowing down* the set of alternatives under consideration to smaller and smaller subsets of the original negotiation set. That is, the players by mutual agreement always gradually replace the original bargaining game G by much smaller bargaining games G^* whose negotiation sets are restricted to smaller and smaller neighborhoods of $\bar{u}$. Hence, in order that a given point $\bar{u}$ can emerge as the solution of the original game G, it is necessary that $\bar{u}$ should also be the solution of these smaller games G^*, which are obtained from G by restricting the original payoff space P of G to smaller sets P^* (without, however, excluding $\bar{u}$ or c from these new payoff spaces P^*).[7]

Nash [1950b, p. 159] has also shown that a solution point $\bar{u}$ satisfying Postulates 1 to 4 always *exists*, is always *unique*, and can be mathematically characterized as follows:

Theorem 8.1. The solution $\bar{u} = (\bar{u}_1, \bar{u}_2)$ is the point satisfying the requirement

$$(\bar{u}_1 - c_1) \cdot (\bar{u}_2 - c_2) = \max \left[(u_1 - c_1) \cdot (u_2 - c_2) \right] \tag{8.1}$$

$$u \in P \tag{8.1a}$$

$$u_i \geq c_i \quad i = 1, 2 \tag{8.1b}$$

where c_1 and c_2 are the *constant* conflict payoffs specified by the rules of the game. That is, $u = \bar{u}$ is the point where the Nash product $\pi(u) = (u_1 - c_1) \cdot (u_2 - c_2)$ is maximized, subject to (8.1a) and (8.1b).

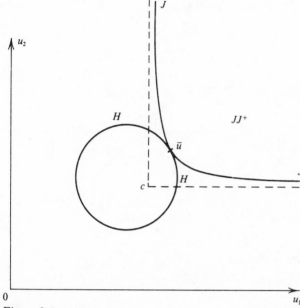

Figure 8.4

Geometrically this means that the solution $\bar{u}$ is the unique point of *tangency* between the upper right boundary HH of the payoff space P, and a rectangular hyperbola JJ asymptotic to the horizontal line $u_1 = c_1$ and to the vertical line $u_2 = c_2$ (see Figure 8.4). The equation of JJ is $\pi(u) = (u_1 - c_1) \cdot (u_2 - c_2) = \text{const.} = \pi(\bar{u})$. Hence the product $\pi(u)$ takes the value $\pi(\bar{u})$ only on JJ itself; and only in the area JJ^+ *above* the curve JJ (as well as in the area below the other branch of the hyperbola JJ) does it take even higher values.

Now suppose that $\bar{P}$ (i.e., the triangular area cab) is the area where conditions (8.1a) and (8.1b) are both satisfied. Since $\bar{P}$ has no point in common with area JJ^+, and since its only point in common with the curve JJ itself is $\bar{u}$, the point $\bar{u}$ is the only point at which the product $\pi(u)$ takes the value $\pi(\bar{u})$ over the set $\bar{P}$; this is its *maximum* value over $\bar{P}$.

Proof. Let $u = \bar{u}$ be the point where product $\pi(u)$ is maximized subject to (8.1a) and (8.1b). Because of the compactness of the payoff space P, such a point will always exist; and because of the convexity of P, it will always be unique.

Let us subject both players' utility functions to order-preserving linear transformations carrying the conflict point $c = (c_1, c_2)$ into the origin $c^* = (0, 0)$ while carrying the point $\bar{u} = (\bar{u}_1, \bar{u}_2)$ into the point $\bar{u}^* = (1, 1)$ (see Figure 8.5).

Let P^* be the image of the payoff space P under this transformation T. Finally let G^* be the game whose payoff space is P^* and whose conflict point is c^*.

Consider the Nash product $\pi^*(u^*) = (u_1^* - c_1^*) \cdot (u_2^* - c_2^*) = u_1^* u_2^*$ for this new game G^*. Suppose that $u^* = (u_1^*, u_2^*)$ is the image of some given point $u = (u_1, u_2)$ of the original payoff space P. Then $\pi^*(u^*) = \gamma \pi(u)$ where γ is the

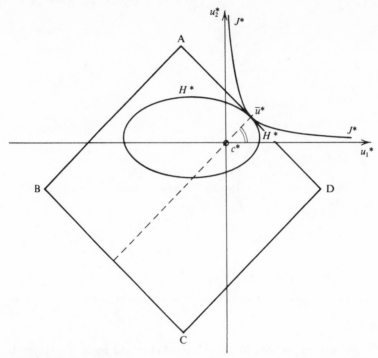

Figure 8.5

positive constant

$$\gamma = \frac{1}{(\bar{u}_1 - c_1)(\bar{u}_2 - c_2)}$$

Hence the transformation simply multiplies the Nash product for every point u by the same positive constant γ. Consequently, if $\pi(u)$ took its maximum value at the point $u = \bar{u}$, then $\pi^*(u^*)$ must take its maximum value at $u^* = \bar{u}^*$, the image of $\bar{u}$ under transformation T.

The point $\bar{u}^* = (1, 1)$ obviously lies on the line $u_1^* + u_2^* = 2$ (line AD of Figure 8.5). This line is the common tangent (or common supporting line) of the curves H^*H^* and J^*J^* at the point $\bar{u}^*$. Since the set P^* is convex, no point u^* of P^* can lie above this line AD. Therefore we can always construct a rectangle $ABCD$ symmetric with respect to the $45°$ line $c^*\bar{u}^*$, and wholly containing the payoff space P^*, so that the line AD will be the upper right boundary of the rectangle $ABCD$.

Let G^{**} be the game whose payoff space is the rectangle $ABCD$, while its con-flict point is c^*. By Postulates 1 and 2, since G^{**} is a symmetric game, the solution of G^{**} must be $\bar{u}^*$. Consequently, by Postulate 4, the point $\bar{u}^*$ must be the solu-tion also of G^*. But then, by Postulate 3, the point $\bar{u}$, which is the image of $\bar{u}^*$ under the inverse of our original transformation T, must be the solution of the original game G, as desired.

8.4 Zeuthen's model of the bargaining process

Another important model of the bargaining process was developed by a Danish economist, Frederik Zeuthen [1930, Chap. IV]. Zeuthen's approach is quite different from that of Nash, but, as we shall see, it is mathematically equivalent to it. Zeuthen's own analysis was restricted to collective bargaining on the labor market but can be easily extended to any other bargaining situation.[8]

Consider a bargaining process between players 1 and 2. If they can reach some agreement A, then they will obtain the corresponding payoffs $U_1(A)$ and $U_2(A)$.[9] If they fail to reach an agreement, then a conflict situation C will develop, and the two players will obtain the conflict payoffs $U_1(C)$ and $U_2(C)$. The bargaining proceeds in stages. At stage k player 1 has proposed an agreement $A_1{}^k = A_1$ to player 2, while player 2 has proposed another agreement $A_2{}^k = A_2$ to player 1. We will assume that

$$U_i(C) < U_i(A_j) < U_i(A_i) \qquad i,j = 1,2 \text{ and } i \neq j \tag{8.2}$$

That is, each player i would prefer his own last proposal A_i to his opponent's last proposal A_j but would prefer *either* proposal to the conflict situation C.

At the next stage $k + 1$, each player i has three alternatives:

α: He may simply repeat his last offer A_i.

β: He may accept his opponent's last offer A_j in full.

γ: He may make some *new* proposal $A_i{}^{k+1} = A_i{}'$, more favorable to the opponent than his own last offer A_i but less favorable than the opponent's own last offer A_j. Thus any new proposal $A_i{}'$ by player i will satisfy

$$U_j(A_i) < U_j(A_i{}') < U_j(A_j) \tag{8.3}$$

If player i chooses alternative β or γ, then we say that he is making a *concession*, whereas, if he chooses alternative α, then we say that he *refuses* to make a concession. We will assume that, if at any given stage k, $k \geq 2$, the players have not yet reached an agreement, yet *both* of them refuse to make concessions; then the negotiations will break down, and the conflict situation C will arise.

Now the following cases are possible:

$\alpha\alpha$: Both players choose alternative α, refusing to make a concession. Then a *conflict* will occur, and the players will receive the payoffs $U_1(C)$ and $U_2(C)$.

$\alpha\beta$: One player, say, player i, chooses alternative α while the other player chooses alternative β. This means that the two players will reach an *agreement* by accepting player i's last proposal A_i. This will yield them the payoffs $U_1(A_i)$ and $U_2(A_i)$, respectively.

$\beta\beta$: Both players choose alternative β, i.e., both of them express a willingness to accept the other player's last offer. This means that player 1 is willing to accept the payoff $U_1(A_2)$, while player 2 is willing to accept the payoff $U_2(A_1)$. This we will interpret as an *agreement* between the two players to accept the payoffs $U_1(A_2)$ and $U_2(A_1)$ and will assume that the players will, in fact, obtain these payoffs.[10]

$\alpha\gamma$: One player chooses alternative α, while the other player chooses alternative γ. This means that the players have reached no agreement but that the bargaining can go on because one player has made a concession. Therefore the bargaining process will move to stage $k + 2$.

$\beta\gamma$: One player, say, player i, chooses alternative β, while the other player chooses alternative γ. This means that player i would be willing to accept player j's previous offer A_j but that, in the meantime, player j himself has abandoned A_j in favor of a new offer $A_j{}'$. Thus player i is willing to accept the payoff $U_i(A_j)$, whereas player j is willing to accept the payoff $U_j(A_j{}') < U_j(A_j)$. This makes case $\beta\gamma$ somewhat similar to case $\beta\beta$. We interpret case $\beta\gamma$ as an *agreement* between the two players to accept the payoffs $U_i(A_j)$ and $U_j(A_j{}')$ and assume that the players will, in fact, obtain these payoffs.

$\gamma\gamma$: Both players choose alternative γ. This case is similar to $\alpha\gamma$: There is no agreement between the players, but there is no conflict either, because both players have made concessions. Thus the bargaining process can move to stage $k + 2$.

The question that Zeuthen tries to answer is this: Given the two players' utility functions U_1 and U_2, and given their last offers $A_1{}^k = A_1$ and $A_2{}^k = A_2$ at stage k, *which player will have to make the next concession* at stage $k + 1$? Zeuthen argues that the next concession must always come from the player *less willing to face the risk of a conflict* – in order to obtain an agreement on his own terms rather than on the opponent's terms. But how can we measure a given player's willingness to risk a conflict rather than accept the opponent's terms? Zeuthen proposes the following measure.

Because we want to measure each player's willingness to stick to his own terms rather than to accept his opponent's terms, we should consider a simplified bargaining situation in which each player i is restricted to a choice between alternatives α and β – that is, between full insistence on his own last offer, A_i and full acceptance of his opponent's last offer, A_j. How can he decide whether to choose α or β?

If he is a Bayesian expected-utility maximizer, then he must start with assigning *subjective probabilities* to the two possible choices that his opponent can make. Let p_{ji} be the subjective probability that i assigns to the hypothesis that j will choose alternative α; and let $q_{ji} = 1 - p_{ji}$ be the subjective probability that i assigns to the hypothesis that j will choose alternative β.

If player i himself chooses alternative β, then under our assumptions he will obtain the payoff $U_i(A_j)$ with certainty, regardless of what j will do. On the other hand, if i chooses alternative α, then he *may* obtain the higher payoff $U_i(A_i) > U_i(A_j)$, but he *may* also obtain the lower payoff $U_i(C) < U_i(A_j)$. The former possibility will occur with probability $q_{ji} = 1 - p_{ji}$, while the latter possibility will occur with probability p_{ji}. Consequently, if player i wants to maximize his expected utility, then he can choose alternative α, i.e., he can stand on his own last offer A_i, only if

$$(1 - p_{ji}) \cdot U_i(A_i) + p_{ji} \cdot U_i(C) \geq U_i(A_j) \tag{8.4}$$

that is, if

$$p_{ji} \leqq r_i = \frac{U_i(A_i) - U_i(A_j)}{U_i(A_i) - U_i(C)} \tag{8.5}$$

The quantity r_i ($i = 1, 2$) defined by (8.5) is called player i's *risk limit,* since it represents the *highest risk* (the highest subjective probability of a conflict) that player i would be willing to face in order to obtain an agreement on his own terms A_i rather than on his opponent's terms A_j. This is so because, if player i sticks to his own last offer A_i, then he must expect a conflict to occur with probability p_{ji} (this is the probability that his opponent will also stick to his own last offer A_j, so that neither player will make a concession). But, by (8.5), the highest value of the probability p_{ji} that i can face, without switching over to accepting the opponent's last offer, is $p_{ji} = r_i$.

In view of Equation (8.2), the quantity r_i must always satisfy

$$0 \leqq r_i \leqq 1 \tag{8.6}$$

The case $r_i = 0$ can occur only if $U_i(A_i) = U_i(A_j)$, which would mean that the two players have already essentially reached an agreement. On the other hand, the case $r_i = 1$ can only occur if $U_i(A_j) = U_i(C)$, which would mean that player j had made a completely unacceptable – and therefore unreasonable – offer A_j to player i, giving the latter no advantage over the conflict situation C.

The quantity r_i can also be interpreted as a ratio of two utility differences. The numerator, the difference $U_i(A_i) - U_i(A_j)$, is the *cost* to player i *of reaching an agreement on the opponent's terms* instead of an agreement on player i's own terms. The denominator, the difference $U_i(A_i) - U_i(C)$, is the *cost* to player i *of reaching no agreement* at all. In other words, the first difference is the *cost of a total concession*, while the second is the *cost of a conflict*. Therefore the ratio of these two differences, the quantity r_i itself, is a measure of the strength of player i's incentives for insisting on his own last offer rather than accepting his opponent's last offer.

To sum up, the quantity r_i measures the *highest risk* that player i is willing to take rather than to accept his opponent's terms; and it also measures player i's *incentives* to take a high risk rather than to accept his opponent's terms. Under either interpretation r_i is exactly the measure that is needed for Zeuthen's purposes. If $r_i < r_j$, this means that player i is *less willing* than player j is to risk a conflict and that he has *weaker incentives* to do so. Moreover, both players will know that this is the case. Therefore player i will be under strong psychological pressure to make the next concession, while player j will feel he can afford not to make any concession at this point. On the other hand, if $r_i = r_j$, this means that the two players are *equally willing* to make a concession, and have *equally strong incentives* to do so. Zeuthen argues that in this case *both* of them will be under psychological pressure to make concessions in order to avoid a breakdown in their negotiations, which would lead to a conflict. Thus Zeuthen proposes the following decision rule, which we will call *Zeuthen's Principle*:

(α) If $r_1 > r_2$, then player 2 has to make the next concession;

(β) If $r_1 < r_2$, then player 1 has to make the next concession;

(γ) If $r_1 = r_2$, then *both* players have to make some concessions.

In all of these cases the player or players who have to make concessions are free to make quite small concessions. Within certain limits (which will be discussed) the bargaining process will lead to the *same* final outcome, regardless of how large concessions the players will make to each other at each stage, as long as they follow Zeuthen's Principle in deciding *who* should make the next concession at each stage of the bargaining process. More specifically, as we will see in the next section, this bargaining process will always lead to the Nash solution.

8.5   Mathematical equivalence of Zeuthen's and Nash's theories

We make the following assumptions:

1. Neither player will make concessions *going beyond* the Nash solution of the game. That is, if the payoff vector $\bar{u} = (\bar{u}_1, \bar{u}_2)$ is the Nash solution, then any offer A_i by either player i will satisfy

$$U_i(A_i) \geq \bar{u}_i \tag{8.7}$$

This is a reasonable assumption because, as we will see, the player can always achieve the Nash solution. Therefore it would be irrational for him to propose an agreement giving him a payoff lower than the Nash solution would.

2. If either player makes a concession, the latter must be no smaller than some *minimum size* – except when a concession of this size would already take him beyond the Nash solution. Thus assumption 1 takes precedence over assumption 2. For example, if the bargaining is about money, then we may assume that any concession must involve giving up at least one monetary unit (say, 1 cent). More generally we may assume that any new offer A_i' be player i must increase the utility payoff offered to his opponent at least by ϵ, where ϵ is some small positive number. That is

$$U_j(A_i') \geq U_j(A_i) + \epsilon \tag{8.8}$$

The purpose of this assumption is to ensure that the players' offers will converge to some agreement after a finite number of stages (i.e., after a finite number of bargaining moves).

Thus assumption 1 sets an upper bound for the size of admissible concessions, while assumption 2 sets a lower bound to it.

We will now prove the following theorem.

Theorem 8.2. Under assumptions 1 and 2, if the two players follow Zeuthen's Principle during the bargaining process, then they will eventually reach an agreement corresponding to the Nash solution.

Proof. According to Zeuthen's Principle, player i ($i = 1, 2$) will always make a concession to the other player j whenever

$$r_i = \frac{U_i(A_i) - U_i(A_j)}{U_i(A_i) - U_i(C)} \leqq \frac{U_j(A_j) - U_j(A_i)}{U_j(A_j) - U_j(C)} = r_j \tag{8.9}$$

This condition is equivalent to

$$\pi(A_i) = [U_i(A_i) - U_i(C)] \cdot [U_j(A_i) - U_j(C)]$$
$$\leqq [U_i(A_j) - U_i(C)] \cdot [U_j(A_j) - U_j(C)]$$
$$= \pi(A_j) \tag{8.10}$$

That is, player i will always make a concession whenever $\pi(A_i)$, the *Nash product* associated with his *own* last offer A_i, is smaller than (or is equal to) $\pi(A_j)$, the *Nash product* associated with his *opponent's* last offer A_j. This means that player i will have to make *further* concessions until he comes to propose an offer $A_i{}^*$ associated with a *larger* Nash product $\pi(A_i{}^*)$ than was the Nash product $\pi(A_j)$ associated with his opponent's last offer A_j. At this point player j will have to take over the task of making concessions, and so on.

Thus at every stage of the bargaining process, of the two parties' last offers, the offer corresponding to the *smaller* value of the Nash product π will always be eliminated, and the offer corresponding to the *larger* value of π will always be retained until the next stage. Then at the next stage one of the two parties will introduce a new offer associated with an *even larger* π value than the offer surviving from the previous stage, and so on. This process will continue until one of the two parties introduces an offer corresponding to the *largest possible* value of π; this offer then will be accepted by *both* parties (since the other party will not be able to counter this by an offer corresponding to a still larger value of π). Hence under Zeuthen's model the final agreement will be reached at the point where the Nash product π takes its *maximum* value – which is the Nash solution point of the game, as desired.

8.6 Derivation of Zeuthen's Principle from our "strong" rationality postulates

In Zeuthen's original discussion the decision rule, which we have called Zeuthen's Principle, has the nature of an independent axiom, accepted because of its intrinsic plausibility. But we now show that this principle, in fact, directly *follows* from our "strong" rationality postulates for game situations, being the *only* possible decision rule consistent with these rationality postulates.

For convenience, we shall here repeat the five rationality postulates that we will use to derive Zeuthen's Principle. (For a full list of our eight rationality postulates for game situations, see Section 6.2)

A3. *Subjective-best-reply postulate (Bayesian expected-utility maximization postulate).* In a bargaining game $B(G)$ associated with a game G profitable to you, as far as your binding agreements with the other players allow, always use a bargaining strategy β_i representing your *subjective* best reply to the mean bargaining-strategy combination $\tilde{\beta}^i$ that you expect the other players to use.

A4. *Acceptance-of-higher-payoffs postulate.*

Part I. Let σ and σ^* be two joint strategies available to the n players, both of them consistent with our other rationality postulates. Suppose that σ^* would yield you (player i) a higher payoff $U_i(\sigma^*) > U_i(\sigma)$. Let us assume that, at a given stage of the bargaining game $B(G)$, the set $A_i(\beta_i)$ of all joint strategies acceptable to you would include the joint strategy σ. Then this set $A_i(\beta_i)$ must also include the joint strategy σ^* more favorable to you.

Part II. Let $\beta = (\beta_1, \ldots, \beta_i, \ldots, \beta_n)$ and $\beta^* = (\beta_1^*, \ldots, \beta_i^*, \ldots, \beta_n^*)$ be two possible n-tuples of bargaining strategies for the n players, both of them consistent with our other rationality postulates, but β^* yielding you (player i) a higher payoff than β would. Suppose that, in the absence of any special agreement to the contrary, you and all the other players would use bargaining strategies corresponding to the n-tuple β. Then you must be willing to enter into an agreement under which you and all the other players will shift to bargaining strategies corresponding to the n-tuple β^*.

B1. *Mutually expected-rationality postulate.* In the same way as you yourself will follow the present postulates (i.e., Postulates A3, A4, B1, B2, and B3), if you are a rational player, you must expect, and act on the expectation, that *other* rational players will likewise follow these rationality postulates.

B2. *Symmetric-expectations postulate.* You cannot choose your bargaining strategy β_i on the expectation that a rational opponent will choose a *different* bargaining strategy from your own and, in particular, that he will choose a bargaining strategy *more concessive* than you yourself would choose in the same situation.

B3. *Expected-independence-of-irrelevant-variables postulate.* You cannot expect a rational opponent to make his bargaining strategy β_j dependent on variables whose *relevance* for bargaining behavior *cannot be established* on the basis of the present rationality postulates. (This postulate will be restated presently in a more specific form.)

Let us again consider a bargaining process (i.e., a bargaining game) subject to the rules stated in Section 8.4. We first analyze the special case where – for any reason whatever – each player i restricts his choice to alternatives α and β. Thus he will *either* stick to his own last offer A_i *or* will accept his opponent's last offer A_j in full. This special case we will call *restricted bargaining*.

We have already seen that if player i is a Bayesian expected-utility maximizer – i.e., if he follows our Postulate A3 – then he can choose alternative α only if Condition (8.4) is satisfied. This means that his bargaining behavior will depend only on the quantity r_i and on the subjective probability p_{ji}. Thus player 1's behavior will depend on r_1 and on p_{21}, while player 2's behavior will depend on r_2 and on p_{12}. In other words, Postulate A3 makes these four variables *relevant* for the two players' bargaining behavior. Careful reading of our rationality postulates will show that none of our postulates establishes the relevance of any other variables.[11] Thus we can now restate Postulate B3.

B3*. *Expected-independence-of-irrelevant-variables postulate – specific form.* In restricted two-person bargaining, we cannot expect a rational opponent to make his choice between alternatives α and β dependent on any other variables than the four quantities r_1, r_2, p_{12}, and p_{21}.

Returning to Condition (8.5), the latter could serve as a decision rule for player i, if he could assign a specific numerical value to the probability p_{ji}. We will now try to show that, if he tries to assign such a numerical value to p_{ji}, consistent with our rationality postulates, then he will necessarily arrive at Zeuthen's Principle.

By Postulate B1, each player will know that the other player's behavior will also be guided by Condition (8.5). Hence, for instance, player 1 will know that his assessment of probability p_{21} (i.e., his assessment of the probability that player 2 will stick to his last offer A_2) will be realistic only if he uses the following p_{21} values:

$$p_{21} = 0 \quad \text{if} \quad p_{12} > r_2$$
$$p_{21} = 1 \quad \text{if} \quad p_{12} < r_2 \tag{8.11}$$

Therefore he will look for a decision rule consistent with (8.11).

On the other hand, player 1 will know that, by the same token, player 2 will assess the probability p_{12} as follows:

$$p_{12} = 0 \quad \text{if} \quad p_{21} > r_1$$
$$p_{12} = 1 \quad \text{if} \quad p_{21} < r_1 \tag{8.12}$$

However, Conditions (8.11) and (8.12) together allow only the following three possible cases:

$$\text{Either} \quad \text{(i)} \; p_{12} = 0 \quad \text{and} \quad p_{21} = 1$$
$$\text{Or} \quad \text{(ii)} \; p_{12} = 1 \quad \text{and} \quad p_{21} = 0$$
$$\text{Or} \quad \text{(iii)} \; p_{12} = r_2 \quad \text{and} \quad p_{21} = r_1 \tag{8.13}$$

But it still has to be decided *when* each of these cases will apply.

Now (8.12) makes p_{12} a step function of p_{21} and r_1, so that

$$p_{12} = F(p_{21}, r_1) \tag{8.14}$$

Likewise (8.11) makes p_{21} a step function of p_{12} and r_2, so that

$$p_{21} = F(p_{12}, r_2) \tag{8.15}$$

In view of our symmetry postulate, Postulate B2, the function F in (8.14) must be the same as the function F in (8.15).

Equations (8.14) and (8.15) are simultaneous in the two unknowns p_{12} and p_{21}. Therefore p_{12} and p_{21} must be functions of the variables r_1 and r_2. Indeed, by Postulate B3*, they must be functions of r_1 and r_2 *alone*. Therefore we can write

$$p_{12} = G(r_1, r_2)$$

$$p_{21} = G(r_2, r_1) \tag{8.16}$$

Again, by Postulate B2, the function G determining p_{12} must be the same as the function G determining p_{21}.

By Part I of Postulate A4, p_{12} must be a *nondecreasing* function of $U_1(A_1)$ if all the other utilities are kept constant, while p_{21} must be a nondecreasing function of $U_2(A_2)$ if all other utilities are kept constant. Therefore G must be a monotone nondecreasing function of its first argument.

All functions G satisfying this monotonicity requirement, and also satisfying the symmetry postulate (Postulate B2), as well as Condition (8.13), must be of the following form: They must be defined over the square $0 \leq r_1 \leq 1; 0 \leq r_2 \leq 1$. They must divide this square into three regions corresponding to cases (i), (ii), and (iii) of Condition (8.13) (see Figure 8.6). Region (i) must include the r_1 axis, while region (ii) must include the r_2 axis. Region (iii) must include the $r_1 = r_2$ line and must be symmetric with respect to this line. Any straight line running parallel to the r_1 axis in the positive direction must go through regions (ii), (iii), and (i) in this order; any straight line running parallel to the r_2 axis in the positive direction must go through them in the opposite order.

Any such function G corresponds to a possible decision rule R for the players to the effect that:

1. In region (i) player 1 should stick to his last offer A_1, while player 2 should yield.

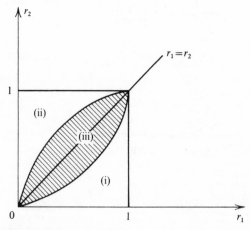

Figure 8.6

2. In region (ii) player 2 should stick to his last offer A_2, while player 1 should yield.

3. In region (iii) the players should use mixed strategies so that player 1 is sticking to his last offer A_1 with probability r_1 and is yielding with probability $(1 - r_1)$, while player 2 is sticking to his last offer A_2 with probability r_2 and is yielding with probability $(1 - r_2)$.

Different functions G, of course, will define different regions (i), (ii), and (iii) and so will furnish different decision rules R. Let S be the set of all decision rules R corresponding to some admissible function G. All decision rules R in set S will be consistent with Postulates A3, B1, B2, and B3, as well as with Part I of Postulate A4. But they will not be equally consistent with Part II of Postulate A4, which requires that the players should use jointly efficient joint strategies in the bargaining game.

Adoption by the players of any decision rule R in set S will give rise to conflicts between them in region (iii), with probability $\bar{p} = r_1 r_2$. Therefore, by the joint-efficiency requirement imposed by Part II of Postulate A4, they will try to reduce region (iii) to its smallest possible size, i.e., to the line $r_1 = r_2$ itself. This means that all points satisfying $r_1 > r_2$ will be assigned to region (i), while all points satisfying $r_1 < r_2$ will be assigned to region (ii). Let us denote this decision rule by R^*. By Part II of Postulate A4, among the decision rules belonging to set S, R^* is the only one that the players can adopt.

However, R^* still does not represent a completely efficient joint bargaining strategy, because in the case $r_1 = r_2$ it will still result in conflicts between the players with probability $\bar{p} = r_1 r_2 = (r_1)^2$. These conflicts can be avoided if the players agree that in region (iii), i.e., on the line $r_1 = r_2$, both of them will *always* yield, instead of using mixed strategies. Let us denote this modified form of rule R^* by R^{**}.

If we disregarded the qualifying clause in Postulate A3 (viz., "as far as your binding agreements with other players allow"), then decision rule R^{**} would be inconsistent with Postulate A3. This is so because R^{**} requires *both* players to make concessions when $r_1 = r_2$. Yet, if the players choose their bargaining moves by the criterion of expected-utility maximization, then, as we have seen, Condition (8.4) follows. Consequently the possibility of simultaneous concessions by *both* players, corresponding to $p_{12} = p_{21} = 1$, is ruled out (except at the point $r_1 = r_2 = 1$). Intuitively speaking, if the players are trying to maximize their expected utilities, then each player will make a concession only because he expects the other player *not* to make a concession.

However, once we take account of the qualifying clause, decision rule R^{**} becomes consistent with Postulate A3. Consequently, by Part II of Postulate A4, we can conclude that the players will agree to replace decision rule R^* by decision rule R^{**}, which will be mutually beneficial by eliminating the possibility of conflicts between them. This means that the players will use the expected-utility maximization criterion in a literal sense in regions (i) and (ii) only, corresponding to the cases $r_1 > r_2$ and $r_1 < r_2$. But in region (iii), i.e., in the case $r_1 = r_2$, they will shift to an agreed joint strategy of mutual concessions.

Thus our rationality postulates lead to decision rule R^{**}, which requires that:

1. Player 1 should stick to his last offer A_1, while player 2 should yield if $r_1 > r_2$.

2. Player 2 should stick to his last offer A_2, while player 1 should yield if $r_1 < r_2$.

3. *Both* players should make concessions if $r_1 = r_2$.

This decision rule, however, has been obtained under the restrictive assumption that both players will restrict their choices to alternatives α and β. Now let us drop this restrictive assumption. Moreover, let us assume that the two players' last offers A_1 and A_2 have been such that $r_1 > r_2$. Then it still will be true that, *as long as neither player makes a new offer*, our rationality postulates will require player 2 to make a concession, accepting player 1's last offer A_1 *in full*. But now player 2 can avoid this extreme move by making a new offer A_2', representing a concession going beyond player 2's last offer A_2, yet falling short of full acceptance of player 1's last offer A_1. Because player 2 will prefer making a small concession rather than making a large one, making such a new offer A_2' will be the rational thing for him to do.

Hence, if $r_1 > r_2$, then player 2 will have to make the next concession (though he need not go as far as fully accepting his opponent's last offer).

By similar reasoning, if $r_1 < r_2$, then player 1 has to make the next concession; and if $r_1 = r_2$, then both players have to make some concessions (but again in neither case need concessions go as far as full acceptance of the other player's last offer).

This is the final form of the decision rule that we obtain on the basis of our "strong" rationality postulates. But this is precisely the decision rule that we have called Zeuthen's Principle. Hence we can state:

Theorem 8.3. If the two players follow our "strong" rationality postulates (i.e., Postulates A3, A4, B1, B2, and B3*), then their bargaining behavior will conform to Zeuthen's Principle.

Theorems 8.2 and 8.3 in turn imply:

Theorem 8.4. If the two players follow our "strong" rationality postulates, then they will agree on terms corresponding to the Nash solution of the game.

We feel that deriving the Nash solution from our rationality postulates by way of Zeuthen's Principle has some advantages over Nash's own original approach. In our view, our own rationality postulates possess greater intuitive appeal than Nash's and represent more fundamental criteria for rational behavior. In particular, our own approach, based on Zeuthen's model of the bargaining process, explains *why* the solution must depend on the two players' *cardinal* utility functions, defined in terms of their attitudes toward risk. It also explains *why* the solution must be *in-*

variant with respect to order-preserving linear transformations of either player's utility function. Under Nash's original approach these properties have to be *assumed* without explanation in terms of more basic rationality postulates.

Zeuthen's model makes it clear that the reason for the use of cardinal utility is that bargaining by its very nature represents behavior in the face of *risk* (uncertainty). The quantities r_1 and r_2 governing the two players' behavior express their attitudes toward risk (they represent the highest risk each player is willing to face), and therefore they must depend on their *cardinal* utility functions. Moreover, the solution must be *invariant* with respect to order-preserving linear transformations of either player's utility function, because the quantities r_i ($i = 1, 2$) themselves, governing the two players' behavior, are invariant with respect to such transformations. For example, if we replace player i's utility function U_i by the new utility function $V_i = aU_i + b$ with $a > 0$, then r_i will not change, because

$$r_i = \frac{U_i(A_i) - U_i(A_j)}{U_i(A_i) - U_i(C)} = \frac{V_i(A_i) - V_i(A_j)}{V_i(A_i) - V_i(C)} \tag{8.17}$$

Likewise, Zeuthen's model provides the independence-of-irrelevant-alternatives property (Postulate 4 of Section 8.3) automatically without requiring a special postulate to this effect.

In actuality the heuristic justification that we proposed in Section 8.3 for Nash's Postulates 3 and 4 (by our numbering) were equivalent to using Zeuthen's bargaining model in an informal way.

Our rationality postulates also have the advantage of making explicit the dependence of the Nash solution on certain consistency requirements (rationality postulates) regarding the players' *expectations* (subjective probabilities) about each other's behavior.

While Zeuthen's model provides a more explicit rationale for the Nash solution, Nash's results also supplement Zeuthen's results in an important way: They provide an explicit mathematical characterization of the solution point to which the bargaining process postulated by Zeuthen eventually converges.

8.7 The role of the "strong" postulates of rational expectations

We now propose to give closer consideration to the role that the three rational-expectations postulates (Postulates B1, B2, and B3) have played in the proof of Theorem 8.3.

As we saw in Chapter 6, the postulate of mutually expected rationality (Postulate B1) is an essential assumption not only in the theory of bargaining-determined games but also in the theory of games determined by payoff-dominance. Even in the simple cases of games with strictly identical or strictly opposite interests (two-person zero-sum games), our analysis had to assume this postulate. In effect, one may argue that the essential difference between game theory and the theory of individual rational behavior (in situations of individual independence) lies primarily in the use of this postulate, which sets up a general rationality requirement for the players' mutual expectations.

In contrast, the symmetry postulate and the irrelevant-variables postulate (Postulate B2 and B3) are needed only in the analysis of bargaining-determined games. The main purpose of the symmetry postulate is to rule out bargaining strategies based on the expectation that a rational opponent facing a given player will use a bargaining strategy *less rational* than this player himself would use in the other player's position. In particular the postulate serves to point out that one cannot consistently expect a rational opponent to make a concession in a situation in which one would oneself refuse such a concession according to one's own criteria of rational bargaining behavior.

The irrelevant-variables postulate, on the other hand, aims to exclude from the players' decision rules all variables extraneous to rational decision making based on expected-utility maximization. If we dropped this postulate, then our remaining five postulates would not rule out some quite arbitrary, or even quite silly, decision rules. For instance, it would be fully compatible with our other five postulates that the players should divide any joint profit in proportion of their telephone numbers, or in proportion to the logarithm of their waist measurements, and so forth. (You can easily convince yourself that such rules of division would be *symmetric* between the two players; they could be made *efficient*, and so on, and therefore would not violate any of our first five postulates.)

The irrelevant-variables postulate is based on the following consideration. If the two players' behavior is guided fundamentally by the criterion of expected-utility maximization, and if they mutually *expect* each other's behavior to be guided by this criterion, then their behavior will depend only on those variables which enter into expected-utility maximization. All other variables will be intrinsically irrelevant for the players' strategy choices.

In our view the only reason that rational players might introduce into their decision rules additional variables unrelated to utility maximization would be the impossibility of choosing between alternative possible agreement points on the basis of rational criteria alone. If all ways of dividing the payoffs were *equally* rational, then one could not exclude the possibility that even very rational players might conceivably agree on a division, e.g., in proportion to their telephone numbers. For under this assumption all possible arrangements would be equally rational or equally arbitrary, and that particular one would be no less rational than alternative arrangements. But, as we have seen, a bargaining game does have a unique rational solution based on a decision rule involving only the variables r_1 and r_2 directly connected with utility maximization. Hence the need for introducing additional variables into the players' decision rules does not arise.[12]

More particularly we have seen [Condition (8.5)] that, if the players' behavior is based on expected-utility maximization, then their behavior will be guided by the variables r_1, r_2, p_{12}, and p_{21}. But, of these four quantities, only r_1 and r_2 have the nature of independent variables, since the probabilities p_{12} and p_{21} themselves depend on r_1 and r_2. (In the case of player 1, for instance, his behavior will depend on r_1, because r_1 is related to his own utility function U_1. Yet his behavior will also depend on r_2, related to his *opponent's* utility function U_2, because player 1's expectations about his opponent's behavior, i.e., the probability p_{21}, will depend also on r_2.) However, neither player's behavior will depend on *other* variables, because there is simply no way for other variables to enter into a rational strategy choice by either player.

If we examine the proof of Theorem 8.3, we will find that, of the five rationality postulates that we used, Postulates B2 and B3* (or B3) have been the most important assumptions. In particular, it is the use of Postulate B3* that distinguishes our theory from alternative theories of bargaining such as those of Raiffa [1953], Braithwaite [1955], and Schelling [1960]. In contrast, the use of Postulate B2 – or, at least, of *some* symmetry postulate for the two players – is common to *all* possible theories of bargaining as a matter of strict logical necessity.

Every theory must make the outcome or "solution" a function of certain independent variables, which the theory regards as *relevant* for characterizing the two players' bargaining positions – though different theories, of course, will consider a different set of variables as "relevant." But once the "relevant" variables have been designated, the solution must be made a *symmetric* function of all these relevant variables. That is, if we interchange *all* relevant variables associated with the two players, then each theory must predict that the two players' payoffs will also be interchanged. (This is true by the definition of "relevant" variables: If in such a case a given theory does not predict a reversal of the two players' payoffs, this must mean that not *all* relevant independent variables have yet been interchanged between the two players.)

Our own theory differs from alternative theories in restricting the set of "relevant" variables to those variables which directly enter into rational choice based on expected-utility maximization. This is accomplished by Postulate B3*. In contrast, Schelling's theory assigns "relevance" in this sense also to certain *psychological* variables that have "prominence" for the players, while Raiffa's and Braithwaite's theories assign relevance to certain *ethical* variables. Since our model is meant to represent bargaining behavior governed only by a *rational* pursuit of individual *self-interest* (or more generally by a rational pursuit of individual *utility*[13]), we want to exclude all these variables from our model by means of Postulate B3*.

From a formal standpoint it would be very natural to combine Postulates B2 and B3 into *one* statement having the nature of a symmetry postulate (of course, it would be a *stronger* symmetry postulate than Postulate B2 in its present form). Postulate B2 makes the two players' decision rules, taken in conjunction, a *symmetric* function of the variables associated with the two players, while Postulate B3 makes these decision rules a function of the "relevant" variables only. The combined postulate could state as *one* proposition that these decision rules must be a symmetric function of the "relevant" variables, containing no other variables. However, we prefer to state Postulates B2 and B3 as two independent axioms in order to make it easier to distinguish between assumptions peculiar to our theory and assumptions that our theory shares with other theories dealing with bargaining situations.

8.8 The compressed Zeuthen model

We noted in Section 8.3 that Nash's bargaining model is a bargaining game in normal form, in which each player has only one move, viz., stating his payoff demand. In contrast, Zeuthen's model is a bargaining game in extensive form, in which each player typically has a large number of moves (offers and counteroffers). We now propose to show that Zeuthen's model can be restated, without major changes, so that it becomes a much shorter bargaining game in which each player has (at most) *two* moves.

The proposed model will be called the *compressed Zeuthen model*. It is a bargaining game with two stages. In stage 1 each player i ($i = 1, 2$) makes some offer A_i to the other player. The two players have to make these offers simultaneously and independently of each other. We say that these two offers are mutually *compatible* if

$$\text{both} \quad U_1(A_2) \geq U_1(A_1) \quad \text{and} \quad U_2(A_1) \geq U_2(A_2) \tag{8.18}$$

If the two players' offers are compatible, then the game comes to an end at stage 1, and the two players will receive the payoffs $u_1 = U_1(A_1)$ and $u_2 = U_2(A_2)$ corresponding to their *own* offers. In particular, if $A_1 = A_2 = A$, then they will receive the payoffs $u_1 = U_1(A)$ and $u_2 = U_2(A)$.

If the two players' offers are *not* compatible, then the game will proceed to stage 2, where each player i can *either* repeat his own offer A_i *or* can accept the other player's offer A_j, but neither player can propose any *new* offer $A_i' \neq A_i$ and $\neq A_j$. That is, at stage 2 each player can choose between what we have called alternatives α and β in Section 8.4. Consequently the two players' moves at stage 2 can give rise to three possible cases, which we have called cases $\alpha\alpha$, $\alpha\beta$, and $\beta\beta$. We will assume that in each of these three cases the players' payoffs will be as specified in Section 8 4. This means that:

1. If a given player i accepts his opponent's offer A_j, then he will obtain the payoff $U_i(A_j)$, regardless of what move his opponent will make at stage 2.

2. If player i repeats his own offer A_i and the opponent accepts this offer, then player i will obtain the *higher* payoff $U_i(A_i)$.

3. If player i repeats his own offer A_i while the opponent likewise repeats his own offer A_j, then a conflict will result, and player i will receive the lower payoff $U_i(C)$.

In view of Theorem 8.3, if the two players follow our "strong" rationality postulates, then at stage 2 of the bargaining game they will act in accordance with Zeuthen's Principle. But, by (8.10), this is the same as saying that at stage 2 each player i will accept his opponent's offer A_j if

$$\pi(A_i) \leqq \pi(A_j) \tag{8.19}$$

but will repeat his own offer A_i if

$$\pi(A_i) > \pi(A_j) \tag{8.20}$$

where $\pi(A_i)$ and $\pi(A_j)$ are the Nash products associated with A_i and A_j, respectively.

Therefore we can assume that at stage 2 both players' behavior will be governed by (8.19) and (8.20) and that both of them will know this already at stage 1. How will they then choose the offers A_1 and A_2 that they will make to each other at stage 1?

To answer this question, we consider a *constrained* bargaining game, in which at stage 1 each player i is free to choose any feasible agreement A as his offer $A_i = A$, but in which at stage 2 he *must* act according to (8.19) and (8.20).

Lemma 1. In a constrained bargaining game, the maximin strategy of each player i is to choose an offer $\bar{A}_i$ proposing an agreement corresponding to the Nash solution $\bar{A}$ so that we can write $\bar{A}_i = \bar{A}$. The maximin payoff of each player i is the payoff $\bar{u}_i = U_i(\bar{A})$, which he would obtain under the Nash solution.

Proof. By choosing the offer $A_i = \bar{A}_i = \bar{A}$, each player i can assure the payoff $\bar{u}_i = U_i(\bar{A}_i) = U_i(\bar{A})$. Two cases are possible. If $A_i = \bar{A}_i$ is *compatible* with the opponent's offer A_j, then the game will end at stage 1, and player 1 will receive the payoff $U_i(\bar{A}_i) = \bar{u}_i$. If $\bar{A}_i$ is *incompatible* with A_j, then player j will have to accept $\bar{A}_i$ at stage 2, since $\pi(\bar{A}_i) \geqq \pi(A_2)$, because $\bar{A}_i$ is the Nash solution and is therefore associated with the highest possible Nash product. But if player j accepts $\bar{A}_i$, then player i will again receive the payoff $U_i(\bar{A}_i) = \bar{u}_i$.

On the other hand, player i cannot assure a payoff higher than $\bar{u}_i$, whatever offer A_i he may choose. This is so because player j may always choose the offer $\bar{A}_j = \bar{A}$, which will assure him the payoff $\bar{u}_j = U_j(\bar{A})$. Yet if player j obtains the payoff $\bar{u}_j$, then player i cannot obtain a payoff higher than $\bar{u}_i$, because the payoff vector $(\bar{u}_i, \bar{u}_j)$ corresponding to the Nash solution is an efficient payoff vector. Thus player i's payoff cannot be increased above $\bar{u}_i$ without decreasing player j's payoff below $\bar{u}_j$.

Lemma 2. The only equilibrium point in the constrained bargaining game is the strategy pair (or offer pair) $(A_1, A_2) = (\bar{A}_1, \bar{A}_2)$, where $\bar{A}_1 = \bar{A}_2 = \bar{A}$ are offers corresponding to the Nash solution.

Proof. We first show that $(\bar{A}_1, \bar{A}_2)$ is, in fact, an equilibrium point, i.e., that $\bar{A}_1$ and $\bar{A}_2$ are best replies to each other. Suppose that player j's offer is $\bar{A}_j$. Then, if player i chooses the offer $\bar{A}_i$, the game will end at stage 1, and player i will receive the payoff $U_i(\bar{A}_i) = \bar{u}_i$. On the other hand, if player i chooses some other offer $A_i \neq \bar{A}_i$, he cannot obtain a payoff higher than $\bar{u}_i$ because by choosing the offer $\bar{A}_j$ player j is assured to obtain at least $\bar{u}_j$, which makes it impossible for player i to obtain more than $\bar{u}_i$. Hence $\bar{A}_i$ is, in fact, a best reply to $\bar{A}_j$ for $i, j = 1, 2$ and $i \neq j$, and so $(\bar{A}_1, \bar{A}_2)$ is an equilibrium point.

Moreover, $(\bar{A}_1, \bar{A}_2)$ is the *only* equilibrium point in the game. It is easy to verify that $(\bar{A}_1, \bar{A}_2)$ is the only offer pair yielding the Nash payoff vector $\bar{u} = (\bar{u}_1, \bar{u}_2)$. Any other offer pair (A_1, A_2) will yield at least one of the players a lower payoff $u_i < \bar{u}_i$. But, in view of Lemma 1 of Section 5.10, no equilibrium point can yield either player a payoff lower than his maximin payoff $\bar{u}_i$. Therefore no other offer pair (A_1, A_2) can be an equilibrium point.

Lemmas 1 and 2 indicate that the constrained bargaining game shows some similarity to a two-person zero-sum game with a unique equilibrium point (saddle point) in pure strategies. In particular, the two players' equilibrium strategies have maximin properties.

Theorem 8.5. If the two players follow our "strong" rationality postulates in the *compressed* Zeuthen bargaining model, then both of them will propose the Nash solution $\bar{A}$ already at stage 1 of the game. Hence the game will end at stage 1, and both players will receive their Nash payoffs $\bar{u}_1 = U_1(\bar{A})$ and $\bar{u}_2 = U_2(\bar{A})$.

Proof. By Theorem 8.3, if the two players follow our "strong" rationality postulates, then the compressed Zeuthen model will be equivalent to a constrained bargaining game. But, by Lemmas 1 and 2, the latter will have the nature of an unprofitable game, since its only equilibrium point is unprofitable to both players, yielding them only their maximin payoffs. Therefore, by Postulate A1, the players must use their maximin strategies, i.e., must make the offers $\bar{A}_1$ and $\bar{A}_2$ at stage 1 of their game. As a result the game will end at stage 1, yielding the players the Nash payoffs $\bar{u}_1$ and $\bar{u}_2$.

Thus the *compressed* Zeuthen model, like the *extensive* Zeuthen model, yields the Nash solution as outcome of the bargaining game.

8.9   Risk-dominance relations

As we saw in Section 8.5, Zeuthen's Principle has the following implication. If the two players have to choose between two alternative offers A_1 and A_2, they will always choose that offer A_i which corresponds to a higher risk limit r_i, or equivalently they will choose that offer A_i which yields a higher Nash product $\pi(A_i)$. We can express this by saying that Zeuthen's Principle establishes a dominance-like relation between any offer A_i corresponding to a higher risk limit r_i [or a higher Nash product $\pi(A_i)$] and any offer A_j corresponding to a lower risk limit r_j [or a lower Nash product $\pi(A_j)$]. We will call this dominance-like relation *risk-*

dominance, as distinguished from the payoff-dominance relations discussed in Chapter 5.

More formally let $u^1 = (u_1{}^1, u_2{}^1) = U(A_1)$ and $u^2 = (u_1{}^2, u_2{}^2) = U(A_2)$ be the payoff vectors associated with player 1's last offer A_1 and with player 2's last offer A_2, respectively. In view of (8.2) this means that

$$u_1{}^1 \geq u_1{}^2 \geq c_1 \quad \text{and} \quad u_2{}^2 \geq u_2{}^1 \geq c_2 \tag{8.21}$$

where $c_1 = U_1(C)$ and $c_2 = U_2(C)$ are the two players' conflict payoffs.

We will say that u^i $(i = 1, 2)$ *weakly risk-dominates* u^j if

$$r_i = \frac{u_i{}^i - u_i{}^j}{u_i{}^i - c_i} \geq \frac{u_j{}^j - u_j{}^i}{u_j{}^j - c_j} = r_j \tag{8.22}$$

or equivalently if

$$\pi(u^i) = (u_i{}^i - c_i) \cdot (u_j{}^i - c_j) \geq (u_i{}^j - c_i) \cdot (u_j{}^j - c_j) = \pi(u^j) \tag{8.23}$$

We say that u^i *strongly risk-dominates* u^j if the $\geq$ signs in (8.22) and (8.23) can be replaced by $>$ signs.

We also introduce the concept of risk-equivalence. We will say that u^i and u^j are *risk-equivalent* if they mutually risk-dominate each other in a weak sense, i.e., if $r_i = r_j$ and $\pi(u^i) = \pi(u^j)$. In this case, as you will recall, Zeuthen's Principle requires *both* players to make concessions.

It is convenient to extend the concept of risk-dominance also to cases in which Condition (8.21) is not satisfied. First of all we can replace (8.21) by the weaker condition

$$u_1{}^1 \geq c_1 \quad u_1{}^2 \geq c_1 \quad u_2{}^1 \geq c_2 \quad u_2{}^2 \geq c_2 \tag{8.24}$$

We can say that u^i risk-dominates u^j if Conditions (8.23) and (8.24) are satisfied. This means that we no longer require that one player should prefer one payoff vector under consideration while the other player should prefer the other. Our new definition covers the case where *both* players prefer (say) u^i to u^j. In this case we will always have $\pi(u^i) \geq \pi(u^j)$, and so u^i will risk-dominate u^j.

Indeed it is sometimes convenient to extend the concept of risk-dominance to cases where even the weaker Condition (8.24) is not satisfied. In particular let $u = (u_1, u_2)$ be a payoff vector such that

$$u_i < c_i \quad \text{for} \quad i = 1, i = 2, \text{ or both} \tag{8.25}$$

Then u can never be accepted by mutual agreement between the players. Therefore we can say that such a payoff vector u will be strongly risk-dominated by *any* other payoff vector $u' = (u_1{}', u_2{}') \neq u$.

Let σ^* and σ^{**} be two joint strategies yielding the payoff vectors $u^* = U(\sigma^*)$ and $u^{**} = U(\sigma^{**})$. We will say that σ^* weakly (or strongly) risk-dominates σ^{**} whenever u^* weakly (or strongly) risk-dominates u^{**}.

Under this terminology Zeuthen's Principle essentially says that, if the payoff vector u^i proposed by player i is risk-dominated, even if only in a weak sense, by the payoff vector u^j proposed by his opponent, then player i must propose some new payoff vector $(u^i)'$ more favorable to the opponent.

On the other hand, Nash's theory essentially says that in any simple bargaining game G there is always one payoff vector $\bar{u} = (\bar{u}_1, \bar{u}_2)$ with the following properties:

1. It *strongly* risk-dominates all other feasible payoff vectors u' in the game.

2. It is itself *not* risk-dominated, even in a *weak* sense, by any other feasible payoff vector u'. Thus $\bar{u}$ is a maximal element under risk-dominance relations.

This payoff vector $\bar{u}$ is the Nash solution.

8.10   Formal definition of the solution

Formally, we define the *payoff solution* of a simple bargaining game G as the Nash solution $\bar{u} = (\bar{u}_1, \bar{u}_2)$. We define the *strategy solution* $\bar{\Sigma}$ as the set of all joint strategies $\bar{\sigma}$ that will yield the Nash solution $\bar{u}$ so that $U(\bar{\sigma}) = \bar{u}$.

9

General two-person cooperative games

THE PROBLEM OF OPTIMAL THREATS

9.1 Games with and without binding threats

In a general cooperative game the rules of the game do not uniquely determine the conflict payoffs c_1 and c_2 the players would receive in a conflict situation, if they could not agree on their final payoffs $\bar{u}_1$ and $\bar{u}_2$. Instead these disagreement payoffs will depend on the *conflict strategies* θ_1 and θ_2 which players 1 and 2 would actually use against each other in case of a conflict. Thus we can write

$$c_1 = U_1(\theta_1, \theta_2) \qquad c_2 = U_2(\theta_1, \theta_2) \tag{9.1}$$

where U_1 and U_2 are the two players' payoff functions.

We can distinguish two cases: games with and games without *binding threats*. In the former the players will announce their conflict strategies θ_1 and θ_2 at the beginning of the game; once these have been announced the players are *bound* to implement them if they later fail to reach agreement on their final payoffs. Accordingly θ_1 and θ_2 can now be called *threat strategies*. Since θ_1 and θ_2 would have to be fully carried out in a conflict situation, they will have the nature of fully credible threats rather than mere *bluffs*.

In general each player can implement a threat, i.e., can damage his opponent, only at a certain *cost* to himself. In a conflict situation each player would prefer to save the cost of implementing a threat if he could (unless implementation of this threat would yield some direct benefit for him). Therefore it is important to know whether the rules of the game leave him a free choice in this matter.

In a cooperative game it is a natural assumption that the players can make *binding threats* which would have to be carried out if a conflict situation arose, for this is simply an extension of the general assumption that all agreements and promises made by the players have binding force – the defining characteristic of cooperative games. We will, however, also briefly consider the alternative case, in which the players *cannot* make binding threats.

In a cooperative game *with* binding threats the players have to choose their conflict strategies (threat strategies) θ_1 and θ_2 at the beginning of the game. These conflict strategies will then define their disagreement payoffs c_1 and c_2 in accordance with Equation (9.1). These disagreement payoffs c_1 and c_2 will in turn determine the final payoffs $\bar{u}_1$ and $\bar{u}_2$ in accordance with Equation (8.1) of Section 8.3, which defines the Nash solution. Since both players are assumed to consider each other as rational individuals, they will have full confidence in being able to reach agreement. Hence they will expect that their final payoffs will be the payoffs $\bar{u}_1$ and $\bar{u}_2$ resulting from such an agreement, which may be called agreement payoffs, rather than the disagreement payoffs c_1 and c_2 that they would obtain in a hypothetical conflict situation. Consequently, in choosing his threat strategy θ_i, each player i will try to maximize his agreement payoff $\bar{u}_i$ instead of trying to maximize his disagreement payoff c_i.

We can express the same conclusion also by saying that in a game G *with* binding threats the threat subgame G^* (in which the two players choose their threat strategies θ_1 and θ_2 and thereby determine their disagreement payoffs c_1 and c_2) is a *dependent game,* subordinated to the bargaining subgame G^{**} in which the players agree on their final payoffs (agreement payoffs) $\bar{u}_1$ and $\bar{u}_2$.

In contrast, in a cooperative game *without* binding threats, if the negotiations broke down and a conflict situation arose, the players' freedom of action would not be restricted by any threats possibly made at earlier stages. Yet once a conflict situation arose, the agreement payoffs $\bar{u}_1$ and $\bar{u}_2$ would have been irretrievably lost to the players. Hence they would concentrate on what still could be saved, and each of them would choose his conflict strategy θ_i in order to maximize his disagreement payoff c_i.

Thus in a game G *without* binding threats the conflict subgame G^* (in which the players choose their conflict strategies θ_1 and θ_2, and thereby determine their disagreement payoffs c_1 and c_2) will be an *independent game,* not subordinated to the bargaining subgame G^{**} (in which the players agree on $\bar{u}_1$ and $\bar{u}_2$). Consequently G^* will have the nature of an independent strictly noncooperative game between the two players, where each player i tries to maximize his payoff c_i from this game G^*. (The solution of G^* will be determined by our general theory of noncooperative games, to be discussed in Chapter 14.) Although rational players will again expect to reach an agreement and will hope that they will never have to actually play the conflict subgame G^*, their disagreement payoffs in the bargaining game G^{**} will be the payoffs c_1 and c_2 determined by the solution of the independent noncooperative game G^*. This will be so because the players will know that, in case they did fail to reach an agreement in G^{**}, they would have to play the conflict game G^* and would obtain the payoffs c_1 and c_2 resulting from G^*.

In what follows we will concentrate on cooperative games *with* binding threats. In an abstract model we can assume that in a conflict situation implementation of the players' mutual threats would be enforced by the same enforcement agency which also enforces agreements concluded by the players. In the real world, of course, the implementation of threats is usually enforced by fear of losing face and of decreasing the credibility of one's threats in the future in similar situations.

Depending on whether we use Nash's one-bid model or Zeuthen's many-bids model for analyzing the bargaining subgame G^{**} of the cooperative game, we obtain two different but equivalent models. Under Nash's model the two players announce their threat *strategies* θ_1 and θ_2 at the beginning of the game. (It can be shown that it does not matter whether the two players have to choose their threat strategies *independently* of each other, or whether one of them has to announce his threat strategy *first* while the other is allowed to choose his own threat strategy *after* learning his opponent's choice.) When both threat strategies have been announced, each player i decides on his *demand,* specifying the final payoff $\bar{u}_i$ on which he insists. Now it is essential that each player should choose his own demand *independently,* without knowing his opponent's demand. (Otherwise the player specifying his demand *first* would have a great advantage: Once he had committed himself to any agreement point within the negotiation set, the other player could not rationally refuse to accept his terms. This would transform the *bargaining game* into an *ultimatum game* – see Section 9.8.) For instance, we may assume that each player has to put his demand into a sealed envelope without being able to observe the other player's demand.

Finally the two players' demands are compared. If they are *compatible,* that is, if the payoff vector $(\bar{u}_1, \bar{u}_2)$ is a point within the payoff space P, then each player i obtains the payoff $\bar{u}_i$ for which he has asked. On the other hand, if the two demands are *incompatible,* then the players are forced to implement their threat strategies θ_1 and θ_2 against each other, which will result in their receiving the disagreement payoffs c_1 and c_2.

If we want instead to use Zeuthen's model (now supplemented with Nash's concept of threat strategies), then again we have to assume that the two players will announce their threat strategies θ_1 and θ_2 at the beginning of the game. But this will now be followed by a sequence of offers and counteroffers by the two players. This process will continue until an agreement is reached or alternatively until at one stage *both* players refuse to make further concessions, giving rise to a conflict situation in which both players will have to carry out their threats and will receive the disagreement payoffs c_1 and c_2 as a result.

Thus we use the same concept of threat strategies in both models. The only difference is in the nature of the assumed bargaining process. Since Nash's and Zeuthen's models for a bargaining process are equivalent, this equivalence is, of course, preserved if we enlarge both models by adding a threat game of the same nature in both cases.

9.2 Mutually optimal threat strategies

We have seen that, given the two players' disagreement payoffs c_1 and c_2, the Nash solution $\bar{u} = (\bar{u}_1, \bar{u}_2)$ is defined by maximization of the product $\pi(u)$ subject to certain constraints [Equation (8.1)]. We will first derive an alternative but equivalent definition which is mathematically more convenient for our purposes.

Let $H(u_1, u_2) = 0$ be the equation of the upper right boundary of the payoff space P. Let H_1 and H_2 be the first derivatives of the function H with respect to u_1 and u_2.[1] Using Lagrange's multiplier method we find that the constrained maximum problem stated in Equation (8.1) is equivalent to the following three simultaneous equations:

$$H(\bar{u}_1, \bar{u}_2) = 0 \tag{9.2}$$

$$a_1 \cdot (\bar{u}_1 - c_1) = a_2 \cdot (\bar{u}_2 - c_2) \tag{9.3}$$

$$a_i = H_i(\bar{u}_1, \bar{u}_2) \quad i = 1, 2 \tag{9.4}$$

In view of the convexity of the payoff space P, the second-order conditions of maximization are always satisfied. Therefore Equations (9.2) through (9.4) give a sufficient and necessary condition for the Nash solution.

Since on the upper right boundary H the payoffs u_1 and u_2 are *strictly decreasing* functions of each other, the derivatives H_1 and H_2 must always have the *same* signs. Without loss of generality we can assume that both are nonnegative. Hence

$$a_i = H_i \geqq 0 \quad i = 1, 2 \tag{9.5}$$

where the sign of equality can possibly apply only at the end points of the upper right boundary H.

Given his opponent's threat strategy $\theta_j = \theta_j^o$, each player i will choose his own threat strategy $\theta_i = \theta_i^o$ in order to maximize his own final payoff $\bar{u}_i$, subject to Equations (9.2) through (9.4), as well as (9.1). Any threat strategy θ_i^o maximizing $\bar{u}_i$ subject to these constraints will be called *optimal* against θ_j^o. If θ_1^o and θ_2^o *both* satisfy this requirement in relation to each other, then they are called *mutually optimal*. Clearly any pair of mutually optimal threat strategies θ_1^o and θ_2^o will represent an *equilibrium point* in the threat game G^* between the two players (if we regard G^* as a dependent game subordinated to the bargaining game G^{**} – see Section 9.1).

Nash has shown that in any cooperative game with binding threats such a pair of mutually optimal threat strategies *always exists*. The proof is based on Kakutani's [1941] fixed-point theorem [Nash, 1953]. There may possibly exist several pairs of mutually optimal threat strategies, but *all* of them yield the same *unique* solution $\bar{u} = (\bar{u}_1, \bar{u}_2)$ for the game. Moreover, all pairs of mutually optimal threat strategies are *interchangeable:* If θ_1 and θ_2 are mutually optimal, and if the same is true for θ_1^o and θ_2^o, then θ_1 and θ_2^o as well as θ_1^o and θ_2 will again form mutually optimal pairs of threat strategies.

Mathematically these convenient properties of mutually optimal threat strategies are attributable to the fact that a threat game G^* is in many ways similar to a two-person zero-sum game. This is so because the solution $\bar{u} = (\bar{u}_1, \bar{u}_2)$ is always a point on the upper right boundary H. Hence $\bar{u}_1$ and $\bar{u}_2$ are decreasing functions of each other. Consequently, maximizing $\bar{u}_1$ is equivalent to maximizing $y_1 = \bar{u}_1 - \bar{u}_2$; whereas maximizing $\bar{u}_2$ is equivalent to maximizing $y_2 = \bar{u}_2 - \bar{u}_1$. Therefore we can assume that player 1 tries to maximize y_1, while player 2 tries to maximize y_2. Yet $y_1 + y_2 = 0$, which makes the game a zero-sum game.[2]

Intuitively an optimal threat strategy in Nash's sense is the threat strategy maximizing the relative strength of one's bargaining position against the opponent. It represents the best possible compromise between trying to *maximize* the costs of a conflict to the *opponent* and trying to *minimize* the costs of a conflict to *oneself*. (Or equivalently it is the best possible compromise between trying to *minimize* the opponent's conflict payoff c_j and trying to *maximize* one's *own* conflict payoff c_i.)

We now propose to derive sufficient and necessary mathematical conditions for mutually optimal threat strategies and by this means to find a mathematical definition of the Nash solution for the two-person general cooperative game (with binding threats).

We first prove the following lemma.

Lemma 1. Let

$$c = (c_1, c_2) = U(\theta_1{}^o, \theta_2{}^o) \tag{9.6}$$

and let $\bar{u} = (\bar{u}_1, \bar{u}_2)$ be the Nash solution corresponding to this disagreement payoff vector c so that $\bar{u}$ and c satisfy Equations (9.2) through (9.4).

Then, in order that threat strategy $\theta_i{}^o (i = 1, 2)$ of player i be *optimal* against threat strategy $\theta_j{}^o (j = 1, 2$ and $\neq i)$ of player j, it is both necessary and sufficient that

$$a_i c_i - a_j c_j = \max_{\theta_i \in \Sigma_i} \ [a_i U_i(\theta_i, \theta_j{}^o) - a_j U_j(\theta_i, \theta_j{}^o)] \tag{9.7}$$

$$a_i, a_j = \text{const.}$$

where Σ_i is the set of all strategies available to player i in the game.

Proof. Take any point $u^* = (u_1{}^*, u_2{}^*)$ on the upper right boundary H of the payoff space P. Consider the set $C(u^*)$ of all possible disagreement payoffs $c^* = (c_1{}^*, c_2{}^*)$ such that would make this point u^* the Nash solution of the game. By (9.3) and (9.4) the set $C(u^*)$ is given by the intersection of the payoff space P and the straight line $L(u^*)$ whose points c^* satisfy the linear equation

$$H_i(u^*) \cdot c_i{}^* = H_j(u^*) \cdot c_j{}^* = H_i(u^*) \cdot u_i{}^* - H_j(u^*) \cdot u_j{}^* = \text{const.} \tag{9.8}$$

Now any point c^* will define a unique Nash solution u^*. Therefore any point c^* will belong to one and only one set $C(u^*)$. Consequently the family of all sets $C(u^*), u^* \in H$, represents a partitioning of the payoff space P into these sets $C(u^*)$ as equivalence classes. Clearly the mapping C of all points u^* of H into the family of all sets $C(u^*)$ is continuous, and so is the inverse mapping C^{-1}.

Comparing two possible disagreement payoff vectors $c = (c_1, c_2)$ and $c^* = (c_1{}^*, c_2{}^*)$, we call c^* *more favorable* than c for player i if

$$c \in C(u) \quad c^* \in C(u^*) \tag{9.9}$$

and

$$u_i{}^* > u_i \tag{9.10}$$

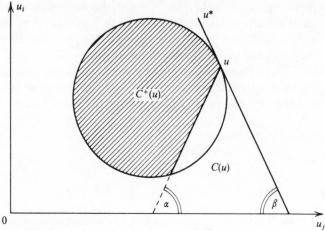

Figure 9.1

For a graphic interpretation refer to Figure 9.1. Here the line $C(u)$ and the tangent of the boundary curve H at point u must have equal but opposite slopes, in view of Equations (9.3) and (9.4). Hence $\alpha = \beta$.

Let $C^+(u)$ be the set of all points c^* in the payoff space P such that

$$H_i(u) \cdot c_i{}^* - H_j(u) \cdot c_j{}^* > H_i(u) \cdot u_i - H_j(u) \cdot u_j \qquad (9.11)$$

or equivalently such that

$$a_i c_i{}^* - a_j c_j{}^* > a_i u_i - a_j u_j = a_i c_i - a_j c_j \qquad (9.12)$$

where the equivalence of (9.11) and (9.12) follows from (9.3) and (9.4). We will now show that all points c^* of $C^+(u)$ are for player i *more favorable* disagreement payoff vectors than are the points c of $C(u)$.

Choose any point $u^* = (u_1{}^*, u_2{}^*)$ on the upper right boundary H such that

$$u_i{}^* > u_i \qquad (9.13)$$

Since $a_i \geqq 0$ we can write

$$a_i u_i{}^* \geqq a_i u_i \qquad (9.14)$$

By the convexity of P we have

$$a_i u_i + a_j u_j \geqq a_i u_i{}^* + a_j u_j{}^* \qquad (9.15)$$

By (9.14) and (9.15),

$$a_i u_i{}^* - a_j u_j{}^* \geqq a_i u_i - a_j u_j \qquad (9.16)$$

Hence the point u^* must lie either in the set $C^+(u)$ or in the set $C(u)$. But it cannot lie in $C(u)$, because then, in view of (9.8), we would have $u^* = u$, which would be inconsistent with (9.13). Consequently

$$u^* \in C^+(u) \tag{9.17}$$

Now for player i the point $c^* = u^*$ as disagreement payoff vector would be clearly more favorable than any point c in $C(u)$, because obviously $u^* \in C(u^*)$; and, by (9.13), $u_i^* > u_i$. But, in view of the continuity of the mapping C^{-1}, by the Bolzano-Weierstrass theorem, if *any* point u^* of $C^+(u)$ is more favorable for player i than are the points c of $C(u)$, then *all* points c^* of $C^+(u)$ must be more favorable than are the points c of $C(u)$.[3]

Hence if player i had any threat strategy θ_i^* yielding a disagreement payoff vector $c^* = U(\theta_i^*, \theta_j^o)$ belonging to $C^+(u)$, i.e., satisfying the inequality $a_i c_i^* - a_j c_j^* > a_i c_i - a_j c_j$, then θ_i^o could not be optimal against θ_j^o. Thus θ_i^o can be optimal against θ_j^o only if it *maximizes* the expression in square brackets on the right side of (9.7). This proves the lemma.

Lemma 1 implies:

Lemma 2. In order that θ_i^o and θ_j^o be *mutually* optimal against each other, it is both necessary and sufficient that the point c should satisfy Equations (9.2), (9.3), (9.4), (9.6), and (9.7), as well as the additional equation

$$a_i c_i - a_j c_j = \min_{\theta_j \in \Sigma_j} [a_i U_i(\theta_i^o, \theta_j) - a_j U_j(\theta_i^o, \theta_j)] \tag{9.18}$$

$$a_i, a_j = \text{const.}$$

where Σ_j is the set of all strategies available to player j.

Lemma 2 follows from the fact that *minimizing* the expression $(a_i c_i - a_j c_j)$ is equivalent to *maximizing* the expression $(a_j c_j - a_i c_i)$. Since Nash has shown that a pair of mutually optimal threat strategies always *exists*, there is always a pair of strategies θ_i^o and θ_j^o satisfying Equations (9.2), (9.3), (9.4), (9.6), (9.7) and (9.18). But if such a pair exists, then it must have *maximin* and *minimax* properties. This gives:

Lemma 3. Suppose that strategies θ_i^o and θ_j^o are *mutually optimal* threat strategies and consequently satisfy Conditions (9.2), (9.3), (9.4), (9.6), (9.7), and (9.18). Then

$$a_i c_i - a_j c_j = a_i U_i(\theta_i^o, \theta_j^o) - a_j U_j(\theta_i^o, \theta_j^o) \tag{9.19}$$

$$= \max_{\theta_i \in \Sigma_i} \min_{\theta_j \in \Sigma_j} [a_i U_i(\theta_i, \theta_j) - a_j U_j(\theta_i, \theta_j)]$$

$$a_i, a_j = \text{const.}$$

The lemma remains true even if we reverse the order of the *max* and the *min* operators (i.e., if we use the *minimax* operator instead of the *maximin* operator).

Proof. The proof is based on the fact that Equations (9.7) and (9.18) entail Equation (9.19). Let

$$F(\theta_i, \theta_j) = a_i U_i(\theta_i, \theta_j) - a_j U_j(\theta_i, \theta_j) \tag{9.20}$$

Then for *any* $\theta_i \in \Sigma_i$

$$\min_{\theta_j} F(\theta_i, \theta_j) \le F(\theta_i, \theta_j^{o}) \le \max_{\theta_i} F(\theta_i, \theta_j^{o}) \tag{9.21}$$

$$= F(\theta_i^{o}, \theta_j^{o}) = \min_{\theta_j} F(\theta_i^{o}, \theta_j)$$

where the last two equalities follow from (9.7) and (9.18). Consequently

$$F(\theta_i^{o}, \theta_j^{o}) = \max_{\theta_i} \min_{\theta_j} F(\theta_i, \theta_j) \tag{9.22}$$

as desired. We can prove by similar argument that

$$F(\theta_i^{o}, \theta_j^{o}) = \min_{\theta_j} \max_{\theta_i} F(\theta_i, \theta_j) \tag{9.23}$$

This completes the proof of the lemma.

Lemmas 2 and 3 entail the following theorem:

Theorem 9.1. In a general two-person cooperative game with binding threats, the Nash solution $\bar{u} = (\bar{u}_1, \bar{u}_2)$ can be defined by the following conditions which are both necessary and sufficient:

$$H(\bar{u}_1, \bar{u}_2) = 0 \tag{A}$$

$$a_i = H_i(\bar{u}_1, \bar{u}_2) = H_i(\bar{u}) \quad i = 1, 2 \tag{B}$$

$$a_1 \cdot (\bar{u}_1 - c_1) = a_2 \cdot (\bar{u}_2 - c_2) \tag{C}$$

$$c_i = U_i(\theta_1^{o}, \theta_2^{o}) \quad i = 1, 2 \tag{D}$$

$$a_1 c_1 - a_2 c_2 = a_1 U_1(\theta_1^{o}, \theta_2^{o}) - a_2 U_2(\theta_1^{o}, \theta_2^{o}) \tag{E}$$

$$= \max_{\theta_1 \in \Sigma_1, \theta_2 \in \Sigma_2} \min [a_1 U_1(\theta_1, \theta_2) - a_2 U_2(\theta_1, \theta_2)]$$

$$a_1, a_2 = \text{const.}$$

or equivalently

$$= \min_{\theta_2 \in \Sigma_2, \theta_1 \in \Sigma_1} \max [a_1 U_1(\theta_1, \theta_2) - a_2 U_2(\theta_1, \theta_2)]$$

$$a_1, a_2 = \text{const.}$$

Instead of Equation (E) we can also take the equivalent condition

$$a_1 c_1 - a_2 c_2 = a_1 U_1(\theta_1{}^o, \theta_2{}^o) - a_2 U_2(\theta_1{}^o, \theta_2{}^o) \tag{E*}$$

$$= \max_{\theta_1 \in \Sigma_1} [a_1 U_1(\theta_1, \theta_2{}^o) - a_2 U_2(\theta_1, \theta_2{}^o)]$$

$$a_1, a_2 = \text{const.}$$

$$= \min_{\theta_2 \in \Sigma_2} [a_1 U_1(\theta_1{}^o, \theta_2) - a_2 U_2(\theta_1{}^o, \theta_2)]$$

$$a_1, a_2 = \text{const.}$$

By Lemma 3, Condition (E*) entails (E), and it is easy to verify that the converse is also true. Therefore any pair of strategies $\theta_1{}^o$ and $\theta_2{}^o$ satisfying (E) or (E*) must have the nature of *mutually optimal* threat strategies.

The quantities $a_1 = H_1(\overline{u})$ and $a_2 = H_2(\overline{u})$ will be called the *weights* of the game. We are always free to multiply the function H by any positive constant, because this will leave Equation (A) and Inequality (9.5) unaffected. Therefore the weights a_1 and a_2 are indeterminate up to a positive proportionality factor. To make them fully determinate, one can normalize them so that $a_1 + a_2 = 1$. This can be achieved by replacing Equation (B) by the equation

$$a_i = \frac{H_i(\overline{u})}{H_1(\overline{u}) + H_2(\overline{u})} \qquad i = 1, 2 \tag{B*}$$

This is always legitimate, since H_1 and H_2 can never be *both* zero.

Conditions (D) and (E) can be omitted in the special case of *simple bargaining games*, where c_1 and c_2 (or equivalently $\theta_1{}^o$ and $\theta_2{}^o$) are *constants* directly specified by the rules of the game.

Condition (B) assumes the existence of the derivatives H_1 and H_2 at the solution point $\overline{u}$. To obtain more general conditions which can be used even if $\overline{u}$ happens to be a corner point of the upper right boundary H, we state the following theorem:

Theorem 9.2. We obtain an alternative set of sufficient and necessary conditions for the Nash solution if we replace Conditions (A) and (B) by the new conditions

$$a_i \geqq 0 \qquad i = 1, 2 \tag{AA}$$

$$a_1 \overline{u}_1 + a_2 \overline{u}_2 = \max_{(u_1, u_2) \in P} (a_1 u_1 + a_2 u_2) \tag{BB}$$

$$a_1, a_2 = \text{const.}$$

retaining Conditions (C), (D), and (E) unchanged.

Obviously these conditions do not assume the existence of H_1 and H_2.

If we want to normalize the weights a_1 and a_2, then we can now add the further requirement

$$a_1 + a_2 = 1 \tag{F}$$

Proof. In case the derivatives H_1 and H_2 do exist at the point $\bar{u}$, the equivalence of Conditions (AA) and (BB) to Conditions (A) and (B) follows from the convexity of the payoff space P. In the case where H_1 and H_2 do not exist at $\bar{u}$, we can extend the theorem by using the approximation method outlined in Footnote 1.

In cases where the payoff functions U_1 and U_2 of the two players are sufficiently simple we can compute the solution by directly solving the simultaneous equations of Theorems 9.1 and 9.2. In general, however, their solution requires an iterative procedure. Note that our simultaneous equations form a nonrecursive (i.e., circular) system: To compute $c_1, c_2, \bar{u}_1$, and $\bar{u}_2$ we would have to know a_1 and a_2; on the other hand, a_1 and a_2 themselves are in general functions of $\bar{u}_1$ and $\bar{u}_2$ (except when the upper right boundary H is a straight line). But this nonrecursiveness is not objectionable, because we know that our simultaneous equations always *have* a solution, and indeed this solution is even known to be *unique*, at least as far as the vector $\bar{u} = (\bar{u}_1, \bar{u}_2)$ is concerned. (This follows from Nash's existence and uniqueness theorems for $\bar{u}$.)

9.3 An alternative characterization of mutually optimal threat strategies

We will now propose an alternative mathematical characterization of optimal threat strategies, which will lead to an alternative definition of the Nash solution.

Lemma 1. Let $u = (u_1, u_2)$ be the Nash solution, and suppose that u is *not* a corner point of the upper right boundary H of the payoff space P. Then, in order that a given strategy $\theta_i^{\,o}$ of player i be an optimal threat strategy against some threat strategy $\theta_j^{\,o}$ of player j, it is both necessary and sufficient that $\theta_i^{\,o}$ should satisfy the condition

$$\frac{u_j - U_j(\theta_i^{\,o}, \theta_j^{\,o})}{u_i - U_i(\theta_i^{\,o}, \theta_j^{\,o})} = \max_{\theta_i \in \Sigma_i} \left[\frac{u_j - U_j(\theta_i, \theta_j^{\,o})}{u_i - U_i(\theta_i, \theta_j^{\,o})} \right] \qquad (9.24)$$

Proof. (See Figure 9.1.) Let $c = (c_i, c_j)$ be a point of line $C(u)$, and let $c^* = (c_i^*, c_j^*)$ be a point in the set $C^+(u)$. Then c will satisfy the equation of line $C(u)$ so that

$$a_i c_i - a_j c_j = a_i u_i - a_j u_j \qquad (9.25)$$

while c^* will satisfy the inequality

$$a_i c_i^* - a_j c_j^* > a_i u_i - a_j u_j \qquad (9.26)$$

Hence we can write

$$\frac{u_j - c_j}{u_i - c_i} = \frac{a_i}{a_j} < \frac{u_j - c_j^*}{u_i - c_i^*} \qquad (9.27)$$

or simply

$$\frac{u_j - c_j}{u_i - c_i} < \frac{u_j - c_j^*}{u_i - c_i^*} \tag{9.28}$$

Now from player i's point of view any point c^* in set $C^+(u)$ would be a *more favorable* conflict point than any point c on line $C(u)$ would be, in the sense that the former would lead to a more favorable Nash solution than the latter would. Consequently (9.28) is a sufficient and necessary condition to ensure that, from i's point of view, c^* will be a more favorable conflict point than c.

Let

$$c = U(\theta_i^{\,o}, \theta_j^{\,o}) \tag{9.29}$$

The strategy $\theta_i^{\,o}$ will be optimal against $\theta_j^{\,o}$ if and only if we cannot find an alternative threat strategy $\theta_i \neq \theta_i^{\,o}$ yielding a *more favorable* conflict point

$$c^* = U(\theta_i, \theta_j^{\,o}) \tag{9.30}$$

from i's point of view. But this means that $\theta_i^{\,o}$ will be optimal against $\theta_j^{\,o}$ if and only if no alternative threat strategy θ_i would yield a conflict point c^* satisfying (92.8) and (9.29). However, this is equivalent to Condition (9.24). This proves the lemma.

Lemma 2. Under the assumptions of Lemma 1, two threat strategies $\theta_i^{\,o}$ and $\theta_j^{\,o}$ will be *mutually* optimal if and only if

$$\frac{u_j - U_j(\theta_i^{\,o}, \theta_j^{\,o})}{u_i - U_i(\theta_i^{\,o}, \theta_j^{\,o})} = \max_{\theta_i \in \Sigma_i} \min_{\theta_j \in \Sigma_j} \left[\frac{u_j - U_j(\theta_i, \theta_j)}{u_i - U_i(\theta_i, \theta_j)} \right] \tag{9.31}$$

where we are free to interchange the order of the max and min operators.

Proof. By Lemma 1, $\theta_i^{\,o}$ will be optimal against $\theta_j^{\,o}$ if and only if it satisfies Condition (9.24). Again, by Lemma 1, $\theta_j^{\,o}$ will be optimal against $\theta_i^{\,o}$ if and only if

$$\frac{u_j - U_j(\theta_i^{\,o}, \theta_j^{\,o})}{u_i - U_i(\theta_i^{\,o}, \theta_j^{\,o})} = \min_{\theta_j \in \Sigma_j} \left[\frac{u_j - U_j(\theta_i^{\,o}, \theta_j)}{u_i - U_i(\theta_i^{\,o}, \theta_j)} \right] \tag{9.32}$$

But Equations (9.24) and (9.32) imply Equation (9.31), as desired.

Lemma 3. If the Nash solution $u = (u_1, u_2)$ is a corner point of the upper right boundary H, then Equation (9.31) will still remain a sufficient condition for mutual optimality (though in general it will no longer be a necessary condition).

Proof. The sufficiency of Condition (9.31) can be established by the approximation method outlined in Footnote 1. However, Condition (9.31) will no longer be necessary, because the left side of (9.31) will take different values for different pairs of mutually optimal threat strategies $\theta_1^{\,o}$ and $\theta_2^{\,o}$, corresponding to the different slopes of the various supporting lines L to the payoff space P at the corner point u.

Theorem 9.3. An alternative mathematical definition of the Nash solution $\bar{u} = (\bar{u}_1, \bar{u}_2)$ is as follows:

$$(\bar{u}_1 - c_1) \cdot (\bar{u}_2 - c_2) = \max_{\substack{(u_1, u_2) \in P \\ u_1 \geq c_1 \\ u_2 \geq c_2 \\ c_1, c_2 = \text{const.}}} (u_1 - c_1) \cdot (u_2 - c_2) \tag{α}$$

$$c_i = U_i(\theta_1{}^o, \theta_2{}^o) \quad i = 1, 2 \tag{β}$$

$$\frac{\bar{u}_2 - c_2}{\bar{u}_1 - c_1} = \frac{\bar{u}_2 - U_2(\theta_1{}^o, \theta_2{}^o)}{\bar{u}_1 - U_1(\theta_1{}^o, \theta_2{}^o)} \tag{γ}$$

$$= \max_{\theta_1 \in \Sigma_1} \min_{\theta_2 \in \Sigma_2} \left[\frac{\bar{u}_2 - U_2(\theta_1, \theta_2)}{\bar{u}_1 - U_1(\theta_1, \theta_2)} \right]$$

$$= \min_{\theta_2 \in \Sigma_2} \max_{\theta_1 \in \Sigma_1} \left[\frac{\bar{u}_2 - U_2(\theta_1, \theta_2)}{\bar{u}_1 - U_1(\theta_1, \theta_2)} \right]$$

Proof. Condition (α) is a restatement of Theorem 8.1. Conditions (β) and (γ) follow from Lemmas 2 and 3. It makes no difference that Condition (γ) is in general only a sufficient condition for mutual optimality without being a necessary condition. This means only that by solving Equation (γ) we may not obtain *all* pairs of mutually optimal threat strategies when $\bar{u}$ is a corner point. But to compute $\bar{u}$, all we need is to find *one* pair of mutually optimal threat strategies, and this can be done by solving Equation (γ) together with Equations (α) and (β).

Of course, Conditions (α), (β), and (γ) in general form a nonrecursive system. Conditions (α) and (β) enable one to compute $\bar{u}$ if $\theta_1{}^o$ and $\theta_2{}^o$ are given, whereas Condition (γ) enables one to compute $\theta_1{}^o$ and $\theta_2{}^o$ if $\bar{u}$ is given. This means that in general the three equations must be solved by an iterative procedure.

Equations (α) and (γ) involve the same quantities $v_1 = \bar{u}_1 - c_1$ and $v_2 = \bar{u}_2 - c_2$. But in Equation (α) c_1 and c_2 are regarded as given. Therefore it is natural to interpret v_1 and v_2 as the two players' *net payoffs*, i.e., as the amounts that they will obtain in excess of their conflict payoffs c_1 and c_2, if they can reach an agreement.

In contrast, in Equation (γ) the quantities $\bar{u}_1$ and $\bar{u}_2$ are regarded as given. Therefore it is natural to interpret v_1 and v_2, in this case, as the two players' *conflict costs*, i.e., as the amounts they would lose in a conflict situation compared with what they would obtain in an agreement situation.

Thus Equation (α) may be interpreted as saying that agreement will be reached at the point where the product of the two players' net payoffs is maximized. On the other hand, Equation (γ) and in particular Equation (9.31), which is equivalent to

Equation (γ), may be interpreted as saying that each player i must choose a threat strategy that will maximize the ratio of the *other* player's conflict cost $v_j = \bar{u}_j - c_j$ to his *own* conflict cost $v_i = \bar{u}_i - c_i$.

In other words, suppose that player i is considering whether or not he should switch from one threat strategy θ_i to another threat strategy $\theta_i{}'$. Equation (9.31) says that such a switch will be in player i's interest, if it will increase the conflict cost v_j of his opponent in a *higher proportion* than it will increase his own conflict cost v_i. The same will be true if such a switch from θ_i to $\theta_i{}'$ will decrease player i's own conflict cost v_i in a *higher proportion* than it will decrease the opponent's conflict cost v_j.

Thus in general the relevant comparison is not between *absolute* increases or decreases in the two players' conflict costs; rather it is between *proportional* increases or decreases in their conflict costs.

9.4 Conclusion

To conclude, the Nash-Zeuthen solution for the two-person general cooperative game with binding threats predicts that each player i will achieve a higher final payoff $\bar{u}_i$:

1. The greater his own willingness, and the lesser his opponent's willingness, to *risk* a conflict in order to obtain better terms, as shown by the two players' cardinal utility functions. (This can be best seen by considering Zeuthen's model of the bargaining process.[4])

2. The easier it is to *transfer* utility from the other player to player i, and the harder it is to transfer it the other way around. (If we increase the marginal rate of utility transfer $-du_j/du_i = a_j/a_i$ at the solution point $\bar{u}$ of the game, this will shift the solution point in favor of player i, as can be seen from Condition (C) of Theorem 9.1.)

3. The greater *damage* that player i could cause to his opponent in a conflict situation at a given *cost* to himself and the lesser damage that the opponent could cause to player i at a given cost to himself.

The solution is based on the concept of mutually optimal threat strategies. Intuitively speaking these represent the best possible compromise between trying to *maximize* the *damage* that one can cause to the opponent in a conflict situation and trying to *minimize* the *cost* of the conflict to oneself.[5]

The Nash-Zeuthen theory of two-person bargaining games (and more generally of two-person cooperative games) has applications to a number of economic, political, and other social situations, such as commercial transactions, collective bargaining on the labor market, other types of bilateral monopoly, duopoly, or duopsony, political power situations involving two persons or two social groups, and so forth. But many important social situations involve bargaining among more than two parties; therefore they have to be analyzed in terms of the theory of n-person cooperative games, to be discussed in Chapters 10 and 11 – or possibly in terms of the theory of noncooperative games, to be discussed in Chapter 14.

COMPOSITE BARGAINING GAMES

9.5 Invariance with respect to commensurate changes in the conflict payoffs

The Nash solution has the following important invariance property. Suppose that in a given game G both players' disagreement payoffs are increased (or decreased) from c_1 and c_2 to

$$c_1' = c_1 + \Delta c_1 \quad \text{and} \quad c_2' = c_2 + \Delta c_2 \qquad (9.33)$$

whereas the upper right boundary H of the payoff space P is left unchanged. Then, by Equation (C) of Theorem 9.1, the resulting new game G' will have the same solution $\bar{u} = (\bar{u}_1, \bar{u}_2)$ as did the original game G if and only if

$$a_1 \cdot \Delta c_1 = a_2 \cdot \Delta c_2 \qquad (9.34)$$

where a_1 and a_2 are the weights defined by Equation (B) of Theorem 9.1. If Δc_1 and Δc_2 satisfy (9.34), then they are called *commensurate* increments (or decrements) in the conflict payoffs. [In this case, by (9.5), Δc_1 and Δc_2 must always have the same sign.]

This property can be used in the analysis of composite bargaining games.

9.6 Solution of an "embedded" bargaining game

Let G be a *composite* bargaining game to be played in two stages. In stage 1 the two players have to agree on some payoff vector $u^* = (u_1^*, u_2^*)$ chosen from a given convex and compact set P^*. If they cannot agree, then they receive the conflict payoffs c_1 and c_2. Thus stage 1 itself is a bargaining game G^* with payoff space P^* and with conflict point c.

In stage 2 the two players have to agree on another payoff vector $u = (u_1, u_2)$ now chosen from a larger convex and compact set P, a superset of P^*. If they cannot agree in stage 2, then they receive the payoffs u_1^* and u_2^* already agreed upon in stage 1. Thus stage 2 is again a bargaining game G^{**} with payoff space $P \supseteq P^*$ and with conflict point u^*.

Let H be the upper right boundary of P, and let H^* be the upper right boundary of P^*.

Though under our assumptions game G is actually played in two stages, it is easy to see that it is strategically equivalent to, and has the same normal form as, a one-stage bargaining game $\bar{G}$ with the same payoff space P and the same disagreement point c. Even if G is played in two stages, the players in the end can achieve any payoff vector u in P if they fully cooperate; if they do not cooperate at all, then they will be confined to the point c. Therefore the Nash solution $\bar{u} = (\bar{u}_1, \bar{u}_2)$ of the two-stage game G is the same as that of the corresponding one-stage game $\bar{G}$ and is accordingly defined by Equations (A) through (C) of Theorem 9.1. This means that, if the players follow our rationality postulates, then in the end (i.e., during stage 2) they must come to adopt the payoff vector $u = \bar{u}$ defined by these equations.

Consequently during stage 1 the players must choose a vector u^* which will lead to adoption of $u = \bar{u}$ as the final payoff vector during stage 2, when this vector u^* will be used as conflict point. That is, the same solution $\bar{u}$ must be obtained by using vector u^* as conflict point during the second stage of our two-stage game G as would be obtained in the corresponding one-stage game $\bar{G}$ with vector c as disagreement point. But by Equation (9.34) these two disagreement points u^* and c will yield the same solution $\bar{u}$ if and only if

$$a_1 \cdot (u_1^* - c_1) = a_2 \cdot (u_2^* - c_2) \tag{9.35}$$

where

$$a_i = H_i(\bar{u}_1, \bar{u}_2) \qquad i = 1, 2 \tag{9.36}$$

On the other hand, efficiency requires that u^* should lie on the upper right boundary H^* so that

$$H^*(u_1^*, u_2^*) = 0 \tag{9.37}$$

Intuitively this argument amounts to saying that in stage 1 of the game a rational player i will not agree to a payoff vector u^* which would *worsen* his relative bargaining position in stage 2 with respect to his final payoff $u_i = \bar{u}_i$. Therefore if *both* players act rationally, then in stage 1 they will adopt a payoff vector u^* which will leave *unchanged* their relative bargaining positions with respect to the final outcome of the game. Consequently in stage 1 they will agree on *commensurate* payoff increments $\Delta u_i^* = u_1^* - c_1$ and $\Delta u_2^* = u_2^* - c_2$, in accordance with (9.34).

Thus if a given bargaining game G^* with payoff space P^* and with disagreement point c is *embedded* as a subgame into a larger composite bargaining game G, then the solution of G^* will be in general different from what it would be if G^* were played as an *independent* game. In the former case the solution u^* of G^* will be defined by Equations (9.35) through (9.37). In the latter case, in view of Equations (A) through (C) of Theorem 9.1, its solution u^* would be defined by the equations

$$a_1^* \cdot (u_1^* - c_1) = a_2^* \cdot (u_2^* - c_2) \tag{9.38}$$

$$a_i^* = H_i^*(u_1^*, u_2^*) \qquad i = 1, 2 \tag{9.39}$$

together with Equation (9.37), which applies equally in both cases. The essential difference is that, if G^* were played as an independent game, then its solution u^* would be defined in terms of the weights a_1^* and a_2^*, determined by the mathematical properties of the payoff space P^* of G^* itself. In contrast, if G^* is played as a subgame of the larger game G, then the solution u^* of G^* will be defined in terms of the weights a_1 and a_2, depending on the mathematical properties of the payoff space P of this larger game G. The reason for this difference is that, if G^*

is played as an independent game, then each player's goal will be to maximize his immediate payoff u_i^* from G^* – whereas if G^* is played as a *dependent* game, then each player's main goal will be to maximize his final payoff $u_i = \bar{u}_i$ from the larger game G rather than to maximize his payoff u_i^* from G^* itself.

Extension of this analysis to bargaining games played in more than two stages is straightforward. This gives:

Theorem 9.4. Let G be a composite bargaining game played in k stages. Let $P^1 \subseteq P^2 \subseteq \cdots \subseteq P^k$, where P^j $(1 \leq j \leq k)$ is the payoff space for stage j, with $P = P^k$ the payoff space for stage k as well as for the whole game. The P^j's are convex and compact sets. Let $H^j(u_1, u_2) = 0$ be the equation of the upper right boundary H^j of P^j with $H^k = H$. In each stage j the two players have to agree on some payoff vector $u^j \in P^j$. We will write $u^k = \bar{u}$. In stage 1 the conflict point is a given prearranged payoff vector c. In each later stage j the disagreement point is the payoff vector $u^{(j-1)}$ agreed upon in the previous stage. For convenience we write $c = u^0$. Then in each stage j the players will agree on a payoff vector u^j such that

$$H^j(u_1{}^j, u_2{}^j) = 0 \qquad j = 1, \ldots, k \tag{9.40}$$

$$a_1 \cdot \Delta u_1{}^j = a_2 \cdot \Delta u_2{}^j \qquad j = 1, \ldots, k \tag{9.41}$$

where

$$\Delta u_i{}^j = u_i{}^j - u_i{}^{(j-1)} \qquad i = 1, 2; j = 1, \ldots, k \tag{9.42}$$

and

$$a_i = H_i(\bar{u}_1, \bar{u}_2) \qquad i = 1, 2; j = 1, \ldots, k \tag{9.43}$$

That is, at each stage j the players will agree on *commensurate* payoff increments $\Delta u_1{}^j$ and $\Delta u_2{}^j$. Instead of (9.41) and (9.42) we can also use the equivalent relationship

$$a_1 \cdot (u_1{}^j - c_1) = a_2 \cdot (u_2{}^j - c_2) \qquad j = 1, \ldots, k \tag{9.44}$$

9.7 Negative embedded bargaining games

Let G^* be a bargaining game with disagreement point c. Suppose that the players agree on some payoff vector u^*. Then we may call the quantities $\Delta u_1^* = u_1^* - c_1$ and $\Delta u_2^* = u_2^* - c_2$ the players' *net* payoffs, since they represent the players' net gains above the payoffs that they would receive in a conflict situation.

We call a bargaining game G^* a *negative* bargaining game if under any possible agreement at least one player i must necessarily receive a negative net payoff Δu_i^* from G^*. This will be the case if the payoff space P^* of G^* fails to contain any point u^* satisfying the two conditions $u_1^* \geq c_1$ and $u_2^* \geq c_2$ at the same time (see Figures 9.2 and 9.3). Geometrically this means that no point of P^* lies as *high* as, and at the same time also as much to the *right* as, the point c itself does. If a negative bargaining game G^* is played as an independent game, then it is quite trivial,

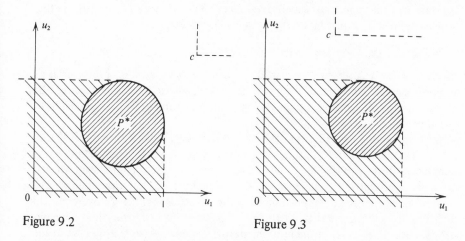

Figure 9.2   Figure 9.3

because neither player will be willing to accept a negative net payoff; therefore the players will always move to the disagreement point c rather than to any point u^* in set P^*.

But the situation is different if a *negative* bargaining game G^* is *embedded* as a preliminary stage into a *positive* bargaining game G, which allows both players to obtain positive net payoffs $\Delta u_1 = u_1 - c_1$ and $\Delta u_2 = u_2 - c_2$ in the end. For instance, suppose that G is played in two stages. In stage 1, corresponding to a negative bargaining game G^*, the players are asked to agree on some payoff vector $u^* \in P^*$. If they do not agree to accept some payoff vector u^* in P^*, then they receive the conflict payoffs c_1 and c_2, and the game ends at this point. But if they do accept some vector u^* in P^* (which means that at least one of them has accepted a *reduction* in his payoff from c_i to some lower level $\cdot u_i^*$), then they are free to play stage 2 of the game. In stage 2 they have to agree on some payoff vector u chosen from a larger set P (a superset of P^*). If they cannot agree on the choice of u, then they receive the payoffs u_1^* and u_2^*, already agreed upon in stage 1.

If we consider this composite bargaining game G as a whole, then its payoff space is again the whole set P, and its disagreement point is c. We assume that P does contain points u such that both $u_1 > c_1$ and $u_2 > c_2$, so that G as a whole (as well as its second stage considered in isolation) is a *positive* bargaining game. Under these assumptions it will be worthwhile for the players to accept a temporary payoff *reduction* during stage 1, i.e., to choose a payoff vector $u^* \in P^*$ rather than to choose c – since this is a preliminary condition for being allowed to participate in stage 2 of the game, where they can *increase* their payoffs above c_1 and c_2.

Yet for the same reasons as in the case where G^* is a positive game (discussed in Section 9.6), the players will try to agree on payoff reductions which leave *unchanged* their relative bargaining positions and therefore also the final solution $\bar{u} = (\bar{u}_1, \bar{u}_2)$ of the game. Hence, by Condition (9.34), whose validity is independent of the signs of Δc_1 and Δc_2, the payoffs u_1^* and u_2^* agreed upon by the players during stage 1 of the game must satisfy Equation (9.35). That is, if a_1 and a_2 are the weights defined by Equation (9.36), then we must have

$$a_1 \cdot (u_1^* - c_1) = a_2 \cdot (u_2^* - c_2)$$

even though now $\Delta u_1^* = u_1^* - c_1 < 0$ and $\Delta u_2^* = u_2^* - c_2 < 0$. [Since G^* is a negative game, at least *one* of the quantities Δu_1^* and Δu_2^* must be negative. But then *both* must be negative, because, in view of (9.36) and (9.37), they must have the same sign.[6]]

However, requirement (9.35) may lead to difficulties, because the payoff space P^*, from which u^* is to be selected, possibly may not have any point u^* in common with the straight line L defined by Equation (9.35). (In the case where G^* was a nonnegative bargaining game, this difficulty could not arise; then we always assumed that the point c would lie in the payoff space P^*.) To overcome this difficulty we will assume that either player i is always free to *reduce* his own payoff u_i^* by any amount, even if the resulting payoff vector $u^* = (u_1^*, u_2^*)$ lies outside the payoff space of the game as originally defined.[7] This assumption is equivalent to replacing the original payoff space P^* by a larger *extended payoff space* $\overline{P}^*$ which contains all points u^* of P^* and in addition contains all points $\overline{u}^*$ (at least) weakly dominated by any point u^* of P^*. (See Figures 9.2 and 9.3 in which the extended payoff space $\overline{P}^*$ includes *both* shaded areas in each figure.)

More formally $\overline{P}^*$ can be defined as follows: For any given utility vector $u = (u_1, \dots, u_n)$, we define the *dominion* of u as the set $D(u)$ of all vectors $\overline{u} = (\overline{u}_1, \dots, \overline{u}_n)$ such that $\overline{u}_i \leq u_i$ for all $i = 1, \dots, n$. Thus $D(u)$ includes exactly u itself as well as all vectors at least weakly dominated by u. For any given set S of utility vectors u we define the *dominion* of S, $D(S)$, as the *union* of all sets $D(u)$, $u \in S$. The extended payoff space $\overline{P}^*$ can be defined as the dominion of the original payoff space P^*, i.e., $\overline{P}^* = D(P^*)$.

We assume that P^* itself is a convex and compact set. Consequently $\overline{P}^*$ will also be a convex set; but it can never be compact, because it extends to negative infinity for both coordinates u_1 and u_2.

We have defined the upper right boundary H^* of P^* as the set of all *strongly efficient* points u^* in P^* (i.e., as a set of all points u^* not subject even to *weak* dominance by other points of P^*). Clearly the set of strongly efficient points in the extended payoff space $\overline{P}^*$ will be the *same* set H^*. Therefore H^* also will be called the *upper right boundary* of $\overline{P}^*$. We reach a different conclusion, however, if we consider the set of *weakly efficient* points (i.e., the set of all points not subject to *strong* dominance, though possibly subject to *weak* dominance). Let H^{**} be the set of weakly efficient points in P^*, and let $\overline{H}^{**}$ be the set of all weakly efficient points in $\overline{P}^*$; then always $H^* \subseteq H^{**} \subset \overline{H}^{**}$. $\overline{H}^{**}$ will be a much larger set then H^* or H^{**}, because it will result from either of these sets by adding an infinite horizontal and infinite vertical half-ray to H^* or H^{**}.[8] We will call this infinite boundary curve $\overline{H}^{**}$ the *extended upper right boundary* of the extended payoff space $\overline{P}^*$.

The line L defined by Equation (9.35) may not intersect the upper right bound-

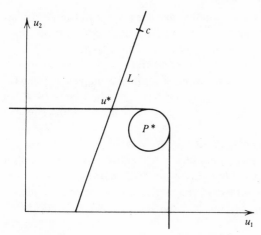

Figure 9.4

ary H^* itself, but it will always intersect the *extended* upper right boundary $\overline{H}^{**}$, at least in the nondegenerate case where a_1 and $a_2 \neq 0$.[9] (See Figure 9.4.) By efficiency, in this case the vector u^* always will lie at least on this extended boundary $\overline{H}^{**}$ and will therefore be the point of intersection between the line L and the extended boundary $\overline{H}^{**}$. Hence it is convenient to redefine the function H^* in (9.37) so that Equation (9.37) now becomes the equation of the entire *extended* upper right boundary $\overline{H}^{**}$ and not only of the shorter curve H^* itself. Then, of course, u^* will always satisfy (9.37). We have already seen that u^* always satisfies (9.35) and (9.36); thus in the nondegenerate case the vector u^* agreed upon by the players in subgame G^* will be defined by the same three equations, irrespective of whether G^* is a negative or a nonnegative embedded bargaining game.

The degenerate case where $a_i = 0$ can arise only when $\overline{u}_j = c_j$ [this follows from Equation (C) of Theorem 9.1]. Since the solution $\overline{u}$ of the main game G must always lie on the upper right boundary H of the payoff space P for G, this is possible only if at the point c player j's payoff c_j is already at the highest level that he can attain in P. Consequently player j can never obtain a positive net payoff $\Delta u_j = u_j - c_j$ under any possible agreement, and so G will not be a *positive* bargaining game. (Indeed, G will not be a true cooperative bargaining game at all, because player j cannot possibly benefit from cooperation with the other player.) Thus we can now state:

Theorem 9.5. Let G^* be a *negative* bargaining game *embedded* into a composite *positive* bargaining game G played in two stages, G^* representing the first stage of G. Then the solution u^* of G^* will be defined by Equations (9.35) through (9.37), the same as in the case of an embedded positive bargaining subgame G^* (except that in the case of a negative subgame G^* we must allow for the possibility that the solution u^* of G^* may lie only on the *extended* upper right boundary $\overline{H}^{**}$ instead of lying on H^*, the upper right boundary proper).

That is, in an embedded *negative* bargaining game the players will agree on *commensurate* payoff *reductions,* in the same way that in an embedded *positive* bargaining game they would agree on *commensurate* payoff *increases.*

This theorem is, of course, true also in the case where a negative bargaining game G^* is embedded as a subgame into a positive composite bargaining game G played in *several* (say, k) stages, G^* corresponding to the jth stage (with $j \neq k$, since the *last* stage of a positive bargaining game must always be itself a *positive* bargaining game).

Our theory of composite bargaining games, discussed in the previous two sections, has direct applications to social situations in which two economic or political units are anxious not only to expand but also to preserve their relative power positions (e.g., the relationship between two rival imperial powers seeking colonial expansion). We will use it as an analytical tool in our theory of n-person cooperative games (Chapters 11 and 12).

SOME CONCEPTS AND THEORIES RELATED TO
BARGAINING GAMES

9.8   Ultimatum games: the Blackmailer's Fallacy

As Nash has pointed out, any bargaining game in "extensive form," involving a *sequence* of offers and counteroffers by the two players, is analytically equivalent to a game in "normal form," allowing each player only one final offer (or demand). But this is true only if in the latter case both players have to make their demands *simultaneously* or at least *independently* of each other.

We obtain a very different type of game if we assume that one player (say, player 1) can irrevocably *commit* himself to some particular demand, called his *ultimatum,* and can inform the other player (player 2) of this fact before the latter has chosen his own demand. In this case player 2 will have a choice only between a conflict situation and the full acceptance of player 1's terms, on a take-it-or-leave-it basis. Thus player 1 will be able to force player 2 to accept *any* agreement point this side of his concession limit – though he cannot force player 2 to return to his concession limit itself[10] and even less to a point beyond that limit. While in a true bargaining game the solution will tend to lie in the middle range of the negotiation set (except if the two players' utility functions, i.e., their attitudes toward risk, are very dissimilar), in an ultimatum game it will always lie very close to one of the two end points of the negotiation set.

An ultimatum game arises if one player can effectively commit himself to some particular agreement point before the other player has had the opportunity to make a similar commitment. For instance, the rules of the game may be such that all communication is cut between the two players as soon as (say) player 1 has stated his own demand, making it physically impossible for him to renege on this demand even if he wanted to. Or player 1 may be able to commit himself under heavy penalty (e.g., by making a bet with a third person to this effect) not to accept any less favorable offer, even if communication between the players remains uninterrupted.

Between two rational players an ultimatum game can occur only if the communication facilities are strongly *biased* in favor of one of them. It can occur only if one of the players can commit himself fully to his demand and can inform his opponent about this before the latter could likewise commit himself to his *own* demand. In contrast, assuming *unbiased* communication facilities, if the use of ultimatums is permitted at all, then *both* players will put forward ultimatums[11] at the very beginning of the game, because neither party can afford to yield the initiative to his opponent. But then we are back to Nash's symmetric one-bid bargaining model. Since the situation is symmetrical, neither party can simply force his own terms on the other party. Rather, both parties will have strong incentives to moderation, because both of them would lose if they committed themselves to mutually incompatible ultimatum demands. (Alternatively we can assume that the players will rule out the use of ultimatums by mutual consent or simply by refusing to consider any ultimatum by the opponent.)

Of course, it may happen that an alert player faced with an unwary opponent will succeed in transforming a true bargaining game, with equal communication facilities, into an ultimatum game biased in his own favor. He may achieve this by manipulating the communication facilities or by merely persuading his opponent to accept an ultimatum even though the latter would be in a position to resist it.[12] But this can happen only if the second player acts irrationally, i.e., makes a strategic mistake.

Empirically we also find that in most bargaining situations neither party succeeds in transforming free bargaining into an ultimatum situation biased in his own favor. Each party has a strong interest in preventing the other party from doing this, not only because this would greatly worsen the terms that he would obtain on this particular occasion but also because a reputation of readily accepting terms "dictated" by the other party in bargaining situations would greatly weaken a given party's bargaining position in future negotiations (with the same opponent or with other opponents). Thus most empirical bargaining situations seem to have the nature of simple bargaining games (or of general cooperative games) rather than ultimatum games.

But no doubt there are important situations in which ultimatum games do arise, even if both parties are proficient players. For example, an asymmetry which may give rise to ultimatum games is a substantial difference in *size* between two bargaining units. Suppose that one party is a large economic or political unit which expects to be involved in many similar bargaining situations, while the other party is a small unit without similar expectations. Then the larger unit will have a strong interest in creating a reputation of toughness which will tend to improve its bargaining position on many future occasions. This will be the case even if in the short run this policy tends to result in a few conflicts with smaller units, which could have been avoided by a more conciliatory policy. Once the reputation of toughness is firmly established, the larger unit will be able to push its weaker bargaining partners very close to their concession limits. Such a larger unit may even refuse to "bargain" at all and may simply set its own condition unilaterally; i.e., it may insist on playing only ultimatum games formally recognized as such. Since any concession granted to one trading partner will tend to create a pressure for similar concessions to others, the larger unit will have an interest in denying concessions even in particularly "justified" cases (with a possible exception of cases where such concessions can be kept secret from the other trading partners).

In the analysis of social situations, it is a common mistake to confuse bargaining situations with ultimatum games. For example, suppose that a would-be blackmailer, B, could cause $1000 damage to a certain rich man, R. Then B may argue that he could extract any ransom short of $1000 from R, who would prefer to pay even $999 rather than suffer a damage of $1000. But this reasoning would be clearly fallacious. R could just as well argue that he could get away with any ransom, however small, since B would prefer to get even a ransom of $1 rather than implement his threat and get nothing. Neither argument would have any validity. They only show that the ransom must lie somewhere *between* zero dollars and $1000, but they allow no inference as to *where* it will lie within this range. In order to have a more definite prediction we must make use of some specific theory of bargaining games. For instance, if we use the Nash-Zeuthen theory, then we obtain the prediction that the size of the ransom – within the range from $0 to $1000 – will depend mainly on the two parties' attitudes toward *risk* (assuming that they have no other conflict strategies or threat strategies than those mentioned, e.g., assuming that R could not get any effective police protection).

B's argument would be valid only if he could convince R that he has irrevocably committed himself not to accept anything *less* than (say) $999, i.e., if he could convert the bargaining game into an ultimatum game. But normally R will have no reason to take seriously any such "commitment" by B – just as B will have no reason to take seriously a possible claim by R that he himself is "committed" not to pay more than $1. I propose to describe the mistake of treating a bargaining game as if it were an ultimatum game as the *Blackmailer's Fallacy*.

An ultimatum game can be regarded as a degenerate case of a bargaining game, where the effective bargaining set is reduced (virtually) to a point. Even if the original negotiation set covered a large number of possible agreement points, the effective negotiation set will shrink to one point once one player has effectively committed himself not to accept any other point as agreement point. But formally under our theory an ultimatum game is not a bargaining game at all, precisely because its one-point negotiation set leaves no room for real bargaining. It is not a "bargaining-determined game" but is rather a "game determined by payoff-dominance relations." It can be reduced to a cooperative game in which one payoff vector strongly dominates all other payoff vectors in the payoff space of the game.

To sum up, since the most interesting analytical problems arise only in bargaining-determined games, ultimatum games are rather trivial from the viewpoint of basic theory. But they are a useful conceptual tool for analyzing empirical social behavior, all the more so because a skillful player can sometimes convert a true bargaining game into an ultimatum game, by manipulating the communication facilities, by entering into unilateral commitments, and so forth – though this can happen only if the other party makes a strategic mistake.

We feel that game theory could make an important contribution to the analysis of empirical social situations if it could make social scientists more conscious of the distinction between free bargaining games and ultimatum games. Confusion of the former with the latter – which we have called the Blackmailer's Fallacy – can result in highly unrealistic predictions and in complete misunderstanding of the relative bargaining power between the parties.

9.9 The game-independence problem: Hicks's theory

We have seen that a clear distinction must be made between an *independent* game G, where each player's goal is to maximize his direct payoff $u_i(G)$ from G *itself*, and a *dependent* game G^*, where each player's goal is to maximize his payoff $u_i(G^{**})$ from some *other* game G^{**} to which G^* is subordinated. In the latter case the players' payoff vector $u(G^*)$ from G^* is important only insofar as it influences the payoff vector $u(G^{**})$ that they will obtain from the main game G^{**}. We have argued that a bargaining game *embedded* into a larger composite bargaining game is a dependent game, and so is a *threat game*, which is part of a cooperative game with binding threats.

Even though this distinction between dependent and independent games is obvious enough in theory, it is easy to lose sight of in empirical applications, treating dependent games as if they were independent. In particular, cooperative games *with* binding threats (where the conflict game is a dependent game) are often treated as if they were cooperative games *without* binding threats (where the conflict game is an independent game). In our view, for instance, Hicks's theory of collective bargaining [1932, Chap. VII] is open to this objection [cf. Harsanyi, 1956, pp. 154-155].

Hicks's basic assumption is that a labor union will undertake, or will seriously threaten to undertake, a strike only if this move will cost the unionists *less* than accepting a lower wage rate would. Likewise an employer will refuse to grant a wage increase only if the strike likely to result from his refusal will cost him *less* than allowing the wage increases would. This principle will determine how long the union would be ready to strike rather than accept a given wage rate w: Suppose that it would be willing to strike for $t_u(w)$ time units. The same principle will determine how long the employer would endure a strike rather than grant a given wage rate w: Suppose that he would endure a strike lasting $t_e(w)$ time units. If for a given possible wage rate w we have $t_u(w) > t_e(w)$; then the employer will be unable to refuse w, since his refusal would give rise to a longer strike than he would be ready to face. On the other hand, if $t_u(w) < t_e(w)$, then the union will be unable to refuse w, since it would not be ready to undertake a strike long enough to extract further concessions from the employer. Hence the two parties must reach an agreement at the wage rate w where $t_u(w) = t_e(w)$.

Thus Hicks's theory is based on the assumption that the quantity that each party tries to maximize is his *net conflict payoff* – that is, the value of the concessions that he will extract by his conflict strategy *less* the costs of this conflict to him. But in our own view this would be an irrational policy objective for either party, at least if both parties expect to reach an agreement. In this case the quantities that they should maximize are the payoffs that they will receive under this *agreement*, quite irrespective of the payoffs that they would receive in a hypothetical conflict situation. Their conflict payoffs are important only to the extent that they influence the strength of the parties' bargaining positions with respect to the payoffs that they will agree upon (if a conflict situation is avoided).

In order to achieve the strongest possible bargaining position, the correct strategy for each party is not to *maximize* his *own* conflict payoff as such but rather to choose an appropriate compromise policy between *maximizing* his *own* conflict payoff and *minimizing* his *opponent's* conflict payoff – as defined by Nash's theory of optimal threats (see Sections 9.2 and 9.3).

For instance, let us assume that a labor union asks for wage increases worth $500,000 up to the end of the contract period. A strike of two months' duration would cost the union $600,000 in lost wages. Then it *may* still pay for the union to commit itself to such a strike in case no agreement would be reached – provided that this strike would also cost the employer substantially more than $500,000 (the cost of granting the wage increases). The prospect of an expensive strike may induce the employer to make further concessions (without an actual strike). The question is only whether such a strike would increase the employer's conflict costs *relatively* more than the union's conflict costs, or conversely (cf. Theorem 9.3 in Section 9.3).

To sum up, if we assume that the parties expect to reach an agreement, then the value of a conflict strategy (threat strategy) must not be judged in terms of its net payoff in a conflict situation (where each party would have to implement its threats). Rather it must be judged in terms of its net payoff in the agreement situation, i.e., in terms of its effect on the two parties' relative bargaining positions in case they do reach an agreement and avoid a conflict (in which case they will not have to implement their threats).

This conclusion, however, is subject to two qualifications:

1. In Nash's model the players are perfectly rational and have full information about each other's utility functions. Therefore they can have full confidence in being able to reach an agreement at the Nash solution of the game. But in the real world there is always some chance that no agreement will be reached because of lack of information or strategical mistakes. Therefore, if u_i is player i's agreement payoff and c_i is his conflict payoff (disagreement payoff), then he should presumably maximize the quantity $u_i^* = (1 - p)u_i + pc_i$ rather than the quantity u_i itself, where p is a certain small probability that he assigns to the possibility that no agreement will be reached.

2. In Nash's model the players have no doubts about the opponent's intention to implement his threats in full in case no agreement is reached. In the real world

the efficacy of threats will be lessened by some small probability p^* that they may not be fully implemented in a conflict situation. Insofar as p and/or $p^* > 0$, the real situation is intermediate between a cooperative game *with* binding threats and one *without* binding threats. That is, the conflict game is neither fully dependent nor fully independent. Yet, insofar as both p and p^* are *small* (as they probably are in most cases), Nash's model retains its approximate validity. We certainly cannot assume without further justification that the two parties' choice of conflict strategies represents an independent game and that they pay no attention to the threat properties (deterrent properties) of their conflict strategy choices, as seems to be implied by Hicks's model.

9.10 Bargaining games and arbitration models

Our analysis of moral value judgments in Chapter 4 and of bargaining games in this chapter now enables us to round off our discussion on the relationship between bargaining games and arbitration models, begun in Chapter 1 (Section 1.5).

Suppose again that players 1 and 2 have to agree on a payoff vector $u = (u_1, u_2)$ chosen from some payoff space P. But, instead of trying to reach an agreement by bargaining, they submit their case to an arbitrator. What payoff vector will the arbitrator choose for the two players? This question cannot be answered without making specific assumptions about the arbitrator's actual task and power in this situation.

1. One extreme assumption would be that the arbitrator has absolute power to impose his own (or society's) moral value judgments on the two parties. In this case his task will be to choose what he regards as the "morally best" solution, irrespective of what the balance of power would be between the two players without his intervention. (For instance, he need not pay any attention to the threat possibilities available to either player.) He must be guided by "right" rather than by "might." According to our argument in Chapter 4, this means that the arbitrator must try to maximize the joint payoff $\tilde{u} = u_1 + u_2$ of the two parties as his social-welfare function. (If there are several solutions yielding the same joint payoff $\tilde{u}$ to players 1 and 2, then the arbitrator may have a free choice among them, or alternatively he may use some subsidiary principle, e.g., symmetry, to decide his choice.)

2. Another extreme assumption would be that the arbitrator has no power whatever for introducing his own value judgments. The only purpose of the arbitration process is to save the parties the costs (including the emotional costs) of actual bargaining. But it is not meant to change the final outcome in any way. Hence the arbitrator's task is to get as close as he can to the solution that presumably would have resulted from actual bargaining between the parties. If it is assumed, for instance, that actual bargaining would have led the two players to the Nash solution, then it will be the arbitrator's task to recommend the Nash solution as agreement point.

3. Of course, many intermediate assumptions may be suggested. We may assume that the arbitrator is free to follow his own value judgments but has no abso-

lute power to impose them on the two players. Instead any agreement requires the consent of all three parties: It must be accepted by both players and also by the arbitrator himself. In this case we have essentially a three-person bargaining game in which player 1 tries to maximize his own individual payoff u_1; player 2 tries to maximize his own individual payoff u_2, whereas the arbitrator tries to maximize the social-welfare function $u_3 = \tilde{u} = u_1 + u_2$. Under our theory of three-person (n-person) bargaining games (to be discussed in Chapter 10), the solution of this game will be at that particular point $u = (u_1, u_2, u_3) = (u_1, u_2, u_1 + u_2)$, where the three-person generalized Nash product, $\pi = (u_1 - c_1)(u_2 - c_2)(u_3 - c_3) = (u_1 - c_1)(u_2 - c_2)(u_1 + u_2 - c_1 - c_2)$, is maximized.

Clearly none of these three interpretations of the arbitration process can be made the basis for a theory of bargaining games. Interpretation 1 would give us a solution selected on the basis of moral considerations alone, which is quite independent of the relative bargaining power of the two parties. In contrast, interpretations 2 and 3 would give us solutions which do reflect their relative bargaining power; but these solutions already presuppose some theory of bargaining games and cannot be used as a basis for constructing such a theory.

Thus our present discussion confirms our previous conclusion that arbitration models cannot serve as a basis for the theory of bargaining games; and, unless the task of the arbitrator is conceived in a very narrow sense (as under interpretation 2), the solution furnished by an arbitration model will in general be different from the solution furnished by the theory of bargaining games.

9.11 Bargaining models and interpersonal utility comparisons

The solution concepts based on ethical criteria, which are usually called "arbitration models," are usually based on interpersonal utility comparisons. We have seen that such utility comparisons are quite essential for making moral value judgments and for constructing a satisfactory social-welfare function. The reason is that, in a world where economic (and other) resources are scarce, we often have to *choose* between increasing one individual's utility level from (say) u_1 to $u_1 + \Delta u_1$ and increasing another individual's utility level from u_2 to $u_2 + \Delta u_2$. Therefore we must be able to *compare* the importance of utility increment Δu_1 to the first individual with the importance of utility increment Δu_2 to the second individual, in terms of some impartial moral criteria (presumably somehow related to the relative psychological intensity of the two individuals' wants and of the satisfactions that they can derive by gratifying these wants). But it is much more questionable why two bargainers interested in obtaining terms as favorable as possible, rather than interested in arriving at a morally "fair" solution, should make their bargaining strategies dependent on such interpersonal comparisons of utility.

The interpersonal-utility-comparison concepts used by various arbitration models, as well as those used by certain theories in ethics and in welfare economics, fall into two main classes. Some of them are supposed to be based on the *intrinsic psychological nature* of the various individuals' utility functions to be compared.

Following Bishop [1963], these we will call *substantive* interpersonal comparisons of utility. Under these approaches, once we establish the "correct" conversion ratio between two individuals' utility functions, this will be given once for all and will remain the same in different social situations (in different game situations) as long as these utility functions themselves remain the same. The utility comparisons assumed by classical utilitarian moral philosophers are such substantive comparisons. The same is true for the utility comparisons that we used in defining a social welfare function (Chapter 4 throughout but in particular Sections 4.2 through 4.4). Raiffa [1953] also uses intrinsic comparisons in some of his arbitration models.[13]

Other concepts of interpersonal utility comparisons are defined in terms of the *game situation* itself: Thus they depend not only on the intrinsic nature of the players' utility functions as such but also on their physical environment – not only on the subjective intensity of their *preferences* but also on the objective *opportunities* available to them. The idea is to select the utility distance between two specified points of the game's payoff space as the *utility unit* for each player (e.g., one may select as the unit the utility distance between the highest and the lowest payoff each player can obtain in a given game, and so on). The utility units chosen in this way for each player are then treated as "equal" utility distances (equal utility increments) in constructing the solution. Using Bishop's terminology we will call these concepts *ad hoc* interpersonal comparisons of utility. Under these concepts the conversion ratio between two individuals' utility functions will in general vary from game to game (e.g., because the highest and the lowest possible payoff for a given player will be different in each game). Some of Raiffa's arbitration models are based on such ad hoc utility comparisons. The same is true for Braithwaite's [1955] arbitration model and for some social-welfare concepts criticized by Arrow [1951].

The Nash-Zeuthen bargaining model is intrinsically independent of interpersonal comparisons of utility. It is certainly independent of *substantive* utility comparisons, because the Nash solution is invariant with respect to order-preserving linear transformations of either player's utility function. Thus the solution remains invariant if we, for example, double our unit of measurement for player 1's utility function (which will reduce all his utility figures by half), leaving player 2's utility unit unchanged – even though this will make the two players' utilities incomparable if they were expressed in comparable units before this transformation. Under Nash's own approach this invariance property is specifically *postulated* precisely in order to make the solution independent of interpersonal utility comparisons. Under our approach this invariance property *follows* from the fact that under expected-utility maximization the players' behavior will depend only on the utility ratios r_1 and r_2 (which, of course, are invariant with respect to linear utility transformations) and on the subjective probabilities p_{12} and p_{21} (which themselves again depend only on r_1 and r_2). (See Section 8.6, as well as our discussion of Postulate 3 in Section 8.3.)

The Nash-Zeuthen solution is also independent of *ad hoc* utility comparisons: As you can easily check, we have made no use even of ad hoc utility comparisons in

deriving the Nash solution from our rationality postulates in Sections 8.4 through
8.8. However, even if this solution does not *presuppose* ad hoc utility comparisons,
it does *establish* a certain type of ad hoc utility comparisons between the two
players – once the solution has been defined independently of such comparisons.
This is true in the sense that the equations of Theorem 9.1 (Section 9.2) defining
the Nash solution take a somewhat simpler form if we subject the two players' utility functions to linear transformations which make the weights a_1 and a_2 defined
by Equation (B), or preferably by Equation (B*), of Theorem 9.1 equal to *unity*.
(Geometrically, in this case the slope of the upper right boundary H at the solution
point $\bar{u}$ will become $-45°$, while the slope of the line connecting the solution $\bar{u}$
with the conflict point c will become $+45°$.) This is equivalent to choosing the two
players' utility units in such a way that, if (starting from the solution point) one
player makes a small side payment to the other player, costing him *one* unit of utility, this payment will yield the other player, also a *one*-unit utility gain (i.e., the
marginal rate of utility transfers[14] between the two players will be unity). Thus
this procedure establishes some basis for comparing the two players' utilities. But
it will be a purely ad hoc comparison: If the same two players will play a different
bargaining game tomorrow under different conditions (e.g., if tomorrow side payments between them will be taxed at a different marginal rate), then the conversion
ratio between their utilities, based on this procedure, may be quite different. Moreover, this utility comparison method is a *consequence* of the Nash solution and is
not a *basis* for it.

For interpersonal comparisons of *utility* Zeuthen's model substitutes interpersonal comparisons of certain *probabilities* (the highest probability of a conflict that
each player would be willing to face) which are equal to certain *utility ratios* r_1 and
r_2 but which are not utilities as such. (Whether we interpret them as probabilities
or as utility ratios, they are pure numbers without dimension.) While the relevance
of these utility ratios for the players' strategy choices follows directly from the
postulate of expected-utility maximization, there is no reason that the players
should be concerned about interpersonal utility comparisons in a game-theoretical
(as distinguished from an ethical) context.

If we go from simple bargaining games to general cooperative games and consider Nash's theory of *optimal threats*, we again find the same independence of interpersonal utility comparisons. In the case of a threat game it is particularly
tempting to base one's analysis on interpersonal comparisons of utility. Intuitively
it is very natural to argue that my threat will be effective against you only if implementing this threat "would hurt you more than it would hurt me" in some appropriate sense. The interesting fact is that Nash's theory does full justice to this intuitive feeling *without* making formal use of interpersonal utility comparisons. It gives
a precise mathematical criterion for measuring the damage that one threatens to
cause to the opponent against the costs of inflicting it, and so for deciding whether
a given threat would strengthen or rather weaken one's bargaining position against
the opponent. But it achieves this without making use of any additional assumption (including utility comparisons). It only assumes that the players know that,
once their threat strategies have determined the conflict point c, the agreement

point will be given by the Nash solution $\bar{u}$ of the resulting simple bargaining game, and that each player will try to maximize his final payoff $\bar{u}_i$ on the basis of this information.

Nash's theory, however, does establish an *ad hoc* interpersonal utility comparison between the two players. If we normalize the two players' utilities so that $a_1 = a_2 = 1$, then Nash's optimal-threat criterion will take a particularly simple form. It will then simply say that it is profitable to intensify one's threats against the opponent as long as the extra damage done to him "would hurt him more" than one would be hurt oneself by the extra cost of inflicting it, if both this damage and this cost are measured in the appropriate normalized utility units (cf. Lemma 1 of Section 9.2). Thus if utilities are measured in the appropriate units, then the intuitive "it-will-hurt-you-more" criterion has quite literal validity under Nash's theory. But this intuitive criterion will be, in any case, a mere corollary of Nash's results and will not have to be introduced as a new independent assumption or as an implication of interpersonal utility comparisons.

9.12 Conclusion

In the first section of this chapter we discussed the Nash-Zeuthen solution for two-person cooperative games with variable threats. (Our results have been summarized in Section 9.4.) In the next section we extended our results to composite bargaining games. In the final section we discussed some alternative approaches to the bargaining problem and have tried to show that some of them are based on what we have called the "Blackmailer's Fallacy." Other approaches have been criticized on the ground that they unnecessarily introduce moral postulates into the analysis of game-theoretical problems and make use of interpersonal comparisons of utility, which have no justification in nonethical contexts.

10

n-Person simple bargaining games

10.1 Introduction

In an *n*-person simple bargaining game the *n* players have to choose a payoff vector $u = (u_1, \ldots, u_n)$ from a compact and convex set P of possible payoff vectors, called the *payoff space* of the game. The choice of u must be by unanimous agreement of all *n* players. If they cannot reach unanimous agreement, then they obtain the *conflict payoffs* $c_1, \ldots, c_n$. The payoff vector $c = (c_1, \ldots, c_n)$ is called the *conflict point* of the game. We will assume that $c \in P$.

That region P^* of the payoff space P which lies in the orthant defined by the *n* inequalities $u_i \geqq c_i$, for $i = 1, \ldots, n$, is called the *agreement space*. Like P itself, P^* is always a compact and convex set.

We will exclude the degenerate case where the payoff(s) of some player(s) is (or are) constant over the entire agreement space P^*. For in this case this player (or these players) would have no interest in cooperating with the other player(s), and so the game would not be a truly cooperative game.

The set of all points u in the payoff space P undominated, even weakly, by any other point u^* in P is called the *upper boundary H* of P. In other words, H is the set of *strongly efficient* points in P. In general the payoff space P is a set of *n* dimensions. Consequently the upper boundary H is typically a hypersurface of $(n - 1)$ dimensions.

10.2 Multilateral bargaining equilibrium

In a simple bargaining game G, a given payoff vector $u = \bar{u}$ will represent the equilibrium outcome of bargaining among the *n* players only if no pair of players *i* and *j* has any incentive to *redistribute* their payoffs between them as long as the other players' payoffs are kept constant. Thus we can define *multilateral bargaining equilibrium* among the *n* players by the requirement that there should be *bilateral bargaining equilibrium* between any two players *i* and *j*.

This means that, in order to define the solution of a given *n*-person simple bargaining game G, we have to consider the various two-person bargaining subgames G_{ij} in which two particular players *i* and *j* bargain with each other about their final payoffs u_i and u_j on the assumption that the final payoffs u_k of all other players $k \neq i, j$ are *given*. The Nash solution of any such subgame G_{ij} will corre-

196

spond to those payoffs $u_i = \bar{u}_i$ and $u_j = \bar{u}_j$ which maximize the Nash product

$$\pi_{ij} = (u_i - c_i)(u_j - c_j) \tag{10.1}$$

subject to the conditions

$$u = (u_1, \ldots, u_i, \ldots, u_j, \ldots, u_n) \in P \tag{10.1a}$$

$$u_i \geq c_i \tag{10.1b}$$

$$u_j \geq c_j \tag{10.1c}$$

$$u_k = \bar{u}_k = \text{const. for all } k \neq i, j \tag{10.1d}$$

$$c_i, c_j = \text{const.} \tag{10.1e}$$

Let $H(u_1, \ldots, u_n) = 0$ be the equation defining the upper boundary of the payoff space P. Then, by Equations (9.2) through (9.4) of Section 9.2, we can define the solution of G_{ij} also by the sufficient and necessary conditions

$$H(\bar{u}_1, \ldots, \bar{u}_i, \ldots, \bar{u}_j, \ldots, \bar{u}_n) = 0 \tag{10.2}$$

$$a_i \cdot (\bar{u}_i - c_i) = a_j \cdot (\bar{u}_j - c_j) \tag{10.3}$$

$$a_m = H_m(\bar{u}_1, \ldots, \bar{u}_i, \ldots, \bar{u}_j, \ldots, \bar{u}_n) \quad m = i, j \tag{10.4}$$

where H_m is the first partial derivative[1] of the function H with respect to its mth argument.

Since we can form all together $n \cdot (n-1)/2$ pairs (i, j) among the n players, this will be the number of subgames G_{ij} that we have to consider. Therefore we obtain $n \cdot (n-1)/2$ equations of form (10.3), but out of these only $(n-1)$ equations will be independent. Moreover, we obtain n equations of form (10.4) and only one equation of form (10.2). These equations together imply the following theorem:

Theorem 10.1. The solution $\bar{u} = (\bar{u}_1, \ldots, \bar{u}_n)$ of an n-person simple bargaining game G is that particular payoff vector $u = \bar{u}$ which maximizes the n-person Nash product

$$\pi = \prod_{i \in N} (u_i - c_i) \tag{10.5}$$

subject to the requirements

$$u \in P \tag{10.5a}$$

$$u_i \geq c_i \quad \text{for all } i \in N \tag{10.5b}$$

$$c_i = \text{const. for all } i \in N \tag{10.5c}$$

This vector $\bar{u}$ always *exists* and is always *unique*.

Proof. Equations (10.2) through (10.4) are the first-order conditions, in terms of Lagrangean multipliers, for maximizing the product π. The second-order conditions are always satisfied because of the convexity of P. The convexity of P also assures the uniqueness of the vector $\bar{u}$ which maximizes π. Finally the existence of $\bar{u}$ follows from the compactness of P.

The amounts $(\bar{u}_i - c_i)$ we will call the players' *net payoffs* from the game (as distinguished from their *gross* payoffs $\bar{u}_i$). By Equations (10.3) and (10.4), the ratios $\rho_{ij} = (\bar{u}_i - c_i)/(\bar{u}_j - c_j)$ of the players' net payoffs will be determined by the quantities $a_1, \ldots, a_n$, corresponding to the first partial derivatives of the function H at the solution point $\bar{u}$. Geometrically they are the slope cosini of the hypersurface H at the point $\bar{u}$. These quantities $a_1, \ldots, a_n$ we will call the *weights* of the game.

Clearly the solution defined by Theorem 10.1 is the most natural generalization of the two-person Nash solution even in a purely formal sense, because it simply replaces maximization of a two-factor product by maximization of an analogous n-factor product. (We will see, however, that this straightforward way of generalizing the Nash solution is restricted to the special case of simple bargaining games. In the case of general cooperative games we will need a more complicated model taking account of the strength of various possible coalitions among the players.)

10.3 Derivation of the solution directly from Nash's postulates

In the previous section we defined our solution concept for n-person simple bargaining games. Our definition was based on the requirement that the solution must represent *bilateral* bargaining equilibrium between any two players i and j. The concept of bilateral bargaining equilibrium itself was defined in terms of the Nash solution for two-person bargaining games. But, in view of Theorem 8.3 of Section 8.6, the Nash solution itself can be derived from our "strong" rationality postulates. Thus our derivation of this solution concept for n-person bargaining games is ultimately based on these rationality postulates.

In this section we will show that the same solution concept can be derived also from Nash's own postulates (see Section 8.3), if we extend their field of application from *two-person* to *n-person* simple bargaining games. Nash's postulates then take the following form:

1. *Joint efficiency.* The solution $\bar{u} = (\bar{u}_1, \ldots, \bar{u}_n)$ of an n-person simple bargaining game lies on the upper boundary H of its payoff space P.

A simple bargaining game is called *symmetric* if all players have the same disagreement payoff $c_1 = \cdots = c_n$ in the game, and if the payoff space P is symmetric with respect to all planes $u_i = u_j$ for any pair of players i and j.

2. *Symmetry.* The solution of a symmetric simple bargaining game yields equal payoffs $\bar{u}_1 = \cdots = \bar{u}_n$ to all n players.

3. *Linear invariance.* Let G be a simple bargaining game with solution $\bar{u}$. Let G^* be the game that results from G if we subject one player's utility function U_i to an order-preserving linear transformation T, leaving all other players' utility functions U_j unchanged. Then the solution $\bar{u}^*$ of this new game G^* will be the image of $\bar{u}$ under this transformation T, i.e., $\bar{u}^* = T\bar{u}$.

4. *Independence of irrelevant alternatives.* Let G again be an n-person simple bargaining game with payoff space P, conflict point $c = (c_1, \ldots, c_n)$, and solution

$\bar{u} = (\bar{u}_1, \ldots, \bar{u}_n)$. Let G^* be a game obtained from G by restricting the payoff space to the smaller set $P^* \subset P$ in such a way that c and $\bar{u}$ remain in the new payoff space P^* and c is also the conflict point for G^*. Then $\bar{u}$ will be the solution also for the new game G^*.

Theorem 10.2. The only payoff vector satisfying Postulates 1 to 4 (the *n*-person analogues of Nash's postulates) is the payoff vector $\bar{u}$ defined by Theorem 10.1.

Proof. The proof is essentially the same as in the two-person case (i.e., as the proof of Theorem 8.1 of Section 8.3).

Let $u = \bar{u}$ be the point at which the product π, defined by Equation (10.5), is maximized subject to conditions (10.5a) through (10.5c). We subject all players' utility functions to order-preserving linear transformations, such that carry the conflict point $c = (c_1, \ldots, c_n)$ into the origin $c^* = (0, \ldots, 0)$ while carrying the point $\bar{u} = (\bar{u}_1, \ldots, \bar{u}_n)$ into the point $\bar{u}^* = (1, \ldots, 1)$.

Let P^* be the image of the payoff space P under this transformation T. Let H^* be the image of H, the upper boundary of P. Finally let G^* be the *n*-person simple bargaining game whose payoff space is P^*, and whose conflict point is c^*. Clearly the upper boundary of P^* will be the hypersurface H^*. Consider the Nash product for this new game G^*, i.e., the expression

$$\pi^*(u^*) = \prod_{i \in N} (u_i^* - c_i^*) = \prod_{i \in N} u_i^*$$

In the same way as in the two-person case we can show that $\pi^*(u^*)$ will take its maximum value, subject to conditions (10.5a) through (10.5c), at the point $u^* = \bar{u}^*$, which is the image of $\bar{u}$ under transformation T.

The point $\bar{u}^* = (1, \ldots, 1)$ obviously lies on the upper boundary hypersurface H^*. It also lies on the hyperplane K^* whose equation is

$$\sum_{i \in N} u_i^* = n$$

Finally it also lies on the rectangular hyperboloid J^* whose equation is

$$\prod_{i \in N} u_i^* = 1$$

More particularly the hyperplane K^* will be tangential (or will be a support) to both H^* and J^* at the point $\bar{u}^*$. Let K_+^* be the half-space defined by the inequality

$$\sum_{i \in N} u_i^* \leq n$$

Since P^* is a convex set, no point u^* of P^* can lie above the supporting hyperplane K^*. Therefore $P^* \subset K_+^*$.

Now let us construct a hypersphere S^* around $\bar{u}^*$ as center point, with a large enough radius so that $P^* \subset S^*$. Since P^* is a compact set this can always be done.

Let P^{**} be the half-hypersphere defined by the intersection of K_+^* and S^*, i.e., $P^{**} = K_+^* \cap S^*$. Clearly $P^* \subset P^{**}$.

Let G^{**} be the n-person simple bargaining game whose payoff space is P^{**} and whose conflict point is c^*. Obviously G^{**} is a fully symmetric game with respect to all n players. Consequently, by Postulates 1 and 2, the solution of G^{**} must be $\bar{u}^* = (1, \ldots, 1)$. Therefore, by Postulate 3, the point $\bar{u}^*$ must be the solution also of G^*. But then, by Postulate 3, the point $\bar{u}$, which is the image of $\bar{u}^*$ under the inverse of the original transformation T, must also be the solution of the original bargaining game G, as desired.

10.4 The n-person bargaining process: risk-dominance relations in the n-person case

Theorem 10.1 defines the solution on the basis of the requirement that it must give rise to bilateral bargaining equilibrium between every possible pair of players i and j if all other players' payoffs are regarded as *given*. Thus the solution can be regarded as the end result of a bargaining process of the following kind.

Suppose that the players reach a *provisional* agreement on accepting the payoff vector $u = (u_1, \ldots, u_n) \in P$, with $u_i \geq c_i$ for all players i. But let us assume that this agreement is purely tentative: Any player i who is dissatisfied with his own payoff u_i can challenge any other player j to *redistribute* his payoff, regarding all other players' payoffs as *given*. Thus player i can suggest some alternative payoff vector $u^* = (u_1^*, \ldots, u_n^*) \in P$, with $u_k^* = u_k$ for all players $k \neq i,j$ but with $u_i^* > u_i$ and $u_j > u_j^* \geq c_j$. According to Zeuthen's Principle [in one of its alternative forms, as stated by Condition (8.9) of Section 8.5], player j will have to make *some* concession to player i whenever

$$(u_i^* - c_i)(u_j^* - c_j) \geq (u_i - c_i)(u_j - c_j) \tag{10.6}$$

Then another player i' may challenge some other player j' in a similar way, and so on. The order in which various players can make such moves must be determined by some suitable rule, but the specific nature of this rule is immaterial for our purposes (as long as it gives every player opportunities to make moves of this kind sooner or later). After every such successful challenge the value of the n-person Nash product $\pi = \Pi(u_i - c_i)$ will *increase*, and eventually the players will tend to converge to the solution where π takes its *maximum* value.

This postulated bargaining process suggests the following definition for risk-dominance relations in the n-person simple bargaining game: Risk-dominance relations are defined between two payoff vectors u and u^* only if u and u^* have at least $(n-2)$ equal components. Suppose, e.g., that $u_k = u_k^*$ for *all* $k \neq i,j$. Then u^* *weakly* risk-dominates u whenever Inequality (10.6) is satisfied; u^* *strongly* risk-dominates u whenever we can replace the $\geq$ sign by a $>$ sign in (10.6). Under this definition the solution payoff vector $\bar{u}$ is the *only* payoff vector in P *not* subject to risk-dominance by any other payoff vector u in P (either in a weak or a strong sense). This concept of risk-dominance will be called *restricted bilateral risk-dominance*, because it is restricted to payoff vectors agreeing in at least $(n-2)$

components, and because it is based on comparing two-person Nash products. The corresponding bargaining process will be called multilateral bargaining based on *restricted bilateral bargaining*.

Of course, once the players realize that this bargaining process will eventually converge to the solution point $\bar{u}$ where the *n*-person Nash product $\pi(u) = \Pi(u_i - c_i)$ is maximized, they can considerably speed the whole process by adopting the following bargaining rules:

Suppose again that the players have reached provisional agreement on accepting the payoff vector $u = (u_1, \ldots, u_n) \in P$ with $u_j \geq c_j$ for all players j. But any player i has the right to suggest an alternative payoff vector $u^* = (u_1^*, \ldots, u_n^*) \in P$ with $u_j^* \geq c_j$ for all $j \in N$. If

$$\pi(u^*) = \prod_{j \in N} (u_j^* - c_j) > \prod_{j \in N} (u_j - c_j) = \pi(u) \tag{10.7}$$

then the players have to accept u^* as their new *provisional* agreement point. A given payoff vector $\bar{u}$ will become the *final* agreement point of the players if no player can suggest any payoff vector $u^* \in P$ with $u_j^* \geq c_j$ such that $\pi(u^*) \geq \pi(\bar{u})$. Clearly this will be the case only when $\bar{u}$ happens to be the *solution* of the game, i.e., the point at which the product π takes its maximum value. A bargaining process conducted according to these rules we will call *direct multilateral bargaining*.

This alternative bargaining model suggests a broader definition for *risk-dominance* relations. Let u^* and $u \in P$, with $u_i^*, u_i \geq c_i$ for all $i \in N$. Then u^* *strongly* risk-dominates u if Inequality (10.7) is satisfied; and u^* weakly risk-dominates u if (10.7) becomes true at least after replacing the $>$ sign by the $\geq$ sign. [For convenience, we also say that u is (both strongly and weakly) risk-dominated by *any* payoff vector u^* if $u_i < c_i$ for at least one player i.] Under this new definition the solution $\bar{u}$ is again the only payoff vector in P *not subject* to risk-dominance by any other payoff vector u in P. But now, in addition, the solution $\bar{u}$ *itself* strongly *risk-dominates* all other payoff vectors u in P, which was not true under the previous definition. This new concept of risk-dominance relations, defined in terms of *n*-person Nash products π, will be called *multilateral risk-dominance*.

Clearly, whenever some given *restricted bilateral* risk-dominance relation exists between two payoff vectors u and u^*, the *same* type of (strong or weak) *multilateral* risk-dominance relation will also exist between them. But while restricted bilateral risk-dominance relations are defined only between two payoff vectors agreeing in at least $(n - 2)$ components, multilateral risk-dominance relations are not limited in this way. Indeed at least a *weak* multilateral risk-dominance relation exists (in one direction or the other) between *every* pair of payoff vectors u and u^* in P.

These concepts of risk-dominance relations can be extended to the *joint strategies* $\sigma(u)$ and $\sigma(u^*)$ corresponding to acceptance of the payoff vectors u and u^*.

As we will see, in *noncooperative* (and in almost-noncooperative) games a third type of risk-dominance concept will be needed – *unrestricted bilateral* risk-dominance. Under this concept two players i and j can be engaged in direct bilateral bargaining, player i advocating adoption of some payoff vector u and player j advocating adoption of some other payoff vector u^*, even if u and u^* do *not* assign the *same* payoffs to the remaining $(n-2)$ players other than i and j. In a cooperative game such "unrestricted" bilateral bargaining cannot take place, because it *would not remain* bilateral. That is, if some given player k is *not* indifferent between u and u^* because $u_k \neq u_k^*$, then he will *side* with one of the two players i or j, so that the bargaining between i and j will be transformed into bargaining between two *coalitions* (or possibly into bargaining between a coalition on one side and an individual player on the other side). Yet Zeuthen's Principle in its original form directly applies only to bargaining between two *individual players* i and j.[2] In contrast, in a noncooperative game the players cannot form coalitions so that every conflict of interest between two players must be settled basically by bargaining between these two players alone, even if it does affect some other players' interests as well.

For example, consider the three-person simple bargaining game G where the payoff space P consists of all payoff vectors u satisfying $u_1 + u_2 + u_3 \leq 30$ and $u_i \geq 0$ for $i = 1, 2, 3$. Suppose that the conflict point of G is $c = (0, 0, 0)$. Clearly the solution of G is $\bar{u} = (10, 10, 10)$, where the Nash product π takes its maximum value $\pi = 1000$. Consider the payoff vector $u^* = (12, 9, 9)$. Under *restricted bilateral* risk-dominance, $\bar{u}$ and u^* are not connected by any risk-dominance relation. Under multilateral risk-dominance, $\bar{u}$ strongly risk-dominates u^* because $\pi(u^*) = 972 < \pi(\bar{u}) = 1000$. Hence in the simple bargaining game G the players will adopt $\bar{u}$ rather than u^*.

But now suppose that $\bar{u}$ and u^* are not payoff vectors in a cooperative game but rather are payoff vectors in some *noncooperative* game G^*. More particularly let $\bar{u}$ and u^* be the payoff vectors corresponding to two stable equilibrium points in G^*. Clearly payoff vector u^* (and the corresponding equilibrium point) will be favored by player 1, while $\bar{u}$ (and the corresponding equilibrium point) will be favored by players 2 and 3. We will again assume (as we did in the case of the cooperative game G) that, if the players cannot reach agreement between adopting $\bar{u}$ or u^*, then they will receive the payoff vector $c = (0, 0, 0)$. Now if we analyze this noncooperative game G^* in terms of *unrestricted bilateral* risk-dominance relations, then u^* will strongly risk-dominate $\bar{u}$, rather than the other way around. That is, since the game is now a noncooperative game, and thus player 1 can bargain *separately* with each of the other two players, he will be able to get each of them to agree to u^*. For instance, if we consider the bargaining between players 1 and 2, by Zeuthen's Principle player 2 will have to accept u^*, because $u_1^* \cdot u_2^* = 108 > \bar{u}_1 \cdot \bar{u}_2 = 100$. Similarly, if we consider the bargaining between players 1 and 3, player 3 will have to accept u^* because $u_1^* \cdot u_3^* = 108 > \bar{u}_1 \cdot \bar{u}_3 = 100$.

Using the alternative version of Zeuthen's Principle [Condition (8.8) of Section 8.5], we of course obtain the same conclusion. The three players' risk limits are

$$r_1 = \frac{u_1^* - \bar{u}_1}{u_1^* - c_1} = \frac{2}{12} = \frac{1}{6} = .17$$

$$r_2 = \frac{\bar{u}_2 - u_2{}^*}{\bar{u}_2 - c_2} = \frac{1}{10} = .10$$

$$r_3 = r_2 = .10$$

Players 2 and 3, bargaining separately with player 1, must yield to him because $r_2 = r_3 = .10 < r_1 = .17$.

To sum up, from a bargaining point of view, the essential difference between a *cooperative* and a *noncooperative* game is this: In a cooperative game the players with similar interests (e.g., players 2 and 3 in our example) can strengthen their bargaining position by acting as a *coalition.* For instance, they may agree that *neither* of them will make a concession to the other side without the consent of his coalition partner. [Intuitively speaking, such an agreement will strengthen their bargaining position against the other player(s), because it will make them less likely to grant concessions than they would be if each of them acted independently.[3]] In contrast, in a noncooperative game such an agreement would be ineffective, because it would have no binding force.

For this reason in a noncooperative game all effective bargaining will remain essentially a two-person affair, taking place between two independent players i and j. On the contrary, in a cooperative game all bargaining will become in general a common concern to all n players and will be guided by *multilateral* risk-dominance relations – except in those special cases where all players other than players i and j happen to be *indifferent* between the two alternatives (in which case the restricted bilateral and the multilateral risk-dominance relations will coincide).

10.5 The joint-bargaining paradox

We have just concluded that our solution concept is in agreement with our common-sense expectations in predicting that the players can improve their bargaining positions by forming coalitions which will act in concert during the bargaining process. While this is true in the contexts just discussed, somewhat paradoxically it turns out not to be true in other contexts. Our purpose in this section is to discover the reasons for this paradox.

Consider again the three-person simple bargaining game G (discussed in the previous section) whose payoff space P is defined by the inequalities $u_1 + u_2 + u_3 \leq 30$ and $u_i \geq 0$ for $i = 1, 2, 3$, and whose conflict point is $c = (0, 0, 0)$. As we have seen if all three players are regarded as *different* and independent players, then the solution is $\bar{u} = (10, 10, 10)$. But suppose that players 2 and 3 decide to act as *one* player and agree that they will split equally the joint payoff that they obtain this way. Then the game will become a two-person game between coalition (23) and player 1. Hence each side will obtain a payoff $u_1 = u_{23} = 15$. If players 2 and 3 later split their joint payoff u_{23}, then the final outcome will become $\bar{u} = (15, 7.5, 7.5)$. Consequently the fact that players 2 and 3 have joined forces has actually *decreased* their payoffs from 10 to 7.5. Clearly we will obtain a similar result in *all n*-person simple bargaining games if two or more players decide to act as one player (except in the trivial case in which *all n* players participate in this agreement). We call this the joint-bargaining paradox. This paradox is not attributable to some peculiarity of our solution concept, because *any* possible solution concept will show this behavior if it satisfies the symmetry and the joint-efficiency postulates (which are obviously necessary ingredients of any acceptable solution for simple bargaining games).

However, we can resolve this paradox if we analyze the situation in greater detail by means of Zeuthen's Principle. First suppose that all three players act as independent players. Then payoff vector $\bar{u}$ will be a *stable* agreement point. Suppose that player 1 tries to exact one more utility unit from (say) player 2, i.e., suggests the payoff vector $\bar{u}' = (11, 9, 10)$. Then in the resulting bargaining player 1's risk limit will be $\bar{r}_1 = 1/11$, while player 2's risk limit will be $\bar{r}_2 = 1/10 > \bar{r}_1 = 1/11$, and so player 1 will have to stop pressing his demand.

In contrast, payoff vector $\bar{\bar{u}}$ will be *unstable*. Suppose that player 2 wants to exact a one-unit concession from player 1, i.e., suggests the payoff vector $\bar{\bar{u}}' = (14, 8.5, 7.5)$ instead of $\bar{\bar{u}}$. Then in the resulting bargaining player 1's risk limit will be $\bar{r}_1 = 1/15$, while player 2's risk limit will be $\bar{r}_2 = 1/8.5 > \bar{r}_1 = 1/15$, and so player 1 will have to yield.

Next take the case where players 2 and 3 decide to act as *one* player and agree to split equally the joint payoff they will obtain. Suppose that the actual bargaining on behalf of coalition (23) will be done by player 2. Now we can make two alternative assumptions (both of which, however, lead to the same results).

One possibility[4] is to assume that, when players 2 and 3 will act as one player, this means that player 2 will regard any payoff received by his partner as his *own* and vice versa, i.e., that both players will act with a view to maximizing their *joint payoff $u_{23} = u_2 + u_3$*. Now payoff vector $\bar{u}$ will become *unstable*, and payoff vector $\bar{\bar{u}}$ will become *stable*. For instance, suppose that the players' provisional agreement point is $\bar{u}$ but that player 1 presses for the alternative payoff vector $\bar{u}'$. In the resulting bargaining player 1's risk limit will still be $\bar{r}_1 = 1/11$. But player 2's risk limit now becomes

$$\bar{r}_2 = \frac{(\bar{u}_2 + \bar{u}_3) - (\bar{u}_2' + \bar{u}_3')}{(\bar{u}_2 + \bar{u}_3) - (c_2 + c_3)} = \frac{20 - 19}{20 - 0} = \frac{1}{20}$$

In contrast, in the case of independent bargaining, player 2's risk limit was

$$\bar{r}_2 = \frac{\bar{u}_2 - \bar{u}_2'}{\bar{u}_2 - c_2} = \frac{10 - 9}{10 - 0} = \frac{1}{10}$$

Hence now $\bar{r}_2 = 1/20 < \bar{r}_1 = 1/11$, and so player 2, acting now on behalf of coalition (23), will have to yield.

On the other hand, $\bar{\bar{u}}$ will now be *stable*. Suppose that player 2 will suggest moving from $\bar{\bar{u}}$ to $\bar{\bar{u}}'$. Then in the resulting bargaining player 1's risk limit will still be $\bar{r}_1 = 1/15$. But player 2's risk limit now becomes

$$\bar{r}_2 = \frac{(\bar{u}_2' + \bar{u}_3') - (\bar{u}_2 + \bar{u}_3)}{(\bar{u}_2' + \bar{u}_3') - (c_2 + c_3)} = \frac{16 - 15}{16 - 0} = \frac{1}{16}$$

In contrast, in the case of independent bargaining, player 2's risk limit was

$$\bar{r}_2 = \frac{\bar{u}_2' - \bar{u}_2}{\bar{u}_2' - c_2} = \frac{8.5 - 7.5}{8.5 - 0} = \frac{1}{8.5}$$

Hence now $\bar{r}_2 = 1/16 < \bar{r}_1 = 1/15$, and so player 2 will have to drop his demand for moving from $\bar{u}$ to $\bar{u}'$.

Comparing the expressions defining $\bar{r}_2$ and $\bar{r}_2$ in the two cases, we can see that the essential difference is in the *denominator,* which approximately doubles when player 2 represents not only his own interests but also those of player 3. Intuitively this means that in this case player 2 will act with *greater caution* than he would act if he did not have to represent player 3 as well. Acting with greater caution decreases his risk limit (i.e., his willingness to risk a conflict); and therefore, by Zeuthen's Principle, he will obtain less favorable terms than those which he and his partner could obtain if they acted independently.

More particularly the reason for player 2's greater caution when he also acts on player 3's behalf will be this: Since agreement always requires the consent of *all* players, an intransigent attitude by any *one* player can always jeopardize the payoffs of *all* players. But if all players act independently, then each player will care only about the losses he *himself* would suffer if no agreement could be reached. In contrast, if player 2 regards player 3's interests as his own, then he will be equally concerned about player 3's possible losses, and this will roughly *double* his *reluctance to risk a conflict* by refusing a concession – which will make him willing to accept *less favorable* terms.

Thus our result is not so paradoxical after all. If two or more players form a coalition for bargaining purposes, this will tend to *strengthen* their bargaining positions if this organizational change *strengthens* their determination to obtain better terms and *weakens* their reluctance to risk a conflict. But if it has the opposite effect, then by forming such a coalition they will actually *weaken* their bargaining positions.

10.6 Bargaining by coalitions

Players 2 and 3 of our example could act as one bargaining unit *without* worsening their bargaining positions vis-à-vis player 1, if they took care that the person representing their coalition should *not* take a more conservative attitude then they would take themselves if they acted independently. Formally this can be achieved if player 2 (or whoever acts on behalf of the coalition) defines the joint payoff (cardinal utility function) to be maximized for the coalition as $u_{23}* = (u_2 - c_2) \cdot (u_3 - c_3)$ rather than as $u_{23} = u_2 + u_3$. If player 1 tries to maximize u_1 while player 2 tries to maximize $u_{23}{}^*$, then the Nash solution of the resulting two-person game will be at the point where the product

$$(u_1 - c_1)(u_{23}{}^* - 0) = (u_1 - c_1)(u_2 - c_2)(u_3 - c_3)$$

is maximized – which means that the solution of this two-person game will coincide with the solution $u = \bar{u}$ of the original three-person game G. More generally, we can state the following theorem.

Theorem 10.3. The joint payoff function of a coalition. Let $u = \bar{u}$ be the solution of a given n-person simple bargaining game G under individual bargaining. Let $u = \bar{u}^*$ be the solution of the same game when s players form a coalition S and act as *one* bargaining unit (i.e., as one player), so that the original n-person game is transformed into an $(n - s + 1)$-person bargaining game G^*. Then the solution $\bar{u}^*$ of G^* will be the same as that of G, i.e., we will have $\bar{u}^* = \bar{u}$, if coalition S will act as one player whose payoff function (or cardinal utility function) is

$$U^S(u) = \prod_{i \in S} (u_i - c_i) \tag{10.8}$$

Proof. The vector $\bar{u}^*$ lies at the point where the product

$$\pi^* = (U^S - 0) \prod_{i \notin S} (u_i - c_i)$$

is maximized subject to Conditions (9.5a) through (9.5c). The vector $\bar{u}$ lies at the point where the product

$$\pi = \prod_{i \in N} (u_i - c_i)$$

is maximized subject to the same conditions. But $\pi^* = \pi$. Therefore $\bar{u}^* = \bar{u}$.

The following theorem is closely related to Theorem 10.3.

Definitions. Let u^* and u^{**} be two payoff vectors in P, satisfying $u_i{}^* \geq c_i$ and $u_i{}^{**} \geq c_i$ for all players i. Suppose that all players i in a given coalition S would prefer u^* to u^{**}, because $u_i{}^* > u_i{}^{**}$ for all $i \in S$, whereas all players j in the complementary coalition $\bar{S} = N - S$ would prefer u^{**} to u^* because $u_j{}^{**} > u_j{}^*$ for all $j \in \bar{S}$. Let us define the *joint payoff functions* of S and $\bar{S}$ as

$$U^S(u) = \prod_{i \in S} (u_i - c_i)$$

and

$$U^{\bar{S}}(u) = \prod_{j \in \bar{S}} (u_j - c_j)$$

in accordance with (10.8).

Moreover, let us define the *joint risk limits* of the two coalitions as

$$r^S = \frac{U^S(u^*) - U^S(u^{**})}{U^S(u^*) - U^S(c)} \tag{10.9}$$

and

$$r^{\overline{S}} = \frac{U^{\overline{S}}(u^{**}) - U^{\overline{S}}(u^*)}{U^{\overline{S}}(u^{**}) - U^{\overline{S}}(c)} \tag{10.10}$$

which are the risk limits that we would obtain if we regarded the game as a *two-person* bargaining game $G_{S\overline{S}}$ between coalition S and coalition $\overline{S}$, with the payoff functions U^S and $U^{\overline{S}}$. We will say that, in this two-person game between coalitions S and $\overline{S}$, the payoff vector u^* favored by coalition S *strongly risk-dominates* the payoff vector u^{**} favored by coalition $\overline{S}$, whenever

$$r^S > r^{\overline{S}} \tag{10.11}$$

Now we can state:

Theorem 10.4. The following two statements are equivalent:
1. In the two-person simple bargaining game $G_{S\overline{S}}$ between coalitions S and $\overline{S}$ the payoff vector u^* favored by coalition S has *strong* (bilateral) *risk-dominance* over the payoff vector u^{**} favored by coalition $\overline{S}$.
2. In the original *n-person* simple bargaining game G payoff vector u^* has *strong multilateral risk-dominance* over payoff vector u^{**}.

A similar relationship holds also between the corresponding *weak* risk-dominance relations.

Proof. Since $U^S(c) = U^{\overline{S}}(c) = 0$, (9.11) is equivalent to the inequality

$$U^S(u^*) \cdot U^{\overline{S}}(u^*) > U^S(u^{**}) \cdot U^{\overline{S}}(u^{**})$$

This is in turn equivalent to

$$\pi(u^*) = \prod_{i \in N} (u_i^* - c_i) > \prod_{i \in N} (u_i^{**} - c_i) = \pi(u^{**})$$

which is the definition of multilateral risk-dominance.

It is of some theoretical interest to redefine the two coalitions' joint risk limits r^S and $r^{\overline{S}}$ in terms of the members' *individual* risk limits. This gives the following theorem.

Theorem 10.5. The joint risk limit of a coalition. Again let u^* be a payoff vector favored by all members i of coalition S, and let u^{**} be a payoff vector favored by all members j of the complementary coalition $\overline{S}$. Then the *joint risk limits* r^S and

$r^{\overline{S}}$ of the two coalitions [defined by (10.9) and (10.10)] can be written as

$$r^S = 1 - \prod_{i \in S} (1 - r_i) \tag{10.12}$$

$$r^{\overline{S}} = 1 - \prod_{j \in \overline{S}} (1 - r_j) \tag{10.13}$$

where r_i and r_j are the *individual risk limits* of all players i and j, defined as

$$r_i = \frac{u_i^* - u_i^{**}}{u_i^* - c_i} \quad \text{for all} \quad i \in S \tag{10.14}$$

and

$$r_j = \frac{u_j^{**} - u_j^*}{u_j^{**} - c_j} \quad \text{for all} \quad j \in \overline{S} \tag{10.15}$$

in accordance with Equation (8.4) of Section 8.4.

Proof. By (10.9),

$$1 - r^S = \frac{U^S(u^{**}) - U^S(c)}{U^S(u^*) - U^S(c)} = \frac{U^S(u^{**})}{U^S(u^*)} \tag{10.16}$$

since $U^S(c) = 0$.
Similarly, by (10.10),

$$1 - r^{\overline{S}} = \frac{U^{\overline{S}}(u^*)}{U^{\overline{S}}(u^{**})} \tag{10.17}$$

On the other hand, by (10.14) and (10.15),

$$1 - r_i = \frac{u_i^{**} - c_i}{u_i^* - c_i} \quad \text{for all } i \in S \tag{10.18}$$

$$1 - r_j = \frac{u_j^* - c_j}{u_j^{**} - c_j} \quad \text{for all } j \in \overline{S} \tag{10.19}$$

Using the definition of U^S and $U^{\overline{S}}$ in (10.8), in view of (10.16) through (10.19), Equations (10.12) and (10.13) follow, as desired.

Theorem 10.5 can be regarded as a *composition law* for the individual risk limits r_i of the members i of a given coalition S. It specifies how the various players' resistance to making concessions is *increased* when they act together as a coalition.

The theorem can be given an intuitive interpretation in terms of the following model. (Notice that our proof of Theorem 10.5 is quite independent of this model, which serves only as a heuristic rationalization of the theorem just proved.)

Suppose that, in bargaining between coalitions S and $\overline{S}$, any member i of S can *veto* the acceptance, by coalition S, of payoff vector u^{**} favored by the opposing coalition $\overline{S}$. Likewise any member j of $\overline{S}$ can veto the acceptance, by coalition $\overline{S}$, of payoff vector u^* favored by coalition S. Suppose also that the highest probability of player i's using his veto power is r_i. Then the highest probability of u^{**} being *rejected* by coalition S (because at least one player i in S uses his veto power) will be

$$r^S = 1 - \prod_{i \in S} (1 - r_i)$$

Thus r^S can be regarded as the *highest probability of a conflict* that coalition S as a whole is willing to face rather than accept the payoff vector u^{**} favored by the opposing coalition $\overline{S}$. That is, r^S can be regarded as the *joint risk limit* of coalition S. The joint risk limit $r^{\overline{S}}$ of the complementary coalition $\overline{S}$ can be interpreted in a similar way.

10.7 The joint-bargaining paradox: a second interpretation

Consider again the three-person simple bargaining game G whose payoff space P is defined by the inequalities $u_1 + u_2 + u_3 \leq 30$ and $u_i \geq 0$ for $i = 1, 2, 3$ and whose conflict point is $c = (0, 0, 0)$. We have seen that, if the three players bargain independently, then the solution of G is $\overline{u} = (10, 10, 10)$. On the other hand, if players 2 and 3 bargain as one player vis-à-vis player 3 and later split equally the joint payoff that they obtain this way, then paradoxically the solution becomes $\overline{\overline{u}} = (15, 7.5, 7.5)$.

In Section 10.4 we explained this result by the assumption that the player representing the coalition (say, player 2) will regard the interests of his coalition partner as his *own*, and this will make him *more cautious* in bargaining with player 1 and will make him willing to accept less favorable terms than he and his coalition partner could obtain if they acted independently.

Now we will show that the same result can also be explained in a different way. Let us assume that player 2, when he bargains with player 1 on behalf of coalition (23), will be concerned only with maximizing his *own* payoff u_2 and will not be concerned with player 3's payoff u_3 as such. But of course his behavior will be influenced by the fact that he is under a commitment to hand over to player 3 *half* of any *gain* resulting from a concession that he may be able to extract from player 1. On the other hand, he can pass over to player 3 *half* of any *loss* resulting from a concession that he may make to player 1. It is easy to verify that this sharing of gains and losses with his coalition partner will *decrease* player 2's risk limit r_2 in bargaining with player 1 just as effectively as would the assumption (used in Section 10.4) that he was interested in maximizing the joint payoff $u_{23} = u_2 + u_3$, rather than in maximizing his own payoff u_2 alone.

For instance, suppose that player 1 suggests to player 2 that the payoff vector $\overline{u} = (10, 10, 10)$ should be replaced by $\overline{u}' = (11, 9, 10)$. In practice this would now mean replacing $\overline{u}$ by $\overline{u}'' = (11, 9.5, 9.5)$, because players 2 and 3 would always split their joint proceeds. Hence in the resulting bargaining player 2's risk limit will be

$$\bar{r}_2 = \frac{10 - 9.5}{10 - 0} = \frac{.5}{10} = .05$$

instead of the risk limit

$$\bar{r}_2 = \frac{10 - 9}{10 - 0} = \frac{1}{10} = .10$$

which player 2 would exhibit if he and his coalition player bargained independently. Since player 1's risk limit will remain $\bar{r}_1 = 1/11 = .09 > \bar{r}_2 = .05$, player 2 will have to yield on behalf of the coalition, and so $\bar{u}$ will be *unstable*.

In contrast, suppose that player 2 suggests to player 1 that the payoff vector $\bar{\bar{u}} = (15, 7.5, 7.5)$ should be replaced by $\bar{\bar{u}}' = (14, 8.5, 7.5)$. In practice this would now mean replacing $\bar{\bar{u}}$ by $\bar{\bar{u}}'' = (14, 8, 8)$, because player 2 must pass on half of the gain to player 3. Therefore in the resulting bargaining player 2's risk limit will be

$$\bar{\bar{r}}_2 = \frac{8.5 - 8.0}{8.5 - 0} = \frac{.5}{8.5} = .06$$

instead of the risk limit

$$\bar{\bar{r}}_2 = \frac{8.5 - 7.5}{8.5 - 0} = \frac{1}{8.5} = .12$$

which player 2 would have under independent bargaining. Since player 1's risk limit will remain $\bar{\bar{r}}_1 = 1/15 = .07 > \bar{\bar{r}}_2 = .06$, player 2 will not be able to insist on the change demanded, and $\bar{\bar{u}}$ will be *stable*.

Compared with the model used in Section 10.4, under our present model, when player 2 is bargaining on behalf of the coalition (23), this will have the effect of *decreasing* the *numerator* of the expression defining his risk limit r_2. In contrast, under our previous model the effect of this was *increasing* the *denominator* of the same expression. But under both models the end result is the same. The value of r_2 will decrease in the same way. In other words, under our previous model player 2 became more cautious in his bargaining behavior, because he felt responsible not only for his own losses in case of a conflict with player 1, but also for player 3's losses: That is, he felt a stronger disincentive against risking a conflict. In contrast, under our present model he will feel a weaker positive incentive to press for better terms, since half of the net gain would go to player 3, which, however, leads to the same end result.

Our new model again suggests a way in which players 2 and 3 could *avoid* weakening their bargaining position in case they wanted to act as *one* bargaining unit. Instead of agreeing that player 2 will pass over to player 3 *half* of any gain that he can exact from player 1, player 2 could guarantee player 3 the fixed amount of $u_3 = 10$ on the condition that he can keep for himself the remainder of the amount that he will obtain from player 1.[5] In this case player 2 will be able to retain the full amount of any *additional* concession that he can extract from player 1. In economic terminology his marginal incentive (marginal private gain) will be equal to the marginal joint gain of the coalition. Consequently for any pair of possible payoff vectors u and u^* player 2's risk limit r_2 will be the same as in the case of independent bargaining by each player. Hence the solution will also be the same, viz., $\bar{u} = (10 \quad 10, 10)$.

To sum up, we have seen that the symmetry and joint-efficiency postulates entail the somewhat paradoxical conclusion that, if two or more players form a coalition and act as *one* bargaining unit, then this will tend to *weaken* their bargaining position vis-à-vis the remaining players (unless they take special steps to prevent this). This we have called the *joint-bargaining paradox*. We have argued that Zeuthen's Principle suggests two alternative models for explaining this paradoxical result. One is based on the assumption that the members of the coalition will act as one player in the full sense of the word and will regard one another's interests as their *own*: We have shown that this will make them less willing to risk a conflict and more willing to accept unfavorable terms. The other model is based on the assumption that each member of the coalition will be concerned only with his *own* interests: But, acting as a member of a coalition, he will have less incentive to press for better terms, because he will have to share with his coalition partners any concession that he can obtain.

11

n-Person cooperative games with transferable utility: the modified Shapley value

11.1 Simple bargaining games with transferable utility

Let G be an n-person simple bargaining game with *transferable utility*. Then its payoff space P will be defined by an inequality of the form

$$\bar{\eta} \le \sum_{i \in N} u_i \le \eta$$

Let its conflict point be $c = (c_1, \ldots, c_n)$. It is easy to verify that the solution of G will be the payoff vector $u = \bar{u}$ where for every player i

$$\bar{u}_i = c_i + \frac{1}{n} \left(\eta - \sum_{j \in N} c_j \right) = \frac{1}{n} \eta + \frac{n-1}{n} c_i + \frac{1}{n} \sum_{\substack{j \in N \\ j \ne i}} c_j \tag{11.1}$$

because this is the point at which the Nash product $\Pi(u_i - c_i)$ will be maximized. (That $\bar{u}$ must be the solution can also be shown more directly by considering the fact that G can be transformed into a fully symmetric game if we subject every player's utility function to the transformation $u_i' = u_i - c_i$.)

In other words, in a simple bargaining game with transferable utility all players will receive the *same net payoff*

$$u_i - c_i = u_j - c_j = \frac{1}{n} \left(\eta - \sum_{k \in N} c_k \right) \tag{11.2}$$

If a simple bargaining game with transferable utility has the conflict point $c = (0, \ldots, 0)$, then we call it an *elementary game*. Clearly an elementary game is always fully symmetric with respect to the various players.

The payoff space P of a bargaining game with transferable utility is not compact. But we can always restrict our attention to the agreement space P^*, which we have defined (Section 10.1) as that region of P which lies in the orthant defined by the n simultaneous inequalities $u_i \ge c_i$ for all $i \in N$. This agreement space P^* is always a compact (and convex) set.

11.2 Characteristic functions

Now we will consider n-person cooperative games with transferable utility, which in general are not simple bargaining games, because the rules of the game do not uniquely specify the conflict payoffs that the players will receive if no agreement is accepted by *all* players.

Suppose that the rules of some game G at least specify the *joint payoff*

$$\sum_{i \in S} u_i = v(S)$$

which the members of any given *coalition* $S \subseteq N$ would achieve if they did cooperate among themselves but did not cooperate with the remaining players. Then the function $v(S)$ is called the *characteristic function* of the game, and the game G itself is called a game *given in the characteristic-function form*. Clearly the function $v(S)$ has as its domain all possible coalitions S, i.e., all *subsets* of the set N of all n players. (Therefore it is called a *set function*.) Its range is the set of all possible joint-payoff values, i.e., the set of all real numbers. Of course, we could specify not only the joint payoff of each coalition S but also the individual payoffs of the players belonging to S. But this would be less appropriate, because we are assuming that G is a game with *transferable utility* in which the members of any coalition S can freely *redistribute* their joint payoff among themselves. Consequently the individual payoffs of the various players belonging to a given coalition S are *variables* under these players' own (joint) control and are not *constants* specified by the rules of the game. Only the joint payoff $v(S)$ of all players in coalition S is a constant directly determined by these rules. This joint payoff $v(S)$ is called the *value* of coalition S.[1]

It is natural to assume that the characteristic function $v(S)$ which specifies the value of every possible coalition S has the following properties

$$v(\phi) = 0 \tag{11.3a}$$

$$v(R \cup S) \geq v(R) + v(S) \quad \text{if} \quad R, S \subseteq N \quad \text{and} \quad R \cap S = \phi \tag{11.3b}$$

Here ϕ denotes the "empty coalition" (or the "empty set") having no members, while $R \cup S$ denotes the *union* of the coalitions R and S. Property (11.3a) states that a "coalition" containing no players will obtain zero payoff. Property (11.3b) states that, if two disjoint coalitions R and S (i.e., two coalitions having no common members) combine their forces, then the members of these two coalitions should be able to obtain payoffs *at least as high* as they could obtain without combining. Because of Property (11.3b) we say that $v(S)$ is a *superadditive* set function.

It is desirable to extend the concept of a characteristic function to all cooperative games with transferable utility, even if they are given not in characteristic-function form but rather in the more general *normal form* [that is, if they are defined by specifying the payoff function U_i for each player i instead of directly specifying the characteristic function $v(S)$]. If we can predict the strategies $\theta^S = \theta_o{}^S$ and $\theta^{\bar{S}} = \theta_o{}^{\bar{S}}$ that each pair of complementary coalitions S and $\bar{S}$ would use against each other in case of a conflict between them, then we can define

$$v(S) = \sum_{i \in S} U_i(\theta_o{}^S, \theta_o{}^{\bar{S}}) \qquad v(\bar{S}) = \sum_{i \in \bar{S}} U_i(\theta_o{}^S, \theta_o{}^{\bar{S}})$$

Von Neumann and Morgenstern [1953, Chap. XI] have argued that in such a conflict situation each side should act on the most pessimistic expectations. That is, coalition S should act on the expectation that coalition $\bar{S}$ would try to minimize the joint payoff of coalition S, and conversely. Thus to minimize the other side's damaging power each coalition should use a *maximin* strategy $\theta_o{}^S$ or $\theta_o{}^{\bar{S}}$. Accordingly von Neumann and Morgenstern define

$$v(S) = \sum_{i \in S} U_i(\theta_o{}^S, \theta_o{}^{\bar{S}}) = \max_{\theta^S \in \Sigma^S} \min_{\theta^{\bar{S}} \in \Sigma^{\bar{S}}} \sum_{i \in S} U_i(\theta^S, \theta^{\bar{S}}) \tag{11.4}$$

where Σ^S and $\Sigma^{\bar{S}}$ are the sets of joint strategies available to coalitions S and $\bar{S}$, respectively, in the game. They have also shown that the characteristic function $v(S)$ defined by (11.4) is *superadditive*, i.e., satisfies (11.3a) and (11.3b).

But this model is open to the following objection: Why should either side expect the other side to choose the strategy of the highest damaging power irrespective of the *costs* to itself? This may be a very natural expectation in a constant-sum game, where one side's loss is necessarily the other side's gain, and vice versa, so that each side must cause the highest possible damage to the other side in order to maximize its own joint payoff. But in a variable-sum game one would rather expect that each side would try to find a suitable compromise between trying to *maximize* the costs of a conflict to the other side and trying to *minimize* the costs of a conflict to itself - in other words, between trying to *minimize* the joint payoff of the opposing coalition and trying to *maximize* the joint payoff of their own coalition. We will see later how this qualitative idea can be translated into quantitative terms and will define an alternative characteristic-function concept in Section (11.8).

Apart from constant-sum games, there is another class of games in which the above objection to the von Neumann–Morgenstern characteristic function has no application. Suppose that, in case of a conflict between any pair of complementary coalitions S and $\bar{S}$, each side's joint payoff is independent of the other side's joint strategy and is dependent only on its *own* joint strategy. Then in case of a conflict we shall have

$$\sum_{i \in S} U_i(\theta^S, \theta^{\bar{S}}) = \sum_{i \in S} U_i(\theta^S) \qquad \sum_{i \in \bar{S}} U_i(\theta^S, \theta^{\bar{S}}) = \sum_{i \in \bar{S}} U_i(\theta^{\bar{S}})$$

Hence we can define

$$v(S) = \max_{\theta^S \in \Sigma^S} \sum_{i \in S} U_i(\theta^S) \qquad v(\bar{S}) = \max_{\theta^{\bar{S}} \in \Sigma^{\bar{S}}} \sum_{i \in \bar{S}} U_i(\theta^{\bar{S}})$$

In this case the definition is equivalent to (11.4), i.e., to the von Neumann–Morgenstern definition. Since now the only damaging action available to either side against the other is simple noncooperation, the problem of how much damage to inflict on the other side does not arise.

It is natural to argue that games given in *characteristic-function form* are really games of this type. That is, they can be identified with games given in normal form such that do not allow other damaging actions than simple noncooperation in conflict situations.

More generally the von Neumann–Morgenstern characteristic function will be appropriate in all games possessing the following property (which is satisfied *both* in constant-sum games *and* in games allowing no positive damaging actions): Let S and $\bar{S}$ be any two complementary coalitions. Let $\theta_o{}^{\bar{S}}$ be any possible joint strategy of coalition $\bar{S}$. Then coalition S must always possess some joint strategy $\theta_o{}^S$ *simultaneously maximizing* its own joint payoff *and minimizing* the other coalition's joint payoff. That is, for every joint strategy $\theta_o{}^{\bar{S}} \in \Sigma^{\bar{S}}$, there must exist some joint strategy $\theta_o{}^S \in \Sigma^S$ simultaneously satisfying

$$\sum_{i \in S} U_i(\theta_o{}^S, \theta_o{}^{\bar{S}}) = \max_{\theta^S \in \Sigma^S} \sum_{i \in S} U_i(\theta^S, \theta_o{}^{\bar{S}})$$

and

$$\sum_{i \in \bar{S}} U_i(\theta_o{}^S, \theta_o{}^{\bar{S}}) = \min_{\theta^S \in \Sigma^S} \sum_{i \in \bar{S}} U_i(\theta^S, \theta_o{}^{\bar{S}})$$

This statement is true for *each* pair of complementary coalitions S and $\bar{S}$ in the game. Whenever this condition is satisfied, there will be no conflict between trying to maximize one's own coalition's joint payoff and trying to minimize the opposing coalition's joint payoff. Thus von Neumann and Morgenstern's definition of a characteristic function [see Equation (11.4)] will be fully appropriate.

11.3 The Shapley value

An intuitively attractive solution concept for n-person cooperative games with transferable utility has been proposed by Shapley [1953] and is called the *Shapley value*. It is defined in terms of the characteristic function $v(S)$ of the game (for the time being we will assume that the game is directly given in characteristic-function form or that, if this is not the case, the problem of defining a satisfactory characteristic function for the game has already been solved). We denote the Shapley value of a given game G to player i by $\bar{u}_i$. It represents the payoff that player i would receive under this solution concept. (Its interpretation in more specific terms will be discussed later.)

The Shapley value can be defined by means of the following postulates:

1. *Joint efficiency.* The n players' payoffs (Shapley values) $\bar{u}_i$ add up to the value of the n-person coalition (which is the highest joint payoff the n players can achieve within the game). That is,

$$\sum_{i \in N} \bar{u}_i = v(N)$$

If a given player i fails to contribute anything to the value of *any* coalition that he may join, i.e., if $v(S + (i)) = v(S)$ for *every* coalition $S \subseteq N$, then he is called a *dummy player*. (He may be regarded as a player who belongs to the game in a purely formal sense but whose behavior has no effect whatever on the course of the game.)

2. *Zero payoff to any dummy player.* If player i is a dummy, then his payoff is $\bar{u}_i = 0$.[2]

Let G be a game given in characteristic-function form. Then G is called a *symmetric* game if the characteristic function remains unchanged when we interchange *any* pair of players i and j. Intuitively speaking, in a symmetric game all players have identical positions.

3. *Symmetry.* If G is a symmetric game, then all n players will obtain the *same* payoffs $\bar{u}_1 = \cdots = \bar{u}_n$.

Let G and G^* be two games played by the *same* n players, with the characteristic functions $v(S)$ and $v^*(S)$. Let G^{**} be again a game played by the same players, with the characteristic function $v^{**}(S) = v(S) + v^*(S)$ for every coalition S. Then G^{**} is called the *sum game* of G and G^*, while G and G^* are called its *component games*. We can regard G^{**} as the composite game which results if the same players play *both* G and G^* (at the same time or one after the other). We will write $G^{**} = G + G^*$.

If G and G^* are *not* played by the *same* players, we can define their sum game G^{**} as follows: Let G be a game played by the n players in set N, and let G^* be a game played by the n^* players in set N^*. (N and N^* may or may not be disjoint sets.) Then we can formally include in game G as *dummy players* all players in set N^* but not in set N, i.e., all players in set $(N^* - N)$. Similarly we can formally include in game G^* as dummy players all players in set N but not in set N^*, i.e., all players in set $(N - N^*)$. Thus we can formally always assume that *both* games will be played by *all* players in the combined set $M = N \cup N^*$, which will have $m \leq n + n^*$ members. Then we can construct the sum game $G^{**} = G + G^*$ according to the definition already given. The concept of a sum game can be extended in an obvious way to the case in which there are more than two component games to be added.

We also introduce the concept of a *difference game*. Let us call G a difference game of G^{**} and G^* and write $G = G^{**} - G^*$, whenever $G^{**} = G^* + G$.

4. *Additivity.* For any given player i, his payoff $\bar{u}_i^{**}$ from a sum game $G^{**} = G + G^*$ equals the *sum* of his payoffs $\bar{u}_i$ and $\bar{u}_i^*$ from the component games G and G^*; that is, $\bar{u}_i^{**} = \bar{u}_i + \bar{u}_i^*$.

In other words, if player i participates in both G and G^*, then his total payoff will be the *sum* of the payoffs he would obtain from G and from G^* if he played each game *separately*.

The joint-efficiency and symmetry postulates (Postulates 1 and 3) are familiar to us and require no further comment. The dummy-player postulate (Postulate 2) states the obvious fact that a dummy player has no bargaining power against the other players, because they do not need his cooperation. Thus only the additivity postulate needs discussion. We will return to it later (Section 11.6).

Shapley has proved the following important theorem:

Theorem 11.1. There is *one* and *only one* set of payoffs $\bar{u}_1, \ldots, \bar{u}_n$ satisfying Postulates 1 to 4. The payoff $\bar{u}_i$ (called the Shapley value of the game to player i)

can be defined as

$$\bar{u}_i = \sum_{\substack{S \ni i \\ S \subseteq N}} \frac{(s-1)!\,(n-s)!}{n!} v(S) - \sum_{\substack{S \not\ni i \\ S \subseteq N}} \frac{s!(n-s-1)!}{n!} v(S) \qquad \text{(I)}$$

where s is the number of players in any coalition S.

Thus the Shapley value is a linear combination of the values $v(S)$ of all possible coalitions S - with *positive* coefficients in the case of all coalitions S containing player i and with *negative* coefficients in the case of all coalitions S *not* containing player i.

The proof of Theorem 11.1 is based on the fact that any n-person cooperative game G with transferable utility can be obtained as a *sum game* (or at least as an algebraic-sum game)[3] of a finite number of elementary games G^S - with one elementary game G^S for every nonempty coalition S [this means $(2^n - 1)$ such elementary games for any n-person game G].

Let $G^S(\eta)$ be an elementary game whose characteristic function $v^S(R)$ is defined as

$$v^S(R) = 0 \quad \text{if} \quad R \subset S$$

$$v^S(R) = \eta \quad \text{if} \quad R = S$$

Let S be a subset of N. We can add all players in N but not in S as dummy players to $G^S(\eta)$. Then the characteristic function $v^S(R)$ must be redefined as

$$v^S(R) = 0 \quad \text{if} \quad R \not\supseteq S$$

$$v^S(R) = \eta \quad \text{if} \quad R \supseteq S$$

That is, $v^S(R) = \eta$ if $R = S$ or if R is a *superset* of S. Otherwise $v^S(R) = 0$.

Before proving Theorem 11.1, we will first prove:

Lemma 1. Let G be an n-person cooperative game with transferable utility, whose characteristic function is $v(S)$. For every possible coalition $S \subseteq N$, let η^S be the quantity

$$\eta^S = \sum_{R \subseteq S} (-1)^{s-r} v(R) \qquad (11.5)$$

where s and r denote the number of players in each coalition S and R.

Suppose that $\eta^S \geq 0$ for *all* $S \subseteq N$.

Then G is the sum game of the $(2^n - 1)$ elementary games $G^S(\eta^S)$; that is,

$$G = \sum_{S \subseteq N} G^S(\eta^S)$$

Proof. We have to prove that

$$\sum_{R \subseteq N} v^R(S) = v(S) \quad \text{for every} \quad S \subseteq N$$

Since $v^R(S) = \eta^R$ if $R \subseteq S$, while otherwise $v^R(S) = 0$, and, in view of (11.5), we can write

$$\sum_{R \subseteq N} v^R(S) = \sum_{R \subseteq S} \eta^R = \sum_{R \subseteq S} \sum_{T \subseteq R} (-1)^{r-t} v(T)$$

where t is the number of players in each coalition T. Let T and S be two *given* coalitions such that $T \subseteq S$, and let r be a *given* positive integer such that $t \leq r \leq s$. Then the number of different r-person coalitions R, such that $T \subseteq R \subseteq S$, will be

$$\binom{s-t}{r-t} = \frac{(s-t)!}{(r-t)!\,(s-r)!}$$

Hence

$$\sum_{R \subseteq N} v^R(S) = \sum_{T \subseteq S} \sum_{r=t}^{s} (-1)^{r-t} \cdot \binom{s-t}{r-t} \cdot v(T)$$

But for every $t < s$, and so for every $T \subset S$, we have

$$\sum_{r=t}^{s} (-1)^{r-t} \cdot \binom{s-t}{r-t} = (1-1)^{s-t} = 0$$

Therefore

$$\sum_{R \subseteq N} v^R(S) = v(S)$$

as desired.

For example, consider the three-person game G whose characteristic function is

$$v((1)) = 10 \qquad v((2)) = 20 \qquad v((3)) = 30$$

$$v((12)) = 40 \qquad v((13)) = 40 \qquad v((23)) = 80$$

$$v((123)) = 160$$

This game G can be regarded as the sum game of the seven elementary games G^1, $G^2, G^3, G^{12}, G^{13}, G^{23}$, and G^{123}, whose characteristic functions are defined as

$$G^1: \ v^1((1)) = v^1((12)) = v^1((13)) = v^1((123)) = 10$$

$$\text{but} \quad v^1((2)) = v^1((3)) = v^1((23)) = 0$$

$$G^2: \ v^2((2)) = v^2((12)) = v^2((23)) = v^2((123)) = 20$$

$$\text{but} \quad v^2((1)) = v^2((3)) = v^2((13)) = 0$$

$$G^3: \ v^3((3)) = v^3((13)) = v^3((23)) = v^3((123)) = 30$$

$$\text{but} \quad v^3((1)) = v^3((2)) = v^3((12)) = 0$$

$$G^{12}: \ v^{12}((12)) = v^{12}((123)) = v((12)) - v((1)) - v((2)) = 10$$

but otherwise $v^{12}(S) = 0$

G^{13} : $v^{13}((13)) = v^{13}((123)) = v((13)) - v((1)) - v((3)) = 0$

and otherwise also $v^{13}(S) = 0$

G^{23} : $v^{23}((23)) = v^{23}((123)) = v((23)) - v((2)) - v((3)) = 30$

but otherwise $v^{23}(S) = 0$

G^{123} : $v^{123}((123)) = v((123)) - v((12)) - v((13)) - v((23)) + v((1)) + v((2))$

$+ v((3)) = 60$

but otherwise $v^{123}(S) = 0$

It is easy to verify that these elementary games exactly add up to the original game G, since

$$v((1)) = v^1((1)) + v^2((1)) + v^3((1)) + v^{12}((1)) + v^{13}((1)) + v^{23}((1)) + v^{123}((1))$$

$$= 10 + 6 \cdot 0 = 10$$

Likewise

$$v((2)) = 20 + 6 \cdot 0 = 20$$

$$v((3)) = 30 + 6 \cdot 0 = 30$$

$$v((12)) = 10 + 20 + 0 + 10 + 3 \cdot 0 = 40$$

$$v((13)) = 10 + 0 + 30 + 4 \cdot 0 = 40$$

$$v((23)) = 0 + 20 + 30 + 2 \cdot 0 + 30 + 0 = 80$$

$$v((123)) = 10 + 20 + 30 + 10 + 0 + 30 + 60 = 160 \quad \text{as it should be}$$

Lemma 1 as it stands does not apply to cases where some of the quantities η^S [defined by Equation (11.5)] are *negative*, since $G^S(\eta^S)$ with a negative η^S would *not* give a legitimate elementary game (because its characteristic function would not be superadditive and because it would yield negative net payoffs to the players participating in it).

We will call any coalition S a *negative coalition* if $\eta^S < 0$. For any negative coalition S we define the quantity $\tilde{\eta}^S = |\eta^S| = -\eta^S > 0$ and use the elementary game $G^S(\tilde{\eta}^S)$ instead of the inadmissible negative game $G^S(\eta^S)$ itself. Let $\tilde{v}^S(R)$ be the characteristic function of $G^S(\tilde{\eta}^S)$. Then we can write $v^S(R) = -\tilde{v}^S(R)$.

We will now show that Lemma 1 remains true, even in the case when some coalitions S are negative coalitions, if for any negative coalition S we *subtract* the elementary game $G^S(\tilde{\eta}^S)$ instead of *adding* the elementary game $G^S(\eta^S)$.

Lemma 2. Irrespective of the sign of the quantities η^S, every n-person cooperative game with transferable utility can be written in the form

$$G = \sum_{S \subseteq N} G^S(\eta^S)$$

provided that in case $\eta^S < 0$ the symbol $G^S(\eta^S)$ is interpreted to mean $G^S(\eta^S) = -G^S(\tilde{\eta}^S) = -G^S(-\eta^S)$.

Proof. We have to prove that the relationship

$$\sum_{R \subseteq N} v^R(S) = v(S)$$

is true even if for some coalition R we have $\eta^R < 0$. The proof of Lemma 1 was based on the fact that

$$v^R(S) = \eta^S \quad \text{if} \quad R \subseteq S$$

whereas otherwise

$$v^R(S) = 0$$

But this relationship is still true for all *nonnegative* coalitions R. Indeed it is also true for all *negative* coalitions R, because in this latter case

$$v^R(S) = -\tilde{v}^R(S) = -\tilde{\eta}^S = \eta^S \quad \text{if} \quad R \subseteq S$$

while otherwise

$$v^R(S) = 0 \quad \text{otherwise}$$

Consequently the proof used for Lemma 1 equally applies to Lemma 2.

As an example for a game containing a negative coalition, consider the three-person game $\bar{G}$ whose characteristic function is

$$v((1)) = 10 \qquad v((2)) = 20 \qquad v((3)) = 30$$
$$v((12)) = 40 \qquad v((13)) = 40 \qquad v((23)) = 80$$
$$v((123)) = 91$$

This is the same game as game G of the previous example, but $v((123)) = 160$ has now been replaced by $v((123)) = 91$. The component games $G^1, G^2, G^3, G^{12}, G^{13}$, and G^{23} remain the same as before. However, if we add them up, we obtain

$$\hat{v}((1)) = 10 \qquad \hat{v}((2)) = 20 \qquad \hat{v}((3)) = 30$$
$$\hat{v}((12)) = 40 \qquad \hat{v}((13)) = 40 \qquad \hat{v}((23)) = 80$$
$$\hat{v}((123)) = 100$$

That is, the value $v((123)) = 100$ that we obtain for the all-player coalition $N = (123)$ is 9 units higher than it should be. We could try to define the seventh component game G^{123} as

$$G^{123}: v^{123}((123)) = -9 \text{ and } v^{123}((1)) = v^{123}((2)) = v^{123}((3))$$
$$= v^{123}((12)) = v^{123}((13)) = v^{123}((23)) = 0$$

But this would not give a legitimate game, since $v^{123}(S)$, as defined above, is not superadditive [e.g., $v((1)) + v((23)) = 0 > v((123)) = -9$]. However, we can define a legitimate game $\tilde{G}^{123}$ by using the negative of v^{123} as its characteristic function. This gives

$$\tilde{G}^{123} : \quad \tilde{v}^{123}((123)) = -9 \quad \text{and otherwise} \quad \tilde{v}^{123}(S) = 0$$

If we now *subtract* $\tilde{G}^{123}$ from the other six component games we achieve the same result as if we had *added* its negative, the "inadmissible" negative game G^{123}. Thus we can write

$$\overline{G} = G^1 + G^2 + G^3 + G^{12} + G^{13} + G^{23} - \tilde{G}^{123}$$

We can easily check that

$$v^1((123)) + v^2((123)) + v^3((123)) + v^{12}((123)) + v^{13}((123)) + v^{23}((123))$$

$$- v^{123}((123)) = 10 + 20 + 30 + 10 + 0 + 30 - 9 = 91 = \tilde{v}((123))$$

Using Lemma 2 we can prove Theorem 11.1.

Proof of Theorem 11.1. First consider the case where R is a *nonnegative* coalition. Then, by Postulates 1 and 3, every player i belonging to coalition R will obtain from the elementary game $G^R(\eta^R)$ the payoff

$$w_i^R = \frac{1}{r} \eta^R = \frac{1}{r} \sum_{S \subseteq R} (-1)^{r-s} v(S) \tag{11.6}$$

which, by Postulate 4, must be *added* to the payoffs player i will obtain from the other component elementary games. We will call the payoff w_i^R player i's *dividend* from coalition R.

Next consider the case where R is a *negative* coalition. Then, by Postulates 1 and 3, every player i belonging to coalition R will obtain from the elementary game $G^R(\tilde{\eta}^R)$ the payoff

$$\tilde{w}_i^R = \frac{1}{r} \tilde{\eta}^R = -\frac{1}{r} \eta^R = -\frac{1}{r} \sum_{S \subseteq R} (-1)^{r-s} v(S)$$

which, by Postulate 4, now has to be *subtracted* from the dividends that player i will obtain from other coalitions $R^* \neq R$. This is, of course, equivalent to *adding* the negative quantity

$$w_i^R = -\tilde{w}_i^R = \frac{1}{r} \eta^R = \frac{1}{r} \sum_{S \subseteq R} (-1)^{r-s} v(S)$$

whose definition is formally the same as the definition of the quantity w_i^R for nonnegative coalitions R. This (negative) quantity w_i^R we again call player i's dividend from coalition R.

Finally, any player *j* *not* belonging to a given coalition *R* will be only a dummy player in the elementary game $G^R(\eta^R)$ or $G^R(\tilde{\eta}^R)$. Therefore, by Postulate 2, he will receive the payoff

$$w_j{}^R = 0$$

irrespective of whether *R* is a nonnegative or a negative coalition.

Consequently, by Postulate 4, the total payoff of any player *i* will be

$$\bar{u}_i = \sum_{\substack{R \subseteq N}} w_i{}^R = \sum_{\substack{R \ni i \\ R \subseteq N}} w_i{}^R = \sum_{\substack{R \ni i \\ R \subseteq N}} \frac{1}{r} \sum_{S \subseteq R} (-1)^{r-s} v(S)$$

For a *given* coalition *S* consisting of *s* players, and for a *given* positive integer *r*, $s \leq r \leq n$, consider all *r*-player coalitions *R* such that $R \ni i$ and $S \subseteq R \subseteq N$. (That is, we require that each coalition *R* should consist of exactly *r* players, that it should contain player *i* as a member, and that it should contain coalition *S* as a subset.) If coalition *S* itself already contains player *i* as a member, then the total number of coalitions *R* satisfying these requirements will be

$$\binom{n-s}{r-s} = \frac{(n-s)!}{(r-s)!\,(n-r)!}$$

If coalition *S* itself does not contain player *i*, then the total number of coalitions *R* satisfying our requirements will be

$$\binom{n-s-1}{r-s-1} = \frac{(n-s-1)!}{(r-s-1)!\,(n-r)!}.$$

Consequently

$$\bar{u}_i = \sum_{\substack{S \ni i \\ S \subseteq N}} \sum_{r=s}^{n} (-1)^{r-s} \cdot \frac{1}{r} \cdot \binom{n-s}{r-s} v(S) + \sum_{\substack{S \not\ni i \\ S \subseteq N}} \sum_{s=r}^{n} (-1)^{r-s} \cdot \frac{1}{r} \cdot \binom{n-s-1}{r-s-1} v(S)$$

$$= \sum_{\substack{S \ni i \\ S \subseteq N}} \frac{(s-1)!\,(n-s)!}{n!} v(S) - \sum_{\substack{S \not\ni i \\ S \subseteq N}} \frac{s!\,(n-s-1)!}{n!} v(S)$$

which is identical with Equation (I) of Theorem 11.1. Hence any set of payoffs $\bar{u}_1, \ldots, \bar{u}_n$ satisfying Postulates 1 to 4 must satisfy Equation (I). It is easy to verify that the converse is also true: Any set of payoffs $\bar{u}_1, \ldots, \bar{u}_n$ defined by Equation (I) will always satisfy Postulates 1 to 4.

The last equality above follows from the following lemma:

Lemma 3.

$$\sum_{k=0}^{m} (-1)^k \cdot \frac{1}{t+k} \cdot \binom{m}{k} = \frac{(t-1)!\,m!}{(m+t)!}$$

Proof. Proof of the lemma is by complete induction. The lemma is obviously true for $m = 1$, because then it gives

$$\frac{1}{t} - \frac{1}{t+1} = \frac{(t-1)!}{(t+1)!} = \frac{1}{t \cdot (t+1)}$$

Now suppose that the lemma is true for some particular value of m. We can show that in this case it will be true also for $(m + 1)$.

If the lemma is true for m, then

$$\sum_{k=0}^{m} (-1)^k \cdot \frac{1}{t+k} \cdot \binom{m}{k} = \frac{(t-1)!\,m!}{(m+t)!}$$

We can replace t by $(t + 1)$ and can write

$$\sum_{k=0}^{m} (-1)^k \cdot \frac{1}{t+k+1} \cdot \binom{m}{k} = \frac{t!\,m!}{(m+t+1)!}$$

Subtracting the last equation from the preceding one, we obtain

$$\sum_{k=0}^{m} (-1)^k \cdot \frac{1}{t+k} \cdot \left[\binom{m}{k} + \binom{m}{k-1} \right] = \frac{(t-1)!\,(m+1)!}{(m+1+t)!}$$

But

$$\binom{m}{k} + \binom{m}{k-1} = \frac{m!}{k!\,(m-k)!} + \frac{m!}{(k-1)!\,(m-k+1)!}$$

$$= [(m-k+1)+k] \cdot \frac{m!}{k!\,(m+1-k)!} = \frac{(m+1)\cdot m!}{k!\,(m+1-k)!}$$

$$= \binom{m+1}{k}$$

After substitution we obtain

$$\sum_{k=0}^{m} (-1)^k \cdot \frac{1}{t+k} \cdot \binom{m+1}{k} = \frac{(t-1)!\,(m+1)!}{(m+1+t)!}$$

which shows that the lemma is true also for $(m + 1)$ – if it is true for m. This establishes the lemma by complete induction for all positive integer values of m.

For instance, again consider the games G and $\overline{G}$ of our two examples. In game G, by Equation (I) of Theorem 11.1, the Shapley values of the game to the three players will be

$$\overline{u}_1 = \tfrac{1}{3} v((1)) + \tfrac{1}{6} v((12)) + \tfrac{1}{6} v((13)) + \tfrac{1}{3} v((123)) - \tfrac{1}{6} v((2)) - \tfrac{1}{6} v((3))$$

$$- \tfrac{1}{3} v((23))$$

$$= \tfrac{1}{3} \cdot 10 + \tfrac{1}{6} \cdot 40 + \tfrac{1}{6} \cdot 40 + \tfrac{1}{3} \cdot 160 - \tfrac{1}{6} \cdot 20 - \tfrac{1}{6} \cdot 30 - \tfrac{1}{3} \cdot 80 = 35$$

$$\overline{u}_2 = 60$$

$$\overline{u}_3 = 65$$

These Shapley values add up to

$$\overline{u}_1 + \overline{u}_2 + \overline{u}_3 = 35 + 60 + 65 = 160 = v((123))$$

in conformity with Postulate 1.

Moreover, each player's Shapley value equals the *sum* of his *dividends* from the various coalitions of which he is a member. Thus

$$\overline{u}_1 = w_1^{(1)} + w_1^{(12)} + w_1^{(13)} + w_1^{(123)}$$

$$= \tfrac{1}{1} \cdot \eta^{(1)} + \tfrac{1}{2} \cdot \eta^{(12)} + \tfrac{1}{2} \cdot \eta^{(13)} + \tfrac{1}{3} \cdot \eta^{(123)}$$

$$= \tfrac{1}{1} \cdot v^1((1)) + \tfrac{1}{2} \cdot v^{12}((12)) + \tfrac{1}{2} \cdot v^{13}((13)) + \tfrac{1}{3} \cdot v^{123}((123))$$

$$= \tfrac{1}{1} \cdot 10 + \tfrac{1}{2} \cdot 10 + \tfrac{1}{2} \cdot 0 + \tfrac{1}{3} \cdot 60 = 35$$

$$\overline{u}_2 = w_2^{(2)} + w_2^{(12)} + w_2^{(23)} + w_2^{(123)}$$

$$= \tfrac{1}{1} \cdot 20 + \tfrac{1}{2} \cdot 10 + \tfrac{1}{2} \cdot 30 + \tfrac{1}{3} \cdot 60 = 60$$

$$\overline{u}_3 = w_3^{(3)} + w_3^{(13)} + w_3^{(23)} + w_3^{(123)}$$

$$= \tfrac{1}{1} \cdot 30 + \tfrac{1}{2} \cdot 0 + \tfrac{1}{2} \cdot 30 + \tfrac{1}{3} \cdot 60 = 65$$

Likewise, in game $\overline{G}$, by Equation (I), the Shapley values of the game will be

$$\overline{u}_1 = \tfrac{1}{3} \cdot 10 + \tfrac{1}{6} \cdot 40 + \tfrac{1}{6} \cdot 40 + \tfrac{1}{3} \cdot 91 - \tfrac{1}{6} \cdot 20 - \tfrac{1}{6} \cdot 30 - \tfrac{1}{3} \cdot 80 = 12$$

$$\overline{u}_2 = 37$$

$$\overline{u}_3 = 42$$

These Shapley values again add up to

$$\overline{u}_1 + \overline{u}_2 + \overline{u}_3 = 12 + 37 + 42 = 91 = v((123))$$

Each player's Shapley value is again equal to the *sum* of his *dividends* from all coalitions of which he is a member. However, in $\overline{G}$ the coalition (123) is a *negative* coalition and its members (i.e., all three players) receive the *negative* dividend $w_1^{(123)} = w_2^{(123)} = w_3^{(123)} = \frac{1}{3}\eta^{(123)} = \frac{1}{3}(-9) = -3$. Thus

$$\bar{u}_1 = \frac{1}{1}\cdot 10 + \frac{1}{2}\cdot 10 + \frac{1}{2}\cdot 0 + \frac{1}{3}\cdot(-9) = 10 + 5 + 0 - 3 = 12$$

$$\bar{u}_2 = \frac{1}{1}\cdot 20 + \frac{1}{2}\cdot 10 + \frac{1}{2}\cdot 30 + \frac{1}{3}\cdot(-9) = 20 + 5 + 15 - 3 = 37$$

$$\bar{u}_3 = \frac{1}{1}\cdot 30 + \frac{1}{2}\cdot 0 + \frac{1}{2}\cdot 30 + \frac{1}{3}\cdot(-9) = 30 + 0 + 15 - 3 = 42$$

In other words, in game $\bar{G}$ the total amount the players can distribute among themselves is $v((123)) = 91$. However, when each player has received his dividends from the one-player and two-player coalitions, then the players will have already distributed the amount

$$v^1((1)) + v^2((2)) + v^3((3)) + v^{12}((12)) + v^{13}((13)) + v^{23}((23)) = 100$$

among themselves. This will give rise to a "deficit" of $100 - 91 = 9$ units, which the three players will bear equally by each of them accepting a *negative dividend* $w_1^{(123)} = w_2^{(123)} = w_3^{(123)} = -3$.

Another possible intuitive interpretation of negative dividends is to regard them as *"entrance fees"* that the members of any negative coalition S have to pay in order to be allowed to play the game at all.

Suppose that the s players belonging to a given set S agree to play an elementary game $G^S(\eta)$ among themselves and agree to raise the prize η among themselves by each of them contributing the amount η/s to a common pool. Clearly this agreement will leave each player's wealth completely unchanged, because he will have to contribute the amount η/s but will receive back exactly the same amount η/s as his payoff from the elementary game $G^S(\eta)$. We will call such a game a *self-financed* elementary game.

Now let G be an n-person cooperative game containing one or more negative coalitions S. Suppose that the members of any negative coalition S are allowed to participate in G only on the condition that they will also play a self-financed elementary game $G^S(\tilde{\eta}^S)$ among themselves. (This assumption is admissible because, as we have seen, a self-financed elementary game does not change the status quo among the participants.) This means that each member i of a given negative coalition S will have to pay into a common pool the amount $\tilde{w}_i^S = \tilde{\eta}^S/s$, which may be regarded as his *entrance fee* to the game. On the other hand, the original game $\bar{G}$ will be replaced by the sum game $\hat{G} = \bar{G} + G^S(\tilde{\eta}^S)$ [or if there is more than one negative coalition S in $\bar{G}$, then $\bar{G}$ will be replaced by the sum game $\hat{G} = \bar{G} + \Sigma G^S(\tilde{\eta}^S)$]. The resulting sum game $\hat{G}$ will contain no negative coalitions. In this new game $\hat{G}$ each player i will receive a payoff $\hat{u}_i$ equal to the Shapley value of $\hat{G}$ to him, i.e., a payoff equal to the sum of all his *positive* dividends $\hat{w}_i^R$ from various coalitions R in $\hat{G}$ – or equivalently a payoff equal to the sum of all his *positive* dividends $w_i^R = \hat{w}_i^R$ from various coalitions R in the original game $\bar{G}$ itself. However, player i's *net* payoff $\bar{u}_i$ will be equal to $\hat{u}_i$ *less* the sum of all *entrance fees* $\tilde{w}_i^S$ that he had to pay before he has been allowed to participate in the game. Consequently each player's *net* payoff $\bar{u}_i$ will be equal to his Shapley value for the original game

$\overline{G}$, that is, to the algebraic sum of all his positive *and* negative dividends w_i^R from *all* coalitions R in $\overline{G}$, because *adding* the negative dividend w_i^S for any negative coalition S is equivalent to *subtracting* the positive entrance fee $\tilde{w}_i^S = |w_i^S|$.

For instance, in the case of the three-person game $\overline{G}$ of our previous example, the three players will have to play the self-financed elementary game $G^{123}(9)$. Hence each of them will have to pay the entrance fee $\tilde{w}_1^{(123)} = \tilde{w}_2^{(123)} = \tilde{w}_3^{(123)} = 3$, which will yield the total amount 9. This will provide the funds needed to replace the original game $\overline{G}$ by the new game $\hat{G} = \overline{G} + G^{123}(9)$, in which the value of the three-player coalition (123) will be increased from $v((123)) = 91$ to $\hat{v}((123)) = 91 + 9 = 100$. The resulting new game $\hat{G}$ will have the Shapley values

$$\hat{u}_1 = 15 \qquad \hat{u}_2 = 40 \qquad \hat{u}_3 = 45$$

But the *net* payoffs of the players will be only

$$\overline{u}_1 = 15 - 3 \qquad \overline{u}_2 = 40 - 5 \qquad \overline{u}_3 = 45 - 3$$

because of the entrance fees that they had to pay. These net payoffs are equal to the Shapely values for the original game $\overline{G}$, already computed above.[4]

11.4   The Shapley values as bargaining-equilibrium payoffs

Shapley [1953, pp. 307, 316] himself did not claim that the Shapley values $\overline{u}_i$ of a given game G will represent the *actual payoffs* that rational players will tend to agree upon in game G. He rather interpreted them as reasonable a priori assessments of the players' *average payoff prospects* (representing the *mathematical expectations* of the players' payoffs under certain assumptions) if we lack (or disregard) any information concerning the coalition structure likely to arise in the game.

Under this interpretation we have no reason to expect that the players of a given game G will agree on any particular occasion on payoffs corresponding to the Shapley values of the game. All that we can expect is that, if the same game G is played on a large number of different occasions (preferably by different sets of players in order to "average out" any special social relations, such as friendships, hostilities, and so on among particular groups of players), then the *average payoff* of the persons playing the role of some particular player i will closely approach the Shapley value $\overline{u}_i$ of the game to player i. We will return to this interpretation of Shapley values as expected average payoffs in Section 11.7.

We will now discuss a stronger interpretation of the Shapley values, which makes them the *actual payoffs* that tend to be agreed upon if the players follow our rationality postulates.

Let G be an n-person cooperative game with transferable utility, having the characteristic function $v(S)$. This means that any given individual player i can obtain the payoff $v((i))$ by himself without any cooperation with the other players. More particularly he will be able to obtain this payoff even in the case of a *conflict* between himself and all remaining $(n-1)$ players.

Likewise any *pair* of players i and j can obtain the *joint* payoff $v((ij))$ even in the case of a conflict between themselves and all other $(n - 2)$ players. But the rules of the game do not specify how this amount $v((ij))$ will be divided between players i and j in this assumed conflict situation: This must be decided by *bargaining* between the two players concerned. Suppose that they agree that player i's payoff would be $u_i^{(ij)}$, while player j's payoff would be $u_j^{(ij)}$. These quantities will be the two players' *conflict payoffs* from coalition (ij). Since players i and j can achieve the payoffs $w_i^{(i)}$ and $w_j^{(i)}$ even without cooperating with each other, their *net* payoffs from cooperating in coalition (ij) will be only $w_i^{(ij)} = u_i^{(ij)} - w_i^{(i)}$ and $w_j^{(ij)} = u_j^{(ij)} - w_j^{(j)}$. These *net* payoffs will be the two players' *dividends* from coalition (ij). [In the case of a one-person (solo) coalition such as (i), we will define both player i's *conflict payoff* $u_i^{(i)}$ and his *dividend* $w_i^{(i)}$ as $u_i^{(i)} = w_i^{(i)} = v((i))$.]

More generally a given sectional coalition S of s players, $S \subset N$, can always achieve the joint payoff $v(S)$ even in the case of a conflict between this coalition S and all other $(n - s)$ players. But the actual distribution of this amount $v(S)$ among the s members of coalition S must be decided by *bargaining*. The total payoff that a given player i in S would receive in case of a conflict between coalition S and the other players will be called his *conflict payoff* u_i^S from coalition S. Since coalition S cannot distribute more than the amount $v(S)$ among its members, we must have

$$\sum_{i \in S} u_i^S \le v(S) \tag{11.7}$$

Of course, joint efficiency implies that the amount $v(S)$ available will be fully distributed among the members of S, which means that the $\le$ sign can be replaced by an $=$ sign in (11.7).

Out of the conflict payoff u_i^S, however, a certain part will represent only player i's dividends w_i^R from various coalitions R which are *subsets* of coalition S. Thus player i's *net* payoff from coalition S as such will be only

$$w_i^S = u_i^S - \sum_{\substack{R \ni i \\ R \subset S}} w_i^R$$

This *net* payoff w_i^S will be called player i's *dividend* from coalition S. The previous equation can also be written in the form

$$u_i^S = \sum_{\substack{R \ni i \\ R \subseteq S}} w_i^R \tag{11.8}$$

Finally, the all-player coalition N can achieve the joint payoff $v(N)$. The distribution of this amount among the n players will again be decided by bargaining. The share that any given player i will receive will be called his *final payoff* $\bar{u}_i$ from the game. Formally it can be regarded as player i's conflict payoff in a "conflict" between the all-player coalition N and the empty coalition ϕ; therefore we can write $\bar{u}_i = u_i^N$. Since the players' joint payoff cannot exceed $v(N)$, we must have

$$\sum_{i \in N} \bar{u}_i = \sum_{i \in N} u_i^N \le v(N) \tag{11.9}$$

By the joint-efficiency postulate, the $\leq$ sign in (11.9) can again be replaced by the = sign. The *net* payoff w_i^N of any player i from the all-player coalition N can be defined as the amount by which u_i^N exceeds the sum of player i's dividends w_i^R from all sectional coalitions R of which he is a member. That is,

$$w_i^N = u_i^N - \sum_{\substack{R \ni i \\ R \subset N}} w_i^R$$

This *net* payoff w_i^N is called player i's *dividend* from the all-player coalition N. Thus we can write

$$\bar{u}_i = u_i^N = \sum_{\substack{R \ni i \\ R \subseteq N}} w_i^R \tag{11.10}$$

That is, every player's final payoff is the sum of the dividends that he receives from *all* coalitions $R \subseteq N$ of which he is a member.

To make our model determinate we need only one further relationship, viz., a rule predicting the *outcome of bargaining* among the s players of each coalition S about their conflict payoffs u_i^S, or equivalently about their dividends w_i^S, from that particular coalition S.

This relationship we obtain by extending our concept of *multilateral bargaining equilibrium*, already used for n-person simple bargaining games in Section 10.2, to *all* n-person cooperative games (or at least, for the time being, to those which have transferable utility). We can now define *multilateral* bargaining equilibrium as a situation where *bilateral* bargaining equilibrium exists between every possible pair of players i and j, if all those payoffs in the game which are *not* subject to bargaining between players i and j are regarded as *given*.

Thus we will consider certain two-person bargaining subgames G_{ij} between any pair of players i and j in which these two players have to agree on their *final payoffs* $\bar{u}_i = u_i^N$ and $\bar{u}_j = u_j^N$ and also on their *conflict payoffs* u_i^S and u_j^S from *all* sectional coalitions S of which *both* of them are members. But the final payoffs $\bar{u}_k = u_k^N$ and the conflict payoffs u_k^S of all other players k are regarded as given; the conflict payoffs u_i^S of player i himself from all coalitions S of which player j is *not* a member are also regarded as *given*. And the same is true for the conflict payoffs u_j^S of player j from coalitions S of which player i is not a member. Or equivalently (and for our purposes, more conveniently) we can define the subgames $\hat{G}_{ij}$ as two-person bargaining games where i and j have to agree on the *dividends* w_i^S and w_j^S from all coalitions $S \ni i,j$ and $\subseteq N$, whereas all dividends w_k^S, $k \neq i, j$, for every coalition $S \subseteq N$ are regarded as *given*; and so are all dividends w_i^S and w_j^S for all coalitions S *not* including *both* players i and j.

In any given n-person game G there are altogether 2^{n-2} possible coalitions S containing *both* players i and j. For each of these coalitions S the two players will have to agree on a pair of dividends w_i^S and w_j^S. Thus the two-person bargaining subgame $\hat{G}_{ij}$ can be regarded itself as a *composite* bargaining game (in the sense defined in Sections 9.6 and 9.7), consisting of 2^{n-2} smaller bargaining subgames

$\hat{G}_{ij}{}^S$. The purpose of each subgame $\hat{G}_{ij}{}^S$ is to agree on the dividends $w_i{}^S$ and $w_j{}^S$ from one particular coalition S. We may assume that these subgames $\hat{G}_{ij}{}^S$ will be played in some particular order (for example, the subgames $\hat{G}_{ij}{}^S$ corresponding to larger coalitions S may be played *after* those corresponding to smaller coalitions S), so that the various subgames $\hat{G}_{ij}{}^S$ can be identified with different "stages" of the composite bargaining game $\hat{G}_{ij}$. But the actual order in which we assume that these subgames $\hat{G}_{ij}{}^S$ will be played is immaterial for our purposes.

If we consider the composite game $\hat{G}_{ij}$ as a whole, then player i's disagreement payoff $\hat{c}_i{}^{ij}$ will be the sum of all his dividends $w_i{}^S$ from coalitions S *not* containing player j; that is

$$\hat{c}_i^{ij} = \sum_{\substack{S \ni i \\ S \not\ni j \\ S \subseteq N}} w_i{}^S \tag{11.11}$$

By the same token, player j's disagreement payoff will be

$$\hat{c}_j^{ij} = \sum_{\substack{S \ni j \\ S \not\ni i \\ S \subseteq N}} w_j{}^S \tag{11.12}$$

The two players can agree on any pair of final payoffs $\bar{u}_i$ and $\bar{u}_j$ satisfying

$$\bar{u}_i + \bar{u}_j \le v(N) - \sum_{k \ne i,j} \bar{u}_k = \eta = \text{const.}$$

Hence the equation of the upper right boundary H of the payoff space for game $\hat{G}_{ij}$ is

$$H(u_i, u_j) = u_i + u_j - \eta = 0$$

Therefore, by Equation (B) of Theorem 9.1 in Section 9.2, we have

$$a_i = a_j = H_i(u) = H_j(u) = 1$$

for every point u of the upper right boundary H. Consequently, by Equation (C) of the same theorem, the solution $\bar{u}^{(ij)} = (\bar{u}_i, \bar{u}_j)$ of $\hat{G}_{ij}$ must satisfy

$$\bar{u}_i - \hat{c}_i{}^{ij} = \bar{u}_j - \hat{c}_j{}^{ij} \tag{11.13}$$

In view of Equations (11.10) through (11.12), this can also be written as

$$\sum_{\substack{S \ni i,j \\ S \subseteq N}} w_i{}^S = \sum_{\substack{S \ni i,j \\ S \subseteq N}} w_j{}^S \tag{11.14}$$

Now let us consider the smaller subgames $\hat{G}_{ij}{}^S$ into which the game $\hat{G}_{ij}$ is divided. By Equation (9.41) of Theorem 9.4, in any particular subgame $\hat{G}_{ij}{}^S$ the two players will agree on dividends $w_i{}^S$ and $w_j{}^S$ such that

$$w_i{}^S = w_j{}^S \tag{11.15}$$

This relationship is true for all coalitions $S \ni i, j$, and $\subseteq N$. In view of Theorem 9.5, this relationship will hold even if w_i^S and w_j^S are *negative* dividends.

In other words, in the composite bargaining game $\hat{G}_{ij}$ the two players' *total net payoffs*,

$$\bar{u}_i - \hat{c}_i^{ij} = \sum_{\substack{S \ni i,j \\ S \subseteq N}} w_i^S \quad \text{and} \quad \bar{u}_j - \hat{c}_j^{ij} = \sum_{\substack{S \ni i,j \\ S \subseteq N}} w_j^S$$

are *equal*. (Intuitively this can be best regarded as a consequence of the fact that the upper right boundary H of the payoff space in $\hat{G}_{ij}$ is a 45° line, and so the game can be transformed into a *symmetric game* if we change the zero points of the two players' utility functions to make the point $\hat{c}^{ij} = (\hat{c}_i^{ij}, \hat{c}_j^{ij})$ our new origin.)

Consequently, according to our theory of composite bargaining games, at any intermediate stage of the game the two players will agree on such dividends (i.e., on such payoff increments or decrements) w_i^S and w_j^S that will *preserve* this basic equality in their bargaining power, which means agreeing on equal dividends w_i^S and w_j^S on each stage.

In view of (11.7) through (11.10), and considering the fact that (11.7) and (11.9) can be regarded as equalities, we can write

$$\sum_{R \subseteq S} \sum_{i \in R} w_i^R = v(S) \quad \text{for all} \quad S \subseteq N \tag{11.16}$$

Consequently

$$\sum_{i \in R} w_i^R = \sum_{S \subseteq R} (-1)^{r-s} v(S) \tag{11.17}$$

The proof of this relationship is similar to the proof of Lemma 1 in Section 11.3.

In view of (11.15) and (11.17),

$$w_i^R = \frac{1}{r} \sum_{S \subseteq R} (-1)^{r-s} v(S) \tag{11.18}$$

Finally, in view of (11.10) and (11.18),

$$\bar{u}_i = u_i^N = \sum_{\substack{R \ni i \\ R \subseteq N}} \frac{1}{r} \sum_{S \subseteq R} (-1)^{r-s} v(S) \tag{11.19}$$

which, according to the proof of Theorem 11.1 in Section 11.3, is equal to the *Shapley value* of the game to player i, as defined by Equation (I) of the same theorem. Thus we can state:

Theorem 11.2. Let G be an n-person cooperative game with transferable utility, given in a characteristic-function form. Suppose that the members i of *every* possible sectional coalition S agree to cooperate in protecting their common interests in the case of a conflict between coalition S and the other players. Let $\bar{u} =$

$(\overline{u}_1, \ldots, \overline{u}_n)$ be a vector consisting of the Shapley values of G. Then $\overline{u}$ is also the payoff vector corresponding to *multilateral bargaining equilibrium* among the n players.

For this reason we will call $\overline{u}$ the *solution* of game G.

Our bargaining model can also be stated in an alternative form, which may bring out certain aspects of its intuitive content more clearly. Let us assume that the game is played in two stages. In stage 1 the players belonging to the various sectional coalitions S agree on the dividends w_i^S from these coalitions. In stage 2 all the n players together agree on the final payoffs $\overline{u}_i$ (or equivalently on the dividends w_i^N from the all-player coalition N). At the end of stage 1 each player i will be guaranteed to receive the payoff

$$c_i = \sum_{\substack{S \ni i \\ S \subset N}} w_i^S$$

Hence we can now regard stage 2 of the game as an n-person simple bargaining game where the players have to agree on some payoff vector $\overline{u} = (\overline{u}_1, \ldots, \overline{u}_n)$, subject to $\Sigma \overline{u}_i \leq v(N)$ and where in case of no agreement they will receive the disagreement payoffs $c_1, \ldots, c_n$. By Equation (11.1), each player i will have a stronger bargaining position (i.e., will obtain a higher final payoff $\overline{u}_i$), the higher his disagreement payoff c_i (i.e., the higher the dividends w_i^S that he has received from the various sectional coalitions S of which he is a member).

Thus we can regard the dividends w_i^S from the various sectional coalitions S as payoffs that the members of each coalition S guarantee one another in order to *improve their bargaining positions* vis-à-vis the other players in the last round of bargaining about the final payoffs $\overline{u}_i$. This dividend-guaranteeing ability of each coalition S is based on the fact that the members of S can achieve the joint payoff

$$\sum_{i \in S} \sum_{\substack{R \ni i \\ R \subseteq S}} w_i^R = v(S)$$

even against the resistance of all other players.

11.5 Further discussion of our bargaining model: the nondiscrimination assumption

Our bargaining model discussed in the previous section has been based on the assumption that the members of *every* possible sectional coalition will fully cooperate in protecting their common interests against the other players. In particular, in the case of a conflict between the two coalitions S and $\overline{S}$, the members of coalition S will cooperate in obtaining the highest possible joint payoff that they can obtain in such a conflict situation, viz., the joint payoff $v(S)$. Technically this assumption has taken the form of assuming that the s members of any coalition S will make full use of their ability to guarantee one another conflict payoffs u_i^S, or equivalently dividends w_i^S, up to the limit defined by the quantity $v(S)$. This amounts to the requirement

$$\sum_{i \in S} u_i^S = \sum_{i \in S} \sum_{\substack{R \ni i \\ R \subseteq S}} w_i^R = v(S) \tag{11.20}$$

Thus under our model each player will be the member of a number of mutually overlapping sectional coalitions. For instance, in a three-person game, for some purposes (viz., for the purpose of guaranteeing the dividends $w_1^{(12)}$ and $w_2^{(12)}$ to each other) players 1 and 2 will form a coalition against player 3; but for other purposes (viz., for the purposes of securing the dividends $w_1^{(13)}$ and $w_3^{(13)}$) players 1 and 3 will form a coalition against player 2; for still other purposes (viz., for the purposes of securing the dividends $w_2^{(23)}$ and $w_3^{(23)}$) players 2 and 3 will form a coalition against player 1. This assumption is a mathematical representation of the fact that in social life the same individual may cooperate with a large number of different social groups, because on some issue he will have common interests with one social group, on other issues with others. For example, the fact that a given individual tries to protect the interests of his own city against the residents of other cities need not prevent him from trying to protect the interests of his own profession against the members of other professions, and again need not prevent him from trying to protect the interests of his own political party against the members of other political parties.

In contrast to our own solution concept, most other solution concepts proposed in the literature for *n*-person cooperative games are based on the assumption that in any given case only a small *subset* of all possible coalitions will be formed and that the coalitions actually formed will always be nonoverlapping. The simplest assumption along these lines would be that the players are divided into two complementary coalitions S and $\bar{S}$ and that the final payoffs are determined by bargaining between these two coalitions. Each of these coalitions may or may not be itself partitioned into sub-coalitions. But no coalition will be formed that contains both S-players and $\bar{S}$-players among its members, except for the all-player coalition N itself, which represents a combination of the *whole* coalition S with the *whole* coalition $\bar{S}$. This means that the members of coalition S will support one another on *all* issues against the members of coalition $\bar{S}$, and conversely.

In terms of our bargaining model this would have to be interpreted as an agreement by the members of each of the two basic coalitions S and $\bar{S}$ not to participate in any other coalition R unless R contained *all* members of their basic coalition S or $\bar{S}$. More pariculary this would mean that the members of S, and again the members of $\bar{S}$, would refuse to participate in guaranteeing dividends w_i^R for any coalition R, except if $R \supseteq S$ or $R \supseteq \bar{S}$. Any such agreement by the members of a given coalition S or $\bar{S}$ will be called a *discriminatory agreement* against the players not belonging to that coalition. Accordingly any solution concept based on the assumption that only a limited number of all possible coalitions will be active in the game will be called a *discriminatory* solution or *biased* solution. On the other hand, our solution, based on active participation by all possible coalitions in the game, will be called the *nondiscriminatory* or *unbiased* solution.[5]

The basic argument in favor of what we call discriminatory solutions is the fact that in many cases, if the members of a given coalition S enter into a discriminatory agreement against the other players, then they can achieve a *higher joint payoff* than if they accept our nondiscriminatory solution. A rather extreme example of this occurs in a three-person constant-sum game. For instance, consider game G with the characteristic function $v((i)) = 0$ for $i = 1, 2, 3$ and $v((12)) = v((13)) = v((23)) = v((123)) = 90$. Since the game is completely symmetric for the three players, the nondiscriminatory solution corresponding to the Shapley values is $\bar{u} = (30, 30, 30)$. But any pair of two players can obtain the amount 90 (i.e., the highest possible joint payoff in the game) without the help of the third player. So it seems natural to argue that (say) players 1 and 2 should form a coalition and should divide the amount 90 between themselves, leaving nothing to the third player. By symmetry the two players will presumably agree on equal shares. This will give the discriminatory solution $(45, 45, 0)$. If players 1 and 3 or players 2 and 3 form a coalition, we would obtain the discriminatory solutions $(45, 0, 45)$ and $(0, 45, 45)$, respectively.

This case is rather extreme because, in order to achieve the highest possible joint payoff, the two-person coalitions need no cooperation by the third player. Hence any discriminatory solution will rest on a mere two-player agreement and will not require the consent of the third player. In contrast, in most three-person games the three-person coalition can in general achieve higher payoffs than any two-person coalition can by acting alone. Hence the final payoffs in a discriminatory solution will depend on bargaining between some two-person coalition and the third player. For instance, consider game G^* with the characteristic function $v((i)) = 0$ for $i = 1, 2, 3$; $v((12)) = v((13)) = v((23)) = 42$ and $v((123)) = 90$. The nondiscriminatory solution will be again $\bar{u} = (30, 30, 30)$. But now it will not be true that a two-person coalition acting alone can achieve the same joint payoff as the three-person coalition can, since the former can achieve only 42 while the latter can achieve 90. Indeed a two-person coalition acting alone cannot achieve a joint payoff equal to the joint payoff of the two players concerned under our nondiscriminatory solution; under the nondiscriminatory solution any pair of two players would obtain $30 + 30 = 60 > 42$.

All the same, one may still argue that any pair of two players can increase their joint payoff *above* the nondiscriminatory joint payoff 60 if they reach a discriminatory agreement against the third player. For instance, let us assume that players 1 and 2 agree to guarantee each other the payoffs $u_1{}^* = u_2{}^* = 42/2 = 21$. Then suppose that they try to reach an agreement with player 3 on how to divide the balance $v((123)) - v((12)) = 90 - 42 = 48$. This will give rise to a simple bargaining game among the three players, yielding the payoffs $u_1{}^{**} = u_2{}^{**} = u_3{}^{**} = 48/3 = 16$. Thus the three players' final payoffs will be $u_1 = u_1{}^* + u_1{}^{**} = 21 + 16 = 37$; $u_2 = u_2{}^{**} = 21 + 16 = 37$; and $u_3 = u_3{}^{**} = 16$. Hence we obtain the discriminatory solution $(37, 37, 16)$, which is more favorable to players 1 and 2 than the nondiscriminatory solution $(30, 30, 30)$.[6] If players 1 and 3 or players 2 and 3 reach a discriminatory agreement, we would obtain the discriminatory solutions $(37, 16, 37)$ and $(16, 37, 37)$, respectively.

Both in our constant-sum example G and in our variable-sum example G^*, the discriminatory solutions described can be formally obtained also from our nondiscriminatory solution model by assuming that two of the three possible two-person coalitions have been assigned the value *zero*. For instance, in either example the discriminatory solution favoring players 1 and 2 can be interpreted as the nondiscriminatory solution of a new game where the original positive values $v((13))$ and $v((23))$ of coalitions (13) and (23) have been reduced to $v^*((13)) = v^*((23)) = 0$, as a result of player 1 and 2's refusal to join player 3 in any two-person coalition.

Contrary to theories based on what we call discriminatory solutions, we will consider the *nondiscriminatory solution,* corresponding to the Shapley value and its generalizations, to be the *basic* solution of the n-person cooperative game. Our reason is that in our view any discriminatory agreement by the members of a given sectional coalition S is inherently *unstable* unless the members of S can finalize their agreement *before* the other players can make any counteroffers to them; and this will be the case only if the communication facilities within the game are strongly *biased* in order to discourage communication between the members of coalition S and the other players, as compared with communication among the various members of coalition S itself.

For instance, let us again consider our three-person constant-sum game example. Suppose that players 1 and 2 are negotiating a discriminatory agreement against player 3, which would result in the discriminatory solution $(45, 45, 0)$. Then in case player 3 can intervene in time, he can always *disrupt* any agreement between players 1 and 2 by offering either of them a payoff higher than 45. For example, he will be able to persuade player 1 to join him in a coalition against player 2 if he offers player 1 the payoff $46 > 45$. Of course, by similar reasoning player 1 or player 2 will also be able to break up any discriminatory agreement by the other two players if he can intervene and overbid before their agreement has been finally confirmed.

In other words, even though in our example any two-person coalition can physically *acquire* the highest possible payoff (viz., 90) without any help from the third player, the latter has what amounts to veto power over any agreement concerning the *distribution* of this amount. Hence he can prevent any discrimination against him just as effectively as he could if even the acquisition of this amount did require his cooperation.

Yet once the players realize that none of them can organize a stable discriminatory solution against another player, they will be ready to settle for the nondiscriminatory solution $(30, 30, 30)$: In other words, the fundamental *symmetry* of the game will reassert itself. Suppose that player 3 first realizes that this is the best solution that he can achieve. Then he can persuade the other two players to accept this solution in the following way: He can approach (say) player 2 and can point out to him that he is in a position to prevent *any* agreement between players 1 and 2 by always offering player 1 a higher payoff than player 2 can offer. Accordingly he can make the threat of continually using this tactic to disrupt any agreement between players 1 and 2, unless player 2 agrees *not* to enter into any discriminatory agreement against him with player 1. In return he may also offer the promise that he himself will not enter into any discriminatory agreement with player 1 against player 2. But once players 2 and 3 have agreed not to participate in discriminatory agreements, player 1 will also have to accept the fact that the best outcome that he can hope for is the nondiscriminatory solution. Thus all three players will now be ready to accept the latter as the only possible stable outcome of the game.

More fundamentally no elaborate argument is really needed to show that in a game defined by a fully symmetric characteristic function, such as both of our examples, only some *asymmetry* or *bias* in the communication network (or possibly in some other aspect of the game situation) can explain the emergence of asymmetric discriminatory solutions such as $(45, 45, 0)$ or $(37, 37, 16)$. But the purpose of our discussion here is to identify the actual *mechanism* which makes all discriminatory solutions basically unstable in cooperative games with free and unbiased communication. This mechanism is, of course, in no way restricted in its operation to games with symmetric characteristic functions.

Under von Neumann and Morgenstern's model [1953],[7] the payoff vectors that we have called discriminatory solutions are not subject to this type of instability. The reason is that under their model the third player could not make an irrevocable *firm* offer to either of the two other players. For instance, suppose again that, in our three-person constant-sum game example, players 1 and 2 are about to agree on the discriminatory solution $(45, 45, 0)$, when player 3 intervenes and offers player 1 the higher payoff of 46 if the latter joins him in a coalition against player 2. That is, player 3 proposes the outcome $(46, 0, 44)$. Under von Neumann and Morgenstern's model it would be unwise for player 1 to accept player 3's offer. If he did, then at the next move player 2, who has lost everything, would surely offer player 3 a higher payoff than 44. Even if he offered only 45, corresponding to the outcome $(0, 45, 45)$, player 3 would probably accept, and player 1 would be left with a zero payoff. This risk would tend to stabilize any discriminatory solution such as $(45, 45, 0)$ against disruptive offers by the third player.

In contrast, under our definition of cooperative games (as distinguished from noncooperative games and various intermediate cases) any player can always make a fully *binding* enforceable commitment. Hence, for instance, player 3 can always make a *firm* offer of a higher payoff to player 1 (or to player 2 if he so chooses), which the latter can accept without any risk of being double-crossed by player 3 at some later stage of the game. Consequently any player in danger of being discriminated against can always disrupt any discriminatory coalition directed against him by making the *firm* offer of a higher payoff to some member(s) of this coalition – provided that he can intervene in time.

To put it differently, in an *n*-person cooperative game with free communication, if the players can make firm offers to each other, then *every* possible sectional coalition S is vulnerable to disruption by outsiders who can bribe one or more members of S into withholding their cooperation from the other members of S. Since every coalition is vulnerable in this way, no stable agreement can arise, unless the players all agree *not* to use such disruptive tactics against *any* possible coalition in the game. More particularly no coalition S can avoid being disrupted by outsiders if the members of S itself try to reach a discriminatory agreement for the very purpose of disrupting some *other* actual or potential coalitions $R \neq S$. To take again the example of a three-person game, players 1 and 2 cannot expect player 3 to refrain from disrupting their own coalition (12), if players 1 and 2 themselves try to prevent player 3 from organizing coalitions (13) and (23), by concluding a discriminatory agreement against him. Consequently the only way of achieving a stable situation is to rule out all discriminatory agreements by mutual consent, which means adopting the nondiscriminatory solution.[8]

11.6   Interpretation of Shapley's additivity postulate in terms of our bargaining model

Theorems 11.1 and 11.2 already imply that, for cooperative games with transferable utility defined in characteristic-function form, Shapley's additivity postulate follows from our general rationality postulates. By Theorem 11.2, if the players act in accordance with our rationality postulates, then they will agree on payoffs equal to the Shapley values of the game. Yet, by Theorem 11.1, these payoffs will satisfy all of Shapley's postulates, including the additivity postulate. But in this section we propose to consider in more specific terms *why* our general rationality postulates entail the additivity postulate for games given in characteristic-function form.

Suppose that the same set N of n players first play some game G^* and then play another game G^{**}, both G^* and G^{**} being games with transferable utility, given in a characteristic-function form. For the sake of simplicity we will assume that both G^* and G^{**} are elementary games [but will allow the possibility that, in the case of either game (or both), *some* players i belonging to set N are only dummy players]. Let us call G the composite game (sum game) consisting of G^* and G^{**} taken together. Then the additivity postulate essentially says that each player's *total payoff* $\bar{u}_i$ (i.e., his payoff from the composite game G) will be equal to the *sum* of the payoffs $\bar{u}_i^*$ and $\bar{u}_i^{**}$ which he would receive if *only* game G^* were played or if *only* game G^{**} were played.

This postulate can be interpreted as involving two statements:

1. The players will agree on the *same* payoffs $\bar{u}_i^*$ in the first game G^* as they would do if G^* were *not followed* by another game G^{**}.

2. The players will agree on the *same* payoffs $\bar{u}_i^{**}$ in the *second* game G^{**} as they would do if G^{**} had *not* been *preceded* by another game G^*.

Now statement 2 is a rather natural assumption. When the players play the second game G^{**}, they do not have to worry about how the outcome of G^{**} will affect their bargaining positions and payoffs in the first game G^*, because by that time G^* will be over and their payoffs from it will have been decided once and for all. The fact that G^{**} has been preceded by G^* will be relevant only because the payoffs that they have received in G^* will affect their *initial wealth* at the moment that they start playing the second game G^{**}. But, since we define the players' payoff functions in *cardinal utility* units, their initial wealth (initial utility levels) will not affect their behavior in the game. This is so because any difference that a given player's initial wealth may make in his behavior has already been *allowed for* when his payoffs have been converted into utility units.

For instance, if a given player has just won \$2000 in a previous game, this admittedly may make him more willing (or possibly less willing) to risk \$100 for a given chance of winning a further \$1000. Whether this will be the case or not will depend on the shape of his cardinal utility function for money, more particularly on how his marginal utility for money changes when his wealth increases by \$2000. But any such effect will be fully allowed for when the value of a possible further \$1000 gain to him is expressed in cardinal utility units. Therefore, by the very definition of our utility concept, a particular player's willingness to risk 100 utility units for a given chance of winning 1000 utility units will be quite independent of his present wealth (or utility level) – even if his willingness to risk \$100 for a given chance of winning \$1000 does depend quite significantly on his present economic situation.

Consequently statement 2 directly follows from our definition of utility payoffs. If we use Nash's solution concept or its *n*-person analogue to define the solution of game G^{**}, then statement 2 also follows from the fact that our solution is *invariant* under order-preserving linear transformations (more particularly under any change of the zero points of the players' utility functions). This implies that we can always choose each player's present utility level as the zero point of his utility. Finally statement 2 also follows from von Neumann and Morgenstern's principle of *strategic equivalence* [1953, Sect. 57.5.1].

In contrast, statement 1 is a much stronger assumption than statement 2. In general it is certainly *not* true that the outcome of a given game G^* will be unaffected by the fact that G^* is to be followed by another game G^{**} among the same players. In playing G^* a rational player will certainly consider the fact that the outcome of G^* may have an important influence on his bargaining position in the second game G^{**}. Hence the players will play G^* as a *dependent game*, i.e., each player's objective will not be to maximize his payoff $\bar{u}_i^*$ from G^* *as such* but will be rather to maximize his total payoff $\bar{u}_i = \bar{u}_i^* + \bar{u}_i^{**}$ from G^* and G^{**} *together*. Therefore in general G^* will be played in a different manner than it would be if it were an *independent game* in which each player's objective would be only to maximize his payoff $\bar{u}_i^*$ from G^* *itself*.

In accordance with this general principle, in the case of *two-person* composite bargaining games (Sections 9.6 and 9.7) we have found that, if a given game G^* is *embedded* into a composite game G, then *in general* the solution of G^* will be *different* from the solution of G^* as an independent game. But our results also imply that in the *special case* where both G^* and G are games with *transferable utility* these two solutions of G^* will *coincide*.

Let $H^*(u_1, u_2) = 0$ be the equation of the upper right boundary H^* of the payoff space P^* of the embedded game G^*, and let $H(u_1, u_2) = 0$ be the equation of the upper right boundary H of the payoff space of the composite game G. By Equations (9.38) and (9.39), if G^* were played as an *independent* game, then its solution would be defined in terms of the weights $a_i^* = H_i^*(\bar{u}_1^*, \bar{u}_2^*)$, $i = 1, 2$, whereas if G^* is played as a *dependent* game embedded into the composite game G, then, by Equations (9.35) and (9.36), its solution will be defined in terms of the weights $a_i = H_i(\bar{u}_1, \bar{u}_2)$, $i = 1, 2$. However, if G and G^* are games with transferable utility, then the upper right boundaries H^* and H will have equations of the form

$$H^*(u_1, u_2) = u_1 + u_2 - \eta^* = 0$$

$$H(u_1, u_2) = u_1 + u_2 - \eta = 0$$

where η^* and η are certain constants. Hence at every point u of H^* we have $a_i^* = H_i^*(u) = 1$; and at every point u of H we have $a_i = H_i(u) = 1$. Consequently $a_i^* = a_i$ for $i = 1, 2$, and the two solution points must *coincide*.

In the more general case, where G^* and G are n-person games, the *same* conclusion applies, since the n-person solution is defined in terms of the relevant two-person bargaining subgames. Let $H^*(u_1, \ldots, u_n) = 0$ be the equation of the upper boundary H^* of G^*, and let $H(u_1, \ldots, u_n) = 0$ be the equation of the upper boundary of H. If G^* were played as an *independent* game, then, by Equations (10.3) and (10.4), its solution would be defined in terms of the weights $a_i^* = H_i^*(u)$; if it is played as a *dependent* game, i.e., as a component game of the composite game G, then its solution will be defined in terms of the weights $a_i = H_i(u)$. However, if G^* and G are games with transferable utility, then the equations of the upper boundaries H^* and H will have the form

$$H^*(u_1, \ldots, u_n) = \sum_{i \in N} u_i - \eta^* = 0$$

$$H(u_1, \ldots, u_n) = \sum_{i \in N} u_i - \eta = 0$$

Hence $a_i^* = H_i^*(u) = a_i = H_i(u) = 1$ for all $i \in N$. Therefore the "independent" and the "dependent" solutions of G^* will *coincide*.

To sum up, Shapley's additivity postulate can be divided into two statements. Statement 2 follows from our definition of *cardinal utility*. Statement 1 is a much stronger assumption. But it nevertheless follows from our theory of *composite bargaining games*, if we consider the fact that we are dealing here with games with *transferable utility*.

11.7   The Shapley values as expected average payoffs

As Shapley [1953, p. 316] has pointed out, the Shapley values $\bar{u}_i$ of a given game G can be interpreted as the expected average payoffs of the players under the following bargaining model.

Theorem 11.3. Suppose that game G is played in the following way: The players build up the all-player coalition N by starting with one given player i, then adding a second player *j*, then adding a third player *k*, and so on until all *n* players have been included. The first player *i* obtains the payoff $v((i))$. The second player *j* obtains $v((ij)) - v((i))$. In general a given player *m* obtains the amount $v(S + (m)) - v(S)$ if *S* is the set of all players admitted to the coalition *before* player *m*. Thus each player obtains the amount by which his own entry increases the value of the coalition (i.e., in economic terminology he obtains the value of his *marginal product*). The order in which the various players are admitted to the coalition is a matter of *chance,* and each possible order is *equally likely*.

Then the mathematical expectation of any given player's payoff will be equal to his Shapley value for game *G*.

Proof. Equation (I) of Theorem 11.1 can also be written as

$$\bar{u}_i = \sum_{\substack{S \ni i \\ S \subseteq N}} \frac{(s-1)!\,(n-s)!}{n!} \, [v(S) - v(S - (i))] \tag{I*}$$

But this expression is precisely the mathematical expectation of player *i*'s payoff under the above model. The probability that the *s* players comprising a given set *S* will enter the coalition *before* the remaining $(n - s)$ players is $p = [s!(n - s)!]/n!$. The probability that, among these *s* players, player *i* will be the *last* one to be admitted is $1/s$. Thus the probability that *both* of these events will occur is the *product* of these two probabilities; that is $p^* = [(s - 1)!\,(n - s)!]/n!$. Hence this expression gives the probability that player *i* will obtain exactly the payoff $[v(S) - v(S - (i))]$. Consequently the mathematical expectation of his payoff is given by the expression on the right side of Equation (I*). This completes the proof of the theorem.

The bargaining model used in Theorem 11.3 gives the Shapley value an intuitive interpretation that is very useful in various social-science applications (see, e.g., Shapley and Shubik [1954]) and also for computation purposes (especially for finding the Shapley values of games containing a very large number of players). But if this model is used as the *primary* rationalization of the Shapley value, then it is open to the objection that, when a given player joins a coalition, he is unlikely to be able to obtain the *whole* increment in the value of the coalition resulting from his entry; we would rather expect some sort of profit-sharing agreement between him and the old members of the coalition.[9] For this reason we will regard Theorem 11.2, rather than Theorem 11.3, as our primary justification in using the Shapley value as our solution concept.

11.8 Games with transferable utility, given in normal form: the "modified" Shapley values

We now consider the question of what characteristic function to use in defining the Shapley values of the game, if the game is not directly given in *characteristic-function* form but is rather given in the more general *normal* form – that is, if the game is defined by specifying its *payoff function* and not by specifying directly its *characteristic function*. In such games Shapley himself has used the von Neumann–Morgenstern characteristic function $v(S)$ for defining the Shapley values.

We will try to show that a more suitable solution concept can be obtained if we redefine the Shapley values of the game in terms of a *modified characteristic function* $\tilde{v}(S)$. Let $U^S = \Sigma u_i{}^S (i \in S)$ be the *joint payoff* of coalition S in the case of a conflict between coalition S and the complementary coalition $\bar{S} = N - S$. Then the von Neumann–Morgenstern characteristic function defines the value $v(S)$ of a given coalition S as the maximin (or minimax) value of this joint payoff U^S *itself* [see Equation (11.4)]. In contrast, our *modified* characteristic function will define the value $\tilde{v}(S)$ of coalition S as that particular value of U^S which corresponds to the maximin (or minimax) value of the *difference* $D^S = U^S - U^{\bar{S}}$ between the joint payoff U^S of coalition S and the joint payoff $U^{\bar{S}}$ of the complementary coalition $\bar{S}$. The Shapley values $\bar{u}_i$ defined in terms of this *modified* characteristic function $\tilde{v}(S)$ will be called *modified* Shapley values.

Let us use the following model: At the beginning of the game, each possible sectional syndicate S will announce its *threat strategy* θ^S, i.e., the joint strategy that the members of coalition S would follow against the members of the complementary coalition $\bar{S}$ in case of a *conflict* between coalitions S and $\bar{S}$, i.e., in case the two coalitions could not agree on the final payoffs $\bar{u}_i$ for the game. The threat strategies θ^S and $\theta^{\bar{S}}$ of any given sectional coalition S and of its complementary coalition $\bar{S}$ will determine the quantity

$$U^S = \tilde{v}(S) = \sum_{i \in S} U_i(\theta^S, \theta^{\bar{S}})$$

which is the joint payoff that coalition S can distribute among its members. In the case of the all-player coalition N, we define

$$U^N = \tilde{v}(N) = \max_{\theta^N \in \Sigma^N} \sum_{i \in N} U_i(\theta^N) = v(N)$$

where Σ^N is the set of all joint strategies θ^N available to the n players.

We assume that, once the quantities $\tilde{v}(S)$ for all coalitions $S \subseteq N$ are determined, the players will agree on all dividends $w_i{}^S$, on all conflict payoffs $u_i{}^S$, and on all final payoffs $\bar{u}_i = u_i{}^N$, in the way described in Section 9.11. Consequently each player's final payoff $\bar{u}_i$ will be defined by Equation (I) of Theorem 11.1, which can also be written as

$$\bar{u}_i = \sum_{\substack{S \ni i \\ S \subseteq N}} \frac{(s-1)!\,(n-s)!}{n!} [\tilde{v}(S) - \tilde{v}(\bar{S})] \tag{I**}$$

Now suppose that all threat strategies θ^R for the various sectional syndicates are *given*, except for the threat strategy θ^S of *one* particular coalition S. Consider the final payoff $\bar{u}_i$ of some particular player i in coalition S, as defined by Equation (I**). The only term depending on the choice of θ^S will be the term containing the difference $D^S = \tilde{v}(S) - \tilde{v}(\overline{S})$. Thus the final payoff $\bar{u}_i$ of every player i in coalition S will be maximized if coalition S tries to *maximize* the difference D^S by its choice of threat strategy θ^S. By similar reasoning the final payoff $\bar{u}_j$ of every player j in the complementary coalition $\overline{S}$ will be maximized if coalition $\overline{S}$ tries to maximize the difference $D^{\overline{S}} = \tilde{v}(\overline{S}) - \tilde{v}(S)$ by its choice of threat strategy $\theta^{\overline{S}}$ – or equivalently if it tries to *minimize* the difference $D^S = -D^{\overline{S}}$.

Hence the choice of threat strategies θ^S and $\theta^{\overline{S}}$ by the two complementary syndicates S and $\overline{S}$ can be regarded as a zero-sum subgame, called the threat game $G_{S\overline{S}}{}^*$ between syndicates S and $\overline{S}$, in which one side tries to *maximize* the difference $D^S = \tilde{v}(S) - \tilde{v}(\overline{S})$ while the other side tries to *minimize* it. This zero-sum threat game will have a unique solution, corresponding to the maximin (or minimax) value of the quantity D^S.

If a given threat strategy $\theta^S = \theta_o{}^S$ is such that it *maximizes* the final payoff $\bar{u}_i$ of every player i in coalition S when all other threat strategies $\theta_o{}^R$ for $R \neq S$ but $\subset N$ are kept constant, then $\theta_o{}^S$ is called *optimal* against all these threat strategies $\theta_o{}^R$. If in a given game G *each* threat strategy $\theta_o{}^S$ is optimal against the other threat strategies $\theta_o{}^R$ in the game, then all threat strategies in the game will be called *mutually optimal*. We can now state:

Theorem 11.4. Let G be an n-person cooperative game with transferable utility, where the players can make binding threats against one another.[10] Suppose that the final payoff $\bar{u}_i$ of each player i is determined by the Shapley-value expression

$$\bar{u}_i = \sum_{\substack{S \ni i \\ S \subseteq N}} \frac{(s-1)!\,(n-s)!}{n!} \tilde{v}(S) - \sum_{\substack{S \not\ni i \\ S \subseteq N}} \frac{s!(n-s-1)!}{n!} \tilde{v}(S) \qquad (\mathrm{I})$$

where each quantity $\tilde{v}(S)$ is itself determined by the threat strategies θ^S and $\theta^{\overline{S}}$ of S itself and of its complement $\overline{S}$, so that

$$\tilde{v}(S) = U^S(\theta^S, \theta^{\overline{S}}) = \sum_{i \in S} U_i(\theta^S, \theta^{\overline{S}})$$

Then a given strategy $\theta^S = \theta_o{}^S$ of coalition S will be *optimal* against a given threat strategy $\theta^{\overline{S}} = \theta_o{}^{\overline{S}}$ of coalition $\overline{S}$, if and only if

$$\tilde{v}(S) - \tilde{v}(\overline{S}) = U^S(\theta_o{}^S, \theta_o{}^{\overline{S}}) - U^{\overline{S}}(\theta_o{}^S, \theta_o{}^{\overline{S}}) \qquad (\mathrm{II}^*)$$

$$= \max_{\theta^S \in \Sigma^S} [U^S(\theta^S, \theta_o{}^{\overline{S}}) - U^{\overline{S}}(\theta^S, \theta_o{}^{\overline{S}})]$$

Moreover, if the threat strategies $\theta_o{}^S$ and $\theta_o{}^{\overline{S}}$ are *mutually optimal*, then

$$\tilde{v}(S) - \tilde{v}(\overline{S}) = U^S(\theta_o{}^S, \theta_o{}^{\overline{S}}) - U^{\overline{S}}(\theta_o{}^S, \theta_o{}^{\overline{S}}) \qquad (\mathrm{II})$$

$$= \max_{\theta^S \in \Sigma^S} \min_{\theta^{\overline{S}} \in \Sigma^{\overline{S}}} [U^S(\theta^S, \theta^{\overline{S}}) - U^{\overline{S}}(\theta^S, \theta^{\overline{S}})]$$

$$= \min_{\theta^{\overline{S}} \in \Sigma^{\overline{S}}} \max_{\theta^S \in \Sigma^S} [U^S(\theta^S, \theta^{\overline{S}}) - U^{\overline{S}}(\theta^S, \theta^{\overline{S}})]$$

We will call the payoff $\bar{u}_i$, defined by Equations (I) and (II), the *modified* Shapley values of the game. The function $\tilde{v}(S)$ will be called the *modified* characteristic function.

Let G be a game with transferable utility, having P as payoff space. Let $\bar{u} = (\bar{u}_1, \ldots, \bar{u}_n) \in P$. Then $\bar{u}$ is called an *imputation* if

$$\sum_{i \in N} \bar{u}_i = \max_{u \in P} \sum_{i \in N} u_i = v(N) \tag{11.21}$$

and

$$\bar{u}_i \geq \check{u}_i = v((i)) \quad \text{for all} \quad i \in N \tag{11.22}$$

where v is the von Neumann–Morgenstern characteristic function of the game and $\check{u}_i$ is the maximin payoff of player i.

It is natural to require that any solution payoff vector should be an imputation, because (11.21) is implied by the joint-efficiency postulate, whereas (11.22) is an individual-rationality requirement for player i: If he is rational, he will never accept a solution that would give him less than $\check{u}_i$, which he can always assure for himself without the cooperation (and even against the resistance) of the other players.

It is easy to see that the original (unmodified) Shapley values $\bar{u}_i$ always form an imputation. They satisfy (11.21) because of Postulate 1. They also satisfy (11.22) because, by superadditivity, for any coalition $S \ni i$ we have

$$v(S) - v(S - (i)) \geq v((i))$$

But

$$\bar{u}_i = \sum_{\substack{S \ni i \\ S \subseteq N}} \frac{(s-1)!\,(n-s)!}{n!} \, [v(S) - v(S - (i))] \geq v((i))$$

because the coefficients $[(s-1)!\,(n-s)!]/n!$ add up exactly to unity.

We will now show that the modified Shapley values also have this property

Theorem 11.5. Let G be a game with transferable utility. Let $\bar{u}_1, \ldots, \bar{u}_n$ be its *modified* Shapley values. Then the latter form an *imputation*.

Proof. (11.21) is again satisfied because $\tilde{v}(N) = v(N)$.

A strategy $\check{\sigma}_i$ of player i is called a *simple* maximin strategy if

$$U_i(\check{\sigma}_i, \sigma^i) \geq \check{u}_i \tag{11.23}$$

for any joint strategy σ^i of the other $(n-1)$ players. We call a strategy $\check{\sigma}_i$ an *exact* maximin strategy if it satisfies Condition (11.23) with an *equality* sign for *any* joint strategy σ^i of the other players. We assume that in game G every player i has at least one exact maximin strategy $\check{\sigma}_i$, because the rules of the game always allow him to reduce his own payoff from any level $u_i > \check{u}_i$ to $\check{u}_i$, so that he can transform any simple maximin strategy into an exact maximin strategy if he so desires. This assumption will result in no loss of generality, because the quantities $\bar{u}_1, \ldots, \bar{u}_n$, $\check{u}_1, \ldots, \check{u}_n$, and $\tilde{v}(N) = v(N)$ do not change if we alter the rules of the game to allow the players to reduce their payoffs to the level of their maximin payoffs $\check{u}_i$.

Let $\check{G}$ be the game which results from G if we restrict player i's strategy space to the exact maximin strategy $\check{\sigma}_i$ as his only strategy. Clearly in this new game $\tilde{v}(S) = v(S - (i)) + \check{u}_i$ for any $S \ni i$. Consequently in $\check{G}$ player i's *modified* Shapley value is exactly $\check{u}_i$.

Now compare the original game G with $\check{G}$. Since in G every coalition $S \ni i$ will have a larger joint-strategy space θ^S than it has in $\check{G}$, the maximin values $U^S - U^{\bar{S}} = \tilde{v}(S) - \tilde{v}(\bar{S})$ appearing in Equation (II) of Theorem 11.4 *cannot decrease* when we move from $\check{G}$ to G. Therefore player i's modified Shapley value $\bar{u}_i$ in G cannot be less than his modified Shapley value $\check{u}_i$ in $\check{G}$. Hence (11.22) is also satisfied, which completes the proof.

Luce and Raiffa [1957, pp. 140 and 252] have shown in a numerical example that the use of the Shapley value in its original form may lead to counterintuitive results, because the Shapley value does not sufficiently reflect the various players' threat possibilities in the game. Our modification of the Shapley value overcomes this difficulty, which is, of course, not surprising, since the modified Shapley value is based on a characteristic function $\tilde{v}(S)$ defined in terms of the *optimal threat strategies* $\theta_o{}^S$ that each coalition S has against the other players.

12

n-Person cooperative games: the general case

12.1 Permissible strategies and the payoff space

We will now generalize our solution concept to n-person cooperative games without transferable utility.

We make the usual assumption that in a cooperative game G the n players are free to use any *jointly randomized* mixed strategy θ^N. The set of all joint strategies θ^N available to the n players, i.e., to the all-player coalition N, will be denoted by Σ^N. In the case of a conflict between two complementary coalitions S and $\bar{S}$, it will be assumed that each side is free to use a jointly randomized strategy θ^S or $\theta^{\bar{S}}$, respectively, where now joint randomization is restricted to the members of the relevant coalition S or $\bar{S}$. The set of all joint strategies θ^S available to coalition S will be denoted by Σ^S.

In general we will not assume that the players can make side payments to each other. But our model does cover games where side payments are allowed: These payments must be simply regarded as moves to be incorporated in the strategies available to the players. Moreover, if side payments are allowed, the payee's utility gain may or may not be equal to the payer's utility loss. That is, in general we are not assuming transferable utility. Our solution for games with transferable utility, discussed in Chapter 11, becomes a special case of the solution concept that we are now going to define. The same is true of our solution for simple bargaining games (with and without transferable utility), discussed in Chapter 10.

Let P be the set of all payoff vectors $u = (u_1, \ldots, u_n)$ that the n players can achieve by any joint strategy $\theta^N \in \Sigma^N$. P will again be called the *payoff space* of the game. Since the players are free to use jointly randomized mixed strategies, P will always be a convex set. We also assume that P is compact. Moreover, we exclude the case where for any player(s) i all payoff vectors u in P yield $u_i = \mathrm{const.}$, because such a player i would have no personal interest in cooperating with the other players; so the game in question would not be a true cooperative game. Thus in general P will be a set of n dimensions.

Let $\tilde{P} = D(P)$ be the *dominion* of P as defined in Section 9.7. Thus $\tilde{P}$ is the set of all points $\tilde{u} = (\tilde{u}_1, \ldots, \tilde{u}_n)$ in the n players' utility space U^n, such that $\tilde{u}$ is either itself a point of P or is at least weakly dominated by some point u of P. Clearly $\tilde{P} \supset P$. $\tilde{P}$ will be called the *extended payoff space*. Let us assume that any player $i \in N$ is always free to reduce his own payoff u_i voluntarily by any amount. We call this the *throwaway assumption.* It essentially makes the set $\tilde{P}$ the effective payoff space of the game.[1]

Let $\check{u}_i$ be player i's maximin payoff. Let P^* be that subset of P which remains if we eliminate all payoff vectors u such that $u_i < \check{u}_i$ for some player(s) i. We will call P^* the *agreement space.* It is obtained by excluding from P all payoff vectors u unacceptable to some player i because of yielding him less than his maximin payoff $\check{u}_i$. Accordingly, if u is in P^*, then

$$u_i \geqq \check{u}_i \quad \text{for all} \quad i \in N \tag{12.1}$$

The dominion of P^*, the set $\tilde{P}^* = D(P^*)$, will be called the *extended agreement space.*

We will assume that the solution $\bar{u} = (\bar{u}_1, \ldots, \bar{u}_n)$ will always lie on the upper boundary H of the agreement space P^*, which we will briefly call the *upper boundary.* We define H as the set of all points u in P^* not dominated, *even weakly*, by any other point u' of P^*. Thus H is the set of strongly efficient points in P^*.

On the other hand, we define the upper boundary $\tilde{H}$ of the *extended* agreement space $\tilde{P}^*$ as the set of all points u in $\tilde{P}^*$ not dominated *strongly* by any other point u' of $\tilde{P}^*$. Thus $\tilde{H}$ is the set of weakly efficient points in $\tilde{P}^*$. We will briefly call $\tilde{H}$ the *extended upper boundary.*

Since in general both P^* and $\tilde{P}^*$ are convex sets of n dimensions, the upper boundary H and the extended upper boundary $\tilde{H}$ are in general hypersurfaces of $(n - 1)$ dimensions, convex to above. Clearly always $H \subset \tilde{H}$. The equation of $\tilde{H}$ (and of H) will be written as $H(u_1, \ldots, u_n) = H(u) = 0$.

The first partial derivative of the function H with respect to u_i will be denoted by H_i.[2]

Since at any given point u of $\tilde{H}$ these partial derivatives must all have the same sign, we can assume without loss of generality that

$$H_i \geqq 0 \quad i = 1, \ldots, n \tag{12.2}$$

At any point u of $\tilde{H}$ at least one of these H_i's must be nonzero. Indeed at any point u of H itself, except for points on the boundary of H, *all* of the H_i's must be nonzero.

The assumption that every player can always reduce his own payoff by any amount, of course, enlarges not only the payoff space from P to $\tilde{P}$ but also the strategy spaces Σ^N and Σ^S available to the various coalitions. These larger strategy spaces will be denoted by $\tilde{\Sigma}^N$ and $\tilde{\Sigma}^S$. Hence any complete joint strategy $\tilde{\theta}^N \in \tilde{\Sigma}^N$ of the all-player coalition N can be regarded as an ordered pair $\tilde{\theta}^N = (\theta^N, \rho^N)$, where θ^N is a joint strategy belonging to the original joint-strategy space Σ^N and ρ^N is a move involving acceptance of certain payoff reduction(s) by some member(s) i of N. Likewise any complete joint strategy $\tilde{\theta}^S$ of a sectional coalition S can be regarded as an ordered pair $\tilde{\theta}^S = (\theta^S, \rho^S)$, where $\theta^S \in \Sigma^S$ and ρ^S is a move involving acceptance of certain payoff reduction(s) by some member(s) i of S. If $\tilde{\theta}^N$ or $\tilde{\theta}^S$ involves no acceptance of payoff reductions, then we can write $\tilde{\theta}^N = \theta^N$ or $\tilde{\theta}^S = \theta^S$.

12.2 The dividend-proportionality rule

Our solution concept will again be based on the assumption that every possible coalition $S \subseteq N$ of the players will cooperate in protecting their common interests against the rest of the players. More particularly we will assume that the s members of every coalition $S \subseteq N$ will guarantee certain payoffs, called *dividends*, to one another and that these dividends w_i^S of every player i in S will be *additional* to the dividends w_i^R that he may receive from other coalitions R of which he is a member. Any dividend w_i^S may be positive, negative, or zero. Any dividend-guaranteeing agreement requires the unanimous consent of *all* members of the relevant coalition.

We also assume that every sectional coalition $S \subset N$ will back its dividend-guaranteeing agreement by announcing a *threat strategy* θ^S, i.e., a joint strategy that the members of S would follow against the other $(n - s)$ players (i.e., against the members of the complementary coalition $\bar{S}$) in case they could not reach an agreement with the latter on the final payoffs $\bar{u}_1, \ldots, \bar{u}_n$. In the case of a conflict between coalition S and its complement $\bar{S}$, a given member i of S would receive the payoff

$$u_i^S = U_i(\theta^S, \theta^{\bar{S}}) \tag{12.3}$$

which will be called his *conflict payoff* from coalition S. For notational symmetry we will write $\bar{u}_i = u_i^N$ to denote player i's final payoff from the game.

Let us again assume that the dividends guaranteed by any given coalition S and all its subsets R can never exceed the payoffs that coalition S can actually *achieve* for its members, even against the resistance of a coalition $\bar{S} = N - S$ containing all the other players. Thus we require for every coalition $S \subseteq N$ that

$$\sum_{\substack{R \ni i \\ R \subseteq S}} w_i^R \leq u_i^S \quad \text{for all} \quad i \in S \tag{12.4}$$

By the joint-efficiency postulate, the $\leq$ sign in (12.4) can be replaced by the $=$ sign. Inequality (12.4) corresponds to Inequalities (11.7) and (11.9), used in the transferable-utility case. But now, since we are not assuming transferable utility, we have to use an inequality referring to each player's *individual* payoff, rather than to the *joint* payoff of the relevant coalition as we did in Section 11.4.

To make our model determinate, we need two further relationships: one to specify how the *dividends* $w_i^S, w_j^S, \ldots$ of different players $i, j, \ldots$ from the same coalition S are related to one another, and one to define the *optimal threat strategies* $\theta^S = \theta_o^S$ for the various sectional coalitions S.

To obtain the first relationship, we will use the same concept of *multilateral bargaining equilibrium* based on *bilateral* bargaining equilibrium between every possible *pair* of players i and j, which we used in Section 11.4. In other words, we assume that there is bargaining equilibrium among all n players only if no two players i and j have an incentive to redistribute their payoffs between them.

More specifically we will consider all possible two-person bargaining subgames

$\hat{G}_{ij}$ in which two particular players i and j may try to reach agreement on their final payoffs $\bar{u}_i$ and $\bar{u}_j$ as well as on their dividends w_i^S and w_j^S from all coalitions S of which *both* of them are members. We assume that for the purposes of any such bargaining subgame $\hat{G}_{ij}$ the dividends w_i^S and w_j^S that either player receives from coalitions S, of which the other player is *not* a member, are regarded as *given*, and that the same is true for all dividends w_k^S that any other player $k \neq i$, j receives from any coalition S whatever. Consequently the final payoffs $\bar{u}_k$ of these other players are also regarded as *given*.

Each subgame $\hat{G}_{ij}$ can be regarded as a *composite* bargaining game, consisting of smaller subgames $\hat{G}_{ij}^S$ in which players i and j try to reach agreement concerning only one particular pair of dividends w_i^S and w_j^S from one particular coalition S of which both of them are members. Hence the solution of each game $\hat{G}_{ij}$ and of its component games $\hat{G}_{ij}^S$ must satisfy Theorems 9.4 and 9.5.

If we consider the composite game $\hat{G}_{ij}$ as a whole, then player i's disagreement payoff $\hat{c}_i^{ij}$ will be the sum of all his dividends w_i^S from coalitions S *not* containing player j; that is

$$\hat{c}_i^{ij} = \sum_{\substack{S \ni i \\ S \not\ni j \\ S \subseteq N}} w_i^S \tag{12.5}$$

Similarly player j's disagreement payoff will be

$$\hat{c}_j^{ij} = \sum_{\substack{S \ni j \\ S \not\ni i \\ S \subseteq N}} w_j^S \tag{12.6}$$

By Theorem 9.1, the solution $\bar{u}^{ij} = (\bar{u}_i, \bar{u}_j)$ of $\hat{G}_{ij}$ is defined by the three equations

$$H(\bar{u}_1, \ldots, \bar{u}_i, \ldots, \bar{u}_j, \ldots, \bar{u}_n) = 0 \tag{12.7}$$

$$a_i \cdot (\bar{u}_i - \hat{c}_i^{ij}) = a_j \cdot (\bar{u}_j - \hat{c}_j^{ij}) \tag{12.8}$$

$$a_m = H_m(\bar{u}_1, \ldots, \bar{u}_i, \ldots, \bar{u}_j, \ldots, \bar{u}_n) \quad m = i, j \tag{12.9}$$

By Condition (12.4), now regarded as an equality, and by Conditions (12.5) and (12.6), we can write (12.8) also in the form

$$a_i \cdot \sum_{\substack{S \ni i,j \\ S \subseteq N}} w_i^S = a_j \cdot \sum_{\substack{S \ni i,j \\ S \subseteq N}} w_j^S \tag{12.10}$$

By Theorem 9.4, a similar relationship applies to each pair of dividends w_i^S and w_j^S taken separately. That is,

$$a_i w_i^S = a_j w_j^S \tag{12.11}$$

for all coalitions $S \subseteq N$ containing *both* players i and j. By Theorem 9.5, Equation (12.11) is true even if w_i^S and w_j^S are *negative*. Intuitively Equation (12.11) again expresses the assumption that in each component game $\hat{G}_{ij}{}^S$ the two players i and j will agree on dividends $w_i{}^S$ and $w_j{}^S$ such that it will not alter their relative bargaining positions with respect to their final payoffs $\bar{u}_i$ and $\bar{u}_j$ in the composite game $\hat{G}_{ij}$ (and in the main game G itself).

Let R be some other coalition containing both players i and j. Then, of course, also

$$a_i w_i{}^R = a_j w_j{}^R$$

where a_i and a_j are again the *same* quantities as in (12.11). Therefore for *all* coalitions S and R containing both i and j we have

$$\frac{w_i{}^S}{w_j{}^S} = \frac{w_i{}^R}{w_j{}^R} = \frac{a_j}{a_i} = \frac{H_j(\bar{u})}{H_i(\bar{u})} \tag{12.12}$$

Obviously we can derive similar relationships for the dividends of any other pair of players k and m, if we analyze the relevant bargaining subgame $\hat{G}_{km}$. Thus we can state:

Theorem 12.1. Dividend-proportionality rule. In every coalition $S \subseteq N$ the distribution of dividends $w_i{}^S$ among the members of S is governed by the same proportionality factors $a_1, \ldots, a_n$, in accordance with Equations (12.9) and (12.11) [or equivalently Equation (12.12)].

These quantities $a_1, \ldots, a_n$ will be called the *weights* of the game. They are the first partial derivatives of the function H at the solution point $\bar{u} = (\bar{u}_1, \ldots, \bar{u}_n)$. Geometrically they are proportional to the slope cosini of the upper boundary H at the point $\bar{u}$; that is, the ratios a_i/a_j represent the slope, in the appropriate direction, of the hypersurface H at the point $\bar{u}$.[3]

12.3   Generalized Shapley-value expressions

Thus far we have obtained the following requirements for the variables $\bar{u}_i = u_i{}^N$, $u_i{}^S$, $w_i{}^S$, and a_i:

$$H(u_1{}^N, \ldots, u_n{}^N) = 0 \tag{12.13}$$

$$a_i w_i{}^S = a_j w_j{}^S \qquad \text{for all } i, j \in S \text{ and } S \subseteq N \tag{12.14}$$

$$a_i = H_i(u_1{}^N, \ldots, u_n{}^N) \quad \text{for all } i \in N \tag{12.15}$$

$$\sum_{\substack{i \ni R \\ R \subseteq S}} w_i{}^R = u_i{}^S \qquad \begin{array}{l} \text{for all } i \in S \\ \text{and all } S \subseteq N \end{array} \tag{12.16}$$

These equations are the same as (12.7), (12.11), (12.9), and (12.4), except that in the last one the $\leq$ sign has been replaced by the $=$ sign.

Since Equation (12.14) remains true if we multiply all weights $a_1, \ldots, a_n$ by the *same* constant, we can redefine these weights by replacing Equation (12.15) with

$$a_i = \frac{H_i(u_1{}^N, \ldots, u_n{}^N)}{\displaystyle\sum_{j \in N} H_j(u_1{}^N, \ldots, u_n{}^N)} \tag{12.17}$$

This is always permissible because some of the a_i's must always be nonzero. This procedure corresponds to "normalizing" the a_i's so that

$$\sum_{i \in N} a_i = 1 \tag{12.18}$$

We have all together $n \cdot 2^{n-1}$ variables of form $u_i{}^S$ (if we include the n variables of form $u_i{}^N = \bar{u}_i$) the same number of variables of form $w_i{}^S$, and n variables of form a_i. This gives a total of $n \cdot (2^n + 1)$ variables. At the same time we have one equation of form (12.13); $(s - 1)$ independent equations of form (12.14) for each coalition $S \subseteq N$, which gives all together $[1 + (n - 2) \cdot 2^{n-1}]$ independent equations of this form; n equations of form (12.17), replacing (12.15); and $n \cdot 2^{n-1}$ equations of form (12.16).

Thus we are still short of $(2^n - 2)$ equations, that is, of one equation for each sectional coalition $S \subset N$. These missing equations we will obtain in Section 12.4 by defining optimal threat strategies θ^S for each sectional coalition S. But first we will derive some further relationships from (12.14) and (12.16).

Let us define

$$\sum_{i \in S} a_i w_i{}^S = W^S \qquad S \subseteq N \tag{12.19}$$

and

$$\sum_{i \in S} a_i u_i{}^S = V^S \qquad S \subseteq N \tag{12.20}$$

Then in view of (12.16),

$$\sum_{R \subseteq S} W^R = V^S \qquad S \subseteq N \tag{12.21}$$

It is easy to verify that the inverse relationship to (12.21) is

$$W^R = \sum_{S \subseteq R} (-1)^{r-s} V^S \tag{12.22}$$

where r and s are the number of players in each coalition R and S, respectively (see proof of Lemma 1 in Section 11.3). Hence, by (12.19) and (12.22),

$$a_i w_i{}^R = \frac{1}{r} W^R = \frac{1}{r} \sum_{S \subseteq R} (-1)^{r-s} V^S \tag{12.23}$$

By (12.16) and (12.23),

$$a_i u_i{}^N = \sum_{\substack{R \ni i \\ R \subseteq N}} \frac{1}{r} \sum_{S \subseteq R} (-1)^{r-s} V^S \tag{12.24}$$

As can be seen from the proof of Theorem 11.1, the result of the double summation is

$$a_i \bar{u}_i = a_i u_i^N = \sum_{\substack{S \ni i \\ S \subseteq N}} \frac{(s-1)!\,(n-s)!}{n!} V^S - \sum_{\substack{S \not\ni i \\ S \subseteq N}} \frac{s!(n-s-1)!}{n!} V^{\bar{S}} \qquad (12.25)$$

$$= \sum_{\substack{S \ni i \\ S \subseteq N}} \frac{(s-1)!\,(n-s)!}{n!} (V^S - V^{\bar{S}})$$

where $\bar{S} = N - S$ is the complementary coalition to S and where we define

$$V^{\bar{N}} = V^\phi = 0 \qquad (12.26)$$

The right side of Equation (12.25) (in either form) will be called a *generalized Shapley-value expression*. It becomes identical to Equation (I) of Theorem 11.1, defining the Shapley value, if we write $a_1 = \cdots = a_n = 1$, and $V^S = v(S)$.

12.4 Optimal threat strategies

In view of Equations (12.3) and (12.20), we can write

$$V^S = \sum_{i \in S} a_i U_i(\theta^S, \theta^{\bar{S}}) \qquad (12.27)$$

where θ^S and $\theta^{\bar{S}}$ are the threat strategies of coalitions S and $\bar{S}$.

Now suppose that the threat strategies θ^R of all sectional coalitions R *other* than one particular coalition S are *given* while coalition S itself is free to choose its own threat strategy θ^S. Then, in view of (12.27), all quantities V^R, except for $R = S$, $R = \bar{S}$ and $R = N$, will be fully specified.

Consequently, in view of (12.23), the dividends w_i^T from any coalition T that is a proper subset of S will also be fully specified. Hence we can define the quantities

$$c_i^S = \sum_{\substack{T \ni i \\ T \subset S}} w_i^T \quad \text{for all} \quad i \in S \qquad (12.28)$$

Coalition S must choose its threat strategy θ^S in order to satisfy (12.14). In view of (12.16) and (12.28), this means that θ^S must be chosen in a way to satisfy

$$a_i \cdot (u_i^S - c_i^S) = a_j \cdot (u_j^S - c_j^S) \quad \text{for all} \quad i, j \in S \qquad (12.29)$$

Since we are assuming that every player is free to reduce his payoff voluntarily, (12.29) can always be satisfied by setting[4]

$$u_i^S = c_i^S + \frac{1}{a_i} \min_{j \in S} [a_j U_j(\theta^S, \theta^{\bar{S}}) - a_j c_j^S] \qquad (12.30)$$

instead of

$$u_i^S = U_i(\theta^S, \theta^{\bar{S}}) \qquad (12.31)$$

Using Equation (12.30) instead of (12.31) for defining $u_i{}^S$ is tantamount to the assumption that, if the conflict payoffs $u_i{}^S$ defined by (12.31) do not satisfy (12.29), then the members of coalition S will accept appropriate payoff reductions – the smallest payoff reductions which will achieve consistency with (12.29).

Let c^S be the s-vector consisting of the quantities $c_i{}^S$ defined for the s members i of S. Let a be the n-vector $a = (a_1, \ldots, a_n)$. We sometimes write (12.30) in the form

$$u_i{}^S = \tilde{U}_i{}^S(\theta^S, \theta^{\bar{S}}, c^S, a) = c_i{}^S + \frac{1}{a_i} \min_{j \in S} [a_j U_j(\theta^S, \theta^{\bar{S}}) - a_j c_j{}^S] \qquad (12.32)$$

Now let us relax the assumption that the threat strategy $\theta^{\bar{S}}$ of the complementary coalition $\bar{S}$ is given while still retaining the assumption that the threat strategy θ^R for every *other* sectional coalition $R \neq S, \bar{S}$ is given. Then the choice of threat strategies θ^S and $\theta^{\bar{S}}$ by the two complementary coalitions S and $\bar{S}$ can be regarded as a two-person threat subgame $G_{S\bar{S}}{}^*$ between these two coalitions.

We will assume that this subgame $G_{S\bar{S}}{}^*$ is played under the following rules: Each coalition will entrust the choice of its threat strategy to one of its members. This will be (say) player i in the case of coalition S and will be (say) player j in the case of coalition $\bar{S}$. Each of these two players will be concerned only with maximizing his *own* final payoff $\bar{u}_i$ and $\bar{u}_j$, respectively, in playing $G_{S\bar{S}}{}^*$ (but this will cause no difficulties because, as we will show, *all* members of coalition S and again *all* members of coalition $\bar{S}$ will have identical interests in $G_{S\bar{S}}{}^*$).

Since for the purposes of subgame $G_{S\bar{S}}{}^*$ all threat strategies θ^R for $R \neq S, \bar{S}$ are given, the quantities V^R are also *given*, except for $R = S, \bar{S}$, and N.

Finally it will be assumed that for the purposes of $G_{S\bar{S}}{}^*$ the weights $a_1, \ldots, a_n$ are also regarded as *given*. The ratio a_i/a_k for any $k \neq i, j$ is decided in a bargaining subgame $\hat{G}_{ik}$ between players i and k, because this ratio determines the distribution of dividends between these two players in all coalitions R of which they are both members. Therefore the ratio a_i/a_k should be regarded as *given* for the purposes of the threat subgame between players i and j. Likewise the ratio a_j/a_k is decided in a bargaining subgame $\hat{G}_{jk}$ between players j and k and therefore should be regarded as *given* for the purposes of the threat subgame between j and i. But if the ratios a_i/a_k and a_j/a_k are *both* given, then the ratio a_i/a_j is also given. Hence all ratios a_k/a_m $(k, m \in N)$ are given, and, in view of (12.18), the weights $a_1, \ldots, a_n$ are fully determined.

Now, according to (12.25), the final payoff $\bar{u}_i$ of *any* player i in coalition S can be written as

$$\bar{u}_i = \frac{1}{a_i} \sum_{\substack{R \ni i \\ R \subset N}} \frac{(r-1)!\,(n-r)!}{n!} (V^R - V^{\bar{R}})$$

$$+ \frac{1}{a_i} \cdot \frac{(s-1)!\,(n-s)!}{n!} (V^S - V^{\bar{S}}) + \frac{1}{a_i} \cdot \frac{1}{n} V^N$$

$$= A_i + \frac{B}{a_i} (V^S - V^{\bar{S}}) + \frac{C}{a_i} V^N \qquad (12.33)$$

where B and C are positive constants, and A_i is also a constant (of either sign). On the other hand, the final payoff $\bar{u}_j$ of *any* player j in $\bar{S}$ can be written as

$$\bar{u}_j = A_j + \frac{B}{a_j}(V^S - V^{\bar{S}}) + \frac{C}{a_j}V^N \tag{12.34}$$

where B and C are the *same* positive constants as in (12.33), while A_j is also some constant (of either sign).

Therefore, as θ^S and/or $\theta^{\bar{S}}$ vary, the final payoffs $\bar{u}_i$ of all members i of coalition S must shift in the *same* direction; and again the final payoffs $\bar{u}_j$ of all members j of coalition $\bar{S}$ must likewise shift in the *same* direction. On the other hand, when the vector $\bar{u}$ moves on the hypersurface H, then the final payoffs $\bar{u}_1, \ldots, \bar{u}_n$ cannot all increase or decrease together because of (12.2). Hence the final payoffs of the members of the two opposing coalitions must move in *opposite* directions.

Consequently any player i in coalition S will maximize his final payoff $\bar{u}_i$ if he *maximizes* the quantity

$$D^S = \frac{1}{B}(a_i\bar{u}_i - a_j\bar{u}_j) = V^S - V^{\bar{S}} \tag{12.35}$$

where j is some player belonging to coalition $\bar{S}$. In contrast, any player j in coalition $\bar{S}$ will maximize his final payoff $\bar{u}_j$ if he maximizes the quantity

$$D^{\bar{S}} = \frac{1}{B}(a_j\bar{u}_j - a_i\bar{u}_i) = V^{\bar{S}} - V^S \tag{12.36}$$

that is, if he *minimizes* the quantity $D^S = -D^{\bar{S}}$.

Consequently the threat subgame $G_{S\bar{S}}^*$ can be regarded as a *two-person zero-sum* game between the two coalitions S and $\bar{S}$, where coalition S will try to choose a threat strategy θ^S in order to *maximize* the difference $D^S = V^S - V^{\bar{S}}$, whereas coalition $\bar{S}$ will try to choose a threat strategy $\theta^{\bar{S}}$ in order to *minimize* the same difference D^S.

In view of Equations (12.29) and (12.32), the nature of this two-person zero-sum game can be defined in two equivalent ways. Either we can assume that the choice of θ^S and $\theta^{\bar{S}}$ by the two coalitions is subject to (12.29), which means that (12.29) is a *constraint* for the maximization or minimization of D^S, or more conveniently we may assume that the choice of θ^S and $\theta^{\bar{S}}$ is free but that the quantities u_i^S and $u_j^{\bar{S}}$ for all $i \in S$ and all $j \in \bar{S}$ are defined by Equation (12.32). Accordingly the quantity D^S must then be defined as

$$D^S = \sum_{i \in S} u_i^S - \sum_{j \in \bar{S}} u_j^{\bar{S}} = \sum_{i \in S} \tilde{U}_i^S(\theta^S, \theta^{\bar{S}}, c^S, a) - \sum_{j \in \bar{S}} \tilde{U}_j^{\bar{S}}(\theta^S, \theta^{\bar{S}}, c^{\bar{S}}, a) \tag{12.37}$$

In view of von Neumann's minimax theorem, this two-person zero-sum game $G_{S\bar{S}}^*$ will always have a unique solution, corresponding to the minimax (or maximin) value of D^S.

On the basis of this analysis we can again define a given threat strategy $\theta^S = \theta_o{}^S$ for some particular sectional coalition S as *optimal* against all other threat strategies $\theta^R = \theta_o{}^R$ chosen by the other sectional coalitions $R \neq S$, if $\theta_o{}^S$ maximizes the final payoff $\bar{u}_i$ of every player i in S under the assumptions of our model. If every coalition's threat strategy $\theta_o{}^S$ is optimal against all other coalitions' threat strategies $\theta_o{}^R$, then we call these threat strategies mutually optimal. We can now state:

Theorem 12.2. Optimality of threat strategies. In a given n-person cooperative game G the threat strategies $\theta^S = \theta_o{}^S$ of the various sectional coalitions S are mutually optimal if and only if for every pair of complementary coalitions S and $\bar{S}$

$$D^S = \sum_{i \in S} \tilde{U}_i^S(\theta_o{}^S, \theta_o{}^{\bar{S}}, c^S, a) - \sum_{j \in \bar{S}} \tilde{U}_j^{\bar{S}}(\theta_o{}^S, \theta_o{}^{\bar{S}}, c^{\bar{S}}, a) \tag{12.38}$$

$$= \max_{\substack{\theta^S \in \Sigma^S \\ \theta_o{}^{\bar{S}} = \text{const.} \\ c^S, c^{\bar{S}}, a = \text{const.}}} \sum_{i \in S} \tilde{U}_i^S(\theta^S, \theta_o{}^{\bar{S}}, c^S, a) - \sum_{j \in \bar{S}} \tilde{U}_j^{\bar{S}}(\theta^S, \theta_o{}^{\bar{S}}, c^{\bar{S}}, a)$$

In view of (12.32), Condition (12.38) can also be written as

$$s \cdot \min_{i \in S} [a_i U_i(\theta_o{}^S, \theta_o{}^{\bar{S}}) - c_i^S] - (n - s) \cdot \min_{j \in \bar{S}} [a_j U_j(\theta_o{}^S, \theta_o{}^{\bar{S}}) - c_j^{\bar{S}}] \tag{12.39}$$

$$= \max_{\substack{\theta^S \in \Sigma^S \\ \theta_o{}^{\bar{S}} = \text{const.} \\ c_i^S = \text{const.}, i \in S \\ c_j^{\bar{S}} = \text{const.}, j \in \bar{S} \\ a_i, a_j = \text{const.}, i, j \in N}} \left\{ s \cdot \min_{i \in S} [a_i U_i(\theta^S, \theta_o{}^{\bar{S}}) - c_i^S] - (n - s) \cdot \min_{j \in \bar{S}} [a_j U_j(\theta^S, \theta_o{}^{\bar{S}}) - c_j^{\bar{S}}] \right\}$$

In view of the minimax theorem, we can also write

$$D^S = \Delta^S(\theta_o{}^S, \theta_o{}^{\bar{S}}, c^S, c^{\bar{S}}, a) = \max_{\substack{\theta^S \in \Sigma^S \\ c^S, c^{\bar{S}}, a = \text{const.}}} \min_{\theta^{\bar{S}} \in \Sigma^{\bar{S}}} \Delta^S(\theta^S, \theta^{\bar{S}}, c^S, c^{\bar{S}}, a) \tag{12.40}$$

$$= \min_{\substack{\theta^{\bar{S}} \in \Sigma^{\bar{S}} \\ c^S, c^{\bar{S}}, a = \text{const.}}} \max_{\theta^S \in \Sigma^S} \Delta^S(\theta^S, \theta^{\bar{S}}, c^S, c^{\bar{S}}, a)$$

where

$$\Delta^S(\theta^S, \theta^{\bar{S}}, c^S, c^{\bar{S}}, a) = \sum_{i \in S} \tilde{U}_i^S(\theta^S, \theta^{\bar{S}}, c^S, a) - \sum_{j \in \bar{S}} \tilde{U}_j^{\bar{S}}(\theta^S, \theta^{\bar{S}}, c^{\bar{S}}, a)$$

12.5   The solution

We can now define our solution concept as follows:

Theorem 12.3.   The solution. The solution $\bar{\bar{u}} = (\bar{u}_1, \ldots, \bar{u}_n) = (u_1{}^N, \ldots, u_n{}^N)$ of an n-person cooperative game G can be defined by the following set of simultaneous equations

$$H(u_1{}^N, \ldots, u_n{}^N) = 0 \tag{α}$$

$$a_i = H_i(u_1{}^N, \ldots, u_n{}^N) \quad i \in N \tag{β}$$

$$u_i{}^S = c_i{}^S + \frac{1}{a_i} \min_{j \in S} \, [a_j \, U_j(\theta_o{}^S, \theta_o{}^{\bar{S}}) - a_j c_j{}^S] \quad S \subseteq N, i \in S \tag{γ}$$

$$c_i{}^S = \sum_{\substack{R \ni i \\ R \subset S}} (-1)^{s-r+1} \, u_i{}^R \quad S \subseteq N, i \in S \tag{δ}$$

$$a_i \cdot (u_i{}^N - c_i{}^N) = a_j \cdot (u_j{}^N - c_j{}^N) \quad i, j \in N \tag{ϵ}$$

$$D^S = \sum_{i \in S} a_i u_i{}^S - \sum_{j \in \bar{S}} a_j u_j{}^{\bar{S}} = \Delta^S(\theta_o{}^S, \theta_o{}^{\bar{S}}, c^S, c^{\bar{S}}, a) \tag{ζ}$$

$$= \max_{\substack{\theta^S \in \Sigma^S \\ c^S, c^{\bar{S}}, a = \text{const.}}} \min_{\theta^{\bar{S}} \in \Sigma^{\bar{S}}} \Delta^S(\theta^S, \theta^{\bar{S}}, c^S, c^{\bar{S}}, a) \quad S \subset N$$

where

$$\Delta^S(\theta^S, \theta^{\bar{S}}, c^S, c^{\bar{S}}, a) = \sum_{i \in S} a_i c_i{}^S - \sum_{j \in \bar{S}} a_j c_j{}^{\bar{S}} + s \cdot \min_{i \in S} \, [a_i \, U_i(\theta^S, \theta^{\bar{S}}) - a_i c_i{}^S]$$

$$- (n - s) \cdot \min_{j \in \bar{S}} \, [a_j \, U_j(\theta^S, \theta^{\bar{S}}) - a_j c_j{}^{\bar{S}}] \quad S \subset N \tag{η}$$

Of course, instead of Equation (β), we could also use Equation (12.17), which would subject the a_i's to the normalizing requirement $\Sigma\, a_i = 1$.

We have chosen Equation (δ) instead of (12.16) to avoid explicit introduction of the variables $w_i{}^S$. These two equations are, however, equivalent, because the inverse relationship to Equation (12.16) is

$$w_i{}^S = \sum_{\substack{i \ni R \\ R \subseteq S}} (-1)^{s-r} \, u_i{}^R \tag{12.41}$$

Hence

$$c_i{}^S = u_i{}^S - w_i{}^S = \sum_{\substack{i \ni R \\ R \subset S}} (-1)^{s-r+1} \, u_i{}^R$$

To compute the $w_i{}^S$'s we can always use Equation (12.41).

In order to obtain conditions which do not assume the existence of the partial derivatives H_i at the solution point $\bar{u}$, we can replace Equations (α) and (β) by the requirements

$$a_i \geqq 0 \tag{$\alpha\alpha$}$$

$$\sum_{i \in N} a_i u_i^N = \max_{\substack{u \in P^* \\ a_i = \text{const.}}} \sum_{i \in N} a_i u_i \tag{$\beta\beta$}$$

where $u = (u_1, \ldots, u_n)$. Because of the convexity of the agreement space P^*, in cases where the derivatives H_i do exist at the point $\bar{u}$, Conditions (α) and (β) and Conditions ($\alpha\alpha$) and ($\beta\beta$) are equivalent. In cases where these derivatives do not exist, the use of Conditions ($\alpha\alpha$) and ($\beta\beta$), as well as Conditions (γ) through (η) for defining the solution can be justified by the argument outlined in Footnote 1 of Section 10.2.

It is easy to see that these conditions contain the equations defining the Nash solution (Theorem 9.1) and the equations defining the modified Shapley value (Theorem 11.4 in Section 11.8) as special cases.

In the case of the two-person game, we have only three coalitions, viz., (1), (2), and (12). We must set $u_1^{(1)} = c_1^{(12)} = c_1$; $u_2^{(2)} = c_2^{(12)} = c_2$; $u_1^{(12)} = \bar{u}_1$; and $u_2^{(12)} = \bar{u}_2$. Then our conditions directly yield the Nash solution.

Our solution, like the Nash solution itself, is invariant with respect to order-preserving linear transformations of the players' utilities. If we disregard the degenerate case where one or more of the a_i's are zero, we can always achieve by appropriate linear transformations to have $a_1 = \cdots = a_n = 1$. After these transformations the close relationship between our solution and the modified Shapley values becomes even more obvious.

Let G be a cooperative game with or without transferable utility, for which $a_1 = \cdots = a_n = 1$. We can *approximate* G by a game $\bar{G}$ with transferable utility as follows: Let U_i be the payoff function of the original game G. In the new game $\bar{G}$, if all n players cooperate in using a joint strategy θ^N, then their joint payoff will be defined as

$$\bar{V}^N(\theta^N) = \sum_{i \in N} U_i(\theta^N) \tag{12.42}$$

On the other hand, if only the s members of a given sectional coalition S cooperate in using a joint strategy θ^S, whereas the other $(n - s)$ players use the joint strategy $\theta^{\bar{S}}$, then the joint payoff of coalition S will be defined as

$$\bar{V}^S(\theta^S, \theta^{\bar{S}}) = \sum_{i \in S} \tilde{U}_i^S(\theta^S, \theta^{\bar{S}}, c^S, e) \tag{12.43}$$

where $\tilde{U}_i^S$ is the function defined in (12.32), while e is the n-vector $e = a = (1, \ldots, 1)$. In the new game $\bar{G}$ each coalition N or $S \subset N$ is assumed to be free to redistribute its joint payoff $\bar{V}^N$ or $\bar{V}^S$ among its members in any way desired, making $\bar{G}$ a game with transferable utility.

Thus the modified Shapley values $\bar{u}_1, \ldots, \bar{u}_n$ for the new game $\overline{G}$ will be equal to the final payoffs $\bar{u}_1, \ldots, \bar{u}_n$ that our solution defines for the original game G. Clearly, if the original game G already has transferable utility, then $\overline{G} = G$, and the final payoffs defined by our solution will be simply the modified Shapley values for G itself.

12.6 Existence of the solution

We will call a game *regular* if its payoff space and its strategy spaces satisfy the assumptions of Section 9.16 above.

Theorem 12.4. Existence theorem. For every regular n-person cooperative game G there exists a solution $\bar{u} = (\bar{u}_1, \ldots, \bar{u}_n)$ defined *either* by Conditions $(\alpha\alpha)$ and $(\beta\beta)$, as well as Conditions (γ) through (η), *or* by a limit process corresponding to these equations.

Proof. We restrict ourselves to the case where all partial derivatives $H_1, \ldots, H_n$ exist at all points u of the extended upper boundary $\tilde{H}$. Our proof can be extended to the general case by the method mentioned in Footnote 1 of Section 10.2.

Suppose that each of the $(2^n - 1)$ coalitions in the game appoints a trustee. The trustee of the n-player coalition N will be called "player N," while the trustee of a given sectional coalition S will be called "player S." We will assume that these $(2^n - 1)$ trustees will play a noncooperative game $G^*(\epsilon)$ among themselves, defined as follows:

Player N has the task of selecting a vector $\bar{a} = (\bar{a}_1, \ldots, \bar{a}_n)$ subject to the conditions

$$\sum_{i \in N} \bar{a}_i = 1 \tag{12.44}$$

and

$$\bar{a}_i \geq \epsilon \quad \text{for all } i \in N \tag{12.45}$$

where ϵ is a small positive number.

Each player S has the task of selecting a joint strategy θ_o^S for his own coalition $S \subset N$, subject to

$$\theta_o^S \in \Sigma^S \tag{12.46}$$

We now define

$$\bar{u}_i^S = U_i(\theta_o^S, \theta_o^{\bar{S}}) \quad \text{for all} \quad S \subset N \tag{12.47}$$

$$\text{and all} \quad i \in S$$

where $\bar{S} = N - S$.

If $S = (i)$ has only one member, then we write

$$\tilde{u}_i^S = a_i \bar{u}_i^S \tag{12.48}$$

whereas, if S has more than one member, then we define

$$\tilde{u}_i^S = \tilde{c}_i^S + \min_{j \in S} (\bar{a}_j \bar{u}_j^S - \tilde{c}_j^S) \quad \text{for all} \quad i \in S \tag{12.49}$$

where

$$\tilde{c}_i^S = \sum_{\substack{R \ni i \\ R \subset S}} (-1)^{s-r+1} \tilde{u}_i^S \quad \text{for all} \quad S \subseteq N \tag{12.50}$$

$$\text{and all} \quad i \in S$$

Here s and r again stand for the number of players in each coalition S and R, respectively.

Clearly Equations (12.47) through (12.50) provide a recursive definition for the variables $\tilde{u}_i^S$ in terms of the quantities $\bar{a}_1, \ldots, \bar{a}_n$ as well as the strategies θ_o^S for all coalitions $S \subset N$. This is so because Equations (12.47) and (12.48) define the variables $\tilde{u}_i^S$ for all one-member coalitions S, and then the remaining equations allow computation of the variables $\tilde{u}_i^S$ first for all two-member coalitions, then for all three-member coalitions, and so on.

We also write

$$Y^S = \sum_{i \in S} \tilde{u}_i^S \quad \text{for all} \quad S \subset N \tag{12.51}$$

$$\hat{u}_i = \frac{1}{\bar{a}_i} \left[\tilde{c}_i^N + \max_{u \in P^*} \min_{j \in N} (\bar{a}_j u_j - \tilde{c}_j^N) \right] \quad \text{for all} \quad i \in N \tag{12.52}$$

$$a_i^* = \frac{H_i(\hat{u}_1, \ldots, \hat{u}_n)}{\sum_{j \in N} H_j(\hat{u}_1, \ldots, \hat{u}_n)} \quad \text{for all} \quad i \in N \tag{12.53}$$

We assume that in this noncooperative game $G^*(\epsilon)$ each player S by his choice of strategy θ_o^S, will try to maximize for his own coalition S the quantity

$$D^S = Y^S - Y^{\bar{S}} \tag{12.54}$$

In contrast, player N by his choice of vector $\bar{a}$ will try to maximize the quantity

$$D^* = \sum_{i \in N} (\bar{a}_i - a_i^*)^2 \tag{12.55}$$

By Debreu's equilibrium-point existence theorem [1952], this noncooperative game $G^*(\epsilon)$ will always have at least one equilibrium point. It is easy to see that $G^*(\epsilon)$, for any small positive ϵ, satisfies the continuity and contractibility conditions of Debreu's theorem.

But for any equilibrium point in $G^*(\epsilon)$ we have

$$|\bar{a}_i - a_i^*| \leqq \epsilon \quad \text{for all} \quad i \in N \tag{12.56}$$

Consequently, as ϵ tends to zero, the vectors $\bar{a}$ and a^* will converge to the same vector $a = (a_1, \ldots, a_n)$. This vector will always correspond to a solution of our original n-person cooperative game G.

We may distinguish the following cases.

A. The *nondegenerate* case, where $a_1 > 0$ for all $i \in N$. In this case all variables converge to well-defined finite limits as ϵ goes to zero. We can write

$$\bar{u}_i = u_i{}^N = \hat{u}_i = \frac{1}{a_i} \left[\tilde{c}_i{}^N + \max_{u \in P^*} \min_{j \in N} (a_j u_j - \tilde{c}_j{}^N) \right] \tag{12.57}$$

$$u_i{}^S = \frac{1}{a_i} \tilde{u}_i{}^S \tag{12.58}$$

$$c_i{}^S = \frac{1}{a_i} \tilde{c}_i{}^S \tag{12.59}$$

The variables $\bar{u}_i$, $u_i{}^S$, and $c_i{}^S$ defined in this way, together with the quantities $a_1, \ldots, a_n$, will satisfy the defining equations of the solution for the original cooperative game G.

B. The *degenerate* case, where for some player(s) i we have $a_i = 0$. Any such player i will be called a zero player. In this case we can still use Equations (12.57) through (12.59) for the nonzero players. Concerning the zero players, we can distinguish two subcases:

B*. The *nonsingular degenerate* case. In this case for all zero players i we have

$$\tilde{c}_i{}^N + \max_{u \in P^*} \min_{j \in N} (a_j u_j - \tilde{c}_j{}^N) = 0 \tag{12.60}$$

In view of (12.57), this makes $\bar{u}_i$ indeterminate. Thus we are free to choose the final payoffs $\bar{u}_i$ of the zero players i, subject to the condition that these payoffs $\bar{u}_i$, together with the payoffs $\bar{u}_j$ computed for the nonzero players j, should give a payoff vector $\bar{u}$ lying on the upper boundary H. This condition can always be satisfied.

B**. The *singular degenerate* case. This case would arise (we do not know for whether it can arise at all) if the left side of (12.60) were negative. (Since $a_i = 0$, the left side of this equation can never be positive.) In this case we must define the payoff $\bar{u}_i$ of the relevant zero player i as being minus infinity, $\bar{u}_i = -\infty$.

Formally the payoff vector $\bar{u}$ defined in this way can still be regarded as a solution.

But clearly player i can always make sure to obtain at least his maximin payoff $\check{u}_i$ (which is, of course, finite, since the payoff space P is a compact set). Indeed, in order to secure player i's cooperation, the other players in general will have an interest in offering him at least the payoff

$$u_i{}^* = \min_{u \in P^*} u_i \tag{12.61}$$

because they can do this without any cost to themselves. In view of (12.1), $u_i{}^* \geq \check{u}_i$. Thus in the singular degenerate case we redefine the solution as a payoff vector $\tilde{u} = (\tilde{u}_1, \ldots, \tilde{u}_n)$ such that

$$\tilde{u}_i \geq u_i{}^* \quad \text{for each zero player } i \tag{12.62}$$

$\tilde{u}_j \geqq \bar{u}_j$ for each nonzero player j $\qquad\qquad\qquad$ (12.63)

where $\bar{u}_j$ is the payoff defined by Equation (12.57) and where

$\tilde{u} \in P*$ $\qquad\qquad\qquad\qquad\qquad\qquad\qquad\qquad$ (12.64)

Such a payoff vector $\tilde{u}$ always exists.

12.7 The question of uniqueness

It is known that the solution $\bar{u}$ is unique at least in the following three special cases:

1. When there are only *two players* (in which case our solution is identical with the Nash solution of the game).

2. When the game is a *simple bargaining game* where the rules of the game uniquely determine the conflict point $c = (c_1, \ldots, c_n)$ of the game (see Section 10.2).

3. When the upper boundary H of the agreement space $P*$ (or of the payoff space P as a whole) is a *hyperplane*. This last case includes all n-person cooperative games with *transferable utility* (in which case the solution consists of the modified Shapley values of the game – see Section 11.8) but is more general than that.

By continuity it is reasonable to assume that this uniqueness property also holds for games which at least "come close" to satisfying cases 2 or 3. But it is known from counterexamples that in general the solution is *not* unique.

For instance, let G be the following three-person cooperative game: Any player i ($i = 1, 2, 3$) acting alone can obtain only the payoff $u_i = 0$. Players 1 and 2 acting together can obtain any payoff vector (u_1, u_2) subject to $u_1 + u_2 \leqq 20$ and u_1, $u_2 \geqq 0$. Player 3 and *either* of the other two players (i.e., player i, with $i = 1, 2$) acting together can obtain any payoff vector (u_i, u_3) subject to $3u_i + u_3 \leqq 480$ and $u_i, u_3 \geqq 0$. Finally all three players acting together can obtain any payoff vector (u_1, u_2, u_3) subject to $3u_1 + u_2 + u_3 \leqq 510; u_1 + 3u_2 + u_3 \leqq 510$; and u_1, u_2, $u_3 \geqq 0$. This game G is obviously symmetric with respect to the two weaker players, viz., 1 and 2.

For this game G the payoff space P and the agreement space $P*$ are identical (they correspond to pyramid $OABCD$ of Figure 12.1). The upper boundary H of P (or of $P*$) consists of the two plane triangles ABD and BCD, as well as the straight-line segment DB where these two triangles meet. ABD lies in the plane $3u_1 + u_2 + u_3 = 510$, while BCD lies in the plane $u_1 + 3u_2 + u_3 = 510$.

This game has three solutions. One (solution α) lies on face ABD and corresponds to the weights $a_1 = 3, a_2 = 1$, and $a_3 = 1$. Another (solution β) lies on face BCD and corresponds to the weights $a_1 = 1, a_2 = 3$, and $a_3 = 1$. The third (solution γ) lies on edge DB and corresponds to the weights $a_1 = a_2 = 2$ and $a_3 = 1$.[5] In all three solutions, of course, $u_i^{(i)} = w_i^{(i)} = 0$ for $i = 1, 2, 3$. Hence $u_i^{(ij)} = w_i^{(ij)}$.

Solution α. $a = (3, 1, 1)$.

$\qquad w_1^{(12)} = 5 \qquad\qquad w_2^{(12)} = 15$

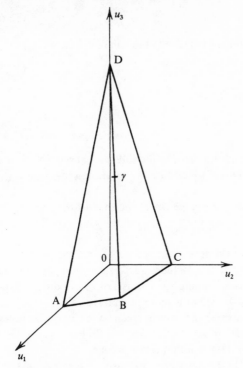

Figure 12.1

$$w_1^{(13)} = 80 \qquad\qquad\qquad w_3^{(13)} = 240$$

$$w_2^{(23)} = 120 \qquad w_3^{(23)} = 120$$

$$w_1^{(123)} = -26\tfrac{2}{3} \qquad w_2^{(123)} = -80 \qquad w_3^{(123)} = -80$$

$$\bar{u}_1 = u_1^{(123)} = 5 + 80 - 26\tfrac{2}{3} = 58\tfrac{1}{3}$$

$$\bar{u}_2 = u_2^{(123)} = 15 + 120 - 80 = 55$$

$$\bar{u}_3 = u_3^{(123)} = 240 + 120 - 80 = 280$$

Solution β. a = (1, 3, 1). Solution β is obtained from solution α if players 1 and 2 are being interchanged. Hence

$$\bar{u}_1 = 55 \qquad \bar{u}_2 = 58\tfrac{1}{3} \qquad \bar{u}_3 = 280$$

Solution γ. a = (2, 2, 1).

$$w_1^{(12)} = 10 \qquad\qquad w_2^{(12)} = 10$$

$$w_1^{(13)} = 96 \qquad\qquad\qquad w_3^{(13)} = 192$$

$$w_2^{(23)} = 96 \qquad w_3^{(23)} = 192$$

$$w_1^{(123)} = -49\tfrac{2}{3} \qquad w_2^{(123)} = -49\tfrac{2}{3} \qquad w_3^{(123)} = -99\tfrac{1}{3}$$

$$\bar{u}_1 = 10 + 96 - 49\tfrac{2}{3} = 56\tfrac{1}{3}$$

$$\bar{u}_2 = 10 + 96 - 49\tfrac{2}{3} = 56\tfrac{1}{3}$$

$$\bar{u}_3 = 192 + 192 - 99\tfrac{1}{3} = 284\tfrac{2}{3}$$

Figure 12.1 shows the position of solution γ on line *DB*. (The other two solutions α and β lie too close to γ on both sides of line *DB* for diagrammatic representation on a figure on this scale.)

According to our basic theory no solution concept can be fully satisfactory if it fails to select a *unique* solution (a unique final payoff vector) for each particular game. Assuming perfect rationality on the part of the players, if any given game had two or more solutions $\bar{u}^1, \ldots, \bar{u}^k$, then none of them would be stable. Each player would try to press for that particular solution which would yield him the highest payoff, and different players would have different interests in this matter. For this reason, in the next section we will develop a criterion always selecting a *unique* "stable solution" $\bar{\bar{u}}$ for any cooperative game.

But in empirical applications it is often desirable to relax the assumption of perfect rationality to various extents. If the players are less than perfectly rational, then *any* particular solution $\bar{u}^i$ *may* be stable, because any such solution by definition satisfies our *local* equilibrium conditions (as stated in Theorem 12.3), and because the players may be simply *unaware* of the existence of alternative solutions, usually corresponding to quite different weights $a_1, \ldots, a_n$ and possibly lying in very different regions of the payoff space. Thus in the real world games possessing several solutions, each of them equally satisfying the conditions of Theorem 12.3, may often be best regarded as social systems with *multiple equilibria*.

12.8 Definition of a unique "stable solution"

Suppose a given *n*-person cooperative game G has two or more solutions $\bar{u}^1, \bar{u}^2, \ldots$ and that the players are aware of this fact. Let Ω be the set of all these solutions. We assume that the players will choose a unique *stable solution* $\bar{\bar{u}}$ for the game by means of the following procedure, which we shall call the *end game* G^o of the cooperative game G.

This end game will consist of two stages. In *stage 1* the players will agree that every player i will receive at least that payoff $u_i^* = \bar{u}_i^j$ which the solution $\bar{u}^j$ least *favorable* to him would grant him, since u_i^* can be regarded as the "noncontroversial part" of his payoff. Thus we write

$$u_i^* = \min_{\bar{u} \in \Omega} \bar{u}_i \qquad i \in N \tag{12.65}$$

In *stage 2* the n players have to reach unanimous agreement on the final payoff vector $\bar{\bar{u}} = (\bar{\bar{u}}_1, \ldots, \bar{\bar{u}}_n)$ subject to

$$\bar{\bar{u}}_i \geq u_i^* \quad i \in N \tag{12.66}$$

and to

$$\bar{\bar{u}} \in P \tag{12.67}$$

Condition (12.66) says that each player i must receive at least the amount u_i^* agreed upon in stage 1, whereas Condition (12.67) says that the payoff vector $\bar{\bar{u}}$ must be feasible, i.e., must lie in the payoff space P of the game.

In other words stage 2 of the end game G^o is an n-person simple bargaining game. Therefore, by Theorem 10.1, its solution will be that particular payoff vector $u = \bar{\bar{u}}$ which maximizes the n-person Nash product

$$\pi = \prod_{i \in N} (u_i - u_i^*) \tag{12.68}$$

subject to/(12.66) and (12.67). This payoff vector $\bar{\bar{u}}$ always exists and is always unique. We will call $\bar{\bar{u}}$ the stable solution of the game. If game G has only one solution $\bar{u}$, then $u_i^* = \bar{u}_i$ for each player i, and so the stable solution is simply this unique solution, i.e., $\bar{\bar{u}} = \bar{u}$. We can now state:

Theorem 12.5. The stable solution $\bar{\bar{u}}$ always exists and is always unique.

From the viewpoint of our formal theory the stable solution $\bar{\bar{u}}$ is the *only* true solution, since, according to our previous argument, "perfectly rational" players will always choose $\bar{\bar{u}}$ as the outcome of the game.

For example, in the three-person game discussed in Section 12.7, we have $u_1^* = u_2^* = 55$ and $u_3^* = 280$. Hence $\Pi = (u_1 - 55\frac{1}{3})(u_2 - 55\frac{2}{3})(u_3 - 280)$. In order to find the stable solution $u = \bar{\bar{u}}$, we have to maximize this quantity π, subject to $u_1, u_2, u_3 \geq 0$; $3u_1 + u_2 + u_3 \leq 510$; and $u_1 + 3u_2 + u_3 \leq 510$. It is easy to verify that the maximum will be reached at the point $\bar{\bar{u}} = (56\frac{2}{3}, 56\frac{2}{3}, 283\frac{1}{3})$, where π takes the value $\pi = (\frac{5}{3})(\frac{5}{3})(\frac{10}{3}) = \frac{250}{27} = 9\frac{7}{27}$. Thus the strong solution of the game is

$$\bar{\bar{u}}_1 = \bar{\bar{u}}_2 = 56\tfrac{2}{3} \quad \bar{\bar{u}}_3 = 283\tfrac{1}{3}$$

Historical note. Shapley first published his definition of the Shapley value (see Section 11.3) in 1953.[6] The "modified" Shapley value (Section 11.8) was introduced by Harsanyi [1959]. The same paper also contained an earlier and less satisfactory version of our solution for general n-person cooperative games. The solution in its present form (as described in this chapter) was first published in Harsanyi [1963].

13

n-Person cooperative games: discriminatory solutions

13.1 Discrimination in games given in characteristic-function form

Let G be an n-person cooperative game with transferable utility, given in characteristic-function form. The Shapley value of G to player i will be

$$u_i = \sum_{\substack{S \ni i \\ S \subseteq N}} \frac{(s-1)!\,(n-s)!}{n!}\, v(S) - \sum_{\substack{S \not\ni i \\ S \subseteq N}} \frac{s!(n-s-1)!}{n!}\, v(S) \tag{13.1}$$

where, for each coalition S, s denotes the number of players in S. By Theorem 11.2, this quantity u_i will be player i's payoff from game G.

Let R be an r-person coalition in G, and let $\bar{R} = N - R$ be the $(n-r)$-person complementary coalition. Using (13.1), it is easy to verify that the joint payoff u_R of the r players in R will be

$$u_R = \sum_{i \in R} u_i = \frac{r}{n} v(N) + \sum_{S \subset N} \frac{s!(n-s-1)!}{(n-1)!} \cdot \left(\frac{s^*}{s} - \frac{r}{n}\right) v(S) \tag{13.2}$$

where, for each coalition S, s again denotes the number of players in S, whereas s^* denotes the number of players in the set $S^* = S \cap R$.

Now suppose that the r players in R insist on dividing up the quantity $v(R)$ among themselves, i.e., they insist on playing an r-person game G^R *before* participating in the n-person game G with the other $(n-r)$ players. In this case we will say that the r players in coalition R *discriminate* against the $(n-r)$ players in the complementary coalition $\bar{R}$. Suppose that the payoff of each player i in R from this game G^R will be u_i^*. Of course,

$$\sum_{i \in R} u_i^* = v(R) \tag{13.3}$$

The $(n-r)$ players in $\bar{R}$, on the other hand, can likewise play an $(n-r)$-person cooperative game $G^{\bar{R}}$ among themselves, in order to divide up the quantity $v(\bar{R})$. This game $G^{\bar{R}}$ will have the characteristic function

$$v^{\bar{R}}(S) = v(S) \quad \text{for all} \quad S \subseteq \bar{R} \tag{13.4}$$

Again, by Theorem 11.2, each player i in $\overline{R}$ will obtain his Shapley value $u_i^{\overline{R}}$ for $G^{\overline{R}}$ as his payoff from $G^{\overline{R}}$, where

$$u_i^{\overline{R}} = \sum_{\substack{S \ni i \\ S \subseteq R}} \frac{(s-1)\,!\,(n-r-s)!}{(n-r)!}\, v(S) - \sum_{\substack{S \not\ni i \\ S \subseteq R}} \frac{s!(n-r-1)!}{(n-r)!}\, v(S) \qquad (13.5)$$

After playing the two "sectional" games G^R and $G^{\overline{R}}$, the n players may play an n-person simple bargaining game G^o in order to divide the remaining balance $\Delta^o = [v(N) - v(R) - v(\overline{R})]$ of the total payoff $v(N)$ available for distribution. It is easy to check that the n-person Nash solution of this game will give every player the *same* net payoff Δ^o/n. Consequently the final payoff u_i^o of each player i will be

$$u_i^o = u_i{}^* + \frac{1}{n}\Delta^o = u_i{}^* + \frac{1}{n}\,[v(N) - v(R) - v(\overline{R})] \quad \text{if} \ \ i \in R \qquad (13.6)$$

and

$$u_i^o = u_i^{\overline{R}} + \frac{1}{n}\Delta^o = u_i^{\overline{R}} + \frac{1}{n}\,[v(N) - v(R) - v(\overline{R})] \quad \text{if} \ \ i \in \overline{R} \qquad (13.7)$$

Therefore, in view of (13.3), the joint payoff u_R^o of the r players in R will be

$$u_R^o = \sum_{i \in R} u_i^o = v(R) + \left(\frac{r}{n}\right) [v(N) - v(R) - v(\overline{R})] \qquad (13.8)$$

$$= \left(\frac{r}{n}\right) v(N) + \left(\frac{n-r}{n}\right) v(R) - \left(\frac{r}{n}\right) v(\overline{R})$$

Obviously discrimination by coalition R against coalition $\overline{R}$ will be profitable only if $u_R^o > u_R$. But even if such behavior would be profitable, as we have argued in Section 11.9, the members of coalition R will be unable to discriminate against the other players *unless the communication network of the game is biased in favor of coalition R*, allowing the r players in R to negotiate with one another and to agree on a joint strategy before their agreement could be disrupted by the other players making counteroffers to them. That is, the members of R must be able to talk to one another and reach an enforceable agreement *before* talking to the other players.

Of course, any agreement by the players in R to discriminate against the other players must specify how the joint profit $\Delta = (u_R^o - u_R)$ achieved by this discrimination will be divided up among the members of R. Bargaining about the division of this quantity Δ will represent an r-person simple bargaining game among the members of R. The r-person Nash solution of this game will give the *same* net payoff Δ/r to every member of R, in addition to the Shapley value u_i that he would receive in the absence of discrimination against the other players.

Consequently the final payoff u_i^o of each player i in R will satisfy

$$u_i^o = u_i + \frac{1}{r}(u_R^o - u_R) \tag{13.9}$$

In view of (13.1), (13.2), and (13.8), this implies that for each player i in R we can write

$$u_i^o = \left(\frac{1}{n}\right)v(N) + \left(\frac{n-r}{n}\right)\cdot\left(\frac{1}{r}\right)v(R) - \left(\frac{1}{n-r}\right)v(\bar{R}) \tag{13.10}$$

$$+ \sum_{\substack{S\in i \\ S \neq R \\ S \subset N}} \frac{(s-1)!(n-s-1)!}{(n-1)!} \cdot \left(\frac{r-s^*}{r}\right)v(S)$$

$$- \sum_{\substack{S \not\ni i \\ S \neq \bar{R} \\ S \subset N}} \frac{(s-1)!(n-s-1)!}{(n-1)!} \cdot \left(\frac{s^*}{r}\right)v(S)$$

In contrast, in view of (13.5) and (13.7), for each player i in $\bar{R}$ we have

$$u_i^o = \left(\frac{1}{n}\right)v(N) + \left(\frac{r}{n}\right)\cdot\left[\left(\frac{1}{n-r}\right)v(\bar{R}) - \left(\frac{1}{r}\right)v(\bar{R})\right] \tag{13.11}$$

$$+ \sum_{\substack{S\ni i \\ S \subset \bar{R}}} \left[\frac{(s-1)!(n-r-s)!}{(n-r)!}\right]v(S)$$

$$- \sum_{\substack{S \not\ni i \\ S \subset \bar{R}}} \left[\frac{s!(n-r-s-1)!}{(n-r)!}\right]v(S)$$

We will call the payoff vector $u^o = (u_1^o, \ldots, u_n^o)$ defined by (13.10) and (13.11) the *discriminating solution* of game G, based on discrimination by coalition R against the complementary coalition $\bar{R}$.

Finally we are now in a position to compute the payoffs u_i^* that the members of coalition R will obtain from the sectional game G^R. The members of R must agree on such payoffs u_i^* from G^R that will give rise to the final payoffs u_i^o defined by (13.10). In view of (13.5) and (13.7), this means that the payoffs u_i^* must be

$$u_i^* = u_i + \frac{1}{r}[v(R) - u_{\bar{R}}] \tag{13.12}$$

This result can be interpreted as follows: If the r players in R play the r-person game G^R among themselves, then they will obtain the joint payoff $v(R)$ and the individual payoffs u_i^*. In contrast, if they participated in the n-person game G

without discriminating against the other $(n - r)$ players, then they would obtain the joint payoff u_R and the individual payoffs u_i. Thus by playing game G^R rather than playing game G without discrimination, their joint gain (or their joint loss) will be $[v(R) - u_R]$. Equation (13.12) says that the r players in R will divide this joint gain (or joint loss) equally among them, so that for each player i in R we have $u_i{}^* - u_i = [v(R) - u_R]/r$.

In view of (13.6) and (13.10), we can also express the payoffs $u_i{}^*$ as

$$u_i{}^* = \left(\frac{1}{r}\right) v(R) + \sum_{\substack{S \ni i \\ S \neq R \\ S \subset N}} \left[\frac{(s - 1)!\,(n - s - 1)!}{(n - 1)!}\right] \left(\frac{r - s^*}{r}\right) v(S) \qquad (13.13)$$

$$- \sum_{\substack{S \not\ni i \\ S \neq \bar{R} \\ S \subset N}} \left[\frac{(s - 1)!\,(n - s - 1)!}{(n - 1)!}\right] \left(\frac{s^*}{r}\right) v(S)$$

We shall now summarize our main result as:

Theorem 13.1. If coalition R discriminates against the complementary coalition $\bar{R} = N - R$ in an n-person cooperative game G with transferable utility, given in characteristic-function form, then the players' final payoffs will correspond to the discriminatory solution $u^o = (u_1{}^o, \ldots, u_n{}^o)$, where for each player i in R his payoff $u_i{}^o$ is defined by (13.10), whereas for each player i in $\bar{R}$ his payoff $u_i{}^o$ is defined by (13.11).

13.2   Discrimination in games with transferable utility, given in normal form

Let G be an n-person cooperative game with transferable utility, given in normal form. Then in the absence of discrimination each player i will still receive a payoff u_i defined by (13.1) if we set

$$v(S) = \sum_{i \in S} U_i(\theta_o{}^S, \theta_o{}^{\bar{S}}) \qquad (13.14)$$

where θ^S and $\theta^{\bar{S}}$ are the optimal threat strategies of the two complementary coalitions S and $\bar{S}$, defined by the optimality condition

$$\sum_{i \in S} U_i(\theta_o{}^S, \theta_o{}^{\bar{S}}) - \sum_{i \in \bar{S}} U_i(\theta_o{}^S, \theta_o{}^{\bar{S}}) \qquad (13.15)$$

$$= \max_{\theta^S \in \Sigma^S} \min_{\theta^{\bar{S}} \in \Sigma^{\bar{S}}} \left[\sum_{i \in S} U_i(\theta^S, \theta^{\bar{S}}) - \sum_{i \in \bar{S}} U_i(\theta^S, \theta^{\bar{S}})\right]$$

$$= \min_{\theta^{\bar{S}} \in \Sigma^{\bar{S}}} \max_{\theta^S \in \Sigma^S} \left[\sum_{i \in S} U_i(\theta^S, \theta^{\bar{S}}) - \sum_{i \in \bar{S}} U_i(\theta^S, \theta^{\bar{S}})\right]$$

By the same token, any coalition R will still receive the joint payoff u_R defined by (13.2), if we interpret the quantities $v(S)$ in accordance with (13.14) and (13.15).

Now suppose that the r players in R decide to discriminate against the other $(n - r)$ players, i.e., they decide to play an r-person game G^R among themselves in order to divide up the quantity $v(R)$. As we argued in Section 13.1, if this happens, then the remaining $(n - r)$ players will play an $(n - r)$-person game $G^{\overline{R}}$ among themselves in order to divide up the quantity $v(\overline{R})$. Finally all n players will play an n-person game G^o in order to divide up the quantity $\Delta^o = v(N) - v(R) - v(\overline{R})$.

In order to make the quantities $v(R)$ and $v(\overline{R})$ determinate we assume that, before playing the games G^R and $G^{\overline{R}}$, the two complementary coalitions R and $\overline{R}$ will announce some threat strategies $\theta_{oo}{}^R$ and $\theta_{oo}{}^{\overline{R}}$ against each other. Moreover in order to make the game $G^{\overline{R}}$ determinate, we have to specify the quantities $v(S)$ for all $S \subset \overline{R}$. Thus we assume that each pair of coalitions $S \subset \overline{R}$ and $\check{S} = \overline{R} - S$ will announce some threat strategies $\theta_{oo}{}^S$ and $\theta_{oo}{}^{\check{S}}$ against each other. As we will see, the optimality conditions for all these threat strategies will be different from Condition (13.15), which applies in the nondiscrimination case. Thus we define

$$v(R) = \sum_{i \in R} U_i(\theta_{oo}{}^R, \theta_{oo}{}^{\overline{R}}) \tag{13.16}$$

$$v(\overline{R}) = \sum_{i \in \overline{R}} U_i(\theta_{oo}{}^R, \theta_{oo}{}^{\overline{R}}) \tag{13.17}$$

and

$$v(S) = \sum_{i \in S} U_i(\theta_{oo}{}^R, \theta_{oo}{}^S, \theta_{oo}{}^{\check{S}}) \tag{13.18}$$

Under these assumptions the final payoff $u_i{}^o$ of each player i in R will be defined by Equation (13.9), whereas the final payoff $u_i{}^o$ of each player i in $\overline{R}$ will be defined by Equation (13.11). In both equations the quantities $v(R)$, $v(\overline{R})$, and $v(S)$ are the quantities defined by (13.16) through (13.18) and *not* the quantities defined by (13.14) and (13.15).

By (13.9) and (13.11), each player i in R will maximize his own final payoff $u_i{}^o$ by choosing the threat strategy $\theta_{oo}{}^R$ of coalition R in a way to *maximize* the quantity

$$D^R = \left(\frac{1}{r}\right) v(R) - \left(\frac{1}{n-r}\right) v(\overline{R}) \tag{13.19}$$

$$= \left(\frac{1}{r}\right) \sum_{i \in R} U_i(\theta_{oo}{}^R - \theta_{oo}{}^{\overline{R}}) - \left(\frac{1}{n-r}\right) \sum_{i \in \overline{R}} U_i(\theta_{oo}{}^R, \theta_{oo}{}^{\overline{R}})$$

In contrast, each player j in $\overline{R}$ will maximize his own final payoff u_j^o by choosing the threat strategy $\theta_{oo}{}^{\overline{R}}$ of coalition $\overline{R}$ in a way to *minimize* the same quantity D^R.

Consequently the choice of the threat strategies $\theta_{oo}{}^R$ and $\theta_{oo}{}^{\overline{R}}$ by coalitions R and $\overline{R}$ will have the nature of a two-person zero-sum game $G_{R\overline{R}}$ between these two coalitions. Any pair of threat strategies $\theta_{oo}{}^R$ and $\theta_{oo}{}^{\overline{R}}$ will be *optimal* against each other if they represent optimal strategies in this game $G_{R\overline{R}}$. Accordingly optimality requires that

$$D^R = \left(\frac{1}{r}\right) \sum_{i \in R} U_i(\theta_{oo}{}^R, \theta_{oo}{}^{\overline{R}}) - \left(\frac{1}{n-r}\right) \sum_{i \in \overline{R}} U_i(\theta_{oo}{}^R, \theta_{oo}{}^{\overline{R}}) \qquad (13.20)$$

$$= \max_{\theta^R \in \Sigma^R} \min_{\theta^{\overline{R}} \in \Sigma^{\overline{R}}} \left[\left(\frac{1}{r}\right) \sum_{i \in R} U_i(\theta^R, \theta^{\overline{R}}) - \left(\frac{1}{n-r}\right) \sum_{i \in \overline{R}} U_i(\theta^R, \theta^{\overline{R}}) \right]$$

$$= \min_{\theta^{\overline{R}} \in \Sigma^{\overline{R}}} \max_{\theta^R \in \Sigma^R} \left[\left(\frac{1}{r}\right) \sum_{i \in R} U_i(\theta^R, \theta^{\overline{R}}) - \left(\frac{1}{n-r}\right) \sum_{i \in \overline{R}} U_i(\theta^R, \theta^{\overline{R}}) \right]$$

At the same time, by (13.11), each player i in any coalition $S \subset \overline{R}$ will maximize his own final payoff u_i^o by choosing the threat strategy $\theta_{oo}{}^S$ of coalition S in a way to *maximize* the quantity

$$D^S = \sum_{i \in S} U_i(\theta^R, \theta^S, \theta^{\check{S}}) - \sum_{i \in \check{S}} U_i(\theta^R, \theta^S, \theta^{\check{S}}) \qquad (13.21)$$

whereas each player j in the corresponding coalition $\check{S} = \overline{R} - S$ will maximize his own final payoff u_j^o by choosing the threat strategy $\theta_{oo}{}^{\check{S}}$ of coalition $\check{S}$ so as to *minimize* the same quantity D^S.

Accordingly, for any pair of coalitions $S \subset \overline{R}$ and $\check{S} = \overline{R} - S$, their threat strategies $\theta_{oo}{}^S$ and $\theta_{oo}{}^{\check{S}}$ will be *optimal* against each other if they satisfy

$$\sum_{i \in S} U_i(\theta_{oo}{}^R, \theta_{oo}{}^S, \theta_{oo}{}^{\check{S}}) - \sum_{i \in \check{S}} U_i(\theta_{oo}{}^R, \theta_{oo}{}^S, \theta_{oo}{}^{\check{S}}) \qquad (13.22)$$

$$= \max_{\theta^S \in \Sigma^S} \min_{\theta^{\check{S}} \in \Sigma^{\check{S}}} \left[\sum_{i \in S} U_i(\theta_{oo}{}^R, \theta^S, \theta^{\check{S}}) - \sum_{i \in \check{S}} U_i(\theta_{oo}{}^R, \theta^S, \theta^{\check{S}}) \right]$$

$$= \min_{\theta^{\check{S}} \in \Sigma^{\check{S}}} \max_{\theta^S \in \Sigma^S} \left[\sum_{i \in S} U_i(\theta_{oo}{}^R, \theta^S, \theta^{\check{S}}) - \sum_{i \in \check{S}} U_i(\theta_{oo}{}^R, \theta^S, \theta^{\check{S}}) \right]$$

where θ^R is a strategy satisfying (13.20).

Thus both optimality conditions (13.20) and (13.22) have forms different from (13.15). The former applies the maximin operator to the quantity $[v(R)/r - v(\overline{R})/n - r]$ rather than to the quantity $[v(R) - v(\overline{R})]$, as (13.15) owuld do. On the other hand, (13.22) applies the maximin operator to $[v(S) - v(S)]$, rather than to $[v(S) - v(\overline{S})]$, where $\check{S} = \overline{R} - S$, while $\overline{S} = N - S$.

We can now state:

Theorem 13.2. In a game G with transferable utility, given in normal form, the discriminating solution $u^o = (u_1{}^o, \ldots, u_n{}^o)$ based on discrimination by coalition R against coalition $\overline{R}$ is defined by (13.9) and (13.11), if the quantities $v(R)$, $v(\overline{R})$, and $v(S)$ are interpreted in accordance with (13.16) through (13.18), (13.20), and (13.22).

13.3 Discrimination in the general case

We again assume that G is an n-person cooperative game given in normal form without, however, assuming that utility is freely transferable in G. Instead we assume, as we did in Chapter 12, that every player i is free to reduce his own pay-off voluntarily by any desired amount. (This "throwaway assumption" is needed to enable the players always to agree on payoffs satisfying the dividend proportionality rule – see below.)

As in Sections 13.1 and 13.2, let us assume that at first the two complementary coalitions R and $\overline{R}$ will separately play the sectional games G^R and $G^{\overline{R}}$, respectively, and then all n players will join in playing the n-person simple bargaining game G^o.

G^R will have the nature of an r-person simple bargaining game, where the conflict payoff of each player i in R is the payoff u_i that he would receive from game G if G were played without discrimination. Hence, by Theorem 12.5 of Section 12.8, we must write

$$u_i = \overline{\overline{u}}_i \quad \text{for all} \quad i \in R \tag{13.23}$$

where $\overline{\overline{u}}_i$ is player i's payoff corresponding to the (nondiscriminatory) *stable solution* of game G. We can write the payoff $u_i{}^*$ of each player $i, i \in R$, from G^R as

$$u_i{}^* = u_i + w_i{}^R \tag{13.24}$$

and can call $w_i{}^R$ player i's *dividend* from coalition R.

In contrast, $G^{\overline{R}}$ will have the nature of an $(n - r)$-person general cooperative game, rather than that of a simple bargaining game. Consequently, in accordance with the model proposed in Chapter 11 and 12, in game $G^{\overline{R}}$ each player i in $\overline{R}$ will receive a dividend $w_i{}^S$ from every coalition $S \subseteq \overline{R}$ containing him as member. Thus the payoff $u_i{}^{\overline{R}}$ of each player i in $\overline{R}$ from game $G^{\overline{R}}$ will have the form

$$u_i{}^{\overline{R}} = \sum_{\substack{S \ni i \\ S \subseteq \overline{R}}} w_i{}^S \quad \text{for all} \quad i \in \overline{R} \tag{13.25}$$

Finally G^o will have the nature of an n-person simple bargaining game. The net payoff $w_i{}^N$ of each player i from G^o will be called his *dividend* from the all-player coalition N. Hence the final payoff $u_i{}^o$ of each player i will be of the form

$$u_i{}^o = u_i{}^* + w_i{}^N = u_i + w_i{}^R + w_i{}^N \quad \text{if} \quad i \in R \tag{13.26}$$

and

$$u_i^o = u_i^{\overline{R}} + w_i^N = \sum_{\substack{S \ni i \\ S \subseteq \overline{R}}} w_i^S + w_i^N \quad \text{if} \quad i \in \overline{R} \tag{13.27}$$

Let $\widetilde{H}$ be the extended upper boundary of the extended agreement space $\widetilde{P}^*$ as defined in Section 12.1. We will write the equation of $\widetilde{H}$ as

$$H(u_1, \ldots, u_n) = H(u) = 0 \tag{13.28}$$

H_i will denote the first partial derivative of H with respect to u_i. We will write

$$a_i = H_i(u_1^o, \ldots, u_n^o) = H(u^o) \quad i = 1, \ldots, n \tag{13.29}$$

By the same reasoning that we used in Chapter 12, in game G^o any pair of players i and j will be in *bargaining equilibrium* only if

$$a_i w_i^N = a_j w_j^N \quad i, j \in N \tag{13.30}$$

Moreover, the two sectional games G^R and $G^{\overline{R}}$ must be regarded as *dependent* games with respect to game G^o. This is so because the players' main objective will be to maximize their final payoffs u_i^o, which will be decided in game G^o, rather than to maximize the payoffs u_i^* and $u_i^{\overline{R}}$ that they will obtain from G^R and from $G^{\overline{R}}$, respectively. Consequently any pair of players i and j, if both i and j are members of coalition R, will be in bargaining equilibrium only if.

$$a_i w_i^R = a_j w_j^R \quad \text{if} \quad i, j \in R \tag{13.31}$$

Likewise any pair of players i and j, if both i and j are members of some coalition S, where $S \subseteq \overline{R}$, will be in bargaining equilibrium only if

$$a_i w_i^S = a_j w_j^S \quad \text{if} \quad i, j \in S \quad \text{and} \quad S \subseteq \overline{R} \tag{13.32}$$

Using the terminology that we used in Chapter 12, we will call (13.30) through (13.32) together the *dividend-proportionality rule*.

Again we assume that, before the games G^R, $G^{\overline{R}}$, and G^o are played, coalitions R and $\overline{R}$ will announce some threat strategies θ_{oo}^R and $\theta_{oo}^{\overline{R}}$ against each other. Similarly each pair of coalitions S and $\check{S}$, where $S \subseteq \overline{R}$ and $\check{S} = \overline{R} - S$, will announce some threat strategies θ^S and $\theta^{\check{S}}$. It is easy to verify that the optimality conditions for these threat strategies are the direct analogues of (13.20) and (13.22), except that the maximin (or minimax) operators have to be constrained by Conditions (13.31) and (13.32). By reasoning similar to that used in Sections 12.4 and 12.5, we can show that the discriminating solution $u^o = (u_1^o, \ldots, u_n^o)$ can be defined by the following requirements:

$$H(u_1^o, \ldots, u_n^o) = 0 \tag{α^o}$$

$$a_i = H_i(u_1^o, \ldots, u_n^o) \quad \text{for all} \quad i \in N \tag{β^o}$$

$$u_i^S = c_i^S + \frac{1}{a_i} \min_{j \in S} [a_j U_j(\theta_{oo}^S, \theta_{oo}^{\check{S}}) - a_j c_j^S] \qquad \text{for all } i \in S \qquad (\gamma^o)$$

$$\text{and for all } S \subseteq \overline{R}$$

$$\text{as well as for } S = R$$

Here $a = (a_1, \ldots, a_n)$, while c^S is the vector consisting of the quantities c_i^S for all $i \in S$.

$$c_i^S = \sum_{\substack{T \ni i \\ T \subset S}} (-1)^{s-t+1} u_i^T \qquad \text{for all } i \in S \qquad (\delta^o)$$

$$\text{and for all } S \subseteq \overline{R}$$

$$c_i^R = u_i = \overline{\overline{u}}_i \qquad \text{for all } i \in R \qquad (\epsilon^o)$$

$$c_i^N = u_i^R \qquad \text{for all } i \in R \qquad (\zeta^o)$$

$$c_i^N = u_i^{\overline{R}} \qquad \text{for all } i \in \overline{R} \qquad (\eta^o)$$

$$a_i(u_i^o - c_i^N) = a_j(u_j^o - c_j^N) \qquad \text{for all } i, j \in N \qquad (\theta^o)$$

$$D^R = \Delta^R(\theta_{oo}^R, \theta_{oo}^{\overline{R}}, c^R, c^{\overline{R}}, a) = \max_{\theta^R \in \Sigma^R} \min_{\theta^{\overline{R}} \in \Sigma^{\overline{R}}} \Delta^R(\theta^R, \theta^{\overline{R}}, c^R, c^{\overline{R}}, a)$$

$$c^R, c^{\overline{R}}, a = \text{const.} \qquad (\iota^o)$$

where

$$\Delta^R(\theta^R, \theta^{\overline{R}}, c^R, c^{\overline{R}}, a) = \left(\frac{1}{r}\right) \sum_{i \in R} a_i u_i^R - \left(\frac{1}{n-r}\right) \sum_{j \in \overline{R}} a_j u_j^{\overline{R}} \qquad (\kappa^o)$$

$$= \left(\frac{1}{r}\right) \sum_{i \in R} a_i c_i^R - \left(\frac{1}{n-r}\right) \sum_{j \in \overline{R}} a_j c_j^{\overline{R}}$$

$$+ \min_{i \in R} [a_i U_i(\theta^R, \theta^{\overline{R}}) - a_i c_i^R]$$

$$- \min_{j \in R} [a_j U_j(\theta^R, \theta^{\overline{R}}) - a_j c_j^{\overline{R}}]$$

$$D^S = \Delta^S(\theta_{oo}^R, \theta_{oo}^S, \theta_{oo}^{\check{S}}, c^S, c^{\check{S}}, a) \qquad (\lambda^o)$$

$$= \max_{\theta^S \in \Sigma^S} \min_{\theta^{\check{S}} \in \Sigma^{\check{S}}} \Delta^S(\theta_{oo}^R, \theta^S, \theta^{\check{S}}, c^S, c^{\check{S}}, a) \quad \text{for all } S \subseteq \overline{R}$$

$$c^S, c^{\check{S}}, a = \text{const.}$$

where

$$\Delta^S(\theta^R, \theta^S, \theta^{\check{S}}, c^S, c^{\check{S}}, a) = \sum_{i \in S} a_i u_i^S - \sum_{j \in \check{S}} a_j u_j^{\check{S}} = \sum_{i \in S} a_i c_i^S - \sum_{j \in \check{S}} a_j c_j^{\check{S}}$$

$$+ s \min_{i \in S} [a_i U_i(\theta^R, \theta^S, \theta^{\check{S}}) - a_i c_i^S]$$

$$- (n - r - s) \min_{j \in \check{S}} [a_j U_j(\theta^R, \theta^S, \theta^{\check{S}}) - a_j c_j^{\check{S}}] \qquad (\mu^o)$$

In Equations (ι^o) and (λ^o) the order of the max and the min operators can be interchanged.

In order to obtain requirements which do not assume the existence of the partial derivatives H_i at the solution point u^o, we can replace (α^o) and (β^o) by

$$a_i \geqq 0 \quad \text{for all} \quad i \in N \tag{$\alpha\alpha^o$}$$

and

$$\sum_{i \in N} a_i u_i^o = \max_{\substack{u \in P_* \\ a_i = \text{const.}}} \sum_{i \in N} a_i u_i \tag{$\beta\beta^o$}$$

Thus we can state:

Theorem 13.3. In the general case the discriminating solution $u^o = (u_1^o, \ldots, u_n^o)$, based on discrimination by coalition R against the complementary coalition $\overline{R}$, is defined by requirements ($\alpha\alpha^o$), ($\beta\beta^o$), and (γ^o) through (μ^o).

The existence of this solution u^o can be shown by the method used in Section 12.6. Again in general this solution u^o is not unique. But we can construct a unique "stable discriminatory solution" u^{oo} essentially in the same way that we constructed the nondiscriminatory stable solution $\overline{\overline{u}}$ in Section 12.7.

14

Noncooperative and
almost-noncooperative games

14.1 Introduction

In this chapter we will define a solution for noncooperative and for almost-noncooperative games (both two-person and n-person). In Section 5.17, we defined a (strictly) *noncooperative* game as a game in which no agreement between the players has any binding force: Thus any player is free to violate any agreement even if he obtains no positive benefit by doing so. In contrast, we defined an *almost-noncooperative* game as a game in which the players are bound by any agreement that they are making as long as they cannot obtain any positive benefit by violating it, though they are free to disregard any agreement if they can achieve a positive gain (however small) by doing so.

Accordingly, whereas in a cooperative game any possible strategy n-tuple (and any possible probability mixture of such strategy n-tuples) will be stable once the players have agreed to adopt it, in a noncooperative or almost-noncooperative game only strategy n-tuples satisfying certain special stability requirements – which we call *eligible*-strategy n-tuples – have sufficient stability to be used by rational players. A strategy n-tuple can be eligible only if it is an equilibrium point or a maximin point (see Sections 5.12 and 5.13). As we have argued, in a strictly noncooperative game a profitable equilibrium point will be eligible only if it is a strong equilibrium point or a centroid equilibrium point, while in an almost-noncooperative game a profitable equilibrium point is always eligible.

More exactly our conclusion has been as follows (see Section 7.2): In a strictly noncooperative game an equilibrium point $\sigma = (\sigma_1, \ldots, \sigma_n)$ is *eligible* if it satisfies the following conditions:

1. It must be profitable to at least one player. That is, for at least one player i we must have $U_i(\sigma) > \check{u}_i$, where $\check{u}_i$ is player i's maximin payoff.

2. If σ is profitable to a given player i, then i's equilibrium strategy σ_i must be a centroid best reply to the other $(n - 1)$ players' strategy combination $\sigma^i = (\sigma_1, \ldots, \sigma_{i-1}, \sigma_{i+1}, \ldots, \sigma_n)$.

3. If σ is unprofitable to a given player j, then j's equilibrium strategy σ_j must be a centroid maximin strategy.

In an almost-noncooperative game an equilibrium point σ is eligible if it satisfies conditions 1 and 3 (but it need not satisfy condition 2). On the other hand, a maximin point is *always* eligible.

As we saw in Section 7.7, in *tacit* and *semivocal* noncooperative and almost-noncooperative games, the strategy-coordination problem further restricts the players' strategy choice to accessible strategy n-tuples. A maximin point is always accessible, because a maximin strategy $\check{\sigma}_i$ will always secure player i his maximin payoff $\check{u}_i$, without any strategy coordination with the other players. In contrast, an equilibrium point will be accessible only if it satisfies the following condition:

Let $\sigma = (\sigma_1, \ldots, \sigma_n)$ be an eligible equilibrium point in a noncooperative or an almost-noncooperative game, yielding the payoff vector $u = U(\sigma)$. Let $\Sigma^*(u)$ be the set of *all* eligible equilibrium points yielding the *same* payoff vector u, and let σ^* be the centroid n-tuple of this set $\Sigma^*(u)$. Then σ will be called an *accessible* equilibrium point if and only if $\sigma = \sigma^*$. Clearly, the set F of accessible strategy n-tuples is always a subset of the set E of eligible-strategy n-tuples.

In the next few sections we will define our solution concept for *vocal* noncooperative and almost-noncooperative games. (*Tacit* and semivocal games will be discussed in Section 14.10.)

14.2 Comparison between Nash's and our own solution concepts for noncooperative games

The concept of noncooperative games was introduced by Nash [1951]; he was also the first to define a solution concept for this class of games, based on the concept of equilibrium points, which also underlies our theory. Our approach, however, does differ from that of Nash in the following respects:

1. In the special case of unprofitable games (where for one reason or another the players cannot rationally expect to obtain more than their maximin payoffs), we consider *maximin points* to have greater stability than equilibrium points do. (Our reasons for this view were stated in Section 7.2.)

2. Unlike Nash, we distinguish between *strictly* noncooperative and *almost-*noncooperative games. Whereas in the latter all profitable equilibrium points are stable, in the former some additional conditions are required to assure stability.

3. Under Nash's definition, noncooperative games are characterized *both* by unenforceability of agreements *and* by lack of communication between the players. Our aim is to study the implications of these two assumptions separately. Therefore we define noncooperative games solely in terms of unenforceability of agreements and then distinguish vocal and tacit (as well as semivocal) games both among cooperative and noncooperative (or almost-noncooperative) games.

4. Nash's solution for noncooperative games exists only in special cases, viz., when all equilibrium points in the game are mutually interchangeable. In contrast, our solution always exists (although in the case of unprofitable games it is merely a "quasi-solution" – see Section 7.8).

5. This last difference itself exists because Nash makes no use of joint-efficiency and of bargaining considerations in defining his solution – presumably because he regards such considerations to be relevant only in cooperative games. In contrast, under our theory both efficiency and bargaining considerations play important

roles also in noncooperative (and in almost-noncooperative) games, but their application is restricted to the set E of eligible joint strategies whereas in cooperative games no such restriction is necessary.[1]

14.3 Efficiency and bargaining considerations

To illustrate point 5, consider the three games in Examples 1 through 3. In Example 1 there are three equilibrium points, viz., the strategy pairs (A_1, B_1), (A_2, B_2), and $(\frac{1}{2} A_1 + \frac{1}{2} A_2, \frac{1}{2} B_1 + \frac{1}{2} B_2)$. All three are eligible,[2] but (A_1, B_1) has strong joint dominance over the other two. Therefore under our theory by the joint-efficiency postulate the players will choose (A_1, B_1), which is (according to the terminology of Section 7.8) the only "rational joint strategy" or the only "particular strategy solution" of the game.

	B_1	B_2		B_1	B_2		B_1	B_2	B_3
A_1	(2, 2)	(0, 0)	A_1	(2, 1)	(-10, -1)	A_1	(10, 10)	(1, 30)	(0, 0)
A_2	(0, 0)	(1, 1)	A_2	(0, 0)	(1, 2)	A_2	(30, 1)	(2, 2)	(1, 1)
						A_3	(0, 0)	(1, 1)	(0, 0)

| Example 1 | Example 2 | Example 3 |

In Example 2 there are only two eligible equilibrium points,[3] viz., $\sigma^1 = (A_1, B_1)$ and $\sigma^2 = (A_2, B_2)$. [There is also a third equilibrium point, viz., $\sigma^3 = (\frac{1}{2} A_1 + \frac{1}{2} A_2, \frac{11}{13} B_1 + \frac{2}{13} B_2)$. But this is unprofitable to both players. Moreover it is an ineligible equilibrium point because the two players' equilibrium strategies are not maximin strategies.] Obviously player 1 will prefer equilibrium point σ^1, while player 2 will prefer equilibrium point σ^2. If both players used their strategies associated with their own favorite equilibrium points, player 1 using strategy A_1 while player 2 using strategy B_2, then player 1 would suffer a much heavier loss (in relation to the payoff difference for him between the two equilibrium points), because $U_1(A_1, B_2) = -10$ while $U_2(A_1, B_2) = -1$ only. Hence it is natural to argue that player 1 will be *more afraid* to use strategy A_1 in defiance of player 2's using strategy B_2, than player 2 will be afraid to use strategy B_2 in defiance of player 1's using strategy A_1. Moreover, both players will know this – which will further discourage player 1 from using strategy A_1 and will further encourage player 2 to use strategy B_2. Hence in the end both players will settle down at equilibrium point $\sigma^2 = (A_2, B_2)$, preferred by player 2.

This type of relationship between two equilibrium points has been pointed out by Luce and Raiffa [1957, p. 110]. Under their terminology equilibrium point σ^2 will have "*psychological dominance*" over equilibrium point σ^1. But their discussion is purely heuristic and qualitative. Our theory will attempt to furnish a general quantitative criterion for this relationship.

Under our theory, the choice between equilibrium points σ^1 and σ^2 will be a matter of *bargaining* between players 1 and 2 and therefore will be subject to Zeuthen's Principle. If the two players try to maximize their expected utilities, then player 1 will stick to strategy A_1 as long as the subjective probability that he attaches to the possibility that player 2 will use strategy B_2 is no greater than

$$r_1 = \frac{U_1(A_1, B_1) - U_1(A_2, B_2)}{U_1(A_1, B_1) - U_1(A_1, B_2)} = \frac{1}{12} = .08$$

Likewise player 2 will stick to strategy B_2 as long as the subjective probability that he attaches to the possibility that player 1 will stick to strategy A_1 is no greater than

$$r_2 = \frac{U_2(A_2, B_2) - U_2(A_1, B_1)}{U_2(A_2, B_2) - U_2(A_1, B_2)} = \frac{1}{3} = .33$$

Thus, in the terminology of Section 8.4, the two players' *risk limits* are $r_1 = .08$ and $r_2 = .33$. By Zeuthen's Principle, since the first number is smaller, player 1 must yield and accept the equilibrium point $\sigma^2 = (A_2, B_2)$ preferred by his opponent. Accordingly we can say that equilibrium point σ^2 will have (strong) *risk-dominance* over equilibrium point σ^1. Thus our concept of risk-dominance in noncooperative and in almost-noncooperative games is essentially a quantitative restatement and generalization of Luce and Raiffa's concept of "psychological dominance."

Example 3 is usually called a Prisoner's Dilemma game (cf. Section 7.3). There is only one equilibrium point, viz., (A_2, B_2), and this is eligible.[4] But strategy pair (A_1, B_1) has strong joint dominance over (A_2, B_2) and indeed over all other possible strategy pairs in the game. Hence if this game were played as a cooperative game, i.e., if the players could make binding agreements, then (A_1, B_1) would be the only rational joint strategy for them. Yet if the game is played as a noncooperative or as an almost-noncooperative game, then either player will be ill-advised to use his "cooperative" strategy A_1 or B_1. Even if he did use his "cooperative" strategy, the other player would still use (and indeed, in our example, would all the more use) his own "noncooperative" strategy A_2 or B_2. This is what we mean by saying that strategy pair (A_1, B_1) would be unstable and is therefore ineligible to rational players. Thus joint-efficiency (as well as bargaining) considerations can operate only *within* the set E of eligible strategies.

14.4   Defining rational behavior in Prisoner's Dilemma situations

Our theory stands on a middle ground between two alternative approaches. Nash's theory disregards all possibilities of *cooperation* (and therefore disregards all joint-efficiency and bargaining considerations) in "noncooperative" games in which agreements are not enforced and have no binding force, while our theory merely *restricts* cooperation among the players to the set E of eligible joint strategies. On the other hand, other authors deny that such "noncooperative" games necessarily require a standard of behavior *different* from cooperative games at all, or that the players' inability to conclude binding agreements necessarily prevents them from attaining a cooperative solution (even if the latter corresponds to a joint strategy outside of what we call the eligible set).

For instance, Rapoport [1966a, p. 94] argues that in a Prisoner's Dilemma game "rational decision theory does not lead to unique, definitive solutions . . . ." In his view such a game possesses two different but equally admissible standards of rationality. One is *individual rationality*, corresponding to what we call the *noncooperative* solution [e.g., strategy pair (A_2, B_2) in Example 3] ; the other is *joint rationality*, corresponding to what we call the *cooperative solution* [strategy pair (A_1, B_1) in Example 3]. Both represent *equally valid* concepts of rationality, so that no choice can be made between them on purely theoretical grounds. All that we can do is to observe empirically under what conditions people do actually follow one or the other. Thus the nature of the game situation itself (whether or not the players can enter into binding agreements) does not uniquely determine which of these two standards of rationality is appropriate in any given case.

The difference between Rapoport's approach and ours may be to a large extent terminological, but this does not make it unimportant. It is a matter of *how to define* rational behavior in Prisoner's Dilemma games in order to maximize the analytical usefulness of this concept of rationality for theoretical and practical purposes. The question concerns what concept of rationality to use in situations where the players have good reasons to expect that the other players would not adhere to mutual agreements (and where each player may know very well that he himself may not adhere to them either).

We fully agree with Rapoport that in practice in a given empirical situation it may often be quite difficult to decide whether a cooperative or a noncooperative standard of rationality is appropriate. The players may not know the other players' utility functions (including their moral attitudes) and their social environment (e.g., the likely reactions of law-enforcing agencies and of public opinion) sufficiently to predict how strong incentives their fellow players would have to maintaining agreements. Thus they may find it very difficult to decide the extent to which the theoretical condition of agreement enforceability[5] differentiating between cooperative and noncooperative games is satisfied in any given case.

Our point is, however, that *given this information* there is always a unique standard of rationality - cooperative or noncooperative (or some combination of the two[6]) as the case may be - appropriate for each particular situation. Indeed, even when this information is not available, our theory at least suggests what the relevant information *would be* for deciding the issue between the two standards of rationality. To put it differently, in order to maximize the explanatory and policy-evaluating value of game-theoretical models we must use models explaining *why* a cooperative standard of rationality is appropriate in one situation and *why* a noncooperative standard is appropriate in another.

Admittedly it will not solve our *entire* problem of theoretical explanation if we know that the choice between these two standards of rationality depends on the existence of effective law-enforcing agencies and of spontaneous attitudes favorable to keeping agreements, since we still have to explain *why* such agencies or attitudes are present in one case and are absent in another. But it will be at least a first step toward an explanatory theory if we know that security of agreements is the central issue in distinguishing between cooperative and noncooperative situations.

Likewise in practical policy making our theory can obviously supply only part of the answer. In many situations it will tell us that, since our opponents cannot be trusted to keep agreements, we can use only a noncooperative standard of rationality in dealing with them, at least in the short run. But in most of these cases the really important policy problem will be the long-run problem of *transforming* this noncooperative game situation into a cooperative one that is to the mutual advantage of all participants. Our theory will tell us that this can be achieved only by establishing effective law-enforcing agencies and/or by inculcating on both (or on all) sides attitudes more favorable to spontaneous law observance; but it does not tell us how such agencies can be best established and how such attitudes can be best imparted. To answer these questions we need a dynamic theory incorporating the laws of individual and social *learning* and containing our present static theory of game situations as a special case. But in the meantime we feel that it is very important both from a theoretical and from a practical policy-making point of view to admit that *there are* truly noncooperative game situations, where a prudent decision maker (on either side) cannot put much confidence in his opponents' willingness to keep agreements and has to choose his own policies in full awareness of this. If we want to transform a noncooperative game situation of justified mutual distrust into a cooperative game situation of warranted mutual trust, then the first step must be to recognize that, *as things are at present*, rationality does require making use of a noncooperative solution – because only if we recognize this can we find out what factors have to be *changed* in order to make the cooperative solution acceptable and attractive to rational participants.[7]

To sum up, a theory of rational behavior in game situations will achieve its highest usefulness both in theoretical analysis and in practical policy making only if it supplies a unique well-defined standard of rationality, i.e., a unique determinate solution, for every possible game situation – at least when we know the players' utility functions and the "rules" of the game, specifying the players' strategy possibilities and their access to information and communication. Among other things this means that our theory of rational behavior must make it clear when a cooperative and when a noncooperative standard of rationality is appropriate.[8]

14.5 Different types of Prisoner's Dilemma situations

To bring out more clearly the treatment of the Prisoner's Dilemma problem under our theory, see Examples 4 through 6. These are Prisoner's Dilemma situations, different from Example 3 of Section 14.2. (They have all been discussed earlier.)

	B_1	B_2
A_1	(2, 2)	(1, 2)
A_2	(2, 1)	(1, 1)

Example 4

	B_1	B_2
A_1	(3, 1)	(0, 0)
A_2	(0, 0)	(1, 3)

Example 5

	B_1	B_2
A_1	(1, 1)	(0, 0)
A_2	(0, 0)	(1, 1)

Example 6

In Example 4 all possible strategy pairs $\sigma = (\sigma_1, \sigma_2)$ are equilibrium points, where σ_1 may be any mixture of A_1 and A_2, while σ_2 may be any mixture of B_1 and B_2. Equilibrium point (A_1, B_1) has (strong or at least weak) joint dominance over all the others. Consequently if the game is played as an almost-noncooperative game (and, of course, even more so if it is played as a cooperative game), the players will choose the strategy pair (A_1, B_1), and no Prisoner's Dilemma problem will arise. But if the game is played as a *strictly noncooperative* game, then (A_1, B_1) will be unstable, because it will involve an *indifference problem* for each player. That is, even if player 2 did stick to strategy B_1, player 1 could deviate from strategy A_1 without penalty; and player 2 could deviate without penalty from B_1 even if player 1 did stick to A_1. The only stable and therefore eligible equilibrium point now is $(\frac{1}{2} A_1 + \frac{1}{2} A_2, \frac{1}{2} B_1 + \frac{1}{2} B_2)$ in which the two players' strategies are centroid-best-reply strategies to each other. Hence under our theory this is the strategy pair that the players will choose if the game is strictly noncooperative. But then this will represent a Prisoner's Dilemma situation (of a type different from Example 3), because this strategy pair is subject to strong joint dominance by the ineligible equilibrium point (A_1, B_1).

In Example 5 there are three equilibrium points, viz., $\sigma^1 = (A_1, B_1)$, $\sigma^2 = (A_2, B_2)$, $\sigma^3 = (\frac{1}{2} A_1 + \frac{1}{2} A_2, \frac{1}{2} B_1 + \frac{1}{2} B_2)$. The first two have strong joint dominance over the third. Moreover, the latter is unprofitable to both players, and so under our definition it is not eligible as an equilibrium point. But it is also a maximin point; as such it is, of course, a member of the eligible set E. Player 1 will obviously prefer equilibrium point σ^1, while player 2 will prefer σ^2. Thus it would be natural to try to decide between them by means of Zeuthen's Principle. Unfortunately Zeuthen's Principle will give no criterion to choose between them, since

$$r_1 = \frac{U_1(A_1, B_1) - U_1(A_2, B_2)}{U_1(A_1, B_1) - U_1(A_1, B_2)} = \frac{2}{3}$$

$$r_2 = \frac{U_2(A_2, B_2) - U_2(A_1, B_1)}{U_2(A_2, B_2) - U_2(A_1, B_2)} = \frac{2}{3} = r_1$$

Indeed, in view of the complete *symmetry* of the game, no *conceivable* rational criterion could decide between σ^1 and σ^2. In such a case we say that there is a *bargaining deadlock* between σ^1 and σ^2. In cases such as this we can apply part of Zeuthen's Principle (see Section 8.4), which says that, if $r_1 = r_2$, then *both* players have to make concessions. That is, player 1 must be ready to accept a payoff less than $U_1(\sigma^1) = 3$, and player 2 must also be ready to accept a payoff less than $U_2(\sigma^2) = 3$. The eligible set E contains only one strategy pair yielding both players less than 3, viz., the maximin point σ^3 which gives both players the payoff $U_1(\sigma^3) = U_2(\sigma^3) = 2 < 3$. Hence σ^3 will be the strategy solution of the game. Intuitively speaking this means that, since the players will not be able to decide between σ^1 and σ^2 and since they cannot adopt a *jointly randomized* mixed strategy representing a probability mixture of σ^1 and σ^2 as a compromise (this is allowed only in a cooperative game), they will have to accept the less desirable strategy pair σ^3 as compromise solution. However, this will involve a Prisoner's Dilemma paradox, because σ^3 is strongly dominated both by σ^1 and by σ^2.

Example 6 has three equilibrium points, viz., $\sigma^1 = (A_1, B_1)$, $\sigma^2 = (A_2, B_2)$, and $\sigma^3 = (\frac{1}{2} A_1 + \frac{1}{2} A_2, \frac{1}{2} B_1 + \frac{1}{2} B_2)$. The first two again have strong joint dominance over the third. Moreover, the latter is unprofitable to both players and is eligible only as a maximin point. If the game is played as a *vocal* game, then the players will obviously choose σ^1 or σ^2 (they will not care which). But if the game is played as *tacit* or *semivocal* game, then the players will be unable to coordinate their strategy choices, and each of them will play both of his pure strategies with equal probability, which will give rise to σ^3. But since σ^3 is strongly dominated by σ^1 and by σ^2, this will represent a kind of Prisoner's Dilemma situation. As the choice of σ^3 will be a result of the players' inability to make a coordinated choice between σ^1 and σ^2 in the absence of communication, we can describe Example 6 as a *coordination deadlock* (coordination problem) between σ^1 and σ^2.

To sum up, a Prisoner's Dilemma situation arises whenever the players have to use some strategy n-tuple σ in spite of the fact that another strategy n-tuple σ^* would yield higher payoffs to all of them. The reason may be that σ^* is *not* an *equilibrium point* at all; that it is an equilibrium point not satisfying the *stability* requirements for eligibility; that it is at a *bargaining deadlock* with another equilibrium point; or (in the case of a tacit or a semivocal game) that it is at a *coordination deadlock* with another equilibrium point.

14.6 The direct and the extended risk functions

Let $\sigma = (\sigma_i, \sigma^i)$ and $\tau = (\tau_i, \tau^i)$ be two eligible equilibrium points in a vocal noncooperative or almost-noncooperative game.[9] Suppose that $U_i(\sigma) > U_i(\tau)$ so that player i would prefer equilibrium point σ to equilibrium point τ. But suppose that all other players prefer τ to σ or at least have expressed their willingness to settle for τ. If now player i tells the other players that he is likewise willing to settle for τ and to use strategy τ_i, then the other players j will immediately agree to use the strategies τ_j; and so player i will obtain the payoff $U_i(\tau)$ with certainty. But if he insists on using strategy σ_i in order to obtain the higher payoff $U_i(\sigma)$, then he *may* in fact obtain $U_i(\sigma)$, because the other players may in the end come around to using the strategies σ_j. Yet he also runs the *risk* of obtaining only $U_i(\sigma_i, \tau^i)$, because the other players j may just as possibly stick to their original intention of using the strategies τ_j, even if player i himself does use strategy σ_i.

We define player i's *risk limit* r_i as the *highest* subjective probability that he can assign to the other players' using the strategies τ_j, without himself being deterred from using strategy σ_i. Assuming that player i is trying to maximize the mathematical expectation of his utility payoff, this risk limit will be

$$r_i = Q_i(\sigma, \tau) = \frac{U_i(\sigma) - U_i(\tau)}{U_i(\sigma) - U_i(\sigma_i, \tau^i)} \tag{14.1}$$

The function Q_i itself will be called player i's *direct risk function*.

Obviously player i will take no risk whatever for the sake of achieving σ if he does not prefer σ to τ. Therefore we will write

$$Q_i(\sigma, \tau) = 0 \quad \text{if} \quad U_i(\sigma) \leqq U_i(\tau) \tag{14.2}$$

Let $T_i(\tau)$ be the set of all eligible equilibrium points ζ such that $U_i(\zeta) \leqq U_i(\tau)$. Thus $T_i(\tau)$ is the set of all equilibrium points ζ *more favorable* than, or *equally favorable* to, equilibrium point τ from player i's point of view, including τ itself.

We can say that player i is *uniformly* willing to take risk r_i in order to achieve a given eligible equilibrium point σ rather than *any* equilibrium point ζ in set $T_i(\tau)$ if

$$Q_i(\sigma, \zeta) \geqq r_i \quad \text{for all} \quad \zeta \in T_i(\tau) \tag{14.3}$$

The largest number r_i satisfying (14.3) is obviously the quantity

$$r_i = R_i(\sigma, \tau) = \min_{\zeta \in T_i(\tau)} Q_i(\sigma, \zeta) \tag{14.4}$$

Thus $R_i(\sigma, \tau)$ is the highest risk that player i would be *uniformly* willing to face in order to achieve σ rather than τ, or any equilibrium point ζ even less favorable than τ (or just as unfavorable as τ). We call the quantity $R_i(\sigma, \tau)$ player i's *uniform-risk limit*. The function R_i itself will be called player i's *extended-risk function*.

Clearly R_i has the monotonicity property

$$R_i(\sigma, \tau) \leqq R_i(\sigma, \tau^*) \quad \text{whenever} \quad U_i(\tau) \geqq U_i(\tau^*) \tag{14.5}$$

where σ, τ, and τ^* are eligible equilibrium points.

We now propose to show that, for the application of Zeuthen's Principle in noncooperative and in almost-noncooperative games and for the definition of risk-dominance relations, the proper risk function to use is the *extended* risk function $R_i(\sigma, \tau)$ rather than the *direct* risk function $Q_i(\sigma, \tau)$.

In Section 8.6, one of the rationality postulates used in deriving Zeuthen's Principle has been the Acceptance-of-Higher-Payoffs Postulate (Postulate A4). By Part I of this postulate, if player i is ready to accept a given equilibrium point ζ as the outcome of the game, then he must be even more ready to accept any other equilibrium point τ yielding him a higher payoff $U_i(\tau) > U_i(\zeta)$ than ζ would yield him. This postulate makes it necessary for us to replace the direct risk function Q_i by the extended risk function R_i as defined by (14.4).

Intuitively a risk function such as $Q_i(\sigma, \tau)$ or $R_i(\sigma, \tau)$ is meant to measure the strength of player i's opposition to some equilibrium point τ as an alternative to a preferred equilibrium point σ. Definition (14.4) expresses the requirement that i's opposition to τ *cannot be any stronger* than his opposition to an *even less favorable* (or to an equally unfavorable) equilibrium point ζ would be. The monotonicity property (14.5) expresses the same requirement in a slightly different form.

More formally, if we interpreted Zeuthen's Principle in terms of any risk function $\overline{R}_i$ lacking property (14.5) – for example, if we used the direct risk function $\overline{R}_i = Q_i$ for this purpose – then we would often obtain conclusions directly violating the Acceptance-of-Higher-Payoffs Postulate. In this case it could easily happen that

$\bar{R}_i(\sigma, \tau)$ would take a *high* value, whereas $\bar{R}_i(\sigma, \zeta)$ would take a *low* value, even though $U_i(\tau) \geqq U_i(\zeta)$. Hence, if we applied Zeuthen's Principle to this risk function $\bar{R}_i$, then we would have to conclude that player i would refuse accepting equilibrium point τ as the outcome of the game, yet would be willing to accept equilibrium point ζ as the outcome, even though ζ would yield him a lower payoff than τ would. Such a conclusion would clearly violate the Acceptance-of-Higher-Payoffs Postulate.

14.7 Primary risk-dominance relations

In terms of the extended risk function R_i, we can define risk-dominance relations – to be called *primary* risk-dominance relations – as follows: Let σ and τ be eligible equilibrium points. We will say that σ *strongly risk-dominates* τ at risk level r^* (in the sense of *primary* risk-dominance) if

$$r^* = \max_{i \in N} R_i(\sigma, \tau) > \max_{j \in N} R_j(\tau, \sigma) = r^{**} \tag{14.6}$$

In other words, among those players who prefer σ to τ, r^* is the highest uniform risk that any player would take in order to achieve σ; and, among those players who prefer τ to σ, r^{**} is the highest uniform risk that any player would take in order to achieve τ. We say that σ strongly risk-dominates τ if the former risk level r^* is higher than the latter risk level r^{**}. By Zeuthen's Principle, other things being equal, if σ strongly risk-dominates τ, then the players favoring τ will have to yield to the players favoring σ, so that σ will have a stronger claim than τ will have to being accepted as the solution.

We can say that σ *weakly risk-dominates* τ at *risk level* r^* (in the sense of *primary* risk-dominance) if

$$r^* = \max_{i \in N} R_i(\sigma, \tau) \geqq \max_{j \in N} R_j(\tau, \sigma) = r^{**} \tag{14.7}$$

If σ and τ satisfy (14.6) or at least satisfy (14.7), then that particular player (or those particular players) $i = i^*$ for whom

$$R_{i^*}(\sigma, \tau) = \max_{i \in N} R_i(\sigma, \tau) = r^* \tag{14.8}$$

will be called the *decisive player(s)* against τ, because it is his (or their) opposition to τ which makes τ to be (strongly or weakly) risk-dominated by σ.

We will also write

$$H(\sigma, \tau) = r^* \quad \text{if } \sigma \text{ has strong or weak primary risk-dominance over } \tau \text{ at} \tag{14.9}$$
$$\text{risk level } r^*$$

and

$$H(\sigma, \tau) = 0 \quad \text{if } \sigma \text{ has neither strong nor weak risk-dominance over } \tau \tag{14.10}$$
$$\text{at any risk level } r^* \text{ at all}$$

If $\sigma = \tau$, then we will always write $H(\sigma, \tau) = 0$.

It will be convenient to use the following terminology: Suppose that a given eligible equilibrium point σ has a certain property (say, strong or weak risk-dominance) with respect to *all* other eligible equilibrium points τ. Then we say that σ has this particular property with respect to the *game* (as a whole).

Lemma 1. A given equilibrium point σ will have *strong* primary risk-dominance over the game if and only if σ has (at least) *weak* primary risk-dominance over the game and is the *only* eligible equilibrium point having this property.

Proof. Let E^* be the set of all eligible equilibrium points, and let $\sigma \in E^*$. We have to show that we have

$$H(\sigma, \tau) > H(\tau, \sigma) \quad \text{for all} \quad \tau \neq \sigma, \tau \in E^* \tag{14.11}$$

if and only if

$$H(\sigma, \tau) \geq H(\tau, \sigma) \quad \text{for all} \quad \tau \neq \sigma, \tau \in E^* \tag{14.12}$$

with σ being the only equilibrium point in E^* satisfying (14.12).

Now clearly (14.11) implies (14.12). Moreover, (14.11) also implies that only σ can satisfy (14.12), because, if another equilibrium point $\sigma' \neq \sigma$ also satisfied (14.12), then we would have

$$H(\sigma, \sigma') = H(\sigma', \sigma) \tag{14.13}$$

which would be inconsistent with (14.11). Conversely, if σ is the only equilibrium point satisfying (14.12), then there cannot be any equilibrium point $\sigma' \neq \sigma$ satisfying (14.13). Consequently (14.12) will always be satisfied as a *strong* inequality, which implies (14.11). This completes the proof.

A given eligible equilibrium point σ will be called the *solution* of the game if σ has *strong* primary risk-dominance over the game. In view of Lemma 1, this is equivalent to saying that σ will be called the solution if σ has *weak* primary risk-dominance over the game, provided that σ is the *only* eligible equilibrium point with this property.

Lemma 2. Let σ and τ be eligible equilibrium points, and suppose that

$$U_j(\sigma) \geq U_j(\tau) \quad \text{for all} \quad j \in N \tag{14.14}$$

Then τ will have at least weak primary risk-dominance over σ.

Proof. By (14.2), (14.4), and (14.14),

$$R_j(\tau, \sigma) = 0 \quad \text{for all} \quad j \in N \tag{14.15}$$

Consequently

$$\max_{i \in N} R_i(\sigma, \tau) \geq \max_{j \in N} R_j(\tau, \sigma) = 0 \tag{14.16}$$

This proves the lemma.

In other words, if σ and τ are equivalent, or if σ has at least weak joint dominance over τ in terms of the corresponding payoff vectors, then σ will have at least weak primary risk-dominance over τ.

14.8 Secondary risk-dominance relations

We have defined the solution in the special case where some eligible equilibrium point σ has strong primary risk-dominance over all other eligible equilibrium points. But the difficulty is that in general – at least if the game contains more than two eligible equilibrium points – none of them will have strong primary risk-dominance over all the others. This fact makes it necessary to introduce *secondary* risk-dominance relations. For example, suppose that a given game G contains three eligible equilibrium points, ζ, σ, and τ, such that:

1. ζ has strong primary risk-dominance over σ at risk level $H(\zeta, \sigma) = r$, player i being the decisive player against σ.
2. σ has strong primary risk-dominance over τ at risk level $H(\sigma, \tau) = r' < r$, player j being the decisive player against τ.
3. τ in turn has strong primary risk-dominance over ζ at risk level $H(\tau, \zeta) = r'' < r' < r$, player k being the decisive player against ζ.

That is, in this game each of the three eligible equilibrium points strongly risk-dominates another eligible equilibrium point but is itself strongly risk-dominated by still another eligible equilibrium point. But ζ is risk-dominated only at the *low* risk level r, whereas σ and τ are risk-dominated at the higher risk levels r' or r''. Accordingly we will argue that ζ should be regarded as the solution of the game. This conclusion can be justified as follows:

By Zeuthen's Principle, in view of the relevant risk-dominance relations, player i is in a position to veto equilibrium point σ, whereas player j is in a position to veto equilibrium point τ, and player k is in a position to veto equilibrium point ζ. But if all three players made actual use of these veto powers, then no solution could be agreed upon. Thus at least one of them must forgo using his veto power, and it must be decided by bargaining which one of the three should do so. This bargaining can be decided by *using Zeuthen's Principle for a second time:* Player k will have to refrain from using his veto power, because the risk level r'' at which he opposes ζ is lower than the risk levels r and r' at which the other two players oppose σ and τ, respectively. In other words, that equilibrium point which arouses the *least intensive* opposition on the part of the players will be accepted as the solution – if the intensity of opposition to any equilibrium point τ is measured by the highest uniform risk that any player is willing to face in order to defeat this particular equilibrium point τ (as well as other equilibrium points no more favorable than τ).

More generally let

$$K(\sigma) = \max_{\zeta \in E^*} H(\zeta, \sigma) \tag{14.17}$$

Let σ and τ be two eligible equilibrium points. Then σ has *strong secondary risk-dominance* over τ if

$$K(\sigma) < K(\tau) \qquad (14.18)$$

We say that σ has *weak secondary risk-dominance* over τ if

$$K(\sigma) \leq K(\tau) \qquad (14.19)$$

We will call a given eligible equilibrium point σ the *solution* of the game if σ has *strong* secondary risk-dominance over the game. Or equivalently we will call σ the solution if σ has *weak* secondary risk-dominance over the game and is the *only* eligible equilibrium point with this property. (The equivalence of these two statements can be shown by a similar argument to that used in the proof of Lemma 1 of Section 14.7.)

Lemma 1. In any finite game G in which the set E^* of eligible equilibrium points is not empty, there is always at least one equilibrium point with weak secondary risk-dominance over the game.

Proof. We have to show that the function $K(\sigma)$ always reaches a minimum value $K(\sigma) = K_o$ over the set E^* if E^* is not empty.

1. *The case of strictly noncooperative games.* In this case the lemma follows from the fact that E^* is a finite set. This fact itself can be verified. In a finite game G a given player i can have only a finite number of centroid-best-reply strategies. This is so because the set $\Sigma_i(\sigma^i)$ of all the best replies σ_i that player i has against any given strategy combination $\sigma^i = (\sigma_1, \ldots, \sigma_{i-1}, \sigma_{i+1}, \ldots, \sigma_n)$ of the other $(n-1)$ players, is always a convex set spanned by a finite number of his pure strategies. Therefore, if player i has k pure strategies, then he cannot have more than $(2^k - 1)$ different centroid-best-reply strategies, since the number of different sets $\Sigma_i(\sigma^i)$ cannot be more than that.

2. *The case of almost-noncooperative games.* If game G has only a finite number of equilibrium points, then E^* will again be a finite set, and we are done. So we only have to consider the case where G has infinitely many equilibrium points. (This can happen even if G is a finite game.) Let E^{**} be the closure of E^*. We extend the function $K(\sigma)$ to all points of E^{**} in the obvious way. As E^{**} is a compact set, the function $K(\sigma)$ will always reach a minimum value $K(\sigma) = K_o$ over E^{**}. It is easy to verify that, for every point σ where $K(\sigma) = K_o$, $\sigma \in E^*$. Therefore $K(\sigma)$ will reach the value K_o already within E^*. This completes the proof.

Lemma 2. Let σ be an eligible equilibrium point having strong *primary* risk-dominance over the game. Then σ will also have strong *secondary* risk-dominance over the game.

Proof. By assumption

$$H(\sigma, \tau) > 0 \quad \text{and} \quad H(\tau, \sigma) = 0 \quad \text{for all} \quad \tau \neq \sigma, \tau \in E^* \qquad (14.20)$$

Consequently, by (14.17),

$$K(\tau) > 0 \quad \text{for all} \quad \tau \neq \sigma, \tau \in E^* \tag{14.21}$$

whereas

$$K(\sigma) = 0 \tag{14.22}$$

Therefore

$$K(\sigma) < K(\tau) \quad \text{for all} \quad \tau \neq \sigma, \tau \in E^* \tag{14.23}$$

which proves the lemma.

Lemma 2 shows that our first definition of the solution (in terms of primary risk-dominance) is a special case of our second definition (in terms of secondary risk-dominance).

Let Ω be the set of all eligible equilibrium points having weak secondary risk-dominance over the game. Let Ψ be the set of all equilibrium points σ in Ω such that they are not subject to joint dominance (whether weak or strong) by any other equilibrium point τ in Ω. That is, a given equilibrium point σ in Ω belongs to Ψ if and only if there is *no* equilibrium point τ in Ω such that

$$U_i(\tau) \geq U_i(\sigma) \quad \text{for all} \quad i \in N \tag{14.24}$$

and

$$U_i(\tau) > U_i(\sigma) \quad \text{for some} \quad i \in N \tag{14.25}$$

In other words, Ψ is the set of all *strongly efficient* elements of Ω.

A given nonempty set of equilibrium points will be called *admissible* if it contains only one equilibrium point – or if it does contain two or more equilibrium points, yet all of them are *equivalent* (i.e., all of them yield the same payoff vector).

So far we have defined a solution only for games where Ω contains only one equilibrium point. But we can easily extend our definition to all games where Ω is admissible – and indeed to all games where at least set Ψ is admissible. As the latter case contains the former as a special case (since if Ω is admissible then $\Omega = \Psi$), it is sufficient to discuss the case where Ψ is admissible. This is so because:

1. Efficiency considerations (cf. Part II of Postulate A4) require the players to restrict their strategy choice to set Ψ.

2. We are now considering vocal noncooperative and almost-noncooperative games: But in vocal games the players will never have any difficulty in choosing between equivalent-strategy n-tuples (cf. Section 7.5).

Accordingly, if the set Ψ is admissible, then we can define the *complete strategy solution* as Ψ itself and can define each equilibrium point σ in Ψ as a *particular strategy solution*. The payoff vector $U(\sigma)$ uniformly associated with every equilibrium point σ in Ψ can be designated as the *payoff solution*.

14.9 Bargaining deadlocks: final definition of the solution

Now suppose that Ψ contains two or more nonequivalent equilibrium points σ, σ', ... Since the function K will take the same minimum value $K_o = K(\sigma) = K(\sigma') = \cdots$ at all of these equilibrium points, Zeuthen's Principle will not enable us to choose among them. Neither will efficiency considerations or any other rationality requirements. Consequently Part (γ) of Zeuthen's Principle (as stated in Section 8.4) will apply, forcing the players to choose some eligible equilibrium point associated with a higher value $K(\tau) > K_o$ of the function K. For example, consider the game in Example 7. Suppose that this game is played as a strictly noncooperative game. Then only the three pure strategy equilibrium points, $\zeta = (A_1, B_1)$, $\sigma = (A_2, B_2)$, and $\tau = (A_3, B_3)$, are eligible, since none of the four mixed-strategy equilibrium points are centroid equilibrium points. We have

$$H(\zeta, \sigma) = H(\sigma, \zeta) = \tfrac{1}{3}$$

$$H(\zeta, \tau) = \tfrac{2}{3}$$

$$H(\sigma, \tau) = \tfrac{1}{2}$$

$$H(\tau, \zeta) = H(\tau, \sigma) = 0$$

Consequently $K(\zeta) = K(\sigma) = \tfrac{1}{3}$, while $K(\tau) = \tfrac{2}{3}$.

	B_1	B_2	B_3
A_1	(6, 4)	(0, 0)	(0, 0)
A_2	(0, 0)	(4, 6)	(0, 0)
A_3	(0, 0)	(0, 0)	(2, 3)

Example 7

Thus the set Ω consists of ζ and σ. Moreover, $\Psi = \Omega$. But the set $\Psi = \Omega$ is inadmissible, since ζ and σ are not equivalent: Player 1 would prefer ζ, while player 2 would prefer σ. As $K(\zeta) = K(\sigma)$, the two players are in equally strong bargaining positions. Therefore Part (γ) of Zeuthen's Principle will apply: *Both players have to make a concession,* accepting the third eligible equilibrium point τ, which accordingly becomes the solution of the game [even though both $U(\zeta) = (6, 4)$ and $U(\sigma) = (4, 6)$ strongly dominate the payoff vector $U(\tau) = (2, 3)$].

More generally let $\Omega^*(z)$ be the set of all eligible equilibrium points σ with $K(\sigma) = z$. Let $\Psi^*(z)$ be the set of all equilibrium points σ in $\Omega^*(z)$ such that no equilibrium point τ in $\Omega^*(z)$ has properties (14.24) and (14.25) with respect to these σ's. In other words, $\Psi^*(z)$ is the set of all *strongly efficient* elements of $\Omega^*(z)$.

Let Z be the set of all numbers z for which the set $\Psi^*(z)$ is *not empty*. Let Z^* be the set of all numbers z for which the set $\Psi^*(z)$ is admissible. If this set Z^* is not empty, then it will always contain a smallest number $z = z_o$, because Z^* is a closed subset of the interval $[0, 1]$.

We now define the *complete strategy solution* as the set $\Psi^*(z_o)$. Each equilibrium point σ in $\Psi^*(z_o)$ will be a particular strategy solution, and $U(\sigma)$ will be the solution payoff vector.

Intuitively speaking the set $\Psi^*(z_o)$ again is the set of those eligible equilibrium points which arouse least opposition among the players, subject to efficiency considerations and to the need of avoiding bargaining deadlocks.

The definition that we proposed in Section 14.8 is of course a special case of our present definition. It amounted to defining the complete strategy solution as the set $\Psi = \Psi^*(z_{oo})$, where z_{oo} is the smallest number in set Z, provided that $z_{oo} \in Z^*$. As $Z^* \subseteq Z$, if $z_{oo} \in Z^*$, then $z_{oo} = z_o$, and so $\Psi = \Psi^*(z_{oo}) = \Psi^*(z_o)$.

Finally, if the set Z^* is empty – or if already the set E^* of eligible equilibrium points is empty – then we define the complete strategy solution as the set M of all maximin points. Each maximin point will be a particular strategy solution. The solution payoff vector will be the vector $\check{u} = (\check{u}_1, \ldots, \check{u}_n)$, where $\check{u}_1, \ldots, \check{u}_n$ are the players' maximin payoffs. (In the terminology of Section 7.8, in this case the solution just defined will be a mere "quasi-solution.")

14.10   Tacit and semivocal games

This solution concept can be extended to tacit and semivocal noncooperative and almost-noncooperative games without any difficulty, if in the preceding discussion the term "eligible" is everywhere replaced by the term "accessible" and in particular the set E^* of all eligible equilibrium points is replaced by the set F^* of all accessible equilibrium points. Note that any admissible set of accessible equilibrium points will always contain only *one* equilibrium point, because, if σ and τ are accessible equilibrium points and $U(\sigma) = U(\tau)$ then, by the definition of accessibility, $\sigma = \tau$. This means that our solution will never create problems of strategy coordination, because in profitable games it assigns to every player a unique rational strategy σ_i.

As you will recall, in deriving our solution we have assumed that the players can bargain with one another about the equilibrium point to be used. Actually under our assumptions this bargaining can really occur only in vocal and in semivocal games. But the solution defined for semivocal games can be extended to tacit games, by virtue of the Principle of Tacit Bargaining (see Section 7.5).

15

Conclusion

In the preceding chapters I have tried to propose a precise definition – or more exactly a family of precise definitions – for the concept of rational behavior. In the case of individual pragmatic decisions I have argued that rational behavior can be defined in terms of utility maximization, or expected-utility maximization, in accordance with modern decision theory (and modern economic theory). In the case of moral decision I have suggested the utilitarian criterion as the appropriate rationality criterion, involving maximization of the average utility of all individuals in the society.

Finally, in the case of game situations I have argued that we need a concept of rational behavior yielding a determinate solution (i.e., a unique solution payoff vector) for each specific game. For various classes of cooperative and of noncooperative games I have suggested a number of solution concepts, all related to the Nash-Zeuthen bargaining solution, to the modified Shapley value, and to their various generalizations. Though the solution concepts suggested for different game classes have differed in specific detail, all have been based on the same general rationality postulates. My discussion, however, has been restricted to what I have called "classical" games (i.e., to games with complete information, either fully cooperative or fully noncooperative in character, and admitting of representation by their normal form) – even though, as I have shown in other publications, one can extend this analysis also to certain classes of "nonclassical" games (e.g., to games with incomplete information [Harsanyi, 1967, 1968a, 1968b; Harsanyi and Selten, 1972]).

Eventually it may be possible to derive the various specific solution concepts discussed in this book from *one* general solution concept, equally applicable to "classical" and to "nonclassical" games. But this will require significant further developments in our analytical tools.

Our preceding discussion shows that, in a cooperative game, it is almost always possible for rational players to reach an efficient (Pareto-optimal) outcome. In a noncooperative game in general this is not possible, because of the Prisoner's Dilemma problem; but, even so, a surprising amount of cooperation is possible in most cases. This result is in sharp contrast with the view taken by many social scientists, who seem to assume (apparently without even noticing that they are making a strong and very questionable assumption) that, whenever there is a *conflict of interest* between two players, this is a sufficient explanation for a *behavioral conflict* between them – as if no explanation were needed for the players' inability to reach a peaceful compromise agreement that would benefit both (or all) of them. In my view any major deviation from Pareto-optimality always requires a specific explanation, such as unenforceability of agreements, unsurmountable barriers to communcation, ignorance, and so on.

Our analysis also shows that in a cooperative game, without special reasons to the contrary, all possible subsets of the players will form coalitions to protect their common interests against all other players, so that the game will become a complicated network of (typically) a large number of mutually overlapping coalitions, in agreement with the pluralistic model of society. Therefore any significant departure from this model requires a special explanation. This special explanation is required (for instance, in terms of the communication network among the players) if we find that society partitions itself into two or more disjoint major coalitions, with little or no sectional coalition formation across the boundaries between these major coalitions, as predicted, e.g., by Marxist theory.

Our theory also identifies the major factors determining each player's bargaining strength in any given game, such as the extent to which he is willing to risk a conflict rather than to accept unfavorable terms (as determined by his cardinal utility function); his ability, individually or in various coalitions, to inflict high damages on the opposing players, without high costs to himself or to his coalition partners; the costs and the difficulty of organizing coalitions favorable to him.

As I have argued before, the present theory greatly increases the usefulness of game-theoretical models in the social sciences by defining a determinate solution for any specific game. The solution concepts described in this book have already been used for analyzing social power [Shapley and Shubik, 1954; Harsanyi, 1962a, 1962b], social status [Harsanyi, 1966b], international politics [Harsanyi, 1965], and also for pointing out some common fallacies in analyzing bargaining situations [Harsanyi, 1956, 1961b]. No doubt many other social-science applications will be found if more social scientists can be interested in using the analytical tools discussed in this book.

Notes

Chapter 1 Bargaining-equilibrium analysis: a new approach to game theory and to the analysis of social behavior

1 Subject only to some rather mild regularity requirements. For a definition of "classical" games, see Section 1.2.

2 A more comprehensive theory, of course, will have to introduce many additional variables, e.g., the costs of organizing and enforcing various coalitions, the reaction speeds of different players in accepting offers and in making counter offers, and the degree of mutual trust among various subsets of the players.

3 The distinction between games with *complete* and with *incomplete* information must not be confused with the distinction between games with *perfect* and with *imperfect* information (see Section 5.2). Under our definition, a classical game must involve *complete* information, but it may involve either *perfect* or *imperfect* information.

4 For definition of the normal form, see Section 5.3.

5 According to this definition, any fully *cooperative* game will be necessarily a game with *immediate commitment*, because one way in which the players can commit themselves to certain strategies before playing the game is to reach a firm agreement with one another to use particular strategies. In contrast, noncooperative games, and games which are neither fully cooperative nor fully noncooperative, can be either games with immediate commitment *or* games with delayed commitment.

6 It happens that the analysis of a game with *incomplete information* can often be reduced to the analysis of an equivalent game with delayed commitment, so that any solution defined for the latter will also be a solution for the former and conversely [Harsanyi, 1968a, p. 334].

7 Under this definition, *welfare economics* becomes a subdivision of ethics, dealing with a rational pursuit of the economic interests of society as a whole.

8 However, in some cases the primary definition of the relevant rational–behavior concept is not based on a set of rationality postulates but is based rather on some analytical model that reduces the rational–behavior concept in question to another rational–behavior concept already defined. Thus one way in which we will analyze moral value judgments (case B2) will be to propose an analytical model that reduces them to rational choice under risk (case A2). (See Chapter 4.)

Chapter 2 Rational-choice models of social behavior

1 However, our theory is not normative in the sense in which moral and political philosophy are normative disciplines: It is not concerned with the question of how any player should act in order to achieve any particular *moral* (or polit-

ical) values (see Section 1.5). Thus the word "should" italicized in the text is not a *moral* "should" but rather is what moral philosophers call a purely *prudential* "should."

2   We speak of an understandable intentionally suboptimal response when the decision maker intentionally chooses a reasonably effective but, strictly speaking, nonoptimal response, because finding a truly optimal response would entail prohibitive computation costs or would be beyond the decision maker's intellectual capacity altogether. An example would be choosing a reasonably effective but nonoptimal strategy in chess – which is, of course, in practice the best thing that any human chess master or any chess–playing computer program can do in any case.

3   An interesting simple psychological model for the analysis of what we call the problem of *dominant loyalties* has been proposed by Homans [1950, 1961]. His model is based on the assumption that the liking that an individual A has for some other individual B, and the friendly interest that A takes in B's well-being, are an increasing function of the amount of *common activity* and of verbal and nonverbal *interaction* (communication) that A and B have had with each other – and in particular they are an increasing function of the extent to which this common activity and this interaction have been *pleasant experiences* for A.

Chapter 3   Rational behavior under certainty, risk, and uncertainty

1   At this point we have not yet assigned probabilities (whether objective or subjective) to the events e and f. Therefore we cannot define their statistical independence in terms of the relevant probabilities in the usual way. Instead we have to define it as an absence of any significant *causal interaction* between e and f (as judged by the decision maker).

2   For easier reference we shall use the term "Axiom" to describe the rationality postulates that we are using in individual decision theory (Chapter 3) and in ethics (Chapter 4) and shall reserve the term "Postulate" for the rationality postulates that we will use in game theory (Chapters 6 ff.).

3   These axioms are essentially identical to those proposed by Herstein and Milnor [1953].

4   This theorem is often called the (weak) expected–utility maximization theorem. (The "strong" expected–utility-maximization theorem is a generalization of the former to uncertain prospects; see below.)

5   Lemma 1 is often called the Substitution Principle.

6   "Postulate S4" indicates "Savage's Postulate 4."

7   Any proposal of systematic criteria for a rational choice of subjective probabilities (more particularly of prior probabilities) can be regarded as an attempt to restate the principle of best information in a more precise and more specific manner. Classical probability theory tried to use the principle of insufficient reason (principle of indifference) to define prior probabilities, but we now know that this approach often yields inconsistent or indeterminate results. More sophisticated criteria for defining prior probabilities were suggested by Jeffreys [1939], Carnap [1950], and other authors, but thus far no fully satisfactory solution to this problem exists. Our theory, of course, deals only with the much narrower problem of how to assign prior probabilities rationally to alternative strategies available to an intelligent opponent in game situations.

Chapter 4 Morality and social welfare

1   In Section 4.2 we shall define a third preference scale, representing what we shall call individual *i*'s *extended preferences*. As we shall see, a person's *extended* preferences in some way have an intermediate position between his *personal* preferences and his *moral* preferences.

2   More exactly a morally sensitive individual *i* may assign high positive utility to achieving social situations associated with high values of his social welfare function W_i. Under our model his extended preferences will play an important role in defining his social welfare function W_i. Thus, through *this* causal channel, his extended preferences *may* have a significant indirect effect on his behavior.

3   Here we are assuming that this common utility function U would be a von Neumann–Morgenstern *cardinal* utility function, which allows intraperson comparisons between the utility *increments* (utility differences) that the same person would enjoy in two different situations. Let A and B stand for having a heavy meal with and without an apple, respectively. Let C and D stand for having a light meal with and without an apple. We want to compare the utility differences $\Delta U = U(A) - U(B)$ and $\Delta^* U = U(C) - U(D)$. We can accomplish this comparison by a direct experimental test. Let E and F denote the risky prospects $E = (A, \frac{1}{2}; D, \frac{1}{2})$ and $F = (B, \frac{1}{2}; C, \frac{1}{2})$. If the decision maker prefers E to F, then $U(E) = \frac{1}{2} U(A) + \frac{1}{2} U(D) > U(F) = \frac{1}{2} U(B) + \frac{1}{2} U(C)$, which implies that $\Delta U = U(A) - U(B) > \Delta^* U = U(C) - U(D)$. By the same token, if he is indifferent between E and F, then $\Delta U = \Delta^* U$, whereas if he prefers F to E, then $\Delta U < \Delta^* U$.

4   Rothenberg [1961, pp. 268–269] has criticized my model of moral value judgments, because it requires that individual *i* "should put himself in the place" of other individuals and should try to judge the world partly in terms of these *other* individuals' utility functions. He argues that, if *i* assesses various social situations partly in terms of other individuals' utility functions, then we can no longer say that in choosing among these social situations he is trying to maximize his *own* expected utility. Actually, according to our preceding analysis, the utility that *i* would assign to a given social situation A if he were "put in the place" of another individual *j* remains "individual *i*'s utility" in the required sense, because it is the utility that *i himself* would assign to situation A under certain hypothetical conditions, viz., if he had the same taste and the same personal characteristics (the same "causal variables") that *j* has.

  There is admittedly something seemingly paradoxical in asking individual *i* to assess a given situation through the preferences and the utility function of *another* individual *j*. But, as we have seen, this requirement – which we have called the principle of acceptance (consumers' sovereignty) – is inherent in the nature of interpersonal utility comparisons, which all of us are making continually in everyday life. It is not the task of ethics or of welfare economics to *deny* this obvious fact. Rather their task is to *explain* what it means, and in what sense it is possible, for one individual to judge another individual's well-being through the latter's own utility function. This is precisely what our theory attempts to do.

5   I have presented all three arguments in Harsanyi [1955]. However, some critics of my concept of an additive social welfare function have apparently failed to notice the fact that in order to refute my conclusions they would have to refute *all three* arguments. Criticizing one or two of our arguments will not do, because, as long as any one of these arguments stands, so do my conclusions.

6 However, as we will see, from this family of *ordinal* social–welfare functions W_i^*, our four axioms together will select a two–parameter family of *cardinal* social–welfare functions W_i for individual i.

7 However, as we will see, from this family of *ordinal* utility functions U_j^*, our four axioms together will select a two–parameter subfamily of *cardinal* utility functions U_j for each individual j.

8 By the utility distribution in a given industry we mean the utility levels of workers, managers, shareholders, consumers, and so forth.

9 It may be noted that our construction procedure so far has made use only of Axioms 1^{ooo}, 2^{ooo}, and 3^{ooo}. But the lemmas below will make essential use also of Axiom 4^{ooo}.

10 Even if we do impose this requirement, it will be a matter of taste whether we choose to set $a_1 = \cdots = a_n = 1/n$ as we did in Equation (4.1) or choose to set $a_1 = \cdots = a_n = 1$ as we did in Equation (4.46). In the former case the social–welfare function W_i will be the *arithmetic mean* of individual utilities, while in the latter case it will be their *sum*.

11 Axiom 4^{oo} would require that individual i base his decision *completely* on interpersonal utility comparisons. We are trying to show that, even if he does not accept Axiom 4^{oo}, he will have to pay *some* attention to such comparisons.

Chapter 5 Some basic concepts of game theory

1 For a more detailed and more formal discussion, see Luce and Raiffa [1957, Chap. 3]. My own exposition is indebted to theirs and to Kuhn's [1953].

2 Note that, besides the technical sense just defined, we are using the term "outcome" also informally in its everyday meaning, e.g., when we speak of the outcome of a chance event, or when we speak of the outcome of a bargaining process so that it includes not only the *physical outcome* in the above technical sense but also the *utility payoffs* of the players. In fact we will use the term "outcome" in this technical sense only in Section 5.2, where we discuss the game–tree representation of the game.

3 Omitting, of course, the fictitious player 0, who receives no payoff.

4 Actually it is usually sufficient if the players have full information about the normal form of the game, which abstracts from some less essential features of the extensive form (see below).

5 A game in which all players have only a finite number m_i of different (pure) strategies is called *finite*; if at least one player has infinitely many (pure) strategies, we speak of an *infinite* game. In an infinite game a player's strategies may range not only over a *denumerable* set (e.g., the set of all positive integers) but even over a *continuum* (e.g., over the set of all real numbers, as when in economic games a given firm can buy or sell any nonnegative amount of a given commodity) or even over a *function space* (e.g., when the game involves several moves, *each* of which itself ranges over a continuum).

6 At the same time, both from the viewpoint of empirical applications and from a pure theoretical standpoint, considerable interest attaches also to a more direct study of the players' strategical possibilities in games stated in their *extensive form* (or in forms *intermediate* between the full extensive form and the one–move normal form). Even a more systematic "translation" of certain conclusions of the theory of normal–form games, into the language of extensive–form games, will often considerably increase our understanding of empirical game situations.

For example, Schelling [1960, especially Chap. 5] has obtained suggestive results about the effects of threats, promises, delegation of decision making, and so forth, in two-person game situations, by considering *matrix games*, which differ from standard normal-form models only in allowing the players one or two communication moves (with or without the possibility of making irrevocable commitments *prior* to choosing a final strategy). Although his conclusions can be easily restated in terms of strict normal-form models, his use of more flexible matrix-game models has been of evident heuristic value.

Recent work on *computer programs* for playing chess and other games of strategy [e.g., Newell, Shaw, and Simon, 1958] is another important step toward a better understanding of the players' strategical possibilities in games in extensive form.

The bargaining models that we will discuss are also at levels of abstraction intermediate between the normal-form and the full extensive-form representation, ranging from Nash's bargaining model with threats, where each player has *two* moves, to Zeuthen's bargaining model, where he can have *any number* of moves.

7 In other words, when subscripted roman capital letters are used to denote strategies, the subscripts will be used to distinguish *different strategies* of the *same player*. Thus A_1, A_2, A_3 will be different strategies of player 1. In contrast, when subscripted lowercase Greek letters are used, then the subscripts will identify the *players* whose strategies we are discussing. Thus $\sigma_1, \sigma_2, \sigma_3$ will be strategies of players 1, 2, and 3, respectively. In this notation different strategies of the same player will be distinguished by superscripts or by asterisks, and so forth. Thus different strategies of player 1 will be denoted as $\sigma_1^{\,1}, \sigma_1^{\,2}, \ldots$, or as $\sigma_1, \sigma_1^{\,*}$, and so forth.

8 In earlier publications I used the term "syndicate," rather than von Neumann and Morgenstern's term "coalition," to emphasize the distinction between their and my assumptions concerning the coalition structures of cooperative games. But in this book I will use the term "coalition" in common use in game-theoretical literature.

9 In earlier publications I used the term "prospect space." However, in this book the term "prospect" itself refers not to a *utility vector* (payoff vector) but to a *physical result* (sure prospect) or to certain concepts defined in terms of such physical results (risky and uncertain prospects). Therefore it seems less appropriate to call a set of payoff vectors a "prospect space."

10 As the players' cardinal utility functions are unique only up to order-preserving linear transformations, it is natural to adopt the postulate that such transformations will not affect the players' strategical possibilities within the game. But in fact the equivalence of constant-sum and constant-weighted-sum games to zero-sum games does not have to be established by a special postulate but rather follows automatically from the general rationality postulates that we will use.

11 It is often convenient to say that a given game G has the transferable-utility property even though, in general, the second payoff vector u^* cannot be achieved even by the players in S by *individually* switching to alternative strategies $\sigma_i^{\,*}$ – provided that u^* can be achieved by these players by switching to some *jointly randomized* mixed strategy $\sigma_*^{\,S}$.

Under this wider definition, transferable utility may arise, e.g., as follows: Suppose that the game can have n possible outcomes when each of the n players in general prefers a different outcome. The players can agree on any single outcome or on any probability mixture of these outcomes, the probability weights assigned to different outcomes to be decided by bargaining among the players. This game will have transferable utility under the wider definition. Interestingly, utility transfers between the players in this game will not involve transfers of money or other "real" commodities but will rather involve concessions regarding the probabilities associated with various outcomes. This model can be used in the analysis of political power [Harsanyi, 1962a, 1962b].

12   Apart from various payoff-dominance relations, later we will also introduce dominancelike concepts of a different kind, which will be called *risk–dominance* relations.

13   With apologies to Bob Aumann, who has used the term "strong equilibrium point" in a different sense in Aumann [1959]. I could not find a convenient alternative name for the concept for which this term will be used in this book.

14   The term "maximin point" is meant to indicate that such strategy n–tuples play a role somewhat similar to equilibrium points in our theory.

15   This terminology expresses the fact that "not being *strongly* dominated" is a *weaker* property than "not being (even) *weakly* dominated" is, in the sense that the latter implies the former, while the former does not imply the latter.

16   "Strong dominance" and "weak dominance" between payoff vectors were defined in Section 5.5.

17   Cf. Schelling [1960, p. 89] for a similar classification of games.

18   To my knowledge the first clear statement of the principle of tacit bargaining is in Fellner [1949] (in an economic rather than an explicitly game-theoretical context). He calls tacit bargaining "quasi-bargaining" and calls tacit agreements "quasi-agreements."

Chapter 6   Rationality postulates for game situations

1   More particularly Postulate A1 is based on simple dominance in what we shall call the *truncated game* (see Section 6.5), whereas Postulate A4 is based on simple dominance in the *bargaining game* (see further in this section; see also Section 6.6 for further discussion of both postulates).

2   We could have also phrased Postulate A4 to assert the relevant maximality property, viz., that a rational player's bargaining strategy will be such that he will accept the *highest* possible payoff that may be offered to him. Actually, for reasons of analytical convenience, the postulate has been phrased in a manner that makes no explicit reference to this maximality property. But this property does follow from the postulate.

3   Of course, in decision theory it is important to show that the utility and the expected–utility maximization theorems can be derived from more fundamental axioms (see discussion in Chapter 3). But here we can take this for granted and for convenience will treat Postulates A2 and A3 as if they were axioms in their own right.

4   More exactly, in general these probabilities will be generated by random processes inside player i *together* with an external mechanical device used by him. If the strategy σ_i that he chooses from set Σ_i^* happens to be a mixed strategy, then he will presumably use a mechanical device for generating the probabilities prescribed by this mixed strategy σ_i. However, his choice of this strategy σ_i itself from the set Σ_i^* of "equally good" strategies will be governed by random processes inside his brain.

5   However, if the main game G is a two-person zero-sum game in which there

is no scope for cooperation or for agreements between the players, the bargaining game $B(G)$ will be empty: It will be a "game" without moves.

6 For further discussion of the symmetric–expectations postulate, see Harsanyi [1961b].

7 There is no payoff higher than 2 for player 1 in column B_2 of the payoff matrix.

8 There is no payoff higher than -2 for player 2 in row A_1 of the payoff matrix.

Chapter 7 The four basic problems facing the players of a game

1 We are considering a pure strategy as a special case of mixed strategies.

2 See Section 5.15.

3 The name arose from the first example displaying this paradox, suggested by A. W. Tucker: the story involved two prisoners [cf. Luce and Raiffa, 1957, p. 95].

4 You may object that it does not matter if the recombinations ζ of the strategy n-tuples $\sigma^1, \sigma^2, \ldots$ yield *higher* payoffs $U_i(\zeta) > U_i(\sigma^1) = U_i(\sigma^2) = \ldots$ than these strategy n-tuples themselves would yield. What matters is only the possibility that these recombinations may yield *lower* payoffs. Actually there will be a strategy coordination problem in either case. If the ζ's yield higher payoffs, then the players will find it advantageous to *avoid* coordinating their strategies and will try to choose their strategies from *different* strategy n-tuples σ^k in set Σ^*. But this will be just as much of a problem as trying to choose their strategies from the *same* strategy n-tuple σ^k.

5 As Schelling [1960, Chaps. 3 and 4] has pointed out, intelligent players may be able to *guess* each other's intentions even without explicit communication and may be able to coordinate their strategies in a much higher proportion of all cases than mere chance would allow. But for the purposes of a formal theory such guessing games can be regarded as involving some kind of "implicit communication" and thus coming under the category of (fully or partially) *vocal* games. On a less formal level of analysis, of course, the question remains: Under what conditions, and to what an extent, do physically *tacit* games allow successful "implicit communication" so that they can be treated as if they were *vocal* games? For a discussion of this question refer to Schelling [1960].

6 Solutions for games profitable to *some* of the players but unprofitable to the *other* players have an intermediate status. But since in such games our theory requires that the players use strategies corresponding to equilibrium points satisfying two stability requirements, in these games the players are *able* to form stable expectations so that the solutions of such games are basically similar to solutions for games *profitable* to *all* players. Even in games *unprofitable* to *all* players, the players are able to form stable expectations in those special cases where the centroid–maximin–strategy n-tuple (which our theory recommends for use by the players) happens to be an equilibrium point.

7 In fact, the term "noncooperative game" is rather misleading, because it seems to suggest that in such games there is no scope for rational cooperation among the players, which is quite incorrect. An alternative term, such as "games without commitments," may be preferable, but the term "noncooperative games" is now so well entrenched that it would be hard to replace it by another name.

Chapter 8   Two-person simple bargaining games: the Nash solution

1   In welfare economics they did sometimes use cardinal utility (more particularly the assumption of decreasing marginal utility for income) in an essential way, in order to support a demand for a more equal income distribution (e.g., for progressive taxation). [Cf. Harsanyi, 1953.]

2   This is so because, if a purely ordinal theory furnished a unique agreement point $\bar{u}$, then this point $\bar{u}$ would have to be invariant under all monotone transformations of the two players' utility functions. But this is impossible.

   For instance, let triangle *OAB* be the payoff space of the game, and let *O* be the conflict point (see Figure 8.7). Suppose that a given theory defines $\bar{u}$ as the unique agreement point. Then it is clearly always possible to find (continuous) monotone transformations of the two players' utility functions, such that carry the triangle *OAB* into itself but carry the point $\bar{u}$ into some other point $\bar{u}'$ on the upper right boundary *AB*, which means that $\bar{u}$ will *not* be invariant under these transformations.

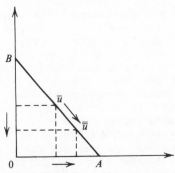

Figure 8.7

3   The term "risk" is used here in a more general sense so that it includes both "risk" and "uncertainty" in the sense of Chapter 3; i.e., it includes both risks corresponding to known objective probabilities and risks corresponding to subjective probabilities.

4   Let $\bar{u} = (\bar{u}_1, \bar{u}_2)$, with $\bar{u}_1 = \bar{u}_2$, be the symmetric solution of a symmetric game (see Figure 8.7). This symmetry in general will not be invariant under monotonic transformations; i.e., it will not be an ordinal property. This is so because we can easily construct monotonic transformations of the two players' utility functions, which will map the symmetric payoff space *BOA* onto itself, preserving its symmetry, but will at the same time map the symmetric point $\bar{u}$ into an asymmetric point $\bar{u}' = (\bar{u}_1', \bar{u}_2')$, with $\bar{u}_1' \neq \bar{u}_2'$.

   This means that our symmetry postulate will lead to self–contradiction unless the two players are assumed to possess *cardinal* utility functions, permitting only *linear* monotonic transformations. (It is easy to verify that any linear monotonic utility transformation that preserves the symmetry of the payoff space *BOA* will map the symmetric point $\bar{u}$ into a symmetric point $\bar{u}'$ in the transformed payoff space so that $\bar{u}_1' = \bar{u}_2'$.)

5   We will analyze the players' choice of bargaining strategies, based on expected–utility maximization, in greater detail when we discuss Zeuthen's model of the bargaining process in Sections 8.4 through 8.6.

6   The postulate of *independence of irrelevant alternatives* was first introduced by Arrow [1951] in welfare economics and in the analysis of social decision

making. It has since been used also in many other contexts. The telling name, *irrelevance of unchosen alternatives*, was suggested by Jacob Marschak for the postulate.

7 In Sections 8.4 and 8.5 we will see that the Nash solution can be derived from our own "strong" rationality postulates also by using Zeuthen's bargaining model, *without* making use of Nash's Postulates 3 and 4 (in our own numbering) just discussed. Thus these postulates are not essential for our theory.

8 Zeuthen's original treatment also made use of various restrictive assumptions which, however, can be easily relaxed. For example, he assumed that two parties will maximize their expected *money* payoffs, instead of assuming that they will maximize their expected *utility* payoffs (which will be our own assumption). He also restricted his discussion to symmetric bargaining situations. Finally his treatment, unlike that of Nash [1953], was restricted to what we call *simple* bargaining games.

9 Mathematically an agreement A may be interpreted as a *joint strategy* (possibly as a jointly randomized mixed strategy) agreed upon by the two players, provided that two joint strategies yielding the same payoff vector are regarded as representing the *same* agreement. Or we may interpret an agreement A simply as a *payoff vector* agreed upon by the two players.

10 Of course, in case $(\beta\beta)$ many alternative assumptinos could be made. For example, we could assume that the two players would flip a coin to decide between proposals A_1 and A_2, which would yield each player i ($i = 1, 2$) the expected payoff $u_i = \frac{1}{2} U_i(A_1) + \frac{1}{2} U_i(A_2)$, and so on. But it can be shown that most of these alternative assumptions would lead to the same solution concept, though they would make some of our mathematical proofs a little more complicated.

11 Of course, besides the quantities r_1, r_2, p_{12}, and p_{21}, the quantities $U_1(A_1)$, $U_1(A_2)$, $U_1(C)$, $U_2(A_1)$, $U_2(A_2)$, and $U_2(C)$, have also played essential roles in our analysis. But the point is that, as Condition (8.5) shows, these latter quantities will influence the players' behavior only through their effects on r_1 and r_2 – and possibly on p_{12} and p_{21}.

12 Thus Postulate B3* on the one hand, and Theorems 8.3 and 8.4 on the other, provide *mutual* logical support for each other. We need Postulate B3* to prove Theorems 8.3 and 8.4. But, conversely, we would not accept Postulate B3* if it did not enable us to prove Theorems 8.3 and 8.4 – that is, if it did not enable us to show that the two variables r_1 and r_2, without introducing any additional variables, are, in fact, *sufficient* to furnish a well-defined decision rule for the players and to specify a unique solution for the game. Of course this situation is not at all unusual: Our acceptance of rationality postulates (and of other axioms) always depends on their yielding reasonable implications.

13 Regarding the distinction between behavior guided by self-interest and behavior guided by individual utility (which may possibly give some weight to altruistic considerations), see Section 1.5. For further discussion of Schelling's theory and his criticism of our symmetry postulate, see Harsanyi [1961b].

Chapter 9 General two-person cooperative games

1 We assume, wherever convenient, that the function H possesses these first derivatives everywhere, i.e., that the upper right boundary H has no corner points. This will result in no loss of generality, since our results can easily be extended to any game G, in which H does have corner points, by making

G a limit of a sequence of certain games $G_1, G_2, \ldots$ in which H has no corner points and in which these first derivatives exist everywhere.

2   This is true only for a two-person cooperative game *with* binding threats. If the players *cannot* make binding threats, then their conflict game G^*, played as an *independent* game, will be in general *nonzero-sum*, because c_1 and c_2 need not add up to zero.

3   The Bolzano-Weierstrass theorem states that a continuous function $y = f(x)$ cannot take the values $y_1 = f(x_1)$ and $y_2 = f(x_2)$ at the points $x = x_1$ and $x = x_2$, unless at some point $x = x_o$ lying *between* x_1 and x_2 it also takes a given value $y_o = f(x_o)$ *intermediate* between y_1 and y_2. In our case this implies that we cannot move from a point c^* *more favorable* than the points c of the line $C(u)$ to a point c^{**} *less favorable* than the latter without crossing the line $C(u)$ itself. Therefore, since the whole set $C^+(u)$ lies on the same side of $C(u)$, the points c^* in set $C^+(u)$ must be either *all* of them *more* favorable or *all* of them *less* favorable than the points lying on the line $C(u)$ itself.

4   For instance, as far as a progressive income tax makes high-income taxpayers less willing to take risks, our theory predicts that they will also become readier to make concessions in bargaining situations, e.g., in collective bargaining with labor unions. This prediction seems to be borne out by experience.

5   The formal definition of our solution concept for the general cooperative game is a direct extension of the definition given in Section 8.10 for the two-person simple bargaining game and need not be described here.

6   We are disregarding the degenerate case in which $a_1 = 0$ and so $\Delta u^*{}_2 = 0$, or where $a_2 = 0$ and so $\Delta u^*{}_1 = 0$.

7   If physical limitations in the situation do not allow a given player i to reduce his payoff u_i^* physically to the required extent, then we will assume that the players will agree to act in later stages of the game *as if* this reduction had been achieved, i.e., to *disregard* that part of player i's payoff which is in excess of the theoretically required equilibrium level.

8   If the boundary of the original payoff space P^* contains no horizontal and vertical segments on top and on the right side, then $H^{**} = H^*$. Otherwise H^{**} will consist of H^* itself and of these finite straight-line segments adjoining it.

9   To show this, it is sufficient to show that the intersection K of the line L and the extended payoff space $\overline{P}^*$ is *never empty*. In this case since the point c itself always lies on the line L and always lies outside the set P^*, the line L must cross the boundary line $\overline{H}^{**}$ of $\overline{P}^*$ at some point u^*.

Take any point $u = (u_1, u_2)$ of the original payoff space P^*. Let

$$\Delta u_1 = u_1 - c_1 \qquad \Delta u_2 = u_2 - c_2$$

and

$$\overline{u}_i = c_i + \frac{1}{a_i} \cdot \min(a_1 \cdot \Delta u_1, a_2 \cdot \Delta u_2) \qquad i, j = 1, 2$$

Clearly the point $\overline{u} = (\overline{u}_1, \overline{u}_2)$ lies in $D(u)$, the dominion of u and therefore also in the set $\overline{P}^* = D(P^*)$. Moreover, $\overline{u}$ lies on the line L. Therefore $\overline{u}$ lies in $K = \overline{P}^* \cap L$. Consequently the set K is not empty, and thus L must intersect $\overline{H}^{**}$ at some point u^*.

10   If player 2 agreed to return to his concession limit, he would be no better off than if he became involved in a conflict with player 1. Thus he will have no reason to do this.

Therefore in an ultimatum game the player who can use an ultimatum has no strictly optimal strategies but has only ϵ-optimal strategies: He can insist on terms very close to his opponent's concession limit but cannot insist on terms coinciding with this concession limit. But for practical purposes ϵ-optimal strategies are just as good as optimal strategies. Moreover, if we introduce indivisibilities (e.g., an indivisible smallest monetary unit), then we obtain optimal strategies even in the stricter sense (e.g., "Ask for 1 cent less than your opponent's concession limit.").

11 Here we are using the term "ultimatum" informally. Strictly speaking, we will not call a given final demand an "ultimatum" if *both* players can simultaneously state their final demands. Technically we define an ultimatum as a final demand to which one player has fully committed himself *before* the other player could make a contrary commitment. Only when this is possible do we call the resulting game an *ultimatum game*.

12 Schelling [1960, Chap. 2] discusses many interesting examples of how a clever player may be able to create an ultimatum situation if he catches his opponent off guard.

13 Social scientists and philosophers questioning the possibility of interpersonal utility comparisons have been questioning the possibility of *substantive* comparisons. Nobody denies the possibility of purely *ad hoc* comparisons (see the next paragraph in the text), since this means only the possibility of adopting certain conventions of measurement for various individuals' utility functions. But it is, of course, controversial whether such ad hoc utility comparisons involve anything *more* than conventions of measurement, e.g., whether they have any ethical or game-theoretical significance.

14 The marginal rate of utility transfers (*MRUT*) is then defined as the number of utility units that player 1 has to give up in order to increase player 2's utility level by one unit. At any point u of the upper right boundary H, $MRUT = H_2(u)/H_1(u)$. If $a_1 = a_2 = H_1(\bar{u}) = H_2(\bar{u}) = 1$, then at the solution point $\bar{u}$ the $MRUT = 1$.

In case the players can transfer money to each other free of transfer costs of any kind (e.g., freedom from income tax), then we can always achieve $MRUT = 1$ by choosing utility units which equalize their *marginal utilities for money* (e.g., by making each player's utility for \$1 equal to unity).

Chapter 10   *n*-Person simple bargaining games

1 We will assume, wherever convenient, that the derivatives $H_1, \ldots, H_n$ *exist* at all points u of the upper boundary H. Our results can be easily extended to games G where the upper boundary H has corner points by making any such game G the limit of a sequence of games $G_1, G_2, \ldots$, in which H has *no* corner points.

2 This is so because the derivation of Zeuthen's Principle from our rationality postulates was based on the assumption that the bargaining strategies of players i and j will depend *only* on *these two players'* potential payoffs u_i, u_j, u_i^*, u_j^*, c_i, and c_j. But if either player i or j (or both) act as members of a *coalition*, then their bargaining strategies in general will necessarily depend also on their *coalition partners'* interests, i.e., on the payoffs u_k, u_k^*, and c_k for some $k \neq i, j$. Hence Zeuthen's Principle will have no direct application.

3 This intuitive idea will be restated more formally in Theorem 10.5 of Section 10.6 and in the subsequent discussion.

4 An alternative model will be discussed in Section 10.7.

5 More exactly, to keep player 2's disagreement payoff constant at the level
$c_2 = 0$, we must assume that player 2 has to pay player 3 the full amount
$u_3 = 10$ only if he himself can obtain from player 1 at least the same amount
$u_{23} = 10$. Thus we shall assume that player 2 will have to hand over to player
3 the amount

$$u_3 = u_{23} \quad \text{if he obtains} \quad u_{23} \leqq 10 \quad \text{from player 1}$$

but has to hand over

$$u_3 = 10 \quad \text{if he obtains} \quad u_{23} > 10 \quad \text{from the latter}$$

**Chapter 11 *n*-Person cooperative games with transferable utility: the modified
Shapley value**

1 It is customary to denote the set or coalition S having player i as its only
member by $S = (i)$ and to denote the set or coalition S having players i
and j only as its members by $S = (ij)$, and so on. Accordingly the value of
coalition $S = (i)$ must be written as $v(S) = v((i))$, while the value of coalition
$S = (ij)$ as $v(S) = v((ij))$, and so on.

2 Under Shapley's [1953] original approach, our Postulates 1 and 2 are combined into one postulate. This is motivated by the fact that in effect our
Postulate 2 also expresses a joint-efficiency requirement (similar to Postulate 1) from the standpoint of the non-dummy players. They do not need,
and have no use for, cooperation by a dummy player. Therefore, if they
act efficiently in terms of their own interests, then they will not grant a
dummy player any positive payoff. We state the two postulates as separate
axioms merely in order to make more explicit the assumptions underlying
the Shapley value.

3 By an *algebraic–sum game* we mean a game obtained from a finite number of component games by means of the "sum" and the "difference"
operations. Any algebraic-sum game can always be written as the difference of *two* sum games; e.g., $G = G_1 - G_2 + G_3 - G_4$ can be written
as $G = (G_1 + G_3) - (G_2 + G_4)$.

4 Our preceding discussion concerning negative dividends is meant to serve
only heuristic purposes. Our formal justification for negative dividends
will be in terms of our bargaining model for the Shapley value and in particular in terms of our theory of composite bargaining games (see Section
11.4).

5 Since the terms "discriminatory" and "nondiscriminatory" solutions have
been used by von Neumann and Morgenstern [1953] in a different sense,
we will employ the adjectives "biased" and "unbiased" as our "official"
technical terms. However, where no danger of confusion with von Neumann
and Morgenstern's terminology arises, we will feel free to use the more suggestive terms "discriminatory" and "nondiscriminatory" for our own purposes in the sense just defined. In this sense, of course, even the imputations belonging to the nondiscriminatory solutions of von Neumann and
Morgenstern are "biased" or "discriminatory" solutions, because they
assume that only a limited number of all possible coalitions will come into
existence. For instance, under this theory in a three-person game only *one*
of the three possible two-person coalitions will be formed by the players
in any given case.

6 An alternative assumption would be that the amount $v((123)) - v((12)) = 48$
would be divided not in a *three*-person game among players 1, 2, and 3 but

rather in a *two*-person simple bargaining game between coalition (12) (regarded as *one* player) and player 3. Under this model, coalition (12) and player 3 would each receive the amount 48/2 = 24. Accordingly player 3 would obtain the final payoff 24, while players 1 and 2 would each obtain the final payoff 21 + 24/2 = 33. But in our view the model suggested in the text is preferable, because there is no reason to assume that coalition (12) would act as *one* player in bargaining with player 3.

7 The same is true, and for the same reason, under Aumann and Maschler's "bargaining set" model [1964].

8 Discriminatory solutions for n–person cooperative games with *biased* communication will be discussed in Chapter 13.

9 According to economic theory it is true only under *perfect competition* that each participant receives the full value of his marginal product. Of course, in a bargaining situation, such as the one assumed under Theorem 11.3, there is no perfect competition.

10 Even in the case of games *without* binding threats, one may wish to define the Shapley values in terms of a characteristic function different from that of von Neumann and Morgenstern. In such games it is natural to regard the conflict strategies θ^S and $\theta^{\bar{S}}$ of two complementary coalitions as corresponding to equilibrium points in a *nonzero–sum* noncooperative game between the two coalitions, where each side would try to maximize its own joint payoff, $v(S)$ or $v(\bar{S})$. Cf. our discussion for the two-person case in Section 9.1.

Chapter 12 n-Person cooperative games: the general case

1 As will become clear later, the purpose of the throwaway assumption is to enable us to use our theory of *composite* bargaining games with possibly negative bargaining subgames (as defined in Sections 9.6 and 9.7), for the analysis of bargaining between any two players i and j.

2 See Footnote 1, Section 10.1.

3 If $\bar{u}$ happens to be a corner point, then the a_i's will be the slope cosini of one particular supporting hyperplane going through $\bar{u}$ (see below).

4 We are here disregarding the degenerate case where $a_i = 0$.

5 These weights correspond to the slope cosini of the supporting plane $2u_1 + 2u_2 + u_3 = 510$, which contains the line *DB*. (It is the only plane which *both* contains *DB and* has an equation symmetric in u_1 and u_2.)

6 The present writer discovered the Shapley value independently in 1953.

Chapter 14   Noncooperative and almost-noncooperative games

1 Indeed in tacit and semivocal noncooperative and almost-noncooperative games their application is further restricted to the set F of accessible strategy n–tuples.

2 This is true irrespective of whether this game is played as a strictly noncooperative or as an almost-noncooperative game.

3 See Footnote 2.

4 See Footnote 2.

5 For the purposes of empirical applications it may be more appropriate to call this theoretical condition "security of agreements" rather than "enforceability of agreements," since it is meant to cover situations where compliance with agreements is secured by the players' spontaneous inner attitudes (e.g., by their interiorized moral standards) rather than by external penalties from

law-enforcing agencies. However, in abstract theory the term "enforceability" is quite appropriate, because such inner attitudes can be represented in the payoff matrix by assuming that the players assign high *disutilities* to violations of agreements, in the same way as if these violations were subject to heavy external penalties.

6 Between the two extremes of fully cooperative and fully noncooperative games, our theory deals explicitly only with one intermediate case, viz., that of almost-noncooperative games. Most other intermediate cases (e.g., cases where law enforcement exists but is uncertain) can be treated formally as special cases of noncooperative (or of almost-noncooperative) games. (For instance, uncertain penalties can be represented in the payoff matrix by taking their actuarial disutility values.) However, future research providing a more explicit analysis of such intermediate cases would be very desirable.

7 On the dangers of dismissing noncooperative behavior in international life (e.g., wars) simply as irrational behavior, instead of considering how to eliminate the conditions which can make such behavior quite rational, see my review article on Lewis F. Richardson's work [Harsanyi, 1962c, esp. pp. 696–699].

8 We should like to stress again that what we call "noncooperative" standard of rationality, corresponding to our solution concept for noncooperative games, does not completely exclude cooperation among the players but merely restricts it to the set of eligible joint strategies. Thus the term "noncooperative" must not be taken literally but must be understood as a technical term having a meaning as defined above.

9 In a tacit or semivocal game σ and τ would have to be *accessible* equilibrium points. Moreover, in all of our subsequent discussion, the term "eligible" would have to be replaced by the term "accessible" (see Section 14.10).

References

Anscombe, F. J., and R. J. Aumann, "A Definition of Subjective Probability," *Annals of Mathematical Statistics* **34** (1963), pp. 199–205.

Archibald, Kathleen (ed.), *Strategic Interaction and Conflict*, Institute of International Studies, University of California: Berkeley, 1966.

Arrow, Kenneth J., *Social Choice and Individual Values*, Wiley: New York, 1951.

Aumann, Robert J., "Acceptable Points in General Cooperative n-Person Games," in A. W. Tucker and R. D. Luce (1959), pp. 287–324.

and Michael Maschler, "The Bargaining Set for Cooperative Games," in M. Dresher, L. S. Shapley, and A. W. Tucker (1964), pp. 443–476.

"Repeated Games with Incomplete Information," *Final Report to the U.S. Arms Control and Disarmament Agency*, Contract ST-143, MATHEMATICA: Princeton, N.J., November 1968, pp. 25–108.

Bishop, Robert L., "Game-Theoretic Analysis of Bargaining," *Quarterly Journal of Economics* **77** (1963), pp. 559–602.

Braithwaite, R. B., *Theory of Games as a Tool for the Moral Philosopher*, Cambridge University Press: Cambridge, England, 1955.

Carnap, Rudolf, *Logical Foundations of Probability*, University of Chicago Press: Chicago, 1950.

Dahrendorf, Ralf, "Out of Utopia: Toward a Reorientation of Sociological Analysis," *American Journal of Sociology* **64** (1958), pp. 115–127.

Debreu, Gerard, "A Social Equilibrium Existence Theorem," *Proceedings of the National Academy of Sciences of the U.S.A.* **38** (1952), pp. 886–893.

Theory of Value, Wiley: New York, 1959.

Dresher, M., A. W. Tucker, and P. Wolfe (eds.), *Contributions to the Theory of Games, III* (Annals of Mathematics Studies 39) Princeton University Press: Princeton, N.J., 1957.

L. S. Shapley, and A. W. Tucker (eds.), *Advances in Game Theory* (Annals of Mathematics Studies 52), Princeton University Press: Princeton, N.J., 1964.

Edgeworth, F. Y., *Mathematical Psychics*, Routledge & Kegan Paul: London, 1881.

Fellner, William, *Competition Among the Few*, Augustus M. Kelley: New York, 1960 (1st ed. published in 1949).

Fleming, Marcus, "A Cardinal Concept of Welfare," *Quarterly Journal of Economics* **66** (1952), pp. 366–384.

Harsanyi, John C., "Cardinal Utility in Welfare Economics and in the Theory of Risk-taking," *Journal of Political Economy* **61** (1953), pp. 434–435.

"Cardinal Welfare, Individualistic Ethics, and Interpersonal Comparisons of Utility," *Journal of Political Economy* **63** (1955), pp. 309–321.

"Approaches to the Bargaining Problem Before and After the Theory of Games," *Econometrica* **24** (1956), pp. 144–156.

"Ethics in Terms of Hypothetical Imperatives," *Mind* **47** (1958), pp. 305–316.

"A Bargaining Model for the Cooperative *n*-Person Game," in A. W. Tucker and R. D. Luce (1959), pp. 325–355.

"Theoretical Analysis in Social Science and the Model of Rational Behavior," *Australian Journal of Politics and History* **7** (1961a), pp. 60–74.

"On the Rationality Postulates Underlying the Theory of Cooperative Games," *Journal of Conflict Resolution* **5** (1961b), pp. 179–196.

"Measurement of Social Power, Opportunity Costs, and the Theory of Two-Person Bargaining Games," *Behavioral Science* **7** (1962a), pp. 67–80.

"Measurement of Social Power in *n*-Person Reciprocal Power Situations," *Behavioral Science* **7** (1962b), pp. 81–91.

"Mathematical Models for the Genesis of War" (a review article on Lewis F. Richardson's work), *World Politics* **14** (1962c), pp. 687–699.

"A Simplified Bargaining Model for the *n*-Person Cooperative Game," *International Economic Review* **4** (1963), pp. 194–220.

"Game Theory and the Analysis of International Conflicts," *Australian Journal of Politics and History* **11** (1965), pp. 292–304.

"A General Theory of Rational Behavior in Game Situations," *Econometrica* **34** (1966a), pp. 613–634.

"A Bargaining Model for Social Status in Informal Groups and Formal Organizations," *Behavioral Science* **11** (1966b), pp. 357–369.

"Games with Incomplete Information Played by 'Bayesian' Players, Part I," *Management Science* **14** (1967), pp. 159–182.

"Games with Incomplete Information Played by 'Bayesian' Players, Part II," *Management Science* **14** (1968a), pp. 320–334.

"Games with Incomplete Information Played by 'Bayesian' Players, Part III," *Management Science* **14** (1968b), pp. 486–502.

"Individualistic vs. Functionalistic Explanations in the Light of Game Theory," in I. Lakatos (ed.), *Problems in the Philosophy of Science*, North Holland: Amsterdam, 1968c, pp. 305–321, 337–348.

"Rational-Choice Models of Political Behavior vs. Functionalist and Conformist Theories," *World Politics* **21** (1969), pp. 513–538.

"An Equilibrium-Point Interpretation of Stable Sets and a Proposed Alternative Definition," *Management Science* **20** (1974), pp. 1472–1495.

and Reinhard Selten, "A Generalized Nash Solution for Two-Person Bargaining Games with Incomplete Information," *Management Science* **18** (1972), no. 5, part II, pp. 80–106.

Herstein, I. N., and J. W. Milnor, "An Axiomatic Approach to Measurable Utility," *Econometrica* **21** (1953), pp. 291–297.

Hicks, J. R., *The Theory of Wages*, Macmillan: London, 1932.

Homans, George C., *The Human Group*, Harcourt Brace Jovanovich: New York, 1950.

Social Behavior: Its Elementary Forms, Harcourt Brace Jovanovich: New York, 1961.

Howard, Nigel, *Paradoxes of Rationality: Theory of Metagames and Political Behavior*, M.I.T. Press: Cambridge, Mass., 1971.

Jeffreys, H., *Theory of Probability*, Oxford University Press: Oxford, 1939.

Kakutani, S., "A Generalization of Brouwer's Fixed Point Theorem," *Duke Mathematical Journal* **8** (1941), pp. 457–459.

Kuhn, H. W., "Extensive Games and the Problem of Information," in H. W. Kuhn and A. W. Tucker (1953), pp. 193–216.

and A. W. Tucker (eds.), *Contributions to the Theory of Games, I* (Annals of Mathematics Studies 24), Princeton University Press: Princeton, N.J., 1950.

Contributions to the Theory of Games, II (Annals of Mathematics Studies 28), Princeton University Press: Princeton, N.J., 1953.

Luce, R. Duncan, and Howard Raiffa, *Games and Decisions*, Wiley: New York, 1957.

Marschak, Jacob, "Rational Behavior, Uncertain Prospects, and Measurable Utility," *Econometrica* 18 (1950), pp. 111–141.

Nash, John F., "Equilibrium Points in *n*-Person Games," *Proceedings of the National Academy of Sciences of the U.S.A.* 36 (1950a), pp. 48–49.

"The Bargaining Problem," *Econometrica* 18 (1950b), pp. 155–162.

"Non-cooperative Games," *Annals of Mathematics* 54 (1951), pp. 286–295.

"Two-Person Cooperative Games," *Econometrica* 21 (1953), pp. 128–140.

Newell, A., J. C. Shaw, and H. A. Simon, "Chess-Playing Programs and the Problem of Complexity," *IBM Journal of Research and Development* 2 (1958), pp. 320–335.

Owen, Guillermo, *Game Theory*, Saunders: Philadelphia, 1968.

Pigou, A. C., *The Economics of Welfare*, 4th ed., Macmillan: London, 1960.

Pratt, John W., Howard Raiffa, and Robert Schlaifer, "The Foundations of Decision Making Under Uncertainty," *American Statistical Association Journal* 59 (1964), pp. 353–375.

Raiffa, Howard, "Arbitration Schemes for Generalized Two-Person Games," in H. W. Kuhn and A. W. Tucker (1953), pp. 361–387.

Rapoport, Anatol, "Strategic and Non-strategic Approaches to Problems of Security and Peace," in Archibald (1966a), pp. 88–102.

Two-Person Game Theory: The Essential Ideas, University of Michigan Press: Ann Arbor, 1966b.

N-Person Game Theory: Concepts and Applications, University of Michigan Press: Ann Arbor, 1970.

Rothenberg, Jerome, *The Measurement of Social Welfare*, Prentice-Hall: Englewood Cliffs, N.J., 1961.

Savage, L. J., *Foundations of Statistics*, Wiley: New York, 1954.

Schelling, Thomas C., *The Strategy of Conflict*, Harvard University Press: Cambridge, Mass., 1960.

Selten, Reinhard, "Bewertung strategischer Spiele," *Zeitschrift für die gesamte Staatswissenschaft* 116 (1960), pp. 221–282.

"Valuation of *n*-Person Games," in M. Dresher, L. S. Shapley, and A. W. Tucker (1964), pp. 577–626.

Sen, Amartya K., *Collective Choice and Social Welfare*, Holden-Day and Oliver & Boyd: London, 1970.

Shapley, Lloyd S., "A Value for *n*-Person Games," in H. W. Kuhn and A. W. Tucker (1953), pp. 307–317.

and Martin Shubik, "A Method for Evaluating the Distribution of Power in a Committee System," *American Political Science Review* 48 (1954), pp. 787–792.

Smart, J. C. C., *An Outline of a System of Utilitarian Ethics*, Melbourne University Press: Melbourne, 1961.

Tucker, A. W., and R. D. Luce (eds.), *Contributions to the Theory of Games, IV* (Annals of Mathematics Studies 40), Princeton University Press: Princeton, N.J., 1959.

von Neumann, John, and Oskar Morgenstern, *Theory of Games and Economic Behavior*, 3rd ed., Princeton University Press: Princeton, N.J., 1953 (1st ed. published in 1944).

Zeuthen, Frederik, *Problems of Monopoly and Economic Warfare*, Routledge & Kegan Paul: London, 1930.

Index